THE

OLD FARMER'S ALMANAC

Calculated on a new and improved plan for the year of our Lord

1994

Being 2nd after LEAP YEAR and (until July 4)
218th year of American Independence

FITTED FOR BOSTON, AND THE NEW ENGLAND STATES, WITH SPECIAL
CORRECTIONS AND CALCULATIONS TO ANSWER FOR ALL THE UNITED STATES.

Containing, besides the large number of Astronomical Calculations
and the Farmer's Calendar for every month in the year, a variety of

NEW, USEFUL, AND ENTERTAINING MATTER.

ESTABLISHED IN 1792

BY ROBERT B. THOMAS

*"Beauty is truth, truth beauty" — that is all
Ye know on earth, and all ye need to know.*

– JOHN KEATS

Address all editorial correspondence to

THE OLD FARMER'S ALMANAC, DUBLIN, NH 03444

CONTENTS

The Old Farmer's Almanac • 1994

FEATURES

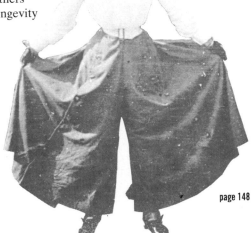

page 148

INDEX OF CHARTS, TABLES, FORECASTS, AND DEPARTMENTS

3

To Patrons

The Almanac presents an interesting challenge to us present-day editors. On one hand, each year's edition must be filled with nothing but brand-new, up-to-date stories, charts, and information. On the other, it must look and feel like what it is, the oldest continuously published periodical in North America. In other words, we need to be both new and old at the same time.

Improvements, then, must be made carefully. When our typesetter used a slightly different style of astronomical symbols one year, a Galveston, Texas, reader wrote to us, saying, "I wish the man who changed the Moon signs in this year's Almanac had died before he'd done it." Nonetheless, over the years since 1939, when the present owners took over (the fourth family since 1792), we've made quite a few improvements that went by virtually unnoticed. Or maybe we should just say they didn't seem to *bother* anyone.

In 1980, for instance, we enlarged the outside dimensions of the Almanac by about a half inch all around. Didn't hear one word from Galveston, Texas. We've also more than doubled the number of annual pages over the past few years; obtained the services of some of the best writers from around the United States and Canada; begun elaborate testing procedures for all published recipes; expanded the weather-forecasting section and, particularly this past year, significantly improved our rate of accuracy; introduced photographs in our stories; and even added some color to our familiar "Four Seasons" cover scene that we first published in 1851 and have used ever since.

This year we've continued our cautious efforts to improve. Little things. For one,

The Old Farmer's Almanac headquarters in Dublin, New Hampshire (population 1,474).

1 **Heatwave Hybrid.** Sets fruit in the hottest weather!

2 **Big Girl® Hybrid VF.** Perfect for slicing or wedges.

3 **Supersteak Hybrid VFN.** Extra-meaty 1-2 lb. fruits.

4 **Super Sweet 100 Hybrid.** Long season, extra sweet.

5 **Early Girl Hybrid.** Produces fruit early and often.

6 **Delicious.** Its seed grew the world's largest tomato!

7 **Long-Keeper.** Keeps up to five months!

8 **Viva Italia Hybrid.** Tastes great fresh and in sauces.

9 **Gardener's Delight.** An old time favorite.

10 **Tumbler Hybrid.** Very early, great for containers!

11 **Yellow Pear.** Mild and pleasing, great for salads.

12 **Celebrity Hybrid.** Great flavor, disease resistant.

12 Juicy Reasons to Send for a FREE 1994 Burpee Gardens Catalogue!

Tomatoes! Burpee's 1994 Garden Catalogue features 26 different tomato varieties! Early ones, late ones, big beauties and bite-sized gems. All packed full of garden-fresh flavor and *guaranteed* to satisfy. You will be able to choose from over 300 varieties of vegetables and over 400 varieties of flowers. Plus fruit trees, bulbs, shrubs, garden supplies. Your new catalogue will arrive in early January.

☐ YES! Send me my FREE 1994 Burpee Gardens Catalogue
Please mail to:
Burpee, 020941 Burpee Building, Warminster, PA 18974

Name _____

Address_____

City _____

State _____Zip_____

© 1993 W. Atlee Burpee & Co.

BURPEE®

The 1994 Edition of
THE OLD FARMER'S ALMANAC

Established in 1792
and published every year thereafter

ROBERT B. THOMAS *(1766-1846)*
FOUNDER

EDITOR *(12th since 1792)*: JUDSON D. HALE SR.

MANAGING EDITOR: SUSAN PEERY

EXECUTIVE EDITOR: TIM CLARK

ART DIRECTOR: MARGO LETOURNEAU

WEATHER PROGNOSTICATOR: DR. RICHARD HEAD

ASTRONOMER: DR. GEORGE GREENSTEIN

COPY EDITOR: LIDA STINCHFIELD

ASSISTANT EDITORS: ANNA LARSON, DEBRA SANDERSON, JODY SAVILLE, MARY SHELDON

RESEARCH EDITOR: MARE-ANNE JARVELA

ARCHIVIST: LORNA TROWBRIDGE

BUSINESS MANAGER, EDITORIAL: ANN DUFFY

CONTRIBUTING EDITORS: CASTLE FREEMAN JR., *Farmer's Calendar*; FRED SCHAAF, *Astronomy*; JAMIE KAGELEIRY

PRODUCTION DIRECTOR: JAMIE TROWBRIDGE

PRODUCTION MANAGER: PAUL BELLIVEAU

PRODUCTION ARTISTS: LUCILLE RINES, STEVE KUSNAROWIS, CLARE INNES

PRODUCTION SYSTEMS COORDINATOR: STEVE MUSKIE

PUBLISHER: *(22nd since 1792)*: JOHN PIERCE

ASSOCIATE PUBLISHER: SHERIN WIGHT

ADVERTISING DIRECTOR: SHERIN WIGHT

MARKETING RESEARCH MANAGER: MARTHA CAVANAUGH

ADVERTISING PRODUCTION: RITA TROUBALOS, *Manager*; STACY BERNSTEIN, LORI GRAY

NEWSSTAND CIRCULATION: KEMCO PUBLISHERS SERVICES

EDITORIAL, ADVERTISING, AND PUBLISHING OFFICES: P.O. BOX 520, DUBLIN, NH 03444
PHONE: 603-563-8111 • FAX: 603-563-8252

YANKEE PUBLISHING INC., MAIN ST., DUBLIN, NH 03444

JOSEPH B. MEAGHER, *President*; JUDSON D. HALE SR., *Senior Vice President*; BRIAN PIANI, *Vice President and Chief Financial Officer*; BROOKS FISHER, JAMES H. FISHMAN, JOHN PIERCE, and JOE TIMKO, *Vice Presidents*.

The Old Farmer's Almanac cannot accept responsibility for unsolicited manuscripts and will not return any manuscripts that do not include a stamped and addressed return envelope.

the type is, we hope, easier to read. For another, we think you'll find this edition better organized for maximum usefulness and entertainment. Please do let us know if you don't agree. Change, we think, is all right, even in something as traditional as the Almanac, but only if, in the opinion of readers, it's change for the better.

But, don't worry, the hole in the upper left-hand corner (for hanging it up to use all year) remains. The cover is the same scene it's been for 143 years. We remain opposed to liquor and tobacco advertising. And the format and contents, while always new, remain basically true to that of all almanacs going back to the days of the ancient Romans. (Of course, this one is the only survivor of all the late-18th-century American almanacs.) As the 11th editor, Robb Sagendorph, wrote as he was preparing the 1971 edition just before his death on July 4, 1970, "*The Old Farmer's Almanac* has and always will have the astronomy of the Babylonians, the farm calendars of the Sumerians, the prognostications of Virgil and Hesiod, the proverbs of Franklin, the wit of Swift."

And yet, were this edition to be buried in a time capsule for a hundred years, as was last year's in the town of Milesburg, Pennsylvania, people in 2094 would peruse it and have a pretty good idea of what life was like in America back in the year 1994. That's the delicate balance we strive for. Remaining true to hundreds of years of tradition . . . and always brand-spanking new.   *J. D. H.*

However, it is by our works and not our words that we would be judged. These, we hope, will sustain us in the humble though proud station we have so long held in the name of

Your ob'd servant,

JUNE 1993

SUBSTITUTIONS FOR COMMON INGREDIENTS

Item	Quantity	Substitution
Allspice	1 teaspoon	½ teaspoon cinnamon plus ⅛ teaspoon ground cloves
Arrowroot, as thickener	1½ teaspoons	1 tablespoon flour
Baking powder	1 teaspoon	¼ teaspoon baking soda plus ⅝ teaspoon cream of tartar
Bread crumbs, dry	¼ cup	1 slice bread
soft	½ cup	1 slice bread
Buttermilk	1 cup	1 cup yogurt
Chocolate, unsweetened	1 ounce	3 tablespoons cocoa plus 1 tablespoon butter or fat
Cracker crumbs	¾ cup	1 cup bread crumbs
Cream, heavy	1 cup	¾ cup milk plus ⅓ cup melted butter (this will not whip)
Cream, light	1 cup	⅞ cup milk plus 3 tablespoons melted butter
Cream, sour	1 cup	⅞ cup buttermilk **or** plain yogurt plus 3 tablespoons melted butter
Cream, whipping	1 cup	⅔ cup well-chilled evaporated milk, whipped; **or** 1 cup nonfat dry milk powder whipped with 1 cup ice water
Flour, all-purpose	1 cup	1⅛ cups cake flour; **or** ⅝ cup potato flour; **or** 1¼ cups rye **or** coarsely ground whole grain flour; **or** 1 cup cornmeal
Flour, cake	1 cup	1 cup minus 2 tablespoons sifted all-purpose flour
Flour, self-rising	1 cup	1 cup all-purpose flour plus 1¼ teaspoons baking powder plus ¼ teaspoon salt
Garlic	1 small clove	⅛ teaspoon garlic powder or instant minced garlic
Herbs, dried	½ to 1 teaspoon	1 tablespoon fresh, minced and packed
Honey	1 cup	1¼ cups sugar plus ½ cup liquid
Lemon	1	1 to 3 tablespoons juice, 1 to 1½ teaspoons grated rind
Lemon juice	1 teaspoon	½ teaspoon vinegar
Lemon rind, grated	1 teaspoon	½ teaspoon lemon extract
Milk, skim	1 cup	⅓ cup instant nonfat dry milk plus about ¾ cup water
Milk, whole	1 cup	½ cup evaporated milk plus ½ cup water; **or** 1 cup skim milk plus 2 teaspoons melted butter
Milk, to sour	1 cup	Add 1 tablespoon vinegar or lemon juice to 1 cup milk minus 1 tablespoon. Stir and let stand 5 minutes.
Mustard, prepared	1 tablespoon	1 teaspoon dry or powdered mustard
Onion, chopped	1 small	1 tablespoon instant minced onion; **or** 1 teaspoon onion powder; **or** ¼ cup frozen chopped onion
Sugar, granulated	1 cup	1 cup firmly packed brown sugar; **or** 1¾ cups confectioners' sugar (do not substitute in baking); **or** 2 cups corn syrup; **or** 1 cup superfine sugar
Tomatoes, canned	1 cup	½ cup tomato sauce plus ½ cup water; **or** 1⅓ cup chopped fresh tomatoes, simmered
Tomato juice	1 cup	½ cup tomato sauce plus ½ cup water plus dash each salt and sugar; **or** ¼ cup tomato paste plus ¾ cup water plus salt and sugar
Tomato ketchup	½ cup	½ cup tomato sauce plus 2 tablespoons sugar, 1 tablespoon vinegar, and ⅛ teaspoon ground cloves
Tomato puree	1 cup	½ cup tomato paste plus ½ cup water
Tomato soup	1 can (10¾ oz.)	1 cup tomato sauce plus ¼ cup water
Vanilla	1-inch bean	1 teaspoon vanilla extract
Yeast	1 cake (⅗ oz.)	1 package active dried yeast
Yogurt, plain	1 cup	1 cup buttermilk

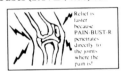
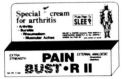

CONSUMER TASTES

WHAT'S HOT, WHAT'S NOT, and What to Expect in '94.

by Jamie Kageleiry

THE RETURN OF THE ELMS: Ever notice how many towns have Elm streets? American cities once had more elms shading them than any other tree, until Dutch

GOOD NEWS

elm disease scoured the country. Plant pathologists now predict that blight-resistant elms will be available in 1994. The new species, called Frontier and Prospector, will turn, respectively, a deep maroon and a deep yellow in autumn.

THE RETURN OF THE WHOOPING CRANE: In 1967 the government listed 78 species in danger of extinction. Today, 44 of those are either stable or increasing, including the bald eagle, the American alligator, and the whooping crane. However, since that first list in 1967, over 300 other animals have been added to the endangered list.

The Differences Between Men and Women
(in 1994)

CHANNEL SURFING: A recent study found that men are twice as likely as women to hold the remote-control device for the television.

DOODLING: People who study such things found that men doodle in straight lines and women in curly ones.

THE WAY TO A MAN'S HEART IS THROUGH HIS STOMACH: Almost two-thirds of all women polled recently believe this. Only 25 percent of men thought that the way to a woman's heart was through her stomach.

WARMTH: No, not all that emotional stuff. Women truly are warmer than men. Recent studies have found that the average temperature of a female is 98.4° F; a male's is 98.1°. (So much for 98.6° . . .)

THE THREE STOOGES: Reactions to the "classic" show are split pretty evenly along gender lines. Males think Moe, Curly, and Larry are funny. Women think they are stupid and violent.

And the

Some records to beat in 1994

Records are always being set and shattered. Here are some of the latest "champs" in various categories.

BIGGEST FEET:

Matthew McGrory, it is said, may just be the only grown man on the planet whose shoe size exceeds his age. Matthew (7' 5") is 20 and his shoes are size 23 (that's 20 inches long, six inches wide, five pounds apiece, $800 the pair).

& TRENDS FOR 1994

GAMBLING — not always such a bad habit: A nun recently won a million dollars in a California lottery. Sister Josephine Contris, 71, has lived under a vow of poverty for 54 years and will use the money to build a new retirement home for her order.

GARBAGE: Americans now throw away about 135 pounds of grocery-product packaging per capita a year. This is good news? In 1980 the per-capita total was 175 pounds.

— David Nelson

FITNESS: For over 15 years, exercise scientists have been telling us that in order to become fit, we must exercise aerobically for at least 20 minutes at least three times a week. Now we can relax. Shorter, more frequent aerobic exercise may be just as beneficial.

Winners Are ...

WORLD'S LARGEST ROSE BUSH: Planted in 1885, the single root of the "White Lady Banksia" has grown to cover more than 8,000 square feet and enables 150 people to sit under it.

The lucky owner is Burton DeVere of Tombstone, Arizona.

LARGEST LIVING THING ON EARTH (so far):

Well, it *was* the 38-acre fungus discovered in Michigan last year, but that one is puny next to the 1,500-acre *Armillaria ostoyae* fungus measured recently in Washington State.

— David Nelson

What's GOOD FOR YOU
in 1994

Red Wine: Scientists believe that phenol, the chemical that makes wine red, can lower the risk of heart disease. Red grape juice is good, too.

Carrots: They always were good for you, but now they're even better — yellow fruits and veggies and dark green leafy ones may even prevent tumor growth.

Naps: They're normal! If you're sleepy midafternoons, it doesn't mean you're lazy or bored — the "slump,"

– David Nelson

it turns out, is deeply ingrained in our biology. And researchers have concluded that giving in to the desire to take a short nap can improve mental performance and mood.

Caffeine: Well, it may not be good for you, but it's no longer the villain it was once thought to be. A recent federal study found that even pregnant women can drink less than three cups a day without harming the baby.

Thumb-sucking: It's no longer one of those nasty childhood habits. Now some psychologists view it as "infant ingenuity" and a sign of motor control. Dentists are reserving judgment for now.

– David Nelson

What's in a Name?

Baby girls' most popular name seems to change every five to ten years, from Jennifer to Jessica to Ashley. Boys just keep getting named Michael, which has been the most popular for decades. The newest trend, though, is the "gender/blender" name (usually used on girls) such as Pat, or Chris, or Jamie.

AGRICULTURE NEWS

☞ New weeds to worry about: Bedstraw, impervious to anything but plowing. Says farmer Ted Hall, 82, "As smart as we're supposed to be, ain't there any other way?" Ted could have it worse. If he lived in Pennsylvania, he'd have to put up with "mile-a-minute" weed, which needs no explanation.

☞ Maybe in 100 years, or maybe 100,000, we'll be planting gardens on Mars. Scientists are looking at ways to transform the environment on Mars to make it more hospitable. After that, there's only the small issue of the commute from Earth.

☞ New fertilizer — from thin air. Moshe Alamaro believes he can create fertilizer by zapping electricity through air-filled chambers. Alamaro's portable system would deliver low-cost fertilizer to parts of the world that could desperately use it.

THE NEW "IN" VIRTUES

Neotraditionalism: *A blend of the traditionalism of their parents and the flexibility and tolerance fostered in the sixties, this is the key baby-boomer characteristic. It includes a hunger for the past:*

☞ Pinball machines are in again.

☞ Toys like Lincoln Logs are being reintroduced for baby boomers' kids.

☞ Virgin-Atlantic Airways entrepreneur Richard Branson is now running charter flights from Orlando to Key West, Florida, using refurbished World War II airplanes, complete with flight attendants appropriately attired (seamed stockings and pillbox caps), and old issues of *Life* and *Saturday Evening Post.*

Simplicity *is another popular virtue:*

☞ People are wearing play clothes to work (sales of suits are slipping, sportswear increasing).

☞ Consumers no longer want "high-tech" gizmos. New ad campaigns such as Reebok's now tout "No Slogans — Just the Basics."

FRUGALITY

People are watching their dollars. It just makes sense. But now it makes for style, too. Watch for evidence of "cheap chic": designer doggie bags for stylish restaurants, and stores selling fancy dress clothes "previously worn" and patronized by well-to-do clients.

☞ Instead of having "everything," people are valuing having less, especially if it means having more time. Many busy people are finding that making lots of money isn't necessarily the best measure of success. Watch for more people making "life-style decisions," choosing perhaps a lower-paying job and doing without some things, but having more time to spend with family. And not feeling guilty about it.

Responsibility

☞ The new 400-store Mall of America in Minneapolis (which has its own zip code and police station) will provide a school for the children of its employees and its own recycling center. Food waste from all 46 restaurants will be composted.

☞ Eberhard Farber has introduced its "EcoWriter" pencil, made of recycled paper instead of wood.

☞ Fidelity Investment's annual report is now distributed on a computer diskette instead of as a glossy magazine. This does more than just cut down on printing costs and the ensuing paper waste. Information on diskettes can be more easily accessible; the diskettes take up less space in new streamlined briefcases; and the next report can be sent to the reader over the phone in minutes.

– David Nelson

FOOD FACTS

Most Expensive Old Cheese

Recently, a British collector paid Sotheby's $1,500 for a spoonful of 200-year-old brown Tibetan cheese. Simon Perry will add the ounce to a collection of several thousand old cheeses he keeps in his basement. "I have always loved cheese ever since I was a kid and started eating cheese triangles," Perry told the Associated Press. "But I won't be eating this. . . . It would taste rather unpleasant, and anyway, it's too valuable."

"Clear" Is Here

Clear soda and beer join clear dishwashing detergent, clear gasoline, and other clear products. Clear, especially in beverages, will stay in style only if the actual purity can match the perceived purity. For now, most of the seeming seltzers contain just as many sweeteners (and calories) as the old brown colas and root beers. What isn't so transparent is why blue foods are in. Most of them are "fun" foods like Jell-O, candies, and even popcorn.

☞ Pizza is about to overtake the hamburger as the national food. About ten percent of all restaurants in the country are pizzerias, and pizza accounts for close to 20 percent of all orders placed in restaurants. If all the pizzas made in the United States in one day were put together into one big pizza, it would cover the city of Boston.

FOOD FUTURE

☞ Scientists are striving to develop a microwavable french fry that has satisfying crispness.

☞ And consumers have led a tomato mutiny of sorts — we want our tomatoes to be "as tasty as they used to be," according to a study done for the Dole food company. This year, we should see a genetically improved tomato that is softer, redder, and more flavorful. But will it be as good as home grown?

☞ Anise will be the "new spice" in 1994.

☞ Caribbean food will be the next rage.

☞ We're moving away from "meat and potatoes" as standard fare and embracing more eclectic, exotic foods as part of a weekly diet. Americans now consume almost 900 million pounds of spices a year.

☞ Looking for a cultural barometer? Keep your eye on sour cream. The more ethnically diverse our diets become, the more sour cream is sold. Since 1977 the market has tripled. Though some of the 600 million pounds of sour cream we eat annually is still used on baked potatoes, the huge increase is due almost entirely to having to cool off spicy fajitas, Indian curries, or Thai peanut sauces.

– David Nelson

Some Manners for the Nineties

Smoking will become like spitting. Just doesn't look right in public.

The etiquette of call-waiting: As Miss Manners (Judith Martin) advises, don't abandon one call to take another.

Blast-Off

"Celestis is a postcremation service. . . . We further reduce and encapsulate them, identify each by name, Social Security number, and a religious symbol, and place them in a payloader."

– John Cherry, in The Boston Globe, *describing a plan to send human remains into permanent orbit 1,900 miles above the Earth.*

DEMOGRAPHICA

OLDIES BUT GOODIES: Some gerontologists predict that by the year 2080 men will live to age 94 on average and women to 100. If this is correct, the number of people aged 85 or older will grow to 72 million (compared with 19 million today), which could have a profound effect on retirement funds.

Look for more attention — fashion, marketing, life-style in general, being paid to "Woopies," the "Well-Off Older Persons" (both aging boomers and youthful elders) who now have money to spend. This means demand for more flattering clothes, more "over 50" fashion models.

News on the Dental Front

Thirty years ago, Americans aged 65 and older had an average of only 7.2 teeth (of their own) in their mouths. Today the same group has an average of 17.8 teeth. And the well-fluoridated mouths of the baby boomers will have even more teeth — two dozen or so — in their golden years.

By the year 2000, there will be a total of 5.6 billion teeth in all of America — double what there is now. That's good news for toothpaste companies. Now the bad news: Because our teeth will last so much longer, we'll have fewer and fewer dentists per tooth. In 1980 there were 48.3 dentists per million teeth. By the turn of the century, that number will drop to only 35.5 dentists per million teeth. Simple supply and demand means that prices of dental services may go up, out of reach of many people. Watch for efforts to have dentistry covered in health packages. Dentistry will become a popular field again.

– David Nelson

Ideas We're Guessing

WON'T CATCH ON

☞ **PERMANENT MAKEUP.** This rather alarming innovation takes the idea of smudge-proof cosmetics and really runs with it. Now women may have makeup tattooed on their faces. No messy nightly cleanups, no time-consuming morning rituals. We have to hand it to the hundreds of women who have so far taken the $1,600 plunge: They must feel very confident about the particular color they choose to have permanently smeared on their lips or above their eyes.

Homes

Bathrooms: ☞ No longer just necessities, bathrooms are growing into rooms where one can go to relax. They must be bigger to accommodate two adults preparing for work at the same time and luxurious enough (steam baths, Jacuzzis) to soothe the busy couples.

☞ Another component of the bathroom: sinkable Ivory soap. Ivory soap is 115 years old, but has always been injected with air to make it float. The air was making people's skin dry, so Procter & Gamble is making a version — "New Ivory Ultra Safe Skin Care Bar" — with less air. Original Ivory will still be available.

Colors: The trend is toward brighter colors in home design. Sunflower yellow instead of off-white, cornflower blue instead of the grayish Williamsburg blue. And green is back.

TVs: We could probably put this under the "Do we really want this?" department. Televisions will soon offer up to 750 cable channels. And once televisions, home phones, computers, and VCRs are merged into a single system, we'll have the chance to order "movies on demand." Our smart TVs will automatically save top-rated shows for days after airing so we can view them at our convenience (that's assuming our televisions have the same taste in shows that we do).

The Kitchen: Baking soda! There is yet one more use for baking soda: To prevent and control mildew and other fungal diseases — it often works better than chemical fungicides.

— David Nelson

SO LONG, FAREWELL

DIAL PHONES: It's only a matter of a year or two before dial phones will look like antiques. (Start saving them!)

TUPPERWARE PARTIES: Tupperware, or its knockoffs, will always be handy, especially in these microwaveable days, but there won't be many classic Tupperware parties — two-earner families just can't spare the time.

Fashion Trends

*T*he words here are sensible and frugal. And what has inspired us to embrace those qualities — the end of the boom years of the 1980s — has also led us to turn away from anything that reeks of "glitz." We saw this anti-fashion look last year in the "grunge" styles. This particular look — flannel shirts tied around waists, greasy, unwashed hair, heavy boots worn with dresses — won't last long. For one thing, it just doesn't look good.

We will continue to wear clothes that are comfortable and practical before anything else. Bell bottoms will be in briefly until the end of this year. The look overall for 1994 is layered and very "vertical" — long tunics worn over skirts or pants with a vest. You can put red away — most colors are muted and austere.

The other major trend informing fashion is a demographic one — the aging of the baby boomers. Watch for clothes that gracefully allow for the not-so-perfect body. Bathing suits with skirts are in again. And Lee Apparel company, the folks who make jeans, are now running ads that feature "pudgy" people (not models). Watch for more "real life" in fashion marketing.

GOOD RIDDANCE!

MALARIA: The British, who were posted at the far, more malarial corners of the Empire, used to joke that if one drank enough gin and tonic (tonic water contains quinine), one would be safe from malaria, which strikes 300 million people a year and has no cure. Chloroquine was used with some degree of effectiveness in preventing malaria — until the mosquito-borne parasites became immune to its effects. Now scientists are gaining knowledge into the genes of the parasite itself, and a cure, or at least a non-resistible prophylactic, is on the horizon.

CHICKEN POX: This will finally be the year in which we get a vaccine against chicken pox.

HASTA LA VISTA, LA CUCARACHA: A final farewell to the cockroach? Maybe, just maybe the newest warfare being waged will diminish the ranks. Pesticide maker Biosys says researchers are using worms as foot soldiers in the battle against the universally hated roach. A trap lures the roach inside (like a "roach motel"). Instead of poisoning them there, it exposes them to microscopic worms called nematodes, which infect them with a lethal bacteria. Biosys hopes to have a commercial product soon.

WAITING LINES: There are scientists who study queues and how to manage them, with the goal of eliminating them altogether. Electronically sensitive pads placed under the places where people most often wait in line — airports, movies, banks — monitor traffic flow. The monitors can even sense "line tolerance" — that's the point at which people in queues give up and go home. Then business owners can schedule more workers to ease the crunch.

WIRES CLUTTERING FLOORS (to speakers, lamps, phones, vacuums): Wires will soon be obsolete.

How to Tell the Future

Economists and other prognosticators watch various indicators for clues to the future. The level of shipments of corrugated cardboard boxes, for example, may show a yet-unreported demand for goods. Or the number of seats booked on business-class flights to Tokyo is a clue to the health of Pacific-rim businesses. These make sense. Other "leading indicators" don't, at first, but they seem to work:

Football: A popular theory holds that in years when a team that was part of the original National Football League (a National Football Conference team) wins the Super Bowl, stocks post gains the following business day. The Super Bowl theory has worked 23 out of 26 times.

Song Lyrics: Harold Zullow, a social psychiatrist in New York, predicted the recession of 1990 by listening to the radio. Harold studied 40 years' worth of song lyrics and correlated types of popular hit songs with news events. He discovered that just when everything in the economy seems peachy, song lyrics suddenly turn pessimistic, becoming, it turns out, a sort of leading indicator of a recession to come. In the prerecession year of 1969, for instance, most songs were "dark," such as "Bad Moon Rising" and "In the Year 2525," which is about the end of the world. When you hear gloom and doom on the radio, it's time to sell your stock, because a recession is on the way. But when things are looking really gloomy, songs start sounding more optimistic, such as 1991's "Coming Out of the Dark," predicting better times to come. ☐☐

— Illustrations by David Nelson

Two centuries of rain,
snow, lightning, accurate
predictions, useful tips, delightful
lore — and more stories than Willard!

ACTS OF GOD

THE OLD FARMER'S ALMANAC
UNPREDICTABLE GUIDE TO WEATHER
& NATURAL DISASTERS

RANDOM HOUSE

BENJAMIN A. WATSON
AND THE EDITORS OF THE OLD FARMER'S ALAMANAC

EPACT?

Here's a little
something
deliciously arcane
for those who
long for the
"simplicity" of
life before
computers . . .

(And what good is it?)

nder the heading "Chronological Cycles for 1994" on page 33 and listed in the Glossary on page 38 is the word *Epact,* expressed as a number from 1 to 30. The number represents the age of the Moon on January 1 and is used to harmonize the lunar and solar calendars. Occasionally (as happened in 1992) a year will have two epacts. What is an epact, and why is one — let alone two — needed at all?

It all goes back to the early years of the Christian era and the need to determine in advance the date for Easter, which is dependent on the vernal equinox and the nearest full Moon. For several hundred years it had been known that the phases of the Moon went through a 19-year cycle, in which no new Moon ever recurred on the same date. After several bouts of trial and error, another regularly repeat-

BY ANDREW ROTHOVIUS

ing cycle of 28 years was discovered, in which every possible day-of-month and day-of-week combination in the Western 12-month calendar occurs at least once. By multiplying these two cycles together (19 x 28), a grand cycle of 532 years was derived, from which it was simple to construct a perpetual almanac that would readily give the date of Easter for any year within it. At the end of the 532 years, the same sequence starts all over again. Problem solved — or so they thought.

Alas, they overlooked the fact that the 19-year lunar cycle falls short by one hour and 29 minutes of being 19 full years. This amounts to one whole day every 308 years. One obvious answer would have been to revise the perpetual almanac every 308 years (and pray for the invention of the computer). But the Middle Ages, suspicious of any intervention in these matters, took no corrective action, and by 1570 the perpetual almanac was already four days in arrears.

In 1572 a commission of astronomers appointed by Pope Gregory XIII undertook a general revision of the calendar. At this point it would have been easy to revise the perpetual almanac for Easter dates, but one member of the commission, a scholar named Christopher Clavius, conceived the idea of scrapping the perpetual almanac and substituting a new mode of calculation he called the epact.

Clavius built a complicated edifice of numbers that could serve for 7,000 years before being recalculated.

Clavius's epact is based on the number of days between the last new Moon in December and January 1. This number varies from 1 to 30 within each 19-year cycle. Upon this foundation, which requires adjustment every three centuries, Clavius built a complicated edifice of numbers that could serve for 7,000 years before being recalculated.

In fact, Clavius's calculations hardly ever agree exactly with the real astronomical full Moon, but are usually a day or two off, either earlier or later. The same is true of the December new Moon, which is the basis of the epact. Nevertheless, the system works after a fashion, and in precomputer times it did provide a rough-and-ready means of determining Easter dates for many years ahead.

Clavius was proud of his complex brainchild, and Western calendar makers adopted it universally. There are no less than 30 different epact sequences, each lasting either 300 or 400 years and all requiring some intermediate corrections. In the current sequence, the 19-year lunar cycle has two years in which the December new Moon would occur 25 days before January 1. Astronomically, however, the new Moon never occurs twice on the same day of any month in a given lunar cycle. To get around that, Clavius devised the use of a second epact, in which a number not already used in the 19-year cycle is used instead.

Confusing? The irony of this curious provision is that even in Clavius's precomputer age, epact was an unnecessary complication; today it is totally unneeded, although still a traditional element of this Almanac (computers can figure the date of Easter for the next million years if need be). As one modern critic said, Clavius shrouded the whole concept in such a mass of erudite detail that "few have really mastered it and fewer have dared to criticize. Like the squid or cuttlefish, Clavius protected his scheme by the cloud of ink with which he surrounded it." □□

HOW TO USE THIS ALMANAC
Anywhere in the U.S.A.

Annually, for the interest and pleasure of our readers, *The Old Farmer's Almanac* provides a variety of astronomical data calculated for the upcoming year. The data cover a wide range of phenomena — the rising and setting times of the Sun and Moon; the declination of the Sun; the astronomical age and placement of the Moon and its monthly phases; the rising and setting times of the visible planets; solar and lunar eclipses; dates and times of meteor showers; rising and setting times of the bright stars; and a monthly summary of astronomical highlights.

THE LEFT-HAND CALENDAR PAGES
(Pages 54-80)

Much of the data is contained in the Left-Hand Calendar Pages (pages 54-80). For the enlightenment of our readers, part of a sample page is reproduced below, with an explanatory text summarizing the individual entries.

☞ **PLEASE NOTE** that all the times given in this edition of the Almanac are calculated for **Boston, Massachusetts.** However, Key Letters accompany much of the data. They are provided so that readers may correct the Boston times to those of their own localities. Several examples are given below to clarify this procedure. (**Eastern Standard Time is used throughout the Almanac.** One hour should be added for Daylight Saving Time between April 3 and October 30.)

SAMPLE LEFT-HAND CALENDAR PAGE
(from November 1993 — page 54)

1993   NOVEMBER, The Eleventh Month

This is a month of close meetings near or at the Sun. A partial solar eclipse on November 13th is seen only in the far southern latitudes. The start of a rare transit of Mercury — the planet passing in front of the Sun — on the 5th is seen from Hawaii and the Aleutians but nowhere else in the nation. All the country gets a look at two conjunctions low in the east before dawn: the bright-planet pair Venus and Jupiter on the 8th; the inner-planet pair Venus and Mercury on the 14th. Mercury puts in a fine morning appearance before and after its greatest elongation on the 22nd. The Leonid meteors are unbothered by moonlight in the hours just before dawn on the 18th. The Moon's total eclipse on the 28th-29th will be visible everywhere.

☾ Last Quarter	7th day	1st hour	37th min.
● New Moon	13th day	16th hour	35th min.
☽ First Quarter	20th day	21st hour	4th min.
○ Full Moon	29th day	1st hour	32nd min.

For an explanation of this page, see "How to Use This Almanac," page 30; for values of Key Letters, see Time Correction Tables, page 209.

Day of Year	Day of Month	Day of Week	⊕ Rises h. m.	Key	⊕ Sets h. m.	Key	Length of Days h. m.	Sun Fast m.	Full Sea Boston A.M.	P.M.	☽ Rises h. m.	Key	☽ Sets h. m.	Key	Declination of Sun °	☽ Place	☽ Age
305	1	M.	6 17	D	4 38	B	10 21	32	12	12	5 57	B	8 18	E	14 s.35	TAU	17
306	2	Tu.	6 19	D	4 37	B	10 18	32	12¼	12¾	6 46	B	9 13	E	14 54	TAU	18
307	3	W.	6 20	D	4 35	B	10 15	32	1¼	1½	7 41	B	10 03	E	15 12	TAU	19
308	4	Th.	6 21	D	4 34	B	10 13	32	2	2	8 41	B	10 49	E	15 31	GEM	20
309	5	Fr.	6 22	D	4 33	B	10 11	32	2¾	2¾	9 45	C	11 29	E	15 49	GEM	21
310	6	Sa.	6 24	D	4 32	B	10 08	32	3½	3¾	10 52	C	12 06	D	16 07	CAN	22
311	7	C	6 25	D	4 31	A	10 06	32	4½	4¾	—	—	12 39	D	16 25	CAN	23

1 2 3 4 5 6 7 8 9 10 11 12 13

1. The text heading the calendar page is a summary of the sky sightings for the month. These astronomical highlights appear on each month's calendar page.

2. The dates and times of the Moon's phases for the month. (For more details, see Glossary, page 38.)

3. The days of the year, month, and week are listed on each calendar page. The traditional ecclesiastical calendar designation for Sunday — the Dominical Letter — C for 1993, B for 1994 — is used by the Almanac. (For further explanation, see Glossary, page 38.)

4. Sunrise and sunset times (EST) for Boston for each day of the month.

5. Key Letter columns. The letters in the two columns marked "Key" are designed to correct the sunrise/sunset times given for Boston to other localities. Note that each sunrise/sunset time has its Key Letter. The values (that is, the number of minutes) of these Key Letters are given in the **Time Correction Tables**, page 209. Simply find your city, or the city nearest you, in the tables, and locate the figure in the appropriate Key Letter column. Add, or subtract, those minutes to the sunrise or sunset time given for Boston. (The result will be accurate to within 5 minutes for latitudes north of 35 degrees, 10 minutes for latitudes 30-35 degrees, and 15 minutes for latitudes 25-30 degrees. See Time Correction Tables for the latitude of your locality.)

Example:

To find the time of sunrise in Cleveland, Ohio, on November 3, 1993:

Sunrise, Boston, with Key Letter D	6:20 A.M., EST
Value of Key Letter D for Cleveland (p. 210)	+ 40 minutes
Sunrise, Cleveland	7:00 A.M., EST

Use the same process for sunset. (Add one hour for Daylight Saving Time between April 3 and October 30.)

6. Length of Days. This column denotes how long the Sun will be above the horizon in Boston for each day of the month. To determine the length of any given day in your locality, follow the procedure outlined in #5 above to determine the sunrise and sunset times for your city. Then, add 12 hours to the time of sunset, subtract the time of sunrise, and you will have the length of day.

Example:

Sunset, Cleveland, Ohio, Nov. 1	5:21
Add 12 hours	+ 12:00
	17:21
Subtract sunrise, Cleveland, Nov. 1	− 6:57
Length of day, Cleveland, Nov. 1 (10 hrs., 24 min.)	10:24

7. The Sun Fast column is designed to change sundial time into local clock time. A sundial reads natural, or Sun, time, which is neither Standard nor Daylight time except by coincidence. Simply *subtract* the minutes given in the Sun Fast column to get local clock time, and use Key Letter C in the Time Correction Tables (page 209) to correct the time for your city. (Add one hour for Daylight Saving Time between April 3 and October 30.)

Example: **Boston, MA**

Sundial reading, Nov. 1	12:00
Subtract Sun Fast	− 32 minutes
Clock time	11:28 A.M., EST

Example: **Austin, TX**

Sundial reading, Nov. 1	12:00
Subtract Sun Fast	− 32 minutes
	11:28
Use Key C for Austin (page 209)	+ 47 minutes
Clock time	12:15 P.M., CST

8. The times of daily high tides in Boston, for morning and evening, are recorded in this column. ("12½" under "Full Sea Boston, A.M." on November 2 means that the high tide that morning will be at 12:30 — with the number of feet of high tide shown for some of the dates on the Right-Hand Calendar Pages). The corrections for tides in a selected number of localities can be found in the **Tide Correction Tables** on page 204.

9. Moonrise and moonset times (EST) for Boston are recorded in these columns for each day of the month.

10. Key Letter columns. These columns designate the letters to be used to correct the moonrise/moonset times for Boston to other localities. As explained in #5, the same procedure for calculating "Sunrise/sunset" is used *except* that an additional correction factor based on longitude (see table below) should be used. For the longitude of your city, consult the Time Correction Tables, page 209.

Longitude of city	Correction minutes
58°- 76°	0
77°- 89°	+1
90°-102°	+2
103°-115°	+3
116°-127°	+4
128°-141°	+5
142°-155°	+6

Example:

To determine the time of moonrise in Madison, Wisconsin, on November 1, 1993:

Moonrise, Boston, with Key Letter B	5:57 P.M., EST
Value of Key Letter B for Madison (page 211)	+ 11 minutes
Correction for Madison longitude 89° 23'	+ 1 minute
Moonrise, Madison	6:09 P.M., CST

Use the same procedure for moonset. (Add one hour for Daylight Saving Time between April 3 and October 30.)

11. This column denotes the declination of the Sun (angular distance from the celestial equator) in degrees and minutes, at *noon,* EST.

12. The Moon's Place denoted in this column is its *astronomical* place, i.e., its *actual* placement, in the heavens. (This should not be confused with the Moon's *astrological* place in the zodiac, as explained on page 160.) *All calculations in* this Almanac, except for the astrological information on pages 160-164, are based on astronomy, not astrology.

In addition to the 12 constellations of the astronomical zodiac, four other abbreviations appear in this column: Cetus (CET) lies south of the zodiac, just south of Pisces and Aries. Ophiuchus (OPH) is a constellation primarily north of the zodiac, but with a small corner between Scorpius and Sagittarius. Orion (ORI) is a constellation whose northern limit first reaches the zodiac between Taurus and Gemini. Sextans (SEX) lies south of the zodiac except for a corner that just touches it near Leo.

13. The last column lists the Moon's age, i.e., the number of days since the previous new Moon. (The lunar month is 29.53 days.)

Further astronomical data may be found on page 42, which lists the eclipses for the upcoming year, details of the principal meteor showers, and dates of the full Moon over a five-year period.

The Visible Planets (page 40) list the rising and setting times for Venus, Mars, Jupiter, and Saturn for 1994; page 43 carries the rising and setting and transit times of the Bright Stars for 1994. Both feature Key Letters, designed to convert the Boston times given to those of other localities (see Nos. 5 and 10 above). Use the letters given, in conjunction with the Time Correction Tables (page 209) to calculate the times for your area.

THE RIGHT-HAND CALENDAR PAGES

(Pages 55-81)

These pages are a combination of astronomical data; specific dates in mainly the Anglican church calendar, inclusion of which has always been traditional in American and English almanacs (though we also include some other religious dates); tide heights at Boston (the Left-Hand Calendar Pages include the daily times of high tides; the corrections for your locality are on page 204); quotations; anniversary dates; appropriate seasonal activities; and a rhyming version of the weather forecasts for New England. (Detailed forecasts for the entire country are presented on pages 114-146.)

The following details some of the entries from this year's Right-Hand Calendar Pages, together with a sample (the first part of November 1993) of a calendar page explained. Also, following the Almanac's tradition, the Chronological Cycles and Eras for 1994 are listed.

MOVABLE FEASTS AND FASTS FOR 1994

Septuagesima Sunday .... Jan. 30
Shrove Tuesday .... Feb. 15
Ash Wednesday .... Feb. 16
Palm Sunday .... Mar. 27
Good Friday .... Apr. 1

Easter Day .... Apr. 3
Low Sunday .... Apr. 10
Rogation Sunday .... May 8
Ascension Day .... May 12
Whit Sunday-Pentecost .... May 22
Trinity Sunday .... May 29
Corpus Christi .... June 2
1st Sunday in Advent .... Nov. 27

THE SEASONS OF 1993-1994

Fall 1993 .... Sept. 22, 7:22 P.M., EST
Winter 1993 .... Dec. 21, 3:26 P.M., EST
Spring 1994 .... Mar. 20, 3:28 P.M., EST
Summer 1994 ... June 21, 9:48 A.M., EST
Fall 1994 .... Sept. 23, 1:19 A.M., EST
Winter 1994 .... Dec. 21, 9:23 P.M., EST

CHRONOLOGICAL CYCLES FOR 1994

Golden Number (Lunar Cycle) 19
Epact 17
Solar Cycle 15
Dominical Letter .... B
Roman Indiction 2
Year of Julian Period 6707

Era	Year	Begins
Byzantine	7503	Sept. 14
Jewish (A.M.)*	5755	Sept. 5
Roman (A.U.C.)	2747	Jan. 14
Nabonassar	2743	Apr. 25
Japanese	2654	Jan. 1
Grecian (Seleucidae)	2306	Sept. 14
		(or Oct. 14)
Indian (Saka)	1916	Mar. 22
Diocletian	1711	Sept. 11
Islamic (Hegira)*	1415	June 9
Chinese (Lunar)	4692	Feb. 10
(Dog)		

Year begins at sunset

DETERMINATION OF EARTHQUAKES

☞ Note, on right-hand pages 55-81, the dates when the Moon (☽) "rides high" or "runs low." The date of the high begins the most likely five-day period of earthquakes in the Northern Hemisphere; the date of the low indicates a similar five-day period in the Southern Hemisphere. You will also find on these pages a notation for Moon on the Equator (☽ on Eq.) twice each month.

At this time, in both hemispheres, is a two-day earthquake period.

NAMES AND CHARACTERS OF THE PRINCIPAL PLANETS AND ASPECTS

☞ Every now and again on these Right-Hand Calendar Pages, you will see symbols conjoined in groups to tell you what is happening in the heavens. For example, ♂ ♃ ☾ opposite November 12, 1993, (see below) means that Jupiter ♃ and the Moon ☾ are on that date in conjunction ♂ or apparently near each other.

Here are the symbols used ...

☉	Sun	♂	Mars
○●☾	Moon	♇	Pluto
☿	Mercury	♃	Jupiter
♄	Saturn	♂	Conjunction, or in the same degree
♀	Venus		
♅	Uranus	☊	Ascending Node
⊕	Earth	☋	Descending Node
♆	Neptune	☍	Opposition, or 180 degrees

EARTH AT APHELION AND PERIHELION 1994

☞ The Earth will be at Perihelion on January 2, 1994, when it will be 91,400,005 miles from the Sun. The Earth will be at Aphelion on July 5, 1994, when it will be 94,512,258 miles from the Sun.

SAMPLE RIGHT-HAND CALENDAR PAGE
(from November 1993 — page 55)

Day of the month.

Day of the week.

For detailed regional forecasts, see pages 114-146.

	D.M.	D.W.	Dates, Feasts, Fasts, Aspects, Tide Heights	Weather
23rd Sunday after Pentecost. (Events in the church calendar generally appear in this typeface.)	1	M.	All Saints • ☾ at ☋ • Earthquake, Lisbon, Portugal, 1755 •	After
The Dominical Letter for 1993 was C because the first Sunday of the year fell on the third day of January. The letter for 1994 is B.	2	Tu.	All Souls • 7° snow, New York City, 1810 • Tides {9.2 {10.2 •	a
	3	W.	☾ high • rides Great flood, Vermont, 1927 • Stephen Austin born, 1793 •	mist,
	4	Th.	Virtues, like essences, lose their fragrance when exposed. Tides {8.9 {10.0	it's
Conjunction — closest approach — of Venus and Jupiter.	5	Fr.	☿ at inf. ♂ • Transit of ♀ • Roy Rogers born, 1912 •	clear and
	6	Sa.	St. Leonard • Edsel Ford born, 1893 • Tides {8.9 {9.8	warm.
The Moon is at perigee, the point in its orbit closest to the Earth.	7	C	23☌ ♁. at ♇. • Bolshevik Revolution began, 1917	Inconsist-
	8	M.	♂♀♃ • The secret of being a bore is to tell everything. • Tides {9.5 {9.8	ent;
	9	Tu.	☾ Eq. • on Auspicious day for travel. • Great Lakes gale, 1913 Tides {10.0 {10.0	now a
Morning tide at Boston, shown to be at 12:15 A.M. on the left-hand page, will be 10.6 feet. The 12:30 P.M. tide will be 11.9 feet.	10	W.	Marine Corps created by Continental Congress, 1775 • Tides {10.7 {10.3	storm.
	11	Th.	St. Martin • Veterans Day • Indian summer begins. •	Hunters
	12	Fr.	☾ at perig. • ♂♃☾ • ♂♀☾ Tides {11.8 {10.8 •	hale
St. Hilda, seventh-century British abbess, founder of the Whitby Monastery. Her wise counsel and advice were sought by rulers and commoners. (Certain religious feasts and civil holidays appear in this typeface.)	13	Sa.	New ● • Eclipse of ☉ • Sadie Hawkins Day Tides {12.2 {10.8 •	and
	14	C	24th ♁. at ♇. • ☾ at ☊ • ♂☿♀ • ☿ stat. • {12.4 {10.8	heavy-booted
	15	M.	45° snow, Water- town, N.Y., 1900 • Tides {12.3	
	16	Tu.	☾ low • −53° F, Lincoln 14NE, Montana, 1959 • Tides {10.6 {11.9	crush
	17	W.	St. Hugh of Lincoln • ♂♇☉ • ♂♅☾ • ♂☾☾ •	the
	18	Th.	St. Hilda • Julia Ward Howe wrote lyrics to "Battle Hymn of the Republic," 1861	leaves,

For a more complete explanation of terms used throughout the Almanac, see Glossary, page 38.

When Your Knees Go Bad...
You're in Trouble!

Now thanks to Coach "Cotton" Barlow, there's an answer

Nobody knows more about crippling knee pain, stiffness and strain than Coach "Cotton" Barlow.

In his many years on and off the field, veteran Coach Barlow realized ordinary knee supports just didn't give enough support. So he set out to make a knee support that could add strength and stability directly to the joint where support and protection are needed the most.

For People Of All Ages

Coach Barlow's fantastic invention uses no metal, yet it provides maximum lateral and cap support. This incredibly lightweight support absorbs shocks, prevents twisting and provides soothing warmth to injured or arthritic joints.

No Risk Offer

We urge you to try the BARLOW Knee Support for 30 days. If it doesn't bring you total pain free relief, we'll refund your purchase price without question.

"My doctor said...'best knee support he'd ever seen. Advised to keep wearing it'!"
Mrs E.L., Fairfield Bay, AR

Custom form-fitting pad prevents slipping and gives maximum mobility and comfort.

Lightweight non-metal construction allows full range of motion and can be worn comfortably for hours.

Improves natural knee function and relieves discomfort.

Patented material insulates, warms, and soothes knee joint.

Machine washable. Non-allergenic

Adds strength, stability, support and protection where needed.

Available in five sizes to ensure proper fit for either left or right knee.

HOLIDAYS, 1994

(*) Recommended as holidays with pay for all employees
(**) State observances only

Jan. 1 (*) New Year's Day
Jan. 6 Epiphany
Jan. 17 (*) Martin Luther King Jr.'s
 Birthday *(observed)*
Jan. 19 (**) Robert E. Lee's Birthday
 (Ark., Fla., S.C., Tenn.)
Feb. 2 Groundhog Day
Feb. 12 (**) Abraham Lincoln's Birthday
Feb. 14 Valentine's Day
Feb. 15 (**) Mardi Gras *(Ala., La.)*
Feb. 16 Ash Wednesday
Feb. 21 (*) Presidents Day
Feb. 22 George Washington's Birthday
Mar. 2 (**) Texas Independence Day
Mar. 15 (**) Andrew Jackson Day *(Tenn.)*
Mar. 17 (**) St. Patrick's Day; Evacuation
 Day *(Boston and Suffolk Co., Mass.)*
Mar. 27 Palm Sunday; Passover
Mar. 28 (**) Seward's Day *(Alaska)*
Apr. 1 Good Friday
Apr. 2 (**) Pascua Florida Day
Apr. 3 Easter
Apr. 13 (**) Thomas Jefferson's Birthday
 (Okla.)
Apr. 18 (**) Patriots Day *(Fla., Me., Mass.)*
Apr. 29 Arbor Day *(except Alaska,
 Georgia, Kansas, Virginia, Wyoming)*
May 1 May Day; Orthodox Easter
May 8 Mother's Day
May 21 Armed Forces Day
May 23 Victoria Day *(Canada)*
May 30 (*) Memorial Day *(observed)*
June 5 World Environment Day

June 11 (**) King Kamehameha I Day
 (Hawaii)
June 14 Flag Day
June 17 (**) Bunker Hill Day *(Boston and
 Suffolk Co., Mass.)*
June 19 Father's Day
June 20 West Virginia Day
July 1 Canada Day
July 4 (*) Independence Day
July 24 (**) Pioneer Day *(Utah)*
Aug. 8 (**) Victory Day *(R.I.)*
Aug. 16 (**) Bennington Battle Day *(Vt.)*
Aug. 26 Women's Equality Day
Sept. 5 (*) Labor Day
Sept. 6 Rosh Hashanah
Sept. 9 (**) Admissions Day *(Calif.)*
Sept. 11 Grandparents Day
Sept. 13 (**) Defenders Day *(observed Md.)*
Sept. 15 Yom Kippur
Sept. 28 (**) Frances Willard Day
 (Minn., Wis.)
Oct. 10 (*) Columbus Day *(observed);*
 Thanksgiving *(Canada)*
Oct. 18 (**) Alaska Day
Oct. 24 United Nations Day
Oct. 31 Halloween; (**) Nevada Day
Nov. 4 (**) Will Rogers Day *(Okla.)*
Nov. 8 Election Day
Nov. 11 (*) Veterans Day
Nov. 19 Discovery Day *(Puerto Rico)*
Nov. 24 (*) Thanksgiving Day
Nov. 27 John F. Kennedy Day *(Mass.)*
Nov. 28 Chanukah
Dec. 10 (**) Wyoming Day
Dec. 15 Bill of Rights Day
Dec. 25 Christmas Day
Dec. 26 Boxing Day *(Canada)*

HOW THE ALMANAC WEATHER FORECASTS ARE MADE

Our weather forecasts are determined both by the use of a secret formula devised by the founder of this Almanac in 1792 and by the most modern scientific calculations based on solar activity. We believe nothing in the universe occurs haphazardly; there is a cause-and-effect pattern to all phenomena, including weather. It follows, therefore, that we believe weather is predictable. It is obvious, however, that neither we nor anyone else has as yet gained sufficient insight into the mysteries of the universe to predict weather with anything resembling total accuracy.

Park Seed®
Flowers and Vegetables
1994

Yours **FREE!**

The Big New Park Seed Catalog

"With color so real you can almost smell the beautiful flowers and taste the luscious vegetables!"

Our big, 132 page catalog is chock-full of delights for your garden . . . Artichokes to Zucchini — Ageratum to Zinnia — from the most advanced new varieties and the rare, to your long-time favorites. Here in one big color catalog you'll find over **2,100 quality products:** flower and vegetable seed, bulbs, plants and garden supplies — many available only from Park. We back each and every one with a solid guarantee of complete satisfaction.

Have more fun gardening this year with **Park High Performer®** **varieties** — flowers more beautiful and easier to grow, vegetables with better taste and higher yield. Park tests thousands each year to make sure you get only the best. **Send for your free copy today and let Park Help You Grow!**

Complete Satisfaction Guaranteed
"Home Garden Seed Specialists Since 1868"

GLOSSARY

Aph. — Aphelion: Planet reaches point in its orbit farthest from the Sun.

Apo. — Apogee: Moon reaches point in its orbit farthest from the Earth.

Celestial Equator: The plane of the Earth's equator projected out into space.

Conj. — Conjunction: Time of apparent closest approach to each other of any two heavenly bodies. **Inf. — Inferior:** Conjunction in which the planet is between the Sun and the Earth. **Sup. — Superior:** Indicates that the Sun is between the planet and the Earth.

Declination: Measurement of angular distance of any celestial object perpendicularly north or south of celestial equator; analogous to terrestrial latitude. The Almanac gives the Sun's declination at noon EST.

Dominical Letter: Used for the ecclesiastical calendar and determined by the date on which the first Sunday of the year falls. If Jan. 1 is a Sunday, the Letter is A; if Jan. 2 is a Sunday, the Letter is B; and so to G when the first Sunday is Jan. 7. In leap year the Letter applies through February and then takes the Letter before.

Eclipse, Annular: An eclipse in which sunlight shows around the Moon.

Eclipse, Lunar: Opposition of the Sun and Moon with the Moon at or near node.

Eclipse, Solar: Conjunction of Sun and Moon with the Moon at or near node.

Epact: A number from 1 to 30 to harmonize the lunar year with the solar year, used for the ecclesiastical calendar. Indicates the Moon's age at the instant Jan. 1 begins at the meridian of Greenwich, England.

Eq. — Equator: A great circle of the Earth equidistant from the two poles.

Equinox, Autumnal: Sun passes from Northern to Southern Hemisphere. **Vernal:** Sun passes from Southern to Northern Hemisphere.

Evening Star: A planet that is above the horizon at sunset and less than 180 degrees east of the Sun.

Golden Number: The year in the 19-year cycle of the Moon. The Moon phases occur on the same dates every 19 years.

Greatest Elongation (Gr. El.): Greatest apparent angular distance of a planet from the Sun as seen from the Earth.

Julian Period: A period of 7,980 Julian years, being a period of agreement of solar and lunar cycles. Add 4,713 to year to find the Julian year.

Moon's Age: The number of days since the previous new Moon.

Moon's Phases: First Quarter: Right half of Moon illuminated. **Full Moon:** Moon reaches opposition. **Last Quarter:** Left half of Moon illuminated. **New Moon:** Sun and Moon in conjunction.

Moon Rides High or Runs Low: Day of month Moon is highest or lowest above the south point of the observer's horizon.

Morning Star: A planet that is above the horizon at sunrise and less than 180 degrees west of the Sun in right ascension.

Node: Either of the two points where the Moon's orbit intersects the ecliptic.

Occultation: Eclipse of a star or planet by the Moon or another planet.

Opposition: Time when the Sun and Moon or planet appear on opposite sides of the sky (El. 180 degrees).

Perig. — Perigee: Moon reaches point in its orbit closest to the Earth.

Perih. — Perihelion: Planet reaches point in its orbit closest to the Sun.

R.A. — Right Ascension: The coordinate on the celestial sphere analogous to longitude on the Earth.

Roman Indiction: A cycle of 15 years established Jan. 1, A.D. 313, as a fiscal term. Add 3 to the number of years in the Christian era and divide by 15. The remainder is Roman Indiction — no remainder is 15.

Solar Cycle: A period of 28 years, at the end of which the days of the month return to the same days of the week.

Solstice, Summer: Point at which the Sun is farthest north of the celestial equator. **Winter:** Point at which the Sun is farthest south of the celestial equator.

Stat. — Stationary: Halt in the apparent movement of a planet against the background of the stars just before the planet comes to opposition.

Sun Fast: Subtract times given in this column from your sundial to arrive at the correct Standard Time.

Sunrise & Sunset: Visible rising and setting of the Sun's upper limb across the unobstructed horizon of an observer whose eyes are 15 feet above ground level.

Twilight: Begins or ends when stars of the sixth magnitude appear or disappear at the zenith; or when the Sun is about 18 degrees below the horizon.

Life after Death

THERE IS NOTHING more certain than death. But what is death? Are those who die really dead, or are they more alive than ever? If they are not dead, where are they— the righteous, the unrighteous, the believers, the unbelievers? The Bible assures us that there is life beyond the grave for all, and that it is the divine purpose to restore the dead to life in the resurrection.

Where will you be in the resurrection?

Will you see and know your loved ones who have died?

You will enjoy the Bible's answer to these questions, as presented in the free booklet, **"Life after Death."** Fill in and mail the coupon below, and obtain your free copy. There is no obligation.

- -

**THE BIBLE ANSWERS, Dept. F
Box 60, General Post Office
New York, NY 10116**

☐ Please send me a FREE copy of
"Life after Death."

NAME. . . . .

ADDRESS. . . . .

City/State/Zip. . . . .

THE VISIBLE PLANETS, 1994

The times of rising or setting of the planets Venus, Mars, Jupiter, and Saturn on the 1st, 11th, and 21st of each month are given below. The approximate time of rising or setting of these planets on other days may be found with sufficient accuracy by interpolation. For an explanation of Key Letters (used in adjusting the times given here for Boston to the time in your town), see page 30 and pages 209-213. Key Letters appear as capital letters beside the time of rising or setting. (For definitions of morning and evening stars, see page 38.)

VENUS is too close to the Sun for observation until the end of February, when it appears as a brilliant object in the evening sky. By late October it again becomes too close to the Sun for observation until the middle of November, when it reappears in the morning sky. Venus is in conjunction with Mercury on November 12.

MARS is too close to the Sun for observation until late February, when it appears in the morning sky in Capricorn. Its westward elongation gradually increases as it passes through Aquarius, Pisces, Aries, Taurus, Gemini, Cancer, and into Leo, where it can be seen for more than half the night. Mars is in conjunction with Mercury on February 26 and April 3 and with Saturn on March 14.

Boldface — P.M.   Lightface — A.M.

Jan. 1 .... rise 7:02 E	July 1 .... set 9:41 D
Jan. 11 .... set 4:21 A	July 11 .... " 9:29 D
Jan. 21 .... " 4:45 A	July 21 .... " 9:13 D
Feb. 1 .... " 5:12 A	Aug. 1 .... " 8:53 C
Feb. 11 .... " 5:38 B	Aug. 11 .... " 8:33 C
Feb. 21 .... " 6:04 B	Aug. 21 .... " 8:11 B
Mar. 1 .... " 6:24 B	Sept. 1 .... " 7:46 B
Mar. 11 ...... " 6:49 C	Sept. 11 ...... " 7:21 B
Mar. 21 ...... " 7:14 D	Sept. 21 ...... " 6:54 A
Apr. 1 .... " 7:41 D	Oct. 1 .... " 6:22 A
Apr. 11 .... " 8:07 D	Oct. 11 .... " 5:45 A
Apr. 21 .... " 8:32 E	Oct. 21 .... " 5:02 A
May 1 .... " 8:57 E	Nov. 1 .... " 4:11 A
May 11 .... " 9:18 E	Nov. 11 ..... rise 5:30 D
May 21 .... " 9:36 E	Nov. 21 ...... " 4:30 D
June 1 .... " 9:48 E	Dec. 1 .... " 3:51 D
June 11 ...... " 9:52 E	Dec. 11 ...... " 3:31 D
June 21 .... set 9:49 E	Dec. 21 ...... " 3:25 D
	Dec. 31 ...... rise 3:27 D

Boldface — P.M.   Lightface — A.M.

Jan. 1 .... rise 7:13 E	July 1 .... rise 1:33 A
Jan. 11 .... " 7:04 E	July 11 .... " 1:17 A
Jan. 21 .... " 6:53 E	July 21 ...... " 1:01 A
Feb. 1 .... " 6:37 E	Aug. 1 .... " 12:46 A
Feb. 11 .... " 6:22 D	Aug. 11 ...... " 12:33 A
Feb. 21 .... " 6:04 D	Aug. 21 .... " 12:21 A
Mar. 1 .... " 5:49 D	Sept. 1 ..... " 12:10 A
Mar. 11 ..... " 5:30 D	Sept. 11 ..... " 12:00 A
Mar. 21 ..... " 5:09 D	Sept. 21 .... rise 11:49 A
Apr. 1 .... " 4:45 C	Oct. 1 .... " 11:38 A
Apr. 11 ...... " 4:23 C	Oct. 11 ...... " 11:27 A
Apr. 21 ...... " 4:01 C	Oct. 21 ...... " 11:14 A
May 1 .... " 3:38 B	Nov. 1 ...... " 10:59 A
May 11 ...... " 3:16 B	Nov. 11 ..... " 10:43 A
May 21 ...... " 2:54 B	Nov. 21 ..... " 10:25 B
June 1 .... " 2:31 B	Dec. 1 .... " 10:03 B
June 11 ...... " 2:11 B	Dec. 11 ..... " 9:38 B
June 21 ... rise 1:52 A	Dec. 21 ...... " 9:07 B
	Dec. 31 ...... rise 8:32 B

JUPITER can be seen in the morning sky in Libra at the beginning of the year, and by early February it is visible for more than half the night. Its westward elongation increases until on April 30 it can be seen throughout the night; its eastward elongation then decreases as it passes into Virgo in late May. By mid-August it is visible in the evening sky in Libra until early November, when it becomes too close to the Sun for observation. At the beginning of December it reappears in the morning sky, passing into Scorpius in midmonth.

SATURN can be seen from the beginning of the year in the evening sky in Aquarius. In early February it becomes too close to the Sun for observation, reappearing in the morning sky in early March. Its westward elongation gradually increases until September 1, when it is visible throughout the night. Its eastward elongation then gradually decreases, and by early December it can be seen only in the evening sky. Saturn is in conjunction with Mercury on February 1 and March 24 and with Mars on March 14.

IVPITER

Boldface — P.M.	Lightface — A.M.	Boldface — P.M.	Lightface — A.M.
Jan. 1 .... rise 2:20 D	July 1........ set 12:38 B	Jan. 1......... set 8:09 B	July 1 .... rise 10:30 D
Jan. 11....... " 1:48 D	July 11..... set 11:55 B	Jan. 11...... " 7:35 B	July 11...... " 9:51 D
Jan. 21........ " 1:15 D	July 21 ...... " 11:16 B	Jan. 21...... " 7:01 B	July 21...... " 9:11 D
Feb. 1......... " 12:37 D	Aug. 1....... " 10:35 B	Feb. 1...... " 6:24 B	Aug. 1 .... " 8:26 D
Feb. 11...... " 12:01 D	Aug. 11..... " 9:58 B	Feb. 11..... " 5:51 B	Aug. 11 .... " 7:46 D
Feb. 21.... rise 11:20 D	Aug. 21..... " 9:22 B	Feb. 21..... " 5:18 B	Aug. 21 .... " 7:05 D
Mar. 1....... " 10:49 D	Sept. 1....... " 8:43 B	Mar. 1...... rise 6:12 D	Sept. 1......... " 6:20 D
Mar. 11...... " 10:08 D	Sept. 11 .... " 8:07 B	Mar. 11 ..... " 5:36 D	Sept. 11..... set 4:31 B
Mar. 21..... " 9:26 D	Sept. 21 .... " 7:33 B	Mar. 21 .... " 4:59 D	Sept. 21..... " 3:48 B
Apr. 1 .... " 8:38 D	Oct. 1 .... " 6:59 B	Apr. 1......... " 4:19 D	Oct. 1 .... " 3:01 B
Apr. 11 ...... " 7:54 D	Oct. 11...... " 6:25 B	Apr. 11..... " 3:42 D	Oct. 11...... " 2:19 B
Apr. 21 ...... " 7:08 D	Oct. 21...... " 5:51 A	Apr. 21..... " 3:05 D	Oct. 21...... " 1:38 B
May 1......... " 6:23 D	Nov. 1 .... " 5:15 A	May 1......... " 2:28 D	Nov. 1 .... " 12:53 B
May 11...... set 4:09 B	Nov. 11 ..... " 4:42 A	May 11..... " 1:50 D	Nov. 11 ...... " 12:14 B
May 21 ...... " 3:26 B	Nov. 21..... rise 6:26 D	May 21...... " 1:13 D	Nov. 21..... set 11:35 B
June 1......... " 2:40 B	Dec. 1......... " 5:58 D	June 1 .... " 12:31 D	Dec. 1......... " 10:58 B
June 11 ...... " 1:59 B	Dec. 11...... " 5:30 E	June 11 .... rise 11:48 D	Dec. 11..... " 10:21 B
June 21..... set 1:18 B	Dec. 21...... " 5:01 E	June 21 .. rise 11:10 D	Dec. 21..... " 9:45 B
	Dec. 31 ...... rise 4:32 E		Dec. 31...... set 9:09 B

MERCURY can be seen only low in the east before sunrise or low in the west after sunset. It is visible mornings between these approximate dates: February 27-April 22, July 4-August 5, and October 28-November 27. The planet is brighter at the end of each period (best viewing conditions in northern latitudes occur the first week of November). It is visible evenings between these approximate dates: January 18-February 14, May 8-June 16, August 23-October 15, and December 30-31. The planet is brighter at the beginning of each period (best viewing conditions in northern latitudes occur early February and the second half of May). *DO NOT CONFUSE 1) Mars with Mercury at the beginning of March, when Mars is the brighter object. The reddish tint of Mars should assist in its identification. 2) Saturn with Mars around mid-March when Saturn is the brighter object. 3) Mercury with Saturn in early February and late March and with Mars late March and early April; on all occasions Mercury is the brighter object. 4) Venus with Mercury mid-November, when Venus is the brighter object.*

ECLIPSES FOR 1994

There will be four eclipses in 1994, two of the Sun and two of the Moon. One of the solar eclipses will not be visible from North America or Hawaii; the others will be seen in certain locations, as specified below. Lunar eclipses technically are visible from the entire night side of the Earth; solar eclipses are visible only in certain areas.

1. Annular eclipse of the Sun, May 10. The eclipse will be visible throughout North America — a rare event. Along the West Coast, the partial phase will begin around 6:45 A.M., PST, in the Southwest; 8:00 A.M., PST, in the Northwest; and end around 9:30 A.M., PST, throughout the region. Along the East Coast, it will begin around 10:15 A.M., EST, in the Southeast; 11:00 A.M., EST, in the Northeast; and end around 2:30 P.M., EST, throughout the region. The annular phase will be visible along a narrow band running from the Southwest to the Northeast, beginning about 8:00 A.M., PST, in the Southwest; 10:30 A.M., CST, in the central regions; and noon EST in the Northeast.

2. Partial eclipse of the Moon, May 24-25. The beginning of the umbral phase will be visible throughout North America, except the Far West, Alaska, Hawaii, and southwestern Canada. The end will be visible throughout North America except Alaska, Hawaii, and northwestern Canada. The Moon enters penumbra at 8:18 P.M., EST (5:18 P.M., PST); the middle occurs at 10:30 P.M., EST (7:30 P.M., PST); the Moon leaves penumbra at 12:43 A.M., EST, on the 25th (9:43 P.M., PST on the 24th).

3. Total eclipse of the Sun, November 3. Not visible from North America or Hawaii.

4. Penumbral eclipse of the Moon, November 17-18. The eclipse will be visible throughout North America and Hawaii. The Moon enters penumbra at 11:26 P.M., EST (8:26 P.M., PST), on the 17th; the middle occurs at 1:44 A.M., EST, on the 18th (10:44 P.M., PST, Nov. 17); the Moon leaves penumbra at 4:02 A.M., EST (1:02 A.M., PST), on the 18th.

FULL MOON DAYS

	1994	1995	1996	1997	1998
Jan.	27	16	5	23	12
Feb.	25	15	4	22	11
Mar.	27	16	5	23	12
Apr.	25	15	3	22	11
May	24	14	3	22	11
June	23	12	1/30	20	9
July	22	12	30	19	9
Aug.	21	10	28	18	7
Sept.	19	8	26	16	6
Oct.	19	8	26	15	5
Nov.	18	7	24	14	4
Dec.	17	6	24	13	3

PRINCIPAL METEOR SHOWERS

Shower	Best Hour (EST)	Radiant Direction*	Date of Maximum**	Approx. Peak Rate (/hr.)	Associated Comet
Quadrantid	5 A.M.	N.	Jan. 4	40-150	—
Lyrid	4 A.M.	S.	Apr. 21	10-15	1861 I
Eta Aquarid	4 A.M.	S.E.	May 4	10-40	Halley
Delta Aquarid	2 A.M.	S.	July 30	10-35	—
Perseid	4 A.M.	N.	Aug. 11-13	50-100	1862 III
Draconid	9 P.M.	N.W.	Oct. 9	10	Giacobini-Zinner
Orionid	4 A.M.	S.	Oct. 20	10-70	Halley
Taurid	midnight	S.	Nov. 9	5-15	Encke
Leonid	5 A.M.	S.	Nov. 16	5-20	1866 I
Andromedid	10 P.M.	S.	Nov. 25-27	10	Biela
Geminid	2 A.M.	S.	Dec. 13	50-80	—
Ursid	5 A.M.	N.	Dec. 22	10-15	—

* Direction from which the meteors appear to come.
** Date of actual maximum occurrence may vary by one or two days in either direction.

BRIGHT STARS, 1994

The upper table shows the Eastern Standard Time when each star transits the meridian of Boston (i.e., lies directly above the horizon's south point there) and its altitude above that point at transit on the dates shown. The time of transit on any other date differs from that on the nearest date listed by approximately four minutes of time for each day. For a place outside Boston the local time of the star's transit is found by correcting the time at Boston by the value of Key Letter "C" for the place. (See footnote.)

Star	Constellation	Magni-tude	Jan. 1	Mar. 1	May 1	July 1	Sept. 1	Nov. 1	Alt.
Altair	Aquila	0.8	**12:50**	8:58	4:58	12:58	**8:50**	**4:50**	56.3
Deneb	Cygnus	1.3	**1:41**	9:49	5:49	1:49	**9:41**	**5:41**	92.8
Fomalhaut	Psc. Austr.	1.2	**3:55**	**12:03**	8:03	4:03	**11:56**	**7:56**	17.8
Algol	Perseus	2.2	**8:06**	**4:14**	**12:14**	8:14	4:10	12:11	88.5
Aldebaran	Taurus	0.9	**9:33**	**5:41**	**1:41**	9:42	5:38	1:38	64.1
Rigel	Orion	0.1	**10:11**	**6:20**	**2:20**	10:20	6:16	2:16	39.4
Capella	Auriga	0.1	**10:13**	**6:21**	**2:21**	10:22	6:18	2:18	93.6
Bellatrix	Orion	1.6	**10:22**	**6:30**	**2:30**	10:31	6:27	2:27	54.0
Betelgeuse	Orion	var. 0.4	**10:52**	**7:00**	**3:00**	11:01	6:57	2:57	55.0
Sirius	Can. Maj.	−1.4	**11:42**	**7:50**	**3:50**	11:50	7:46	3:47	31.0
Procyon	Can. Min.	0.4	12:40	**8:44**	**4:44**	**12:44**	8:40	4:40	52.9
Pollux	Gemini	1.2	12:46	**8:50**	**4:50**	**12:50**	8:46	4:46	75.7
Regulus	Leo	1.4	3:09	**11:13**	**7:13**	**3:13**	11:09	7:09	59.7
Spica	Virgo	var. 1.0	6:25	2:33	**10:29**	**6:29**	**2:26**	10:26	36.6
Arcturus	Bootes	−0.1	7:16	3:24	**11:20**	**7:20**	**3:16**	11:17	66.9
Antares	Scorpius	var. 0.9	9:29	5:37	1:37	**9:33**	**5:29**	**1:29**	21.3
Vega	Lyra	0.0	11:36	7:44	3:44	**11:40**	**7:37**	**3:37**	86.4

Time of Transit (EST) — Boldface — P.M. Lightface — A.M.

RISINGS AND SETTINGS

The times of the star's rising and setting at Boston on any date are found by applying the interval shown to the time of the star's transit on that date. Subtract the interval for the star's rising; add it for its setting. The times for a place outside Boston are found by correcting the times found for Boston by the values of the Key Letters shown. (See footnote.) The directions in which the star rises and sets shown for Boston are generally useful throughout the United States. Deneb, Algol, Capella, and Vega are circumpolar stars — this means that they do not appear to rise or set, but are above the horizon.

Star	Int. hr.m.	Rising Key	Rising Dir.	Setting Key	Setting Dir.
Altair	6:36	B	EbN	D	WbN
Fomalhaut	3:59	E	SE	A	SW
Aldebaran	7:06	B	ENE	D	WNW
Rigel	5:33	D	EbS	B	WbS
Bellatrix	6:27	B	EbN	D	WbN
Betelgeuse	6:31	B	EbN	D	WbN
Sirius	5:00	D	ESE	B	WSW
Procyon	6:23	B	EbN	D	WbN
Pollux	8:01	A	NE	E	NW
Regulus	6:49	B	EbN	D	WbN
Spica	5:23	D	EbS	B	WbS
Arcturus	7:19	A	ENE	E	WNW
Antares	4:17	E	SEbE	A	SWbW

NOTE: The values of Key Letters are given in the Time Correction Tables (pages 209-213).

DEAR MR. ROBERT B. THOMAS ...

A sampling of questions and comments from our readers during the past year.

I would like to comment on the article about the 1893 Chicago World's Fair in the 1993 edition of the Almanac.

It might interest you to know that G. W. G. Ferris was not the inventor of what we now call the Ferris wheel, nor did he even come up with the original idea. Ferris actually got the idea after visiting the man whom many people consider the true inventor of the "Ferris" wheel — William Somers of New Jersey.

In 1891 Somers formed a company to erect an "Observation Roundabout" on the Atlantic City boardwalk. The ride (built of wood, not metal) was a huge hit, and Somers either made contact with or was contacted by officials of the upcoming Columbian Exposition in Chicago.

Fair officials sent Ferris to study the Roundabout's design. Ferris returned to Chicago and built his wheel out of steel for the exposition. Somers sued Ferris; however, Ferris died before the lawsuit was settled. Ironically, the court found for Somers, but it was too late. The ride would be forever known as the Ferris wheel.

– Russell Roberts, Trenton, New Jersey

In the process of moving from New Hampshire to South Dakota, I found a box of Almanacs dated from 1965 to 1991; 1965 was the year I made captain at Eastern Airlines. Now why did a person on the leading edge of technology carry an *Old Farmer's Almanac* with him on every flight? It was good read-

ing for talkative jump-seat riders and FAA inspectors on long trips. It also had the tide tables.

One evening in 1960 we were on our way home to Boston with a scheduled stop in Newark. Boston was closed due to 0-0 [zero ceiling, zero visibility] fog and would remain so until 10:00 A.M. the next day, according to the U.S. Weather Bureau. Captain Van Morris [the pilot] was an old sailor who instinctively knew the tides in Boston. He had me tell the passengers that we would leave Newark at 9:30 P.M. We were the only plane in the New England area. The Boston controller gave us the weather — still 0-0 with holding instructions at the outer marker. The captain proceeded to the outer marker and started down the glide slope in preparation to land. What does this guy think he's doing, I wondered uneasily.

Just as we neared the airport, the Boston tower called: "I don't know how you did this, but we just got 200-½ [200-foot ceiling, ½-mile visibility]." Sure enough, at 200 feet we could see the runway lights. As we taxied into the gate, I got the courage to ask this "Moses" how he knew the fog would break, right to the minute. He told me that about an hour before high tide, regardless of how thick the fog, the ceiling would rise and the visibility would increase. He didn't know why, but it was reliable.

I didn't forget the flying lesson I got that night, and when I became captain, I started carrying the Almanac. I have since amazed many copilots and crew at my "supernatural" ability to predict weather conditions at the Boston airport.

– R. P. Kliegle, Watertown, South Dakota

I am writing about an experience I had at the age of 13. My parents bought a farm in what is now Clifton, New Jersey. Seven acres of good farmland and three acres of stone and brush. My two brothers and I agreed to clear the three acres. While they cleared the field of stone, I, the youngest of the three, arranged a stone wall around the perimeter. It was three feet high by maybe 2½ or three feet wide. We planted the field with a row of tomatoes around the inside of the stone wall.

Much to our surprise, on July 2, which is early for tomatoes because North Jersey has some cold nights, we had a bumper crop. Our seed supplier was Eberly and Company of Albany, New York. Mr. Eberly paid us a visit and brought along an agriculture expert. The expert explained that the heat of the Sun all day warmed the stone wall, which acted as a greenhouse and held the heat until long into the night.

I'm 85 years of age now, and both of my brothers are gone, but I still remember this all so plainly. When I lost the use of my legs a year back, I started to write of my early childhood. It seems that some of the pain is gone, but not the memory of that year in the sun.

– Carmine C. Coppola, Roseland, New Jersey

I notice that in 1993 the dates of aphelion and perihelion were not exactly half a year apart. Was this a typographical error?

– Lars Eighner, Austin, Texas

☞ *Astronomer Dr. George Greenstein replies: It was not. Indeed, the situation has been even stranger other years. In 1992, for instance, aphelion was fully ten*

days late. This would not occur were the Earth orbiting the Sun in a perfect ellipse. But a nearby astronomical object spoils the ellipse. This object is the Moon. Its gravitational tug throws the Earth about, distorting our orbit.

F or how long is the Moon exactly full? *– Marilyn Hauser, Chicago, Illinois*

☞ *Dr. Greenstein: The Moon continuously changes its phase from new to full and back again to new. So this is like asking, "For how long is it exactly 5:00 P.M.?" The correct answer is, "For no time at all," if we really mean "exactly." On the other hand, over the course of a few hours the change in phase is so small that it's hard to notice.*

CALLING ALL OLD FARMER'S ALMANAC COLLECTORS!

W e recently heard from a man in Westport, Massachusetts, who had just filled in the last gap (a 1795 edition) in a full set of *Old Farmer's Almanac*s. He searched for that 1795 Almanac for eight years. We'd love to hear from others who might have complete, or nearly so, collections. If you have duplicates you are willing to sell or swop, we might be able to find someone who is looking for just that edition.

We have a limited number of back issues of *The Old Farmer's Almanac* for sale. Price and availability vary, so please inquire first. Address: Archives, *Old Farmer's Almanac*, P.O. Box 289, Dublin, NH 03444.

ALL ABOUT
The MOON
AND YOU

1994 is as good a year as any to become fully acquainted, at long last, with the personal relationship we all have with the Moon each month . . .

by Martha White

★ TWENTY-FIVE YEARS AGO, ON JULY 20, 1969, Neil Armstrong took his historic steps on the Moon. President Richard M. Nixon, in a moment of national pride, proclaimed it the greatest event since Creation. ★ Some say that the Sun gives life, while the Moon regulates it. The tides, rains, reproduction and fertility, plant life, and even the life cycles of animals and humans all seem affected by the Moon's pull. Without that steady gravitational pull, the Earth's axis would undergo chaotic variations; in keeping the spinning Earth stabilized, the Moon helps regulate the seasons and climate. ★ To many sky watchers, the Moon is home to the gods. Plutarch, a first-century Greek essayist, considered it a way station for the coming and going of souls. Lunar eclipses, some believed, were instances of the Moon being eaten up (1994 has two, in May and November). Various rituals were enacted to bring the Moon back, whether from eclipse or its monthly new Moon phase disappearance. "Shooting the Moon" — now an expression of great ambition — was an attempt to rekindle the light of the Moon with fiery arrows.

Man in the Moon?

★ In our culture, we speak of seeing "the Man in the Moon," an image of a face imposed on the illuminated lunar surface. In Polynesia it is "the Woman in the Moon," and she has her child with her. The Selish Indians of the American Northwest see a toad that escaped to the Moon when a wolf courted her. Other cul-

— illustrated by Rick Geary,
represented by Creative Freelancers

tures see a man with a bundle of sticks on his back, the fingermarks of mischievous boys, Judas, the severed head of an outcast, a giant who controls the tides, or a hunchback. To Japanese viewers it's a rabbit in profile, while Scandinavians see a boy and girl holding a water bucket. From this latter image comes the Jack and Jill nursery rhyme.

Man on the Moon!

★ Two dozen American astronauts have traveled to the Moon, and half of those have walked on its surface. Through all this intensive scientific research, the Moon nevertheless has retained its aura of mystery and romanticism. Colonel James Irwin, pilot of the Apollo 15 lunar module, spoke of "the grand spiritual change of seeing the Earth as God must see it," viewed from the surface of the Moon.

Neil Armstrong is known for his words, "That's one small step for [a] man, one giant leap for mankind." (In his excitement, he forget to say "a," he later confessed.) Charles "Pete" Conrad Jr., in the next Apollo landing (November 1969), was allowed a little more candor. "Whoopee!" he cried. "Man, that may have been a small step for Neil, but that's a long one for me."

Dreams and *Superstitions*

★ To dream of a clear Moon portends success, say some, while a red or "bloody" Moon warns of catastrophe or war. A new Moon in your dreams promises increased wealth or a happy marriage. If a young woman dreams of the Moon growing dimmer, she should mind her sharp tongue, lest happiness elude her. Dreams of an eclipsed Moon are said to predict a contagious disease close at hand.

it's LUCKY to

★ See the first sliver of a new Moon "clear of the brush," or unencumbered by foliage.

★ Own a rabbit's foot, especially if the rabbit was killed in a cemetery by a cross-eyed person at the dark of the Moon.

★ Hold a moonstone in your mouth at the full Moon; it will reveal the future.

★ Have a full Moon on the "Moon day" (Monday).

★ Expose your newborn to the waxing Moon. It will give the baby strength.

★ Move your residence during the new Moon; prosperity will increase as the Moon waxes.

it's UNLUCKY to

★ See the first sliver of a new Moon through a window; you'll break a dish.

★ Point at the new Moon or view any Moon over your shoulder.

★ Sleep in the moonlight, or worse, be born in the moonlight. If a woman must sleep in the moonlight, she should rub spit on her belly or she risks becoming pregnant.

★ See "the old Moon in the arms of the new" or the faint image of the full disk while the new crescent Moon is illuminated, especially if you're a sailor. Storms are predicted.

★ Have a full Moon on Sunday. (Some say Saturday . . .)

Courting, Tomcatting, and Birthing

★ Folklore has it that if a young woman sees a dove and glimpses the new Moon at the same instant, she should repeat: "Bright Moon, clear Moon, Bright and fair, Lift up your right foot, There'll be a hair." When she removes her shoe, she'll find a hair the color of her future husband's. Marriages consummated during the full Moon are most prosperous and happy, according to ancient Greeks, while a waning Moon bodes ill for wedded bliss. The full Moon is an ideal time to accept a proposal of marriage, as well.

Certain plants believed to be ruled by the Moon carry romantic associations. The poppy, particularly, has been considered an inducement for dreams predicting love. Both poppies and cucumbers are folk remedies to enhance fertility. Succulents are thought to attract romance, while eating lettuce has been prescribed for those with an overabundance of lust. (Are your salads giving you mixed messages?)

WEATHER

★ Farmers, sailors, and other sky-watchers have long used the Moon to predict the weather. The waxing Moon is sometimes called the right-hand Moon, its curve following that of the right-hand index finger and thumb. The waning Moon is the left-hand Moon. "In the wane of the Moon, a cloudy morning bodes a fair afternoon," reads one old saw. If the crescent Moon holds its points upward, able to contain water, it predicts a dry spell. If the new Moon stands on its points, expect precipitation to spill out.

In general, the new Moon is considered a time of weather changes,

— Rick Geary

and, indeed, weather records confirm that the days following both the new and full Moons are most likely to be rainy or stormy.

A winter full Moon is a time for long cold snaps. In April it brings frost. Western Kansans claim freedom from storms if the full Moon is near, and sailors agree that the full Moon "eats clouds." Two full Moons in a month increase the chances of flood, a pale full Moon indicates rain, while a red one brings wind, and a Christmas full Moon predicts a poor harvest.

Halos (or rings or "Moon dogs") are another sign. Henry Wadsworth Longfel-

"Tomcatting," whether practiced by felines or humans, is reputed to be most successful at the bright Moon. Carousers will be refreshed rather than exhausted by their exertions and are less apt to suffer physical maladies as a result. Men's virility is enhanced and fertility is at a peak, believe some.

The Navajos, among others, believe that the full Moon's pull on a woman's amniotic fluids increases the chances of birthing at this time. Some nurses and midwives claim the new Moon is also an active time for births.

the RIGHT TIMES to Plant, Wean, Build Fences, Castrate, and Harvest

★ The age-old practice of performing farm chores by the Moon stems from the simple belief that the Moon governs moisture. Pliny the Elder, the first-century Roman naturalist, stated in his *Natural History* that the Moon "replenishes the earth; when she approaches it, she fills all bodies, while, when she recedes, she empties them."

Moonrise occurring in the evening brings fair weather, says one proverb, harking back to the belief that the waning Moon (full and last quarter, which rise in the evening) is dry. New Moon and first quarter, or waxing phases, are considered fertile and wet. For a simple guide to general times of moonrise, remember:

> *The New Moon always rises at sunrise*
> *And the First Quarter at noon.*
> *The Full Moon always rises at sunset*
> *And the Last Quarter at midnight.*

low wrote in "Wreck of the Hesperus":

> *For I fear a hurricane;*
> *Last night the moon had*
> *a golden ring,*
> *And tonight no moon*
> *we see.*

The halo, marking an abundance of moisture in the atmosphere, predicts wet or stormy weather. One should count the number of stars visible within the halo to know the number of days before rain. To others, they signify the number of days of rain. Science confirms that the fewer visible stars, the more moisture in the atmosphere.

The new and first-quarter phases, known as the light of the Moon, are considered good for planting above-ground crops, putting down sod, grafting trees, and transplanting. From full Moon through the last quarter, or the dark of the Moon, is the best time for killing weeds, thinning, pruning, mowing, cutting timber, and planting below-ground crops. (See pages 162, 164, and 206.) The time just before the full Moon is considered particularly wet, best for planting during drought

the RIGHT TIMES to

Plant, Wean, Build Fences, Castrate, and Harvest

(continued)

conditions. Seed germination, some farmers insist, is much better then.

According to folklore, rail fences cut during the dry, waning Moon will stay straighter. Many say wooden shingles and shakes will lie flatter if cut during the dark of the Moon, but others swear by the waxing Moon. Logs cut in the dark of the Moon are thought to sink into the ground quickly, but for a pig fence this is desirable. Similarly, fence posts should be set in the dark of the Moon to resist rotting. Ozark lore adds that fence posts should always be set as the tree grew. To set the root end upward makes a short-lived fence.

Don't commence your weaning when the Moon is waning, nor (ideally) should you be birthing then. Turn your featherbeds to make them smooth; a waxing Moon attracts the feathers too strongly. Castrate and dehorn animals on the Moon's wane for less bleeding, but slaughter on the wax for juicier meat. Crabbing, shrimping, and clamming are thought to be best when the Moon is full, but wait for the days between the new and full Moons for fishing. Mushrooms gathered by the full Moon may be poisonous, even if ordinarily palatable, but dig your horseradish in the full Moon for the best flavor. And always set eggs to hatch on the Moon's increase, but not if a south wind blows.

Lunacy

★ *Paracelsus, the 16th-century physician, said the Moon has "the power to tear reason out of man's head by depriving him of humors and cerebral virtues." There are those who will not sleep in moonlight for fear of courting insanity. In England a distinction was made between lunatics and the insane; lunatics were only affected by the full Moon, while insanity was more permanent. Epilepsy, once called lunaticus or "moonstruck," was believed by early Greeks and Romans to be caused by*

– Rick Geary

moonlight. Lycanthropy, the belief that the full Moon can cause a person to become a werewolf, remains a well-known form of Moon madness and, whether fact or delusion, has its sufferers even today.

Scientific studies over the years have tried to link the full Moon with times of increased violence, suicide, mental disorders, fits and seizures, increased fertility or virility, and times of menstruation and birthing. Some small-scale studies have shown correlations between the full Moon and increased police activity, "hot-line" phone calls, and hospital emergencies.

Healing Powers

★ Not all of the Moon's effects on health are considered negative. The flow of blood, especially, has been suspected of responding to the gravitational tug of the Moon in folklore, astrology, and more recently, even in medicine.

Believers in the influence of the Moon may consider dental care and elective surgery unwise around the times of the full Moon because of the risk of increased bleeding. (Similarly, Civil War doctors noted the tides, suspecting greater blood flow during a flood tide.) A Florida physician, Dr. Edson Andrews, ran an informal study between 1956 and 1958 that pointed to excessive bleeding in operations done between the new Moon and full (waxing) phases, with a peak at the full Moon days.

Lunar folk remedies lean heavily toward myth and superstition. Wart cures, particularly, have relied on lunar magic. For instance, to remove warts, you might blow on them nine times during a full Moon or "wash" your hands in the Moon's rays captured in a shiny metal basin. Be careful not to offend the Moon, however. A surefire route to becoming a witch is to fire a silver bullet at the Moon while spouting obscenities. An even quicker path is to fire seven bullets at the Moon and recite the Lord's Prayer backward.

Do you get the blues on Mondays? Maybe you're engaging in the wrong activities. Literally "the Moon's day," Monday in legend and lore is auspicious for peace and happiness, raising spirits of the dead, water activities and travel, home and family, dreams, medicine, cooking (but watch those salads), love spells and reconciliation, learning the truth, clairvoyance, and becoming invisible. So if it's Monday, shoot for the Moon.

MOON FACTS and Figures

– Rick Geary

★ **Age:** Approximately 4.6 billion years

★ **Circumference:** 6,790 miles

★ **Density:** 3.34 times that of water

★ **Diameter:** 2,160 miles, about 1/4 of the Earth's diameter

★ **Direction of orbit:** Counterclockwise

★ **Distance (mean) from the Earth:** 238,857 miles, with variations of over 30,000 miles

★ **Sidereal period (Moon's mean rotation around the Earth):** 27 days, 7 hours, 43.2 minutes

★ **Surface area:** 23,712,500 miles, or less than 1/13th that of Earth

★ **Surface gravity:** About 1/6th that of Earth

★ **Synodical or lunar month (from one new Moon to the next):** 29 days, 12 hours, 44.05 minutes

★ **Temperature:** 243° F at the lunar equator, with the Sun directly above. At sunset 58° F, and after dark -261° F

★ **Weight:** 81 quintillion tons, or just over 1/10 of the Earth's weight

□ □

1993 NOVEMBER, THE ELEVENTH MONTH

This is a month of close meetings near or at the Sun. A partial solar eclipse on November 13th is seen only in the far southern latitudes. The start of a rare transit of Mercury — the planet passing in front of the Sun — on the 5th is seen from Hawaii and the Aleutians but nowhere else in the nation. All the country gets a look at two conjunctions low in the east before dawn: the bright-planet pair Venus and Jupiter on the 8th; the inner-planet pair Venus and Mercury on the 14th. Mercury puts in a fine morning appearance before and after its greatest elongation on the 22nd. The Leonid meteors are unbothered by moonlight in the hours just before dawn on the 18th. The Moon's total eclipse on the 28th-29th will be visible everywhere.

☾	Last Quarter	7th day	1st hour	37th min.
●	New Moon	13th day	16th hour	35th min.
☽	First Quarter	20th day	21st hour	4th min.
○	Full Moon	29th day	1st hour	32nd min.

For an explanation of this page, see "How to Use This Almanac," page 30; for values of Key Letters, see Time Correction Tables, page 209.

Day of Year	Day of Month	Day of Week	☉ Rises h. m.	Key	☉ Sets h. m.	Key	Length of Days h. m.	Sun Fast m.	Full Sea Boston A.M.	Full Sea Boston P.M.	☽ Rises h. m.	Key	☽ Sets h. m.	Key	Declination of Sun ° '	☽ Place	☽ Age
305	1	M.	6 17	D	4 38	B	10 21	32	12	12	5 PM 57	B	8 AM 18	E	14 S.35	TAU	17
306	2	Tu.	6 19	D	4 37	B	10 18	32	12½	12½	6 46	B	9 13	E	14 54	TAU	18
307	3	W.	6 20	D	4 35	B	10 15	32	1¼	1¼	7 41	B	10 03	E	15 12	TAU	19
308	4	Th.	6 21	D	4 34	B	10 13	32	2	2	8 41	B	10 49	E	15 31	GEM	20
309	5	Fr.	6 22	D	4 33	B	10 11	32	2¾	2¾	9 45	C	11 AM 29	E	15 49	GEM	21
310	6	Sa.	6 24	D	4 32	B	10 08	32	3½	3¾	10 PM 52	C	12 PM 06	D	16 07	CAN	22
311	7	**C**	6 25	D	4 31	A	10 06	32	4½	4¾	— —	–	12 39	D	16 25	CAN	23
312	8	M.	6 26	D	4 30	A	10 04	32	5½	5¾	12 AM 02	C	1 10	D	16 43	LEO	24
313	9	Tu.	6 27	D	4 28	A	10 01	32	6¼	6¾	1 13	D	1 41	C	17 00	SEX	25
314	10	W.	6 29	D	4 27	A	9 58	32	7¼	7¾	2 25	D	2 13	C	17 17	VIR	26
315	11	Th.	6 30	D	4 26	A	9 56	32	8¼	8¾	3 41	E	2 48	B	17 33	VIR	27
316	12	Fr.	6 31	D	4 25	A	9 54	32	9	9¾	4 56	E	3 27	B	17 49	VIR	28
317	13	Sa.	6 32	D	4 24	A	9 52	32	10	10½	6 12	E	4 13	B	18 05	LIB	0
318	14	**C**	6 34	D	4 23	A	9 49	32	10¾	11½	7 24	E	5 05	B	18 21	LIB	1
319	15	M.	6 35	D	4 23	A	9 48	31	11½	—	8 29	E	6 03	B	18 36	OPH	2
320	16	Tu.	6 36	D	4 22	A	9 46	31	12¼	12½	9 26	E	7 06	B	18 51	SAG	3
321	17	W.	6 37	D	4 21	A	9 44	31	1¼	1¼	10 14	E	8 11	B	19 05	SAG	4
322	18	Th.	6 38	D	4 20	A	9 42	31	2	2¼	10 53	E	9 15	C	19 20	SAG	5
323	19	Fr.	6 40	D	4 19	A	9 39	31	3	3¼	11 27	D	10 19	C	19 34	CAP	6
324	20	Sa.	6 41	D	4 19	A	9 38	30	3¾	4	11 AM 56	D	11 PM 20	C	19 48	AQU	7
325	21	**C**	6 42	D	4 18	A	9 36	30	4¾	5	12 PM 23	D	— —	–	20 01	AQU	8
326	22	M.	6 43	D	4 17	A	9 34	30	5¾	6	12 47	D	12 AM 19	D	20 14	PSC	9
327	23	Tu.	6 45	D	4 17	A	9 32	30	6¾	7	1 12	C	1 18	D	20 26	PSC	10
328	24	W.	6 46	D	4 16	A	9 30	29	7½	8	1 38	B	2 16	D	20 38	PSC	11
329	25	Th.	6 47	D	4 15	A	9 28	29	8¼	8¾	2 07	B	3 15	E	20 50	PSC	12
330	26	Fr.	6 48	E	4 15	A	9 27	29	9	9½	2 38	B	4 14	E	21 01	ARI	13
331	27	Sa.	6 49	E	4 14	A	9 25	28	9½	10¼	3 13	B	5 13	E	21 12	ARI	14
332	28	**C**	6 50	E	4 14	A	9 24	28	10¼	10¾	3 54	B	6 11	E	21 23	TAU	15
333	29	M.	6 51	E	4 14	A	9 23	28	11	11½	4 41	B	7 07	E	21 33	TAU	16
334	30	Tu.	6 52	E	4 13	A	9 21	27	11½	—	5 PM 35	B	7 AM 59	E	21 S.43	TAU	17

NOVEMBER hath 30 days. 1993

And the dead leaves lie huddled and still,
No longer blown hither and thither;
The last lone aster is gone;
The flowers of the witch-hazel wither. . .
– Robert Frost

Farmer's Calendar

The multitudes of summer hate to see it end. They keep on coming back. Like an aging tenor or a superannuated generalissimo, a hundred creatures that thrived abundantly in June, then retired with the deep frosts, return on a warm, bright day and take up their careers all over again. But now, although the creatures themselves are real, everything else is different. This is no mere Indian Summer, no simple matter of a mild day in autumn: A summer day in November is more like a mysterious moment in a play or movie — it's a flashback, a memory happening now, a dream.

The summer birds have been gone for eight weeks, the garden closed down for six. The trees are bare. A week or two of winter cold has turned the meadows brown and the earth gray. Often there is a thin cover of snow in the morning, the sun is pale and far off. Then two days of flashback supervene, and forgotten life emerges. Little brown snakes curl on the flagstones by the defunct flower garden. Chipmunks are seen poking about. The paper wasps wake up in their cold cracks and buzz around the eaves. Hibernating butterflies, including my favorites, the big tortoiseshells, bask in the sun on the porch floorboards and fly slowly over the clipped dead flower stalks. Little brown and gray moths suddenly appear in the woods and come to lights at night, just as they did in July. You're in a kind of dream of summer, but as in a real dream, everything that is so convincingly the same is also profoundly changed. It's as though dreams are lit differently over the clipped dead here; summer is back, but it's summer without the colors, summer without green.

D. M.	D. W.	Dates, Feasts, Fasts, Aspects, Tide Heights	Weather ↓
1	M.	**All Saints** • ☾ at ☊ • Earthquake, Lisbon, Portugal, 1755 •	*After*
2	Tu.	**All Souls** • 7" snow, New York City, 1810 • Tides {9.2 {10.2 •	*a*
3	W.	☾ rides Great flood, Stephen Austin high • Vermont, 1927 • born, 1793 •	*mist,*
4	Th.	*Virtues, like essences, lose their fragrance when exposed.* • Tides {8.9 {10.0	*it's*
5	Fr.	☿ at inf. ♂ • Transit of ☿ • Roy Rogers born, 1912 •	*clear and*
6	Sa.	**St. Leonard** • Edsel Ford born, 1893 • Tides {8.9 {9.8	*warm.*
7	C	**23ᵗʰ �§. af. ℙ.** • Bolshevik Revolution began, 1917 •	*Inconsist-*
8	M.	♂♀♃ • *The secret of being a bore is to tell everything.* • Tides {9.5 {9.8	*ent;*
9	Tu.	☾ on Auspicious Great Lakes Eq. • for travel. • gale, 1913 {10.0 {10.0	*now a*
10	W.	Marine Corps created by Continental Congress, 1775 • Tides {10.7 {10.3	*storm.*
11	Th.	**St. Martin • Veterans Day** • Indian Summer begins. •	*Hunters*
12	Fr.	☾ at perig. • ♂♃☾ • ♂♀☾ Tides {11.8 {10.8	*hale*
13	Sa.	New ● • Eclipse of ☉ • Sadie Hawkins Day • {12.2 {10.8	*and*
14	C	**24ᵗʰ �§. af. ℙ.** • ☾ at ☊ • ♂♀♀ • ☿ stat. • {12.4 {10.8 •	*days*
15	M.	45" snow, Water-town, N.Y., 1900 • Tides {12.3 {—	*heavy-booted*
16	Tu.	☾ runs –53° F, Lincoln 14NE, low • Montana, 1959 • Tides {10.6 {11.9	*crush*
17	W.	**St. Hugh of Lincoln** • ♂℞☉ • ♂♅☾ • ♂☌☾ •	*the*
18	Th.	**St. Hilda** • Julia Ward Howe wrote lyrics to "Battle Hymn of the Republic," 1861	*leaves,*
19	Fr.	*Life must be lived forward, but can only be understood backward.* • Tides {9.5 {10.2	*their*
20	Sa.	Indian Prune grape-Summer ends. • ♂♄☾ • vines now. {9.2 {9.6	*colors*
21	C	**25ᵗʰ �§. af. ℙ.** • Mayflower Compact signed, 1620 • {9.1 {9.1	*muted.*
22	M.	**St. Cecilia** • ☾ on Eq. • ☿ Gr. Elong. (20° W.) • {9.1 {8.9 •	*You'll*
23	Tu.	**St. Clement** • *Solitude is impracticable, and society fatal.* •	*have to*
24	W.	☾ at apo. • Joseph Glidden patented barbed wire, 1874 • Tides {9.4 {8.7	*ask*
25	Th.	**Thanksgiving Day** • East Coast blizzard, 57" snow, W. Va., 1950 •	*the*
26	Fr.	*If ice in November will bear a duck, There'll be nothing thereafter but sleet and muck.* •	*Navy*
27	Sa.	Peace march on James Agee Washington, D.C., 1965 • born, 1909 • Tides {10.6 {9.0	*to*
28	C	**1st �§. in Advent** • ☾ at ☊ • Tides {10.2 {9.1	*pass*
29	M.	Full Louisa May Beaver ○ • Eclipse of ☾ • Alcott born, 1832 {10.4 {9.1	*the*
30	Tu.	**St. Andrew** • ☾ rides Thunder this month high • means a fertile year. •	*gravy!*

Arguments are to be avoided: they are always vulgar and often convincing. – Oscar Wilde

1993 DECEMBER, THE TWELFTH MONTH

The Geminid meteor shower peaks around new Moon this year. In clear country skies, observers should see up to 60 per hour late in the evening of the 13th and early after midnight on the 14th. Earlier, Gemini and its two brightest stars, Castor and Pollux, are still low in the northeast. The eastern sky above and to the right of them is decorated with the dipper-shaped Pleiades star cluster and arrowhead-shaped Hyades star cluster in Taurus, and the pentagon-shaped constellation Auriga with its bright star Capella. Rising due east is glorious Orion, with blue Rigel, red Betelgeuse, three-star belt, and nebula-spotted sword. An hour after Orion rises, the brightest star, Sirius, comes up to dominate the sky. Winter begins at 3:26 P.M., EST, on the 21st.

☾ Last Quarter	6th day	10th hour	50th min.
● New Moon	13th day	4th hour	28th min.
☽ First Quarter	20th day	17th hour	26th min.
○ Full Moon	28th day	18th hour	7th min.

For an explanation of this page, see "How to Use This Almanac," page 30; for values of Key Letters, see Time Correction Tables, page 209.

Day of Year	Day of Month	Day of Week	☉ Rises h. m.	Key	☉ Sets h. m.	Key	Length of Days h. m.	Sun Fast m.	Full Sea Boston A.M.	Full Sea Boston P.M.	☽ Rises h. m.	Key	☽ Sets h. m.	Key	Declination of Sun ° '	☽ Place	☽ Age
335	1	W.	6 54	E	4 13	A	9 19	27	12¼	12¼	6 P.M. 35	B	8 A.M. 47	E	21s.52	ORI	18
336	2	Th.	6 55	E	4 13	A	9 18	27	1	1	7 38	B	9 30	E	22 01	GEM	19
337	3	Fr.	6 56	E	4 12	A	9 16	26	1½	1¾	8 44	C	10 07	E	22 09	CAN	20
338	4	Sa.	6 57	E	4 12	A	9 15	26	2¼	2½	9 52	C	10 41	D	22 17	CAN	21
339	5	**C**	6 58	E	4 12	A	9 14	25	3¼	3½	11 P.M. 01	D	11 13	D	22 25	LEO	22
340	6	M.	6 59	E	4 12	A	9 13	25	4	4¼	— —	–	11 A.M. 43	D	22 32	SEX	23
341	7	Tu.	7 00	E	4 12	A	9 12	24	5	5¼	12 A.M. 11	D	12 P.M. 13	C	22 39	LEO	24
342	8	W.	7 01	E	4 12	A	9 11	24	6	6½	1 23	D	12 46	B	22 46	VIR	25
343	9	Th.	7 01	E	4 12	A	9 11	24	6¾	7½	2 35	E	1 21	B	22 51	VIR	26
344	10	Fr.	7 02	E	4 12	A	9 10	23	7¾	8½	3 49	E	2 02	B	22 57	VIR	27
345	11	Sa.	7 03	E	4 12	A	9 09	23	8¾	9½	5 01	E	2 50	B	23 02	LIB	28
346	12	**C**	7 04	E	4 12	A	9 08	22	9½	10¼	6 09	E	3 44	B	23 06	SCO	29
347	13	M.	7 05	E	4 12	A	9 07	22	10½	11¼	7 09	E	4 45	B	23 12	OPH	0
348	14	Tu.	7 06	E	4 12	A	9 06	21	11¼	—	8 03	E	5 50	B	23 14	SAG	1
349	15	W.	7 06	E	4 12	A	9 06	21	12	12¼	8 47	E	6 56	B	23 17	SAG	2
350	16	Th.	7 07	E	4 13	A	9 06	20	12¾	1	9 24	E	8 01	C	23 20	SAG	3
351	17	Fr.	7 08	E	4 13	A	9 05	20	1¾	1¾	9 56	D	9 05	C	23 22	AQU	4
352	18	Sa.	7 08	E	4 13	A	9 05	19	2½	2½	10 24	D	10 06	D	23 23	AQU	5
353	19	**C**	7 09	E	4 14	A	9 05	19	3¼	3½	10 50	C	11 P.M. 06	D	23 25	AQU	6
354	20	M.	7 09	E	4 14	A	9 05	18	4	4¼	11 15	C	— —	–	23 26	PSC	7
355	21	Tu.	7 10	E	4 15	A	9 05	18	5	5¼	11 A.M. 40	C	12 A.M. 05	D	23 26	PSC	8
356	22	W.	7 10	E	4 15	A	9 05	17	5¾	6¼	12 P.M. 08	B	1 03	D	23 26	PSC	9
357	23	Th.	7 11	E	4 16	A	9 05	17	6¾	7¼	12 37	B	2 02	E	23 25	PSC	10
358	24	Fr.	7 11	E	4 16	A	9 05	16	7½	8	1 11	B	3 01	E	23 24	ARI	11
359	25	Sa.	7 12	E	4 17	A	9 05	16	8¼	9	1 49	B	4 00	E	23 22	ARI	12
360	26	**C**	7 12	E	4 18	A	9 06	15	9	9¾	2 34	B	4 57	E	23 20	TAU	13
361	27	M.	7 12	E	4 18	A	9 06	15	9¾	10½	3 25	B	5 52	E	23 17	TAU	14
362	28	Tu.	7 13	E	4 19	A	9 06	14	10½	11	4 24	B	6 42	E	23 14	ORI	15
363	29	W.	7 13	E	4 20	A	9 07	14	11¼	11¾	5 27	B	7 27	E	23 11	GEM	16
364	30	Th.	7 13	E	4 20	A	9 07	13	11¾	—	6 34	B	8 08	E	23 08	GEM	17
365	31	Fr.	7 13	E	4 21	A	9 08	13	12½	12½	7 P.M. 43	C	8 A.M. 44	D	23s.03	CAN	18

DECEMBER hath 31 days. 1993

O World, thou choosest not the better part!
It is not wisdom to be only wise,
And on the inward vision close the eyes,
But it is wisdom to believe the heart.
– George Santayana

D.M.	D.W.	Dates, Feasts, Fasts, Aspects, Tide Heights	*Weather* ↓
1	W.	Marines rescued 1,200 U.S. soldiers, Chosin, Korea, 1950 • Tides {9.2 10.5 •	*It's*
2	Th.	*The finger of God never leaves identical fingerprints.* • John Brown hanged, 1859 •	*sleety,*
3	Fr.	Beware the Pogonip. • Illinois joined Union, 1818 • Tides {9.3 10.4 •	*sweetie.*
4	Sa.	The Grange (Patrons of Husbandry) founded, 1867 • Tides {9.4 10.2 •	*On*
5	**C**	**2nd S. in Adv.** • Walt Disney born, 1901 • {9.5 10.0	*northern*
6	M.	**St. Nicholas** • ☾ on Eq. • Ira Gershwin born, 1896 •	*peaks*
7	Tu.	*Soup and fish explain half the emotions of life.* • Tides {10.0 9.7	*the*
8	W.	**Conception of Virgin Mary** • 100° F, LaMesa, Calif., 1938	*snow*
9	Th.	**Chanukah** • Tanganyika independence, 1961 • {10.8 9.8 •	*is*
10	Fr.	☌♃☾ • ☾ at perig. • 70° F, New York City, 1946 {11.2 9.9	*heaping;*
11	Sa.	☾ at ☊ • First U.S. helicopters and crew arrived in Saigon, Vietnam, 1961 •	*pile*
12	**C**	**3rd S. in Adv.** • Blizzard, New England, 1960 • Tides {11.8 10.2	*on*
13	M.	**St. Lucy** • ☾ runs low • New ● • Tides {11.9 10.2	*blankets*
14	Tu.	*Great riches have sold more men than they have bought.* • Washington died, 1799 •	*for*
15	W.	☌♆☾ • ☌♅☾ • Ember Day • J. Paul Getty born, 1892 • {10.1 11.5	*good*
16	Th.	Great earthquake rocked Miss. River valley near New Madrid, Mo., 1811 •	*sleeping.*
17	Fr.	Ember Day • *Reason is God's gift, but so are the passions.* • Tides {9.8 10.6 •	*Shop*
18	Sa.	☌♄☾ • Ember Day • Battle of Verdun ended with 750,000 casualties, 1916 •	*and*
19	**C**	**4th S. in Advent** • ☾ on Eq. • Tides {9.3 9.4	*shiver —*
20	M.	Halcyon days. • Missouri imposed $1 per year tax on bachelors, 1820 •	*blessed's*
21	Tu.	**St. Thomas** • Winter Solstice • Benj. Disraeli born, 1804 • Tides {9.1 8.5	*the*
22	W.	☾ at apo. • Continental Congress established navy, 1775 • *Snow White* opened, 1937 •	*giver.*
23	Th.	Baseball arbitrator established "free agent" status, 1973 • {9.2 8.2	*Gather nigh*
24	Fr.	Green Christmas, White Easter. • Fire burned ⅔ of Library of Congress collection, 1851 •	*the*
25	Sa.	**Christmas Day** • Wind today brings a fruitful year. {9.6 8.4	*festive*
26	**C**	**1st S. af. Ch.** • **St. Stephen** • ☾ at ☋ • ☌♂☉	*tree,*
27	M.	**St. John** • ☾ rides high • Radio City Music Hall opened, N.Y.C., 1932 •	*and*
28	Tu.	**Holy Innocents** • Full Cold ○ • Tides {10.4 9.1 •	*wave*
29	W.	Battle of Wounded Knee, S.D., 1890 • Pablo Casals born, 1876 • {10.6 9.4	*good-bye*
30	Th.	*Be at war with your vices, at peace with your neighbors, and let every new year find you a better man.* (B. Franklin)	*to*
31	Fr.	**St. Sylvester** • *Begin the new year square with every man.* (R. B. Thomas) {9.6 10.8	*'93!*

Farmer's Calendar

Now, as the season of storms approaches, a bewildering multiplicity of snow shovels has gone on display in practically every store in town. With winter coming, you can buy a snow shovel in a grocery store, a drugstore, a sporting-goods store. Snow shovels are hawked with special fervor at those curious hybrid establishments known as "home centers." (In more plain-spoken times they were called "hardware stores" and "lumberyards.") And what snow shovels they are! There are snow shovels that look like shovels, there are others that look like really large dental tools, there are even snow shovels that look like Eskimo perambulators. There are snow shovels with straight handles, snow shovels with bent handles; with fat blades, with thin blades; with D grips, with T grips. Some snow shovels are plastic and cost a couple of bucks; others are so expensive that it seems wrong to expose them to a substance, like snow, that comes for free. What to do?

It took me a number of winters to discover that very often the best snow shovel is not a shovel at all. Get yourself a simple broom, one with long, stiff straw. A broom will take care of better than half the snow you'll get in a winter, and it won't break your back, burst your heart, or dig up your grass by mistake. For cleaning snow off the car, the broom is far superior to the shovel because it can't scratch your paint job. And if you are equipped with a broom and you should, at last, get a fall of snow too deep for your broom to overcome, you can simply hop on it and fly south until you get to a latitude where snow is unknown and the home centers sell only those shovels that come with pails for use at the beach.

1994   JANUARY, The First Month

The brightest constellations of the year now fill the south sky at mid evening. The central figure is Orion the Hunter with his belt formed by three bright stars in a row and his even brighter stars, Rigel and Betelgeuse. A line drawn to the upper right from Orion's belt brings the eye to the V-shaped face of Taurus the Bull, formed by Aldebaran and the Hyades star cluster. A line drawn to the lower left from the belt takes the gaze to Sirius, most brilliant of all stars. Saturn is the brightest point of light in the southwest in the early evening. Earth is at perihelion on the 2nd, at 1:00 A.M., EST.

☾ Last Quarter	4th day	19th hour	1st min.
● New Moon	11th day	18th hour	11th min.
☽ First Quarter	19th day	15th hour	27th min.
○ Full Moon	27th day	8th hour	24th min.

For an explanation of this page, see "How to Use This Almanac," page 30; for values of Key Letters, see Time Correction Tables, page 209.

Day of Year	Day of Month	Day of Week	☉ Rises h. m.	Key	☉ Sets h. m.	Key	Length of Days h. m.	Sun Fast m.	Full Sea Boston A.M.	Full Sea Boston P.M.	☽ Rises h. m.	Key	☽ Sets h. m.	Key	Declination of Sun ° '	☽ Place	☽ Age
1	1	Sa.	7 14	E	4 22	A	9 08	12	1¼	1¼	8ᴘᴍ52	D	9ᴀᴍ16	D	22s.58	LEO	19
2	2	B	7 14	E	4 23	A	9 09	12	2	2¼	10 02	D	9 47	D	22 53	SEX	20
3	3	M.	7 14	E	4 24	A	9 10	11	2¾	3	11ᴘᴍ13	D	10 17	C	22 47	LEO	21
4	4	Tu.	7 14	E	4 25	A	9 11	11	3½	4	— —	–	10 48	C	22 41	VIR	22
5	5	W.	7 14	E	4 26	A	9 12	10	4½	5	12ᴀᴍ24	E	11 22	B	22 35	VIR	23
6	6	Th.	7 13	E	4 27	A	9 14	10	5½	6	1 35	E	11ᴀᴍ59	B	22 28	VIR	24
7	7	Fr.	7 13	E	4 28	A	9 15	10	6½	7¼	2 46	E	12ᴘᴍ42	B	22 20	LIB	25
8	8	Sa.	7 13	E	4 29	A	9 16	9	7½	8¼	3 54	E	1 32	B	22 12	SCO	26
9	9	B	7 13	E	4 30	A	9 17	9	8½	9¼	4 56	E	2 29	B	22 03	OPH	27
10	10	M.	7 13	E	4 31	A	9 18	8	9½	10	5 52	E	3 31	B	21 54	SAG	28
11	11	Tu.	7 12	E	4 32	A	9 20	8	10¼	11	6 39	E	4 36	B	21 45	SAG	0
12	12	W.	7 12	E	4 33	A	9 21	7	11	11¾	7 20	E	5 42	B	21 35	SAG	1
13	13	Th.	7 12	E	4 34	A	9 22	7	—	12	7 54	E	6 47	C	21 25	CAP	2
14	14	Fr.	7 11	E	4 36	A	9 25	7	12½	12¾	8 24	D	7 51	C	21 15	AQU	3
15	15	Sa.	7 11	E	4 37	A	9 26	6	1¼	1½	8 51	D	8 52	D	21 04	AQU	4
16	16	B	7 10	E	4 38	A	9 28	6	2	2¼	9 17	C	9 52	D	20 53	PSC	5
17	17	M.	7 10	E	4 39	A	9 29	6	2¾	3	9 43	C	10 50	D	20 41	PSC	6
18	18	Tu.	7 09	E	4 40	A	9 31	5	3½	3¾	10 09	C	11ᴘᴍ49	D	20 28	PSC	7
19	19	W.	7 09	E	4 42	A	9 33	5	4¼	4½	10 37	B	— —	–	20 16	PSC	8
20	20	Th.	7 08	E	4 43	A	9 35	5	5	5½	11 08	B	12ᴀᴍ47	E	20 03	ARI	9
21	21	Fr.	7 08	E	4 44	A	9 36	4	6	6½	11ᴀᴍ44	B	1 46	E	19 50	ARI	10
22	22	Sa.	7 07	E	4 45	A	9 38	4	6¾	7½	12ᴘᴍ25	B	2 43	E	19 36	TAU	11
23	23	B	7 06	D	4 47	A	9 41	4	7¾	8¼	1 13	B	3 39	E	19 23	TAU	12
24	24	M.	7 05	D	4 48	A	9 43	4	8½	9	2 08	B	4 31	E	19 08	TAU	13
25	25	Tu.	7 05	D	4 49	D	9 44	3	9¼	9¾	3 10	B	5 19	E	18 53	GEM	14
26	26	W.	7 04	D	4 50	A	9 46	3	10	10½	4 16	C	6 02	E	18 38	GEM	15
27	27	Th.	7 03	D	4 52	A	9 49	3	10¾	11¼	5 26	C	6 41	E	18 23	CAN	16
28	28	Fr.	7 02	D	4 53	A	9 51	3	11½	—	6 37	D	7 16	D	18 07	CAN	17
29	29	Sa.	7 01	D	4 54	A	9 53	3	12	12¼	7 49	D	7 49	D	17 51	SEX	18
30	30	B	7 00	D	4 56	A	9 56	2	12¾	1	9 02	D	8 20	D	17 34	LEO	19
31	31	M.	6 59	D	4 57	A	9 58	2	1½	1¾	10ᴘᴍ14	E	8ᴀᴍ52	C	17s.17	VIR	20

JANUARY hath 31 days. 1994

All day the gusty north-wind bore
The loosening drift its breath before;
Low circling round its southern zone,
The sun through dazzling snow-mist shone.
– John Greenleaf Whittier

D. M.	D. W.	Dates, Feasts, Fasts, Aspects, Tide Heights	Weather ↓
1	Sa.	New Year's Day • Circumcision • {9.9 / 10.9} •	*Lovely,*
2	**B**	2nd S. af. Ch. • ⊕ at perihelion • ☾ on Eq. •	*then*
3	M.	☿ in sup. ☌ • Alaska became 49th state, 1959 • {10.3 / 10.3} •	*shovely.*
4	Tu.	If grass grows in January, it will grow badly the whole year. • Tides {10.4 / 9.9}	*Janus*
5	W.	Twelfth Night • ☾ at perig. • Henry Ford first to offer $5 wage for 8-hour day, 1914 •	*is a*
6	Th.	Epiphany • ☌♃☾ • Tides {10.5 / 9.3} •	*two-faced*
7	Fr.	St. Lucian of Antioch • Fannie Farmer published first cookbook, 1896	*deity;*
8	Sa.	☾ at ☊ • Elvis Presley born, 1935 • Tides {10.8 / 9.3}	*sometimes*
9	**B**	1st S. af. Epiphany • ☾ runs low • {11.0 / 9.5} •	*mild,*
10	M.	Plough Monday • First U.N. Gen. Assembly opened, 1946 •	*sometimes*
11	Tu.	☌♆☉ • New ● • –23° F, Kingston, R.I., 1942 {11.3 / 9.8}	*sleeity.*
12	W.	☌♅☉ • Agatha Christie died, 1976 • Tides {11.2 / 9.9} •	*Gutters*
13	Th.	St. Hilary • *Think much, speak little, and write less.* • {— / 11.0} •	*grow*
14	Fr.	☌♄☾ • Propitious for birth of women. • Loretta Lynn born, 1935 •	*a*
15	Sa.	Vermont declared itself independent state, 1777-1791 • {9.8 / 10.3} •	*beard*
16	**B**	2nd S. af. Epiphany • ♀ in sup. ☌ • ☾ on Eq. • {9.7 / 9.9}	
17	M.	Martin Luther King Jr.'s Birthday • B. Franklin born, 1706 •	*of*
18	Tu.	*Two things a man should not be angry at: What he can help, and what he can't.* •	*icicles;*
19	W.	☾ at apo. • Eleanora R. Sears won 1st U.S. Women's Squash Racquets Singles, 1928 •	*it's*
20	Th.	St. Fabian • Favorable for birth of men. • Tides {9.0 / 8.1} •	*almost*
21	Fr.	St. Agnes • *In January if the Sun appear, March and April pay full dear.* •	*warm*
22	Sa.	St. Vincent • ☾ at ☋ • *The Crucible* premiered on Broadway, 1953	*enough*
23	**B**	3rd S. af. Epiphany • First episode *Roots* airs, 1977 {9.4 / 8.2} •	*for*
24	M.	☾ rides high • Thurgood Marshall, first black Supreme Court justice, died, 1993	*bicycles!*
25	Tu.	Conversion of Paul • *Genius, like water, will find its level.* • {10.1 / 9.0} •	*The*
26	W.	Sts. Timothy & Titus • Michigan statehood, 1837	*rain/snow*
27	Th.	Full Wolf ○ • Univ. of Georgia chartered, 1785 • Samuel Gompers born, 1850 {10.9 / 9.9}	*line*
28	Fr.	St. Thomas Aquinas • Sir Francis Drake died, 1596 • {11.2 / —} •	*is*
29	Sa.	American League of Baseball Clubs formed, 1900 • W. C. Fields born, 1880 • {10.4 / 11.3}	*hard*
30	**B**	Septuagesima • ☾ at perig. • ☾ on Eq. • Tides {10.7 / 11.2} •	*to*
31	M.	*A contented mind is a continual feast.* • 3M Co. began marketing Scotch tape, 1928 •	*divine.*

Farmer's Calendar

Promptly on the bitterest winter mornings there appears at my bird feeder one or more often a pair of purple finches. They are bright, businesslike little birds, and their punctuality is reassuring. Nevertheless, they fill me with puzzlement. For with all its admirable qualities, the purple finch has a curious flaw. Purple it is not.

Why is it that so many of our common birds were evidently given their names not by a sensible observer, certainly not by a scientist, but by the author of *Alice in Wonderland*? The purple finch is the color of an overripe strawberry. The breast of the red-breasted nuthatch, companion of the finch at my winter feeder, is not red. The blue goose isn't blue. The black duck isn't black. Is this a game of some kind? Am I missing something here?

There are plenty of misnomers in the world of birds that are related to behavior. These are well known and easily explained. A whole family of birds of worldwide distribution — in our country including the whippoorwills and nighthawks — has the odd name goatsucker *(Caprimulgidae)* because they were anciently believed to suckle at the teats of milking goats. Sufficiently nutty, all right, but not hard to account for: some Dark Age goatherd with too much mead under his belt discovered a whippoorwill flying around his milking stand one evening, found the nannies dry, and drew a peasant's conclusion.

It's one thing for a bird to be mistakenly associated with an event or action, but what am I to make of a system of names that tells me a red bird is purple, a brown one black? It's the bald effrontery, the unapologetic falsity of the thing. And what about the birds themselves? If I were a purple finch, I would be made quite uncomfortable.

FEBRUARY, THE SECOND MONTH

Mercury puts in a good evening appearance in the first week. It is at its greatest evening elongation from the Sun on the 4th. Jupiter, near the Moon on the 3rd, is the most brilliant point of light in the south at dawn; Venus and Mars remain too nearly in line with the Sun to see clearly. The Big Dipper is bright in the northeast in the early evening, but most of the bright stars are still in the south sky. High above Orion is Capella in Auriga, the Charioteer. Following Orion on his nightly journey are his two dogs, Canis Major and Canis Minor, which feature sparkling Sirius and bright Procyon. Above Procyon glow the heads of Gemini the Twins, marked by stars Castor and Pollux. On clear nights early in the month, observers may note the tilted cone of soft radiance called the zodiacal light, in the west after evening twilight.

☾ Last Quarter	3rd day	3rd hour	7th min.
● New Moon	10th day	9th hour	31st min.
☽ First Quarter	18th day	12th hour	49th min.
○ Full Moon	25th day	20th hour	16th min.

For an explanation of this page, see "How to Use This Almanac," page 30; for values of Key Letters, see Time Correction Tables, page 209.

Day of Year	Day of Month	Day of Week	☉ Rises h. m.	Key	☉ Sets h. m.	Key	Length of Days h. m.	Sun Fast m.	Full Sea Boston A.M.	Full Sea Boston P.M.	☽ Rises h. m.	Key	☽ Sets h. m.	Key	Declination of Sun ° '	☽ Place	☽ Age
32	1	Tu.	6 58	D	4 58	A	10 00	2	2¼	2¾	11 P.M. 26	E	9 A.M. 25	B	17s.00	VIR	21
33	2	W.	6 57	D	4 59	A	10 02	2	3¼	3¾	— —	–	10 01	B	16 43	VIR	22
34	3	Th.	6 56	D	5 01	A	10 05	2	4¼	4¾	12 A.M. 37	E	10 42	B	16 26	LIB	23
35	4	Fr.	6 55	D	5 02	A	10 07	2	5¼	5¾	1 45	E	11 A.M. 29	B	16 08	LIB	24
36	5	Sa.	6 54	D	5 03	A	10 09	2	6¼	7	2 49	E	12 P.M. 22	B	15 50	OPH	25
37	6	**B**	6 52	D	5 05	A	10 13	2	7¼	8	3 45	E	1 21	B	15 32	SAG	26
38	7	M.	6 51	D	5 06	A	10 15	1	8¼	9	4 34	E	2 24	B	15 13	SAG	27
39	8	Tu.	6 50	D	5 07	B	10 17	1	9¼	10	5 17	E	3 28	C	14 54	SAG	28
40	9	W.	6 49	D	5 09	B	10 20	1	10¼	10¾	5 53	E	4 33	C	14 34	CAP	29
41	10	Th.	6 48	D	5 10	B	10 22	1	11	11½	6 24	D	5 36	C	14 15	AQU	0
42	11	Fr.	6 46	D	5 11	B	10 25	1	11½	—	6 53	D	6 38	D	13 55	AQU	1
43	12	Sa.	6 45	D	5 12	B	10 27	1	12	12¼	7 19	D	7 39	D	13 35	PSC	2
44	13	**B**	6 44	D	5 14	B	10 30	1	12¾	1	7 45	C	8 38	D	13 15	PSC	3
45	14	M.	6 42	D	5 15	B	10 33	1	1¼	1¾	8 11	C	9 37	E	12 55	PSC	4
46	15	Tu.	6 41	D	5 16	B	10 35	1	2	2¼	8 39	B	10 35	E	12 35	CET	5
47	16	W.	6 40	D	5 18	B	10 38	1	2¾	3	9 09	B	11 P.M. 33	E	12 14	CET	6
48	17	Th.	6 38	D	5 19	B	10 41	2	3½	4	9 42	B	— —	–	11 53	CET	7
49	18	Fr.	6 37	D	5 20	B	10 43	2	4¼	4¾	10 20	B	12 A.M. 30	E	11 32	TAU	8
50	19	Sa.	6 35	D	5 21	B	10 46	2	5	5¾	11 04	B	1 26	E	11 11	TAU	9
51	20	**B**	6 34	D	5 23	B	10 49	2	6	6¾	11 A.M. 55	B	2 19	E	10 49	TAU	10
52	21	M.	6 32	D	5 24	B	10 52	2	7	7½	12 P.M. 52	B	3 08	E	10 27	ORI	11
53	22	Tu.	6 31	D	5 25	B	10 54	2	7¾	8½	1 55	B	3 53	E	10 05	GEM	12
54	23	W.	6 29	D	5 26	B	10 57	2	8¾	9¼	3 03	C	4 34	E	9 43	CAN	13
55	24	Th.	6 28	D	5 28	B	11 00	2	9½	10	4 14	C	5 11	D	9 21	CAN	14
56	25	Fr.	6 26	D	5 29	B	11 03	2	10¼	10¾	5 27	D	5 45	D	8 59	LEO	15
57	26	Sa.	6 25	D	5 30	B	11 05	3	11¼	11½	6 41	D	6 18	D	8 37	SEX	16
58	27	**B**	6 23	D	5 31	B	11 08	3	—	12	7 56	E	6 51	C	8 14	VIR	17
59	28	M.	6 22	D	5 33	B	11 11	3	12¼	12¾	9 P.M. 11	E	7 A.M. 25	B	7s.51	VIR	18

FEBRUARY hath 28 days. 1994

There's a certain slant of light,
On winter afternoons,
That oppresses, like the weight
Of cathedral tunes.
– Emily Dickinson

D. M.	D. W.	Dates, Feasts, Fasts, Aspects, Tide Heights	Weather ↓
1	Tu.	**St. Brigid** • ☌☿♄ • Clark Gable born, 1901 •	*Groundhog*
2	W.	**Candlemas** • **Purif. of Mary** • Groundhog Day • Windchill –30° F, NYC, 1993	
3	Th.	☌♃☾ • Elizabeth Blackwell, 1st U.S. woman M.D., born, 1821 {10.7 / 9.4	*skeptics*
4	Fr.	☾ at ☊ • ☿ Gr. Elong. (18° E) • Patty Hearst kidnapped, 1974 {10.5 / 9.0	*turn*
5	Sa.	**St. Agatha** • *Liar: one who tells an unpleasant truth.* • {10.4 / 8.9 •	*dyspeptic.*
6	**B**	**Sexagesima** • ☾ runs low • Babe Ruth born, 1895 {10.3 / 8.9	*Plows*
7	M.	Baltimore fire destroyed 2,600 buildings, lasted 30 hours, 1904 • Beatles arrived in NYC, 1964 •	*are*
8	Tu.	☌♆☾ • ☌♅☾ • Tides {10.6 / 9.4	*prerequisite;*
9	W.	*If lying paid a tax It would pay the national debt.* • Tides {10.7 / 9.7 •	*one*
10	Th.	☿ stat. • New ● • –29° F Monterey, Virginia, 1899 •	*more*
11	Fr.	Mount Holyoke Seminary, first U.S. women's college, chartered, 1836 {10.6 / —	*Nor'easter,*
12	Sa.	☾ on Eq. • Abraham Lincoln born, 1809 • Sunshine today good for apples. •	*and*
13	**B**	**Quinquagesima** • Bess Truman born, 1885 • Tides {9.9 / 10.1 •	*we*
14	M.	**St. Valentine** • **Sts. Cyril & Methodius** • *The heart that loves is always young.* •	*say*
15	Tu.	**Shrove Tues.** • ☾ at apo. • Winter's back breaks. • {9.7 / 9.3 •	*the*
16	W.	**Ash Wed.** • Wilt Chamberlain scored 30,000th point, 1972 •	*heckwizit.*
17	Th.	*In the street of by-and-by one arrives at the house of never.* • Geronimo died, 1909 • {9.3 / 8.4 •	*A*
18	Fr.	☾ at ☋ • A February spring is not worth a pin. • Louis C. Tiffany born, 1848	*thaw?*
19	Sa.	Thomas Edison patented phonograph, 1878 • Copernicus born, 1473 • {9.0 / 7.9 •	*Naw!*
20	**B**	**1st S. in Lent** • ☾ rides high • ☿ in inf. ☌ • {9.0 / 7.9 •	*It's*
21	M.	☌♄☉ • First telephone book, New Haven, Conn., 1878 • {9.2 / 8.2	*teasing —*
22	Tu.	George Washington born, 1732 • U.S. acquired Florida from Spain, 1819 •	*rain*
23	W.	Ember Day • *One should go invited to a friend in good fortune, and uninvited in misfortune.* •	*is a*
24	Th.	**St. Matthias** • Dupont began making nylon toothbrush bristles, 1938 {10.6 / 9.9	*pain,*
25	Fr.	Full Snow ○ • Ember Day • Tides {11.1 / 10.6 •	*especially*
26	Sa.	☾ on Eq. • ☌☿♂ • Ember Day • Victor Hugo born, 1802 • {11.4 / 11.1	*when*
27	**B**	**2nd S. in Lent** • ☾ at perig. • *There's no vice like avarice.* •	*it's*
28	M.	♃ stat. • 43" of snow, Rochester, N.Y., 1900 • Tides {11.5 / 11.4	*freezing!*

Men occasionally stumble over the truth,
but most of them pick themselves up
and hurry off as if nothing had happened.
– Winston Churchill

Farmer's Calendar

A week of cold coming straight down from the Pole: 20° below by night, zero at noon, everything freezes solid, and the air makes the inside of your head hurt. You can burn everything you've got that will burn — wood, oil, gas, books, feathers, the cats — and still you won't feel warm. It won't last forever, though, and when the cold drop at last relents, it is a remarkable thing how much satisfaction will flow from a very little warming. The fundamental optimism of animal life is nowhere better displayed.

When the temperature has been down below zero for a few days, it doesn't take much mercury to produce a change of weather in the heart. Let the thermometer hit 10° on the high side, and the birds seem to stand up straighter, the squirrels to breathe more easily. The very trees exhale and let down their arms. As for the people, they practically fall down from relief, especially the young. They forget their coats, emerge in shirtsleeves. Anywhere over 15°, and they'll go about in bathing suits.

The reaction apparently depends not on the high temperature attained but on the interval between the high and low temperatures. Friends of mine in St. Paul, where the winter regularly gets down colder than it does in New England, report that no Minnesota kid worth his or her citizenship wears a coat when the temperature is above minus 10°; at zero you are hard-pressed to keep them decent. The same fact shows that the phenomenon is national and not a mere custom.

For some reason it doesn't work on the warm end of the year. In August, a week in the nineties doesn't make a day at 82° seem cold; it doesn't drive the young indoors to shiver around the stove. They take their relief when they need it.

1994 MARCH, The Third Month

Bright Venus sets in the west soon after dusk; nearly as bright Jupiter dominates the eastern sky after it rises in late evening. Very close conjunctions of Mars and Saturn on the 14th and Mercury and Saturn on the 24th are so low in the east just before dawn that binoculars will be needed to spot them. Mercury's greatest elongation west (28 degrees) of the year takes place on the 18th. In the south between Gemini and Leo a clear moonless night or binoculars can reveal the fuzzy patch of the Beehive star cluster in dim Cancer the Crab. Vernal equinox is at 3:28 P.M., EST, on the 20th.

☾ Last Quarter	4th day	11th hour	55th min.
● New Moon	12th day	2nd hour	6th min.
☽ First Quarter	20th day	7th hour	15th min.
○ Full Moon	27th day	6th hour	11th min.

For an explanation of this page, see "How to Use This Almanac," page 30; for values of Key Letters, see Time Correction Tables, page 209.

Day of Year	Day of Month	Day of Week	☉ Rises h. m.	Key	☉ Sets h. m.	Key	Length of Days h. m.	Sun Fast m.	Full Sea Boston A.M.	Full Sea Boston P.M.	☽ Rises h. m.	Key	☽ Sets h. m.	Key	Declination of Sun ° '	☽ Place	☽ Age
60	1	Tu.	6 20	D	5 34	B	11 14	3	1¼	1½	10ᴾₘ25	E	8ᴬₘ01	B	7s.29	VIR	19
61	2	W.	6 18	D	5 35	B	11 17	3	2	2½	11ᴾₘ36	E	8 42	B	7 06	LIB	20
62	3	Th.	6 17	D	5 36	B	11 19	4	2¾	3½	— —	–	9 28	B	6 43	LIB	21
63	4	Fr.	6 15	D	5 38	B	11 23	4	3¾	4½	12ᴬₘ42	E	10 20	B	6 20	OPH	22
64	5	Sa.	6 13	D	5 39	B	11 26	4	4¾	5½	1 41	E	11ᴬₘ17	B	5 56	OPH	23
65	6	**B**	6 12	D	5 40	B	11 28	4	6	6¾	2 32	E	12ᴾₘ18	B	5 33	SAG	24
66	7	M.	6 10	D	5 41	B	11 31	4	7	7¾	3 16	E	1 21	B	5 10	SAG	25
67	8	Tu.	6 08	D	5 42	B	11 34	5	8¼	8¾	3 53	E	2 24	C	4 47	CAP	26
68	9	W.	6 07	D	5 43	B	11 36	5	9	9¾	4 26	D	3 27	C	4 23	AQU	27
69	10	Th.	6 05	D	5 45	B	11 40	5	10	10¼	4 55	D	4 28	D	4 00	AQU	28
70	11	Fr.	6 03	D	5 46	B	11 43	5	10¾	11	5 22	D	5 29	D	3 36	AQU	29
71	12	Sa.	6 02	C	5 47	B	11 45	6	11¼	11½	5 48	C	6 28	D	3 13	PSC	0
72	13	**B**	6 00	C	5 48	B	11 48	6	—	12	6 15	C	7 27	D	2 48	PSC	1
73	14	M.	5 58	C	5 49	B	11 51	6	12¼	12½	6 42	B	8 26	E	2 25	PSC	2
74	15	Tu.	5 56	C	5 51	B	11 55	6	12¾	1¼	7 11	B	9 24	E	2 01	PSC	3
75	16	W.	5 55	C	5 52	B	11 57	7	1½	1¾	7 43	B	10 21	E	1 38	ARI	4
76	17	Th.	5 53	C	5 53	B	12 00	7	2	2½	8 19	B	11ᴾₘ16	E	1 14	ARI	5
77	18	Fr.	5 51	C	5 54	B	12 03	7	2¾	3¼	9 00	B	— —	–	0 51	TAU	6
78	19	Sa.	5 50	C	5 55	B	12 05	8	3½	4¼	9 47	B	12ᴬₘ09	E	0 27	TAU	7
79	20	**B**	5 48	C	5 56	C	12 08	8	4½	5	10 40	B	12 59	E	0s.03	ORI	8
80	21	M.	5 46	C	5 57	C	12 11	8	5¼	6	11ᴬₘ39	B	1 45	E	0N.20	GEM	9
81	22	Tu.	5 44	C	5 59	C	12 15	8	6¼	7	12ᴾₘ42	C	2 26	E	0 44	GEM	10
82	23	W.	5 43	C	6 00	C	12 17	9	7¼	7¾	1 50	C	3 04	E	1 07	CAN	11
83	24	Th.	5 41	C	6 01	C	12 20	9	8¼	8¾	3 01	D	3 39	D	1 31	LEO	12
84	25	Fr.	5 39	C	6 02	C	12 23	9	9	9½	4 14	D	4 12	D	1 54	SEX	13
85	26	Sa.	5 37	C	6 03	C	12 26	10	10	10¼	5 29	D	4 45	D	2 18	LEO	14
86	27	**B**	5 36	C	6 04	C	12 28	10	10¾	11	6 45	E	5 19	C	2 42	VIR	15
87	28	M.	5 34	C	6 05	C	12 31	10	11½	—	8 02	E	5 55	C	3 05	VIR	16
88	29	Tu.	5 32	C	6 06	C	12 34	11	12	12½	9 17	E	6 36	B	3 28	VIR	17
89	30	W.	5 30	C	6 08	C	12 38	11	12¾	1¼	10 28	E	7 21	B	3 51	LIB	18
90	31	Th.	5 29	C	6 09	C	12 40	11	1½	2¼	11ᴾₘ32	E	8ᴬₘ13	B	4N.15	SCO	19

MARCH hath 31 days. 1994

The little white clouds are racing over the sky,
And the fields are strewn with the gold of the flower of March,
The daffodil breaks under foot, and the tasseled larch
Sways and swings as the thrush goes hurrying by.
– Oscar Wilde

D. M.	D. W.	Dates, Feasts, Fasts, Aspects, Tide Heights	Weather ↓
1	Tu.	**St. David** • President Kennedy created Peace Corps, 1961 •	*Spring*
2	W.	**St. Chad** • ☌ ♃ ☾ • Sam Houston born, 1793 • {11.6 10.6	*preview;*
3	Th.	☾ at ☊ • ♇ stat. • "The Star-Spangled Banner" became national anthem, 1931	*winter*
4	Fr.	☿ stat. • Rep. Jeannette Rankin became first woman in Congress, 1917 •	*review.*
5	Sa.	☾ runs low • *Discussion is the anvil upon which the spark of truth is struck.* {10.4 9.0	*Snow*
6	**B**	**3d S. in Lent** • Fall of the Alamo, 1836 • Elizabeth Barrett Browning born, 1806	*in*
7	M.	**St. Perpetua** • ☌ ♆ ☾ • ☌ ♅ ☾ • Tides {9.9 8.9 •	*the*
8	Tu.	Town Meeting Day, N.H. • New York passed first state dog license law, 1894	*mountains,*
9	W.	☌ ☿ ☾ • Amerigo Vespucci born, 1451 • *Time enough is never enough.*	*raining*
10	Th.	☌ ♂ ☾ • ☌ ♄ ☾ • Harriet Tubman died, 1913 • {10.1 9.7	*coastally.*
11	Fr.	☾ on Eq. • Roxy Theater opened in NYC, 1927 • Lawrence Welk born, 1903	*Mild,*
12	Sa.	**St. Gregory** • New ● • Edward F. Albee born, 1928	*mostally.*
13	**B**	**4th S. in Lent** • ☌ ♀ ☾ • {— 10.1	*Temperatures*
14	M.	**Pure Monday** • ☌ ♂ ♄ • Tides {10.1 9.9	*dropping —*
15	Tu.	☾ at apo. • Turkey buzzards return to Hinckley, Ohio. • Tides {10.1 9.6 •	*it's*
16	W.	*The great pleasure in life is doing what people say you cannot do.* •	*sopping,*
17	Th.	**St. Patrick** • ☾ at ☋ • Golda Meir became Israel's 4th Prime Minister, 1969	*and*
18	Fr.	☿ Gr. Elong. (28° W.) • British Parliament repealed Stamp Act, 1766 • {9.5 8.5	*there's*
19	Sa.	**St. Joseph** • ☾ rides high • Tides {9.3 8.3 •	*no sign*
20	**B**	**5th S. in Lent** • **Passion** • Vernal Equinox • **Sunday of Orthodoxy** •	
21	M.	Sorosis, first U.S. professional Women's Club, founded, 1868 • Alcatraz prison closed, 1963 •	*of it*
22	Tu.	Friendship treaty, Gov. Carver and Chief Massasoit, Mass., 1621 • {9.3 8.6 •	*stopping.*
23	W.	Mussolini founded Fascist Party, 1919 • *To flee from folly is the beginning of wisdom.* •	*We*
24	Th.	☌ ☿ ♄ • *Cat on a Hot Tin Roof* premiered on Broadway, 1955 • {10.1 9.8 •	*sit*
25	Fr.	**Annunciation** • Dr. James Smith, Baltimore, Md., gave free vaccines to poor, 1802	*inside*
26	Sa.	☾ on Eq. • Robert Frost born, 1875 • Nathaniel Bowditch born, 1773 •	*hating*
27	**B**	**Palm Sun.** • **Passover** • Full Worm ○ • {11.4 11.8	*all*
28	M.	☾ at perig. • So many mists in March you see, So many frosts in May will be. • {11.5 —	*this*
29	Tu.	☌ ♃ ☾ • Knights of Columbus chartered, 1882 • Tides {12.1 11.4 •	*pre-*
30	W.	☾ at ☊ • Pencil with attached eraser patented, 1858 • Vincent Van Gogh born, 1853	*cipi-*
31	Th.	*A proverb is a short sentence based on long experience.* • Tides {11.9 10.6 •	*tating.*

Farmer's Calendar

Within a couple of weeks after the new year turns the Spring Equinox, my bailiwick is ready to be visited by two of New England's most cherished institutions: mud and baseball. In my league, where most of the players are under 15 and most of the salaries under seven figures, the two go very much together. My children's school digs out the bats and the softballs as soon as the snow is two-thirds gone. Therefore, spring training gets conducted in conditions some players would find inappropriate.

It's cold work, for one thing. The field is wet and the water that saturates it turns to ice at night. Balls hit sharply on the ground splash through the infield like ducks taking off from a pond. By the second inning, the players, the dog, the fans are as muddy as plow horses. Few mud-time games go the full nine; you can't play well when you can't feel your fingers or feet for cold. We have had more than one game called on account of snow.

I pitch. I chase balls that come near where I am. Balls hit into the outfield, balls hit over the wall into the pasture, balls hit beyond the house must be chased by the batter, after the dog loses interest. Those are the rules. They exist because I am a bit older than the other players and baseball is not really my game. At the Pastime I'm as good as I'm ever going to be, whereas the others each year throw farther, hit harder, run faster. I have noticed that the annual advent of baseball at this changing time of the year seems to gain on me faster than it does on the rest of the squad. Their muscles, their minds switch into spring instantly on the day the bats and the balls come out. Mine take longer.

1994 — APRIL, The Fourth Month

At dusk on the 12th, a crescent Moon is near lustrous Venus. Jupiter rises at nightfall, reaching opposition on the 30th. The brilliant planet burns in Libra, with the star Spica to the right of it. The Moon is at perigee on the 25th, so look for very high tides. High in the north and upside-down at mid evening is the Big Dipper. Extend the curve of its handle outward to find spring's brightest star, Arcturus, high in the east. Some Lyrid meteors from the west may be spotted after moonset and before dawn on the 21st/22nd. Daylight Saving Time begins at 2:00 A.M. on the 3rd.

☾ Last Quarter	2nd day	21st hour	55th min.
● New Moon	10th day	19th hour	18th min.
☽ First Quarter	18th day	21st hour	35th min.
○ Full Moon	25th day	14th hour	46th min.

ADD 1 hour for Daylight Saving Time after 2 A.M., April 3rd.

For an explanation of this page, see "How to Use This Almanac," page 30; for values of Key Letters, see Time Correction Tables, page 209.

Day of Year	Day of Month	Day of Week	☉ Rises h. m.	Key	☉ Sets h. m.	Key	Length of Days h. m.	Sun Fast m.	Full Sea Boston A.M.	Full Sea Boston P.M.	☽ Rises h. m.	Key	☽ Sets h. m.	Key	Declination of Sun ° '	☽ Place	☽ Age
91	1	Fr.	5 27	B	6 10	C	12 43	12	2½	3¼	— —	–	9^A_M10	B	4N38	OPH	20
92	2	Sa.	5 25	B	6 11	C	12 46	12	3½	4¼	12$_M$27	E	10 12	B	5 01	SAG	21
93	3	**B**	5 24	B	6 12	C	12 48	12	4½	5¼	1 14	E	11^A_M15	B	5 24	SAG	22
94	4	M.	5 22	B	6 13	C	12 51	12	5½	6½	1 54	E	12^P_M18	C	5 47	SAG	23
95	5	Tu.	5 20	B	6 14	D	12 54	13	6¾	7½	2 28	E	1 21	C	6 10	AQU	24
96	6	W.	5 18	B	6 15	D	12 57	13	7¾	8½	2 58	D	2 22	D	6 32	AQU	25
97	7	Th.	5 17	B	6 17	D	13 00	13	8¾	9¼	3 26	D	3 22	D	6 55	AQU	26
98	8	Fr.	5 15	B	6 18	D	13 03	14	9½	10	3 52	D	4 21	D	7 17	PSC	27
99	9	Sa.	5 13	B	6 19	D	13 06	14	10¼	10½	4 18	C	5 20	D	7 40	PSC	28
100	10	**B**	5 12	B	6 20	D	13 08	14	11	11	4 45	C	6 18	E	8 02	PSC	0
101	11	M.	5 10	B	6 21	D	13 11	14	11½	11¾	5 13	B	7 16	E	8 24	PSC	1
102	12	Tu.	5 08	B	6 22	D	13 14	15	—	12¼	5 44	B	8 14	E	8 46	ARI	2
103	13	W.	5 07	B	6 23	D	13 16	15	12¼	12¾	6 19	B	9 10	E	9 08	ARI	3
104	14	Th.	5 05	B	6 25	D	13 20	15	1	1½	6 59	B	10 04	E	9 29	TAU	4
105	15	Fr.	5 04	B	6 26	D	13 22	15	1½	2	7 43	B	10 54	E	9 51	TAU	5
106	16	Sa.	5 02	B	6 27	D	13 25	16	2¼	2¾	8 34	B	11$_M$40	E	10 12	TAU	6
107	17	**B**	5 00	B	6 28	D	13 28	16	3	3¾	9 29	B	— —	–	10 33	GEM	7
108	18	M.	4 59	B	6 29	D	13 30	16	3¾	4½	10 29	B	12$_M$22	E	10 54	GEM	8
109	19	Tu.	4 57	B	6 30	D	13 33	16	4¾	5½	11^A_M33	C	1 00	E	11 15	CAN	9
110	20	W.	4 56	B	6 31	D	13 35	17	5¾	6¼	12^P_M40	C	1 35	D	11 36	CAN	10
111	21	Th.	4 54	B	6 32	D	13 38	17	6¾	7¼	1 50	D	2 08	D	11 56	LEO	11
112	22	Fr.	4 53	B	6 34	D	13 41	17	7¾	8¼	3 02	D	2 40	D	12 17	SEX	12
113	23	Sa.	4 51	B	6 35	D	13 44	17	8½	9	4 16	E	3 12	C	12 37	VIR	13
114	24	**B**	4 50	B	6 36	D	13 47	17	9½	9¾	5 32	E	3 47	C	12 57	VIR	14
115	25	M.	4 48	B	6 37	D	13 49	18	10½	10¾	6 49	E	4 25	B	13 16	VIR	15
116	26	Tu.	4 47	B	6 38	D	13 51	18	11¼	11½	8 04	E	5 09	B	13 35	LIB	16
117	27	W.	4 45	B	6 39	D	13 54	18	—	12¼	9 14	E	5 59	B	13 54	LIB	17
118	28	Th.	4 44	B	6 40	D	13 56	18	12½	1	10 16	E	6 56	B	14 13	OPH	18
119	29	Fr.	4 42	B	6 41	D	13 59	18	1¼	2	11 08	E	7 58	B	14 32	SAG	19
120	30	Sa.	4 41	B	6 42	D	14 01	18	2¼	3	11$_M$52	E	9$_M$03	B	14N50	SAG	20

APRIL hath 30 days. 1994

The grass of spring covers the prairies,
The bean bursts noiselessly through the mould in the garden,
The delicate spear of the onion pierces upward,
The apple-buds cluster together on the apple-branches;
– *Walt Whitman*

D. M.	D. W.	Dates, Feasts, Fasts, Aspects, Tide Heights	*Weather* ↓
1	Fr.	**Good Friday** • ☾ runs low • **All Fools** • Tides {11.5 10.0 •	*Just*
2	Sa.	Daylight Saving Time begins tomorrow. • Alec Guinness born, 1914 • {10.9 9.5	*ducky!*
3	**B**	**Easter** • ☌♆☾ • ☌☿♂ • ☌♅☾ •	*Mucky*
4	M.	**Easter Monday (Canada)** • President William Henry Harrison died of pneumonia, 1841	*and*
5	Tu.	Firestone produced first balloon tires, 1923 • Booker T. Washington born, 1856	*yucky.*
6	W.	*He conquers who endures.* • First modern Olympiad opened, Athens, 1896 • {9.5 9.3	*Clouds*
7	Th.	☌♄☾ • Henry Ford died, 1947 • {9.6 9.6 •	*departing —*
8	Fr.	☾ on Eq. • ☌♂☾ • Mary Pickford born, 1893 • {9.7 9.8	*could*
9	Sa.	☌☿☾ • 16" snow, Eastport, Me., 1917 • Tides {9.7 10.0 •	*spring*
10	**B**	**1st S. af. Easter** • New ● • Bataan death march began, 1942	*be*
11	M.	☾ at apo. • Jackie Robinson first black major league baseball player, 1947	*starting?*
12	Tu.	☌♀☾ • 231 mph wind gusts Mt. Washington, N.H., 1934 • Tides {— 9.6 •	*So*
13	W.	☾ at ☋ • Thomas Jefferson born, 1743 • Tides {10.2 9.4 •	*much*
14	Th.	*Let it rain in April and May for me, And all the rest of the year for thee.* •	*sprinkling,*
15	Fr.	First school for deaf, Hartford, Conn., 1817 • President Lincoln died, 1865	*our skin*
16	Sa.	☾ rides high • Lighthouse at Minot Point, Mass., swept away in gale, 1851 • {9.8 8.7 •	*is*
17	**B**	**2nd S. af. Easter** • Tides {9.6 8.6 •	*wrinkling.*
18	M.	San Francisco earthquake, 1906 • First game in Yankee Stadium, 1923 •	*Damper*
19	Tu.	Astronomer John Winthrop made sunspot observations, Cambridge, Mass., 1739 • {9.4 8.8	*and*
20	W.	E. B. Bigelow patented carpet loom, 1837 • *Success is a journey, not a destination.*	*dimmer:*
21	Th.	**St. Anselm** • "Red Baron" shot down, 1918 • Tides {9.7 9.8 •	*Is*
22	Fr.	☾ on Eq. • Germans began using poison gas, WWI, 1915 • **Earth Day** •	*that*
23	Sa.	William Shakespeare born 1564, died 1616 • Hank Aaron hit first home run, 1954 • {10.5 11.2 •	*a*
24	**B**	**3rd S. af. Easter** • Tides {10.9 11.8 •	*glimmer?*
25	M.	**St. Mark** • ♆ stat. • ☾ at perig. • Full Pink ○ • {11.1 12.3	
26	Tu.	☾ at ☊ • ☌♃☾ • Tides {11.2 12.4 •	*Hoist yer*
27	W.	*Sultana* steamship exploded, killing nearly 2,000, 1865 •	*storm warning!*
28	Th.	*To live is to change, and to be perfect is to have changed often.* • {12.4 10.9	*Moisture*
29	Fr.	**St. Catherine** • ☾ runs low • Niagara Falls stopped flowing for 30 hours, 1848	*by*
30	Sa.	♃ at ☍ • ☿ in sup. ☌ • ♅ stat. • {11.5 10.1 •	*morning.*

You cannot do a kindness too soon, because you never know how soon it will be too late.

Farmer's Calendar

One day a couple of years ago, I set out to drive down the hill to the village at a moment when the town crew had lately passed my house grading and evening out the holes, bumps, and ruts that appear in the road each spring. All was well until I got to the steep pitch a mile from home. There my rear end slipped east in the smooth mud while my front slipped west, and the whole rig slithered toward the ditch like a pig at a party, arriving there in the twinkling of an eye. My neighbor pulled me out. As he unhitched his chain, he said to me, "You ought to know better than to try to drive on a road that's been fixed."

Wait, now. That's why they fix them, isn't it? The roads? So you can drive on them? Assuredly it is. But the way they go about mending the roads has a curious progression to it, a kind of dialectic that demands suffering and entails deep lessons about the life of man. As nearly as I can tell, to fix a bumpy, rutted road in Mud Season, you first scrape its surface into an impassable hogback of dirt, mud, and rocks. This ridge you grade down, spreading it across the road and making sure all the biggest rocks, which had migrated to the shoulders, have been put back in the middle. Finally you return with an enormous rake that evens out the top of the road, perking up those big rocks and stirring the surface into a kind of slurry: smooth, pretty, and for a while, as slick as any ice.

Roads, then, are like ourselves in this: Getting fixed is no straight line. There is no royal road to virtue; you must wander through the thorns and thickets. You must enter the dark wood. To become well, you must be made ill; to be right, wrong. Have faith, but take it easy at first.

1994   MAY, THE FIFTH MONTH

On the 10th, a rare annular eclipse of the Sun occurs around midday over a wide band from Mexico and New Mexico to Maine and Nova Scotia; over 94 percent of the Sun's disk will be covered by the Moon. The rest of North America will see a partial solar eclipse. On the evening of the 24th, there will be a partial eclipse of the full Moon, visible from all the 48 states (but joined in progress at moonrise in the westernmost states). Ulysses, a space probe jointly built by NASA and the European Space Agency to study the Sun, will pass over the Sun's south pole during May and June. The probe will provide us with our first close look at the Sun's pole.

☾	Last Quarter	2nd day	9th hour	33rd min.
●	New Moon	10th day	12th hour	8th min.
☽	First Quarter	18th day	7th hour	51st min.
○	Full Moon	24th day	22nd hour	40th min.
☾	Last Quarter	31st day	23rd hour	3rd min.

ADD 1 hour for Daylight Saving Time.

For an explanation of this page, see "How to Use This Almanac," page 30; for values of Key Letters, see Time Correction Tables, page 209.

Day of Year	Day of Month	Day of Week	☉ Rises h. m.	Key	☉ Sets h. m.	Key	Length of Days h. m.	Sun Fast m.	Full Sea Boston A.M.	P.M.	☽ Rises h. m.	Key	☽ Sets h. m.	Key	Declination of Sun ° '	☽ Place	☽ Age
121	1	**B**	4 40	B	6 44	D	14 04	18	3¼	4	— —		10ᴹ08	C	15N.08	SAG	21
122	2	M.	4 38	B	6 45	D	14 07	19	4¼	5	12ᴬ29	E	11ᴹ13	C	15 26	CAP	22
123	3	Tu.	4 37	B	6 46	D	14 09	19	5¼	6	1 01	D	12ᴾᴹ15	C	15 44	AQU	23
124	4	W.	4 36	A	6 47	D	14 11	19	6¼	7	1 29	D	1 16	D	16 02	AQU	24
125	5	Th.	4 34	A	6 48	D	14 14	19	7¼	7¾	1 56	C	2 15	D	16 19	AQU	25
126	6	Fr.	4 33	A	6 49	D	14 16	19	8¼	8½	2 22	C	3 14	D	16 36	PSC	26
127	7	Sa.	4 32	A	6 50	D	14 18	19	9	9¼	2 48	C	4 12	E	16 53	PSC	27
128	8	**B**	4 31	A	6 51	D	14 20	19	9¾	10	3 16	B	5 10	E	17 09	PSC	28
129	9	M.	4 30	A	6 52	D	14 22	19	10½	10½	3 46	B	6 08	E	17 25	ARI	29
130	10	Tu.	4 28	A	6 53	D	14 25	19	11	11¼	4 20	B	7 04	E	17 41	ARI	0
131	11	W.	4 27	A	6 55	D	14 28	19	11¾	11¾	4 58	B	7 59	E	17 56	TAU	1
132	12	Th.	4 26	A	6 56	D	14 30	19	—	12½	5 41	B	8 51	E	18 11	TAU	2
133	13	Fr.	4 25	A	6 57	D	14 32	19	12½	1	6 30	B	9 38	E	18 26	TAU	3
134	14	Sa.	4 24	A	6 58	D	14 34	19	1	1¾	7 24	B	10 21	E	18 41	GEM	4
135	15	**B**	4 23	A	6 59	E	14 36	19	1¾	2½	8 22	B	11 00	E	18 55	GEM	5
136	16	M.	4 22	A	7 00	E	14 38	19	2½	3¼	9 24	C	11ᴾᴹ35	D	19 09	CAN	6
137	17	Tu.	4 21	A	7 01	E	14 40	19	3¼	4	10 28	C	— —		19 22	CAN	7
138	18	W.	4 20	A	7 02	E	14 42	19	4¼	5	11ᴬ35	C	12ᴬ08	D	19 36	LEO	8
139	19	Th.	4 19	A	7 03	E	14 44	19	5¼	5¾	12ᴾᴹ43	D	12 39	D	19 49	SEX	9
140	20	Fr.	4 18	A	7 04	E	14 46	19	6¼	6¾	1 54	D	1 10	D	20 01	LEO	10
141	21	Sa.	4 17	A	7 05	E	14 48	19	7¼	7¾	3 07	E	1 42	C	20 14	VIR	11
142	22	**B**	4 17	A	7 06	E	14 49	19	8¼	8½	4 22	E	2 17	B	20 25	VIR	12
143	23	M.	4 16	A	7 07	E	14 51	19	9¼	9½	5 37	E	2 57	B	20 37	VIR	13
144	24	Tu.	4 15	A	7 08	E	14 53	19	10	10¼	6 50	E	3 43	B	20 48	LIB	14
145	25	W.	4 14	A	7 08	E	14 54	19	11	11¼	7 57	E	4 37	B	20 59	SCO	15
146	26	Th.	4 14	A	7 09	E	14 55	19	—	12	8 55	E	5 37	B	21 10	OPH	16
147	27	Fr.	4 13	A	7 10	E	14 57	19	12	12¾	9 44	E	6 43	B	21 20	SAG	17
148	28	Sa.	4 12	A	7 11	E	14 59	18	1	1¾	10 26	E	7 51	B	21 30	SAG	18
149	29	**B**	4 12	A	7 12	E	15 00	18	1¾	2½	11 01	D	8 58	C	21 39	CAP	19
150	30	M.	4 11	A	7 13	E	15 02	18	2¾	3½	11 31	D	10 03	C	21 48	AQU	20
151	31	Tu.	4 11	A	7 14	E	15 03	18	3¾	4½	11ᴹ59	D	11ᴬ06	C	21N.56	AQU	21

MAY hath 31 days. 1994

May is lilac here in New England,
May is a thrush singing "Sun up!" on a tip-top ash-tree,
May is white clouds behind pine trees
Puffed out and marching upon a blue sky.
– Amy Lowell

D. M.	D. W.	Dates, Feasts, Fasts, Aspects, Tide Heights	Weather ↓
1	**B**	**4th S. af. Easter** • **Orthodox Easter** • ☌♆☾ •	*A*
2	M.	*Reason is the wise man's master; experience is the fool's.* • Tides {10.2 / 9.4 •	*May-*
3	Tu.	Invention of the Cross • First toll bridge, Rowley, Mass., 1654 • Tides {9.7 / 9.3 •	*zing*
4	W.	☌♄☾ • Haymarket Square riot, Chicago, 1886 • Horace Mann born, 1796 •	*grays!*
5	Th.	☾ on Eq. • Napoleon Bonaparte died in exile, 1821 • Carnegie Hall opened, 1891 •	*How*
6	Fr.	Babe Ruth hit first home run, 1915 • Marlene Dietrich, age 90, died in Paris, 1992 • {9.1 / 9.6 •	*sweet*
7	Sa.	☌♂☾ • American Medical Assoc. founded, 1847 • *Lusitania* sunk, 1915 •	*the*
8	**B**	**Rogation S.** • ☾ at apo. • Harry S Truman born, 1884 •	*shine*
9	M.	*He that riseth late must trot all day.* • Howard Carter, discoverer of tomb of King Tut, born, 1873 •	*that*
10	Tu.	☾ at ☋ • New ● • Eclipse ☉ • {9.3 / 10.3	*bathes a*
11	W.	**Three** • American Bible Society formed, 1816 • Bob Marley died, 1981 •	*wretch*
12	Th.	**Ascension** • **Chilly** • Florence Nightingale born, 1820 • {— / 9.2 •	*like*
13	Fr.	☾ rides high • ☌♀☾ • **Saints** • Tides {10.2 / 9.2 •	*me.*
14	Sa.	*After breakfast work a while, after supper walk a mile.* • Antioch College chartered, 1852 •	*'Twas*
15	**B**	**1st S. af. Asc.** • Gasoline rationing began, 1942 • Tides {10.1 / 9.0	*raw*
16	M.	**Shavuot** • First "Oscars" awarded, 1929 • Billy Martin born, 1928 •	*and*
17	Tu.	♇ at ☍ • First Kentucky Derby held, 1875 • Frost, Dedham, Mass., 1748 •	*wet,*
18	W.	Compulsory school attendance, Mass., 1852 • *On a calm sea everyone is a pilot.* • {9.7 / 9.5 •	*but*
19	Th.	**St. Dunstan** • ☾ on Eq. • 99° F New York City, 1962 • {9.7 / 9.9	*now*
20	Fr.	A bushel a day after the middle of May. • Levi Strauss and Jacob Davis patented rivet-pocket pants, 1873	*it's*
21	Sa.	American Red Cross founded, 1881 • *Make today yesterday's pupil.* • {10.0 / 10.9 •	*fine;*
22	**B**	**Whit S.** • **Pentecost** • Associated Press founded, 1900 {10.2 / 11.5	*Cold*
23	M.	☌♃☾ • ☾ at perig. • **Victoria Day, Canada** • Tides {10.5 / 12.0 •	*snap,*
24	Tu.	☾ at ☊ • Full Flower ○ • Eclipse ☾ • Tides {10.7 / 12.3	*but*
25	W.	**St. Bede** • Ember Day • Ralph Waldo Emerson born, 1803 •	*then*
26	Th.	**St. Augustine of Canterbury** • ☾ runs low •	*whoopee!*
27	Fr.	Ember Day • A cold May is kindly, And fills the barn finely. • {12.2 / 10.6 •	*Attention:*
28	Sa.	☌♆☾ • ☌♅☾ • Ember Day • Patrick Henry born, 1736	*We're*
29	**B**	**Trinity** • John F. Kennedy born, 1917 • Bob Hope born, 1903 • {11.4 / 10.1	*due*
30	M.	**Memorial Day** • ☿ Gr. Elong. (23° East) • Tides {10.8 / 9.8 •	*for a*
31	Tu.	**Visit. of Mary** • Johnstown, Pa., flood killed 2,300, 1889 •	*drenchin'.*

Farmer's Calendar

Warm-blooded creatures like ourselves are supposed to have the best of this Earth, but you have to wonder. We go to a lot of trouble. On one of these May mornings, for example, I wake up freezing. I crawl into my two-ton pants and a couple of sweaters. I may even pull on a wool hat — indoors like a fool. I make my way downstairs and put on the water. I wait, blowing on my fingers. Presently I'll be able to start pouring down the hot coffee. All this because I have to make my heat inside myself.

Then, by eleven o'clock the Sun will be high and a day will have arrived that is in reality an early summer day. I'll be tearing off clothing like an Eskimo trapped in a Turkish bath. The fire that I kindled with shivering fingers in the kitchen stove four hours ago will have heated the house intolerably. I'll throw open the windows and sit outdoors on the step. By suppertime I'll be back in my sweaters, and the stove will be cold, the fire out. I'll have to start it all over again. Because I carry my thermostat deep within, I must spend the whole day setting it up or down.

I have never heard snakes, turtles, and lizards praised for their brains. Their magnificent ancestors, the dinosaurs, were long believed to have died out pretty much through sheer stupidity, as I recall the story. On the grand ladder of evolution the reptiles are assigned a fairly humble rung. But who thought up that ladder? We did. Maybe we were jealous. The reptiles, cold-blooded, can get by at whatever temperature's on the market. They don't have to scurry around adjusting themselves. No grass snake has ever been made a fool of by a spring day.

1994

JUNE, THE SIXTH MONTH

Venus shines in the west after nightfall, passing 5 degrees south of Pollux on the 10th and right through the northern edge of the Beehive star cluster on the 21st-22nd. Jupiter is prominent in the southeast as darkness falls and retrogrades back into Virgo late in the month. Spica is the bright star well to the right of Jupiter; Corvus the Crow lies to the right of Spica. High above Jupiter and Spica shines brilliant Arcturus, with the semicircle of Corona Borealis to the upper left of it. Just before dawn, Saturn is the brightest object in the south; a telescope shows its rings the most nearly sideways in many years. Summer solstice arrives at 9:48 A.M., EST, on the 21st.

● New Moon	9th day	3rd hour	28th min.
☽ First Quarter	16th day	14th hour	57th min.
○ Full Moon	23rd day	6th hour	34th min.
☾ Last Quarter	30th day	14th hour	31st min.

ADD 1 hour for Daylight Saving Time.

For an explanation of this page, see "How to Use This Almanac," page 30; for values of Key Letters, see Time Correction Tables, page 209.

Day of Year	Day of Month	Day of Week	☉ Rises h. m.	Key	☉ Sets h. m.	Key	Length of Days h. m.	Sun Fast m.	Full Sea Boston A.M.	Full Sea Boston P.M.	☽ Rises h. m.	Key	☽ Sets h. m.	Key	Declination of Sun ° '	☽ Place	☽ Age
152	1	W.	4 10	A	7 14	E	15 04	18	4¾	5¼	— —	–	12 P.M. 07	D	22N.05	PSC	22
153	2	Th.	4 10	A	7 15	E	15 05	18	5¾	6¼	12 A.M. 26	C	1 06	D	22 12	PSC	23
154	3	Fr.	4 09	A	7 16	E	15 07	18	6¾	7	12 52	C	2 05	E	22 20	PSC	24
155	4	Sa.	4 09	A	7 17	E	15 08	17	7½	8	1 19	B	3 03	E	22 27	PSC	25
156	5	**B**	4 08	A	7 17	E	15 09	17	8½	8¾	1 48	B	4 01	E	22 34	ARI	26
157	6	M.	4 08	A	7 18	E	15 10	17	9¼	9½	2 21	B	4 58	E	22 40	ARI	27
158	7	Tu.	4 08	A	7 19	E	15 11	17	10	10	2 57	B	5 54	E	22 46	TAU	28
159	8	W.	4 08	A	7 19	E	15 11	17	10¾	10¾	3 39	B	6 47	E	22 52	TAU	29
160	9	Th.	4 07	A	7 20	E	15 13	17	11¼	11½	4 26	B	7 36	E	22 56	TAU	0
161	10	Fr.	4 07	A	7 20	E	15 13	16	—	12	5 19	B	8 21	E	23 01	ORI	1
162	11	Sa.	4 07	A	7 21	E	15 14	16	12	12¾	6 16	B	9 02	E	23 05	GEM	2
163	12	**B**	4 07	A	7 21	E	15 14	16	12¾	1¼	7 17	B	9 38	E	23 09	GEM	3
164	13	M.	4 07	A	7 22	E	15 15	16	1½	2	8 21	C	10 11	D	23 13	CAN	4
165	14	Tu.	4 07	A	7 22	E	15 15	16	2¼	2¾	9 26	D	10 42	D	23 16	LEO	5
166	15	W.	4 07	A	7 23	E	15 16	15	3	3½	10 33	D	11 12	D	23 19	SEX	6
167	16	Th.	4 07	A	7 23	E	15 16	15	3¾	4½	11 A.M. 41	D	11 P.M. 43	C	23 21	LEO	7
168	17	Fr.	4 07	A	7 23	E	15 16	15	4¾	5¼	12 P.M. 51	D	— —	–	23 23	VIR	8
169	18	Sa.	4 07	A	7 24	E	15 17	15	5¾	6¼	2 02	E	12 A.M. 16	C	23 24	VIR	9
170	19	**B**	4 07	A	7 24	E	15 17	14	6¾	7¼	3 15	E	12 52	B	23 25	VIR	10
171	20	M.	4 07	A	7 24	E	15 17	14	7¾	8¼	4 27	E	1 33	B	23 25	LIB	11
172	21	Tu.	4 07	A	7 25	E	15 18	14	8¾	9	5 36	E	2 22	B	23 25	SCO	12
173	22	W.	4 08	A	7 25	E	15 17	14	9¾	10	6 39	E	3 18	B	23 25	OPH	13
174	23	Th.	4 08	A	7 25	E	15 17	14	10¾	11	7 33	E	4 21	B	23 25	SAG	14
175	24	Fr.	4 08	A	7 25	E	15 17	13	11½	11¾	8 19	E	5 28	B	23 24	SAG	15
176	25	Sa.	4 08	A	7 25	E	15 17	13	—	12½	8 57	E	6 37	B	23 22	SAG	16
177	26	**B**	4 09	A	7 25	E	15 16	13	12¾	1¼	9 31	D	7 45	C	23 20	AQU	17
178	27	M.	4 09	A	7 25	E	15 16	13	1½	2¼	10 00	D	8 50	D	23 18	AQU	18
179	28	Tu.	4 10	A	7 25	E	15 15	13	2¼	3	10 28	D	9 54	D	23 15	AQU	19
180	29	W.	4 10	A	7 25	E	15 15	12	3¼	3¾	10 55	C	10 55	D	23 12	PSC	20
181	30	Th.	4 11	A	7 25	E	15 14	12	4	4¾	11 P.M. 22	C	11 A.M. 54	E	23N.09	PSC	21

There is a bird in the poplars —
It is the sun!
The leaves are little yellow fish
Swimming in the river;
– William Carlos Williams

Farmer's Calendar

Fireflies wander through the midsummer night. Their strange, cold little lights flash on and off as though they were trying to send signals in a code nobody knows but them. In fact, as I understand it, they're looking for romance like everybody else, but I can't get over the idea that if only I knew how to interpret them, the winking, drifting lights would have something to say to me. Someday I'll get the fireflies' message. I hope it's not an ad.

The fact that there are little beetles flying around out there that can turn themselves on like a flashlight has always seemed to me to come right out of the book of miracles, but in truth creatures that light up are by no means rare. There are luminescent shrimp, jellyfish, squid, clams, snails, worms, and fish — lots of fish — as well as insects. Most are marine, however, perhaps the reason a landsman is so struck by the firefly, which occurs virtually everywhere.

Fireflies themselves may be any of several insects. The ones we see are beetles of the family *Lampyridae*, of which there are 140 different species in North America. Elsewhere in the world there are other, greater light-up bugs. Some are rich in legend. The best one I know concerns the *cucujo (Pyrophorus)*, a large click beetle of Latin America. According to *The Conquest of Mexico*, it was this beetle, shining in the night, that gave the great Cortez a crucial victory over his enemy Narvaez. The soldiers of the latter, besieged in the night by Cortez in one of the temples in the Aztec town of Cempoalla (modern Vera Cruz Province, Mexico), took the lights of the summer fireflies for the matches of the muskets of a vast army and surrendered to Cortez's force, which in fact was tiny. June 1520.

D.M.	D.W.	Dates, Feasts, Fasts, Aspects, Tide Heights	Weather ↓
1	W.	☾ on Eq. • ♂♃☾ • First pay phone New Haven, Conn., 1880 •	*Veiled*
2	Th.	**Corpus Christi** • American Indians granted citizenship, 1924 • Tides {9.1 {9.4	*in*
3	Fr.	*Closed doors are more easily heard through than open ones.* Jefferson Davis born, 1808 •	*mist*
4	Sa.	Battle of Midway began, 1942 • Tiananmen Square massacre, 1989 • Tides {8.7 {9.6	*then*
5	B	2ᵗʰ ☉. af. ℘. • **St. Boniface** • ☾ at apo. • {8.7 {9.8	*sun-*
6	M.	♂♂☾ • D-Day: Allied forces invaded Normandy, 1944 • Nathan Hale born, 1755	*kissed.*
7	Tu.	☾ at �””” • The "$64,000 Question" debuted on TV, 1955 • {8.9 {10.1	*Proud*
8	W.	Frank Lloyd Wright born, 1867 • *Don't laugh at age . . . pray to reach it.*	*Papa*
9	Th.	**Orthodox Ascension** • ☾ high • New ● • rides {9.1 {10.3	*and*
10	Fr.	♂☿☾ • "Pine tree" shilling minted in colonies, 1652 • {— {9.2	*tearful*
11	Sa.	**St. Barnabas** • 11" snow, Berlin, N.H., 1842 • {10.4 {9.2	*Mater*
12	B	3ᵗʰ ☉. af. ℘. • ☿ stat. • ♂♀☾ • Tides {— {9.6	*greet*
13	M.	Yukon Territory formed, 1898 • Miranda Decision, 1966 • Red Grange born, 1903 •	*the*
14	Tu.	**St. Basil** • **Flag Day** • Tides {10.3 {9.6	*grinning*
15	W.	*Lovely flowers fade fast.* Cork center baseball patented, 1909 *Weeds last the season.*	*gradu-*
16	Th.	☾ on Eq. • First "Ladies' Day" baseball game, New York, 1883 • {10.0 {10.1	*ater.*
17	Fr.	Name "GI Joe" coined, 1942 • Polio epidemic broke out, Rutland, Vt., 1894 • {9.8 {10.4	*Cool —*
18	Sa.	Sally Ride became first U.S. woman in space, 1983 • E. W. Scripps born, 1854 •	*no pool.*
19	B	4ᵗʰ ☉. af. ℘. • **Orthodox Pentecost** • ♂♃☾ • {9.7 {11.1	
20	M.	☾ at ☊ • Fanny Brice debuted in Ziegfeld Follies, 1910 • West Virginia statehood, 1863	*Rent*
21	Tu.	☾ perig. • Summer Solstice • Columbia Records introduced LP record, 1948 •	*a tent*
22	W.	**St. Alban** • ☾ low • runs U. S. voting age lowered to 18, 1970 • {10.2 {12.0	*for*
23	Th.	Full Strawberry ○ • ♄ stat. • Tides {10.3 {12.0	*nuptial*
24	Fr.	**Nativ. John the Baptist** • ♂♅☾ • {10.4 {11.9 •	*fests,*
25	Sa.	♂♂☾ • ☿ in inf. ♂ • Rose O'Neill, designer of Kewpie Doll, born, 1874 •	*lest*
26	B	5ᵗʰ ☉. af. ℘. • **Orthodox All Saints** • {11.6 {10.3 •	*your*
27	M.	*If ye cannot see the bottom, do not wade far out.* Helen Keller born, 1880 • {11.1 {10.1	*guests*
28	Tu.	♂♃☾ • 111° F, Camden, S.C., 1954 • Treaty of Versailles ended WWI, 1919 •	*should*
29	W.	**Sts. Peter & Paul** • ☾ on Eq. • Tides {10.0 {9.7 •	*need*
30	Th.	Emile Blondin crossed Niagara Falls on a tightrope, 1859 • Tides {9.4 {9.5 •	*life vests!*

The scales tell us what is light and what is heavy, but not what is gold and what is silver.

1994 JULY, The Seventh Month

Earth is at aphelion (farthest from the Sun) at 2:00 P.M., EST, on the 5th. Also on the 5th, there is a close conjunction of Mars and the Moon. Venus has a striking pairing in the west with the star Regulus on several evenings around the 10th; the Moon is near them on the 11th and 12th and fairly near Jupiter on the 16th. Low in the south, S-shaped Scorpius the Scorpion glitters with its bright, reddish star, Antares. High in the east hangs the Summer Triangle, with bluish Vega at top, Deneb to the lower left, and Altair to the lower right.

● New Moon	8th day	16th hour	39th min.
☽ First Quarter	15th day	20th hour	13th min.
○ Full Moon	22nd day	15th hour	17th min.
☾ Last Quarter	30th day	7th hour	41st min.

ADD 1 hour for Daylight Saving Time.

For an explanation of this page, see "How to Use This Almanac," page 30; for values of Key Letters, see Time Correction Tables, page 209.

Day of Year	Day of Month	Day of Week	☉ Rises h. m.	Key	☉ Sets h. m.	Key	Length of Days h. m.	Sun Fast m.	Full Sea Boston A.M.	P.M.	☽ Rises h. m.	Key	☽ Sets h. m.	Key	Declination of Sun ° '	☽ Place	☽ Age
182	1	Fr.	4 11	A	7 25	E	15 14	12	5	5½	11ᴹ50	C	12ᴹ53	E	23N.05	PSC	22
183	2	Sa.	4 12	A	7 25	E	15 13	12	6	6¼	— —	–	1 51	E	23 01	PSC	23
184	3	**B**	4 12	A	7 24	E	15 12	12	6¾	7¼	12ᴹ21	B	2 49	E	22 56	ARI	24
185	4	M.	4 13	A	7 24	E	15 11	11	7¾	8	12 56	B	3 45	E	22 51	ARI	25
186	5	Tu.	4 13	A	7 24	E	15 11	11	8¾	8¾	1 35	B	4 39	E	22 45	TAU	26
187	6	W.	4 14	A	7 24	E	15 10	11	9½	9½	2 20	B	5 31	E	22 39	TAU	27
188	7	Th.	4 15	A	7 23	E	15 08	11	10¼	10¼	3 11	B	6 18	E	22 33	TAU	28
189	8	Fr.	4 15	A	7 23	E	15 08	11	10¾	11	4 08	B	7 01	E	22 26	GEM	0
190	9	Sa.	4 16	A	7 22	E	15 06	11	11½	11¾	5 08	B	7 39	E	22 19	GEM	1
191	10	**B**	4 17	A	7 22	E	15 05	10	—	12¼	6 12	C	8 14	D	22 12	CAN	2
192	11	M.	4 17	A	7 22	E	15 05	10	12¼	1	7 18	C	8 46	D	22 04	CAN	3
193	12	Tu.	4 18	A	7 21	E	15 03	10	1	1½	8 25	D	9 17	D	21 55	SEX	4
194	13	W.	4 19	A	7 20	E	15 01	10	1¾	2¼	9 33	D	9 47	C	21 47	LEO	5
195	14	Th.	4 20	A	7 20	E	15 00	10	2¾	3¼	10 42	D	10 19	C	21 38	VIR	6
196	15	Fr.	4 21	A	7 19	E	14 58	10	3½	4	11ᴹ52	E	10 53	B	21 28	VIR	7
197	16	Sa.	4 21	A	7 19	E	14 58	10	4½	5	1ᴹ02	E	11ᴹ32	B	21 18	VIR	8
198	17	**B**	4 22	A	7 18	E	14 56	10	5½	6	2 13	E	— —	–	21 08	LIB	9
199	18	M.	4 23	A	7 17	E	14 54	9	6½	7	3 21	E	12ᴹ16	B	20 58	LIB	10
200	19	Tu.	4 24	A	7 16	E	14 52	9	7½	8	4 25	E	1 07	B	20 48	OPH	11
201	20	W.	4 25	A	7 16	E	14 51	9	8½	8¾	5 21	E	2 05	B	20 36	SAG	12
202	21	Th.	4 26	A	7 15	E	14 49	9	9½	9¾	6 10	E	3 09	B	20 25	SAG	13
203	22	Fr.	4 27	A	7 14	E	14 47	9	10½	10¾	6 52	E	4 17	B	20 13	SAG	14
204	23	Sa.	4 28	A	7 13	E	14 45	9	11¼	11½	7 28	D	5 25	C	20 01	CAP	15
205	24	**B**	4 29	A	7 12	E	14 43	9	—	12¼	8 00	D	6 32	C	19 48	AQU	16
206	25	M.	4 30	A	7 11	E	14 41	9	12¼	1	8 29	D	7 37	D	19 35	AQU	17
207	26	Tu.	4 31	A	7 10	D	14 39	9	1	1¾	8 56	C	8 40	D	19 22	PSC	18
208	27	W.	4 31	A	7 09	D	14 38	9	2	2¼	9 24	C	9 41	D	19 09	PSC	19
209	28	Th.	4 32	A	7 08	D	14 36	9	2¾	3	9 52	B	10 41	D	18 55	PSC	20
210	29	Fr.	4 33	A	7 07	D	14 34	9	3½	4	10 22	B	11ᴹ40	E	18 41	PSC	21
211	30	Sa.	4 34	A	7 06	D	14 32	9	4¼	4¾	10 55	B	12ᴹ38	E	18 27	ARI	22
212	31	**B**	4 35	A	7 05	D	14 30	9	5¼	5½	11ᴹ32	B	1ᴹ34	E	18N.12	ARI	23

JULY hath 31 days. 1994

Very good in the grass to lie
And see the network 'gainst the sky,
A living lace of blue and green,
And boughs that let the gold between.
–Katherine Tynan

D. M.	D. W.	Dates, Feasts, Fasts, Aspects, Tide Heights	*Weather* ↓
1	Fr.	**Canada Day** • Prince Edward Island became province of Canada, 1873	*Fireworks*
2	Sa.	♃ stat. • Civil Rights Act signed, 1964 • Tides {8.6 / 9.4 •	*fizzle*
3	**B**	**6th S. af. P.** • ☾ at apo. • Dog Days begin. • {8.4 / 9.5 •	*in the*
4	M.	**Independence Day** • ☾ at ☋ • Tides {8.4 / 9.6 •	*drizzle.*
5	Tu.	☌♂☾ • ⊕ at aphelion • P. T. Barnum born, 1810 •	*Bright*
6	W.	☾ rides high • ☿ stat. • First All-Star baseball game, 1933 • {8.6 / 10.0 •	*and*
7	Th.	☌☿☾ • *No one is rich enough to do without a neighbor.* • Marc Chagall born, 1887	*better; a*
8	Fr.	New ● • Liberty Bell cracked, 1835 • Hail fell, Canterbury, Conn., 1788	*storm,*
9	Sa.	O. J. Simpson born, 1947 • As July (weather), so the next January. • {9.3 / 10.6	*etcetera.*
10	**B**	**7th S. af. P.** • Tides {— / 9.6 •	*Sidewalks*
11	M.	Aaron Burr fatally wounded Alexander Hamilton in duel, 1804 • E. B. White born, 1899	*shimmer*
12	Tu.	☌♀☾ • *Fear is the tax which conscience pays to guilt.* • Tides {10.7 / 10.1 •	*with*
13	W.	☾ on Eq. • Nation's first military draft caused rioting, troops needed to restore order, 1863 •	*the*
14	Th.	♆ at ☍ • Bastille Day • 117° F, E. St. Louis, Ill., 1954 • {10.4 / 10.5	*heat;*
15	Fr.	**St. Swithin** • Rain today means 40 days rain. • Rembrandt born, 1606 • {10.1 / 10.6	*is*
16	Sa.	☌♃☾ • ♅ at ☍ • First parking meters, Oklahoma City, 1935 • {9.8 / 10.7	*this*
17	**B**	**8th S. af. P.** • ☾ at ☊ • ☿ Gr. Elong. (21° West) •	*what*
18	M.	☾ at perig. • Disneyland opened, Anaheim, Ca., 1955 • Nelson Mandella born, 1918 •	*they*
19	Tu.	Rain ceases, wind increases. • Washington Senators stole 8 bases in 1st inning, 1915 • {9.4 / 11.2	*mean*
20	W.	☾ runs low • Armstrong and Aldrich walked on the Moon, 1969 • Tides {9.6 / 11.3 •	*by*
21	Th.	*No need to burn the barn to kill the flies.* • First Battle of Bull Run, 1861 • {9.8 / 11.5 •	*the*
22	Fr.	**St. Mary Magdalene** • ☌♆☾ • ☌♅☾ • Full Buck ○ •	
23	Sa.	Henry David Thoreau arrested for refusing to pay poll tax, 1846 • Tides {10.2 / 11.4	*agony*
24	**B**	**9th S. af. P.** • Amelia Earhart born, 1898 • Tides {— / 10.3 •	*of*
25	M.	**St. James** • ☌♄☾ • Luxury liners *Stockholm* and *Andrea Doria* collided, 1956	*de-*
26	Tu.	**St. Anne** • ☾ on Eq. • U. S. Post Office established, 1775 • {10.8 / 10.2 •	*feet?*
27	W.	Grasshopper plague, Iowa, Neb., S.D., 1931 • Leo Durocher born, 1906 •	*Have a*
28	Th.	*As long as the Sun shines one does not ask for the Moon.* • Tides {9.8 / 9.8 •	*Popsicle;*
29	Fr.	**Sts. Mary & Martha** • First asphalt paved road, Newark, N.J., 1870 •	*the*
30	Sa.	☾ at apo. • Cornscateous air. • Casey Stengel born, 1891 {8.8 / 9.4	*climate's*
31	**B**	**10th S. af. P.** • ☾ at ☋ • Tides {8.4 / 9.3 •	*tropsicle.*

Farmer's Calendar

In July, the bee balm, a native wildflower of the damp woodlands and streamsides, long since domesticated, educated, blooms in the garden. It blooms in the most extraordinary fiery red, an almost fierce color that doesn't seem to belong on a plant at all. The flower is rough and shaggy. It looks like a rag doll, and as the season wears on and the flower drops petals and parts and begins to be somewhat raffish, like a rag doll it looks better and better. Hummingbirds love the bee balm, and so do the monarch butterflies, which appear in numbers around the same time the flower does. No doubt the bees love it too.

The bee balm *(Monarda didyma)*, a member of the mint family, has a long and proud history, traceable through its several names. It was imported from North America to England before 1745 by the botanist John Bartram and became a favorite in the great flower market at Covent Garden, London. The British called it scarlet bergamot, because they believed the plant's aromatic leaves and stems smelled like a popular orange of the day that came to England from the Italian city of Bergamo, north of Milan. In the Colonies the plant was called Oswego tea, for it was said the settlers and Indians around Oswego, New York, drank an infusion of the leaves. Perhaps there was some ridicule in a tea-drinking society's calling this American wildling Oswego tea. Oswego was a fort on the south shore of Lake Ontario, founded as early as 1722. It was a wilderness outpost at the back of beyond. To call *M. didyma* Oswego tea was to say it was what passed for tea at places like Oswego, as we might call a Thompson submachine gun a Chicago piano.

1994   AUGUST, The Eighth Month

The Perseid meteor shower could offer a stupendous display; look especially after midnight in the moonless early hours of the 12th and 13th. In clear country skies, dozens an hour can be seen coming from the northeast, but hundreds or even thousands are not out of the question! Venus is radiant in the west each evening. It reaches greatest elongation east (46 degrees) from the Sun on the 24th and has a superb conjunction with the star Spica on the 31st. As darkness deepens, Vega burns like a sapphire overhead in little Lyra the Lyre. On clear, moonless nights, the Milky Way runs down to the Teapot pattern of Sagittarius in the south.

● New Moon	7th day	3rd hour	46th min.
☽ First Quarter	14th day	0 hour	58th min.
○ Full Moon	21st day	1st hour	48th min.
☾ Last Quarter	29th day	1st hour	41st min.

ADD 1 hour for Daylight Saving Time.

For an explanation of this page, see "How to Use This Almanac," page 30; for values of Key Letters, see Time Correction Tables, page 209.

Day of Year	Day of Month	Day of Week	☉ Rises h. m.	Key	☉ Sets h. m.	Key	Length of Days h. m.	Sun Fast m.	Full Sea Boston A.M.	Full Sea Boston P.M.	☽ Rises h. m.	Key	☽ Sets h. m.	Key	Declination of Sun ° '	☽ Place	☽ Age
213	1	M.	4 36	A	7 04	D	14 28	9	6¼	6½	— —	–	2ᴹ29	E	17N.57	TAU	24
214	2	Tu.	4 38	A	7 03	D	14 25	9	7	7¼	12ᴬᴹ14	B	3 22	E	17 41	TAU	25
215	3	W.	4 39	A	7 02	D	14 23	9	8	8¼	1 03	B	4 11	E	17 25	TAU	26
216	4	Th.	4 40	A	7 00	D	14 20	9	8¾	9	1 56	B	4 56	E	17 10	GEM	27
217	5	Fr.	4 41	A	6 59	D	14 18	10	9½	9¾	2 56	B	5 36	E	16 53	GEM	28
218	6	Sa.	4 42	A	6 58	D	14 16	10	10¼	10½	3 59	B	6 13	D	16 37	CAN	29
219	7	**B**	4 43	A	6 57	D	14 14	10	11	11¼	5 05	C	6 47	D	16 20	CAN	0
220	8	M.	4 44	A	6 55	D	14 11	10	11¾	—	6 13	D	7 19	D	16 03	LEO	1
221	9	Tu.	4 45	A	6 54	D	14 09	10	12	12½	7 22	D	7 51	C	15 46	SEX	2
222	10	W.	4 46	A	6 53	D	14 07	10	12¾	1¼	8 32	D	8 23	C	15 29	LEO	3
223	11	Th.	4 47	A	6 51	D	14 04	10	1½	2	9 42	E	8 56	C	15 11	VIR	4
224	12	Fr.	4 48	A	6 50	D	14 02	10	2¼	2¾	10ᴬᴹ53	E	9 34	B	14 53	VIR	5
225	13	Sa.	4 49	A	6 48	D	13 59	11	3¼	3½	12ᴾᴹ04	E	10 16	B	14 35	VIR	6
226	14	**B**	4 50	A	6 47	D	13 57	11	4¼	4½	1 12	E	11 04	B	14 16	LIB	7
227	15	M.	4 51	B	6 45	D	13 54	11	5¼	5½	2 16	E	11ᴾᴹ58	B	13 58	SCO	8
228	16	Tu.	4 52	B	6 44	D	13 52	11	6¼	6¾	3 14	E	— —	–	13 39	OPH	9
229	17	W.	4 53	B	6 43	D	13 50	11	7½	7¾	4 04	E	12ᴬᴹ59	B	13 20	SAG	10
230	18	Th.	4 54	B	6 41	D	13 47	12	8½	8¾	4 48	E	2 03	B	13 00	SAG	11
231	19	Fr.	4 55	B	6 39	D	13 44	12	9½	9¾	5 26	E	3 10	B	12 41	CAP	12
232	20	Sa.	4 56	B	6 38	D	13 42	12	10¼	10½	5 59	D	4 16	C	12 21	AQU	13
233	21	**B**	4 57	B	6 36	D	13 39	12	11	11¼	6 29	D	5 21	D	12 01	AQU	14
234	22	M.	4 59	B	6 35	D	13 36	13	11¾	—	6 57	D	6 25	D	11 41	PSC	15
235	23	Tu.	5 00	B	6 33	D	13 33	13	12	12½	7 25	C	7 27	D	11 21	PSC	16
236	24	W.	5 01	B	6 32	D	13 31	13	12¾	1	7 53	B	8 28	D	11 00	PSC	17
237	25	Th.	5 02	B	6 30	D	13 28	13	1½	1¾	8 23	B	9 27	E	10 40	PSC	18
238	26	Fr.	5 03	B	6 28	D	13 25	14	2	2½	8 55	B	10 26	E	10 19	ARI	19
239	27	Sa.	5 04	B	6 27	D	13 23	14	3	3¼	9 30	B	11ᴬᴹ23	E	9 58	ARI	20
240	28	**B**	5 05	B	6 25	D	13 20	14	3¾	4	10 10	B	12ᴾᴹ18	E	9 37	TAU	21
241	29	M.	5 06	B	6 23	D	13 17	14	4½	4¾	10 55	B	1 12	E	9 16	TAU	22
242	30	Tu.	5 07	B	6 22	D	13 15	15	5½	5¾	11ᴾᴹ45	B	2 01	E	8 54	TAU	23
243	31	W.	5 08	B	6 20	D	13 12	15	6½	6¾	— —	–	2ᴹ48	E	8N.33	ORI	24

AUGUST hath 31 days. 1994

The sun drew off at last his piercing fires.
Over the stale warm air, dull as a pond
And moveless in the gray quieted street,
Blue magic of a summer evening glowed.
– Lascelles Abercrombie

D.M.	D.W.	Dates, Feasts, Fasts, Aspects, Tide Heights	Weather ↓
1	M.	**Lammas Day** • Summer half over. • Francis Scott Key born, 1779 •	*This*
2	Tu.	♂ ♂ ℂ • Wild Bill Hickok shot and killed, 1876 • Tides {8.2 {9.4	*month,*
3	W.	ℂ rides American Canoe Henry Hudson discovered high • Assoc. formed, 1880 • Hudson Bay, 1610	*they*
4	Th.	*Gossip is the art of saying nothing in a way* {8.5 *that leaves practically nothing unsaid.* {9.9	*say,*
5	Fr.	First electric traffic lights Marilyn Monroe {8.9 installed, Cleveland, Ohio, 1914 • died, 1962 {10.3	*was*
6	Sa.	**Transfiguration** • First Shakers arrived in New York, 1744 •	*named*
7	B	11ᵗʰ ☙. af. ℙ. • Name of Jesus • New ● • {9.7 {10.9	*This*
8	M.	**St. Dominic** • Great Train Robbery, $7 million stolen, England, 1963 • {10.2	*{— for*
9	Tu.	ℂ on Eq. • ☌ stat. • President Nixon resigned, 1974 • Tides {11.0 {10.5	*Caesar.*
10	W.	**St. Laurence** • ♂ ♀ ℂ • Smithsonian Institution est., 1846 •	*(Who's*
11	Th.	**St. Clare** • ℂ at Dog Days Good humor makes end. • all things tolerable. •	*he, sir?)*
12	Fr.	ℂ at perig. • ☿ in sup. ♂ • Diamond Jim Brady born, 1856 • {10.6 {11.0	*Some*
13	Sa.	ℂ at ☋ • ♂ ♃ ℂ • Annie Oakley born, 1860 • {10.2 {11.0	*Roman*
14	B	12ᵗʰ ☙. af. ℙ. • Oregon forest fire destroyed 270,000 acres, 1933 •	*geezer.*
15	M.	**St. Mary** • Will Rogers killed in Edna Ferber {9.4 airplane crash, 1935 • born, 1885 • {10.7	*He*
16	Tu.	ℂ runs Children more more need Frank Gifford low • of models than of critics. • born, 1930 •	*ruled*
17	W.	Cat Nights Solyman Merrick {9.2 begin. • patented the wrench, 1835 • {10.7 •	*the*
18	Th.	♂ ♄ ℂ • ♂ ☌ ℂ • Meriwether Lewis {9.4 born, 1774 {10.8	*Earth;*
19	Fr.	Gail Borden patented process Bill Clinton {9.7 for condensed milk, 1856 • born, 1946 • {10.9	*they*
20	Sa.	William S. Burroughs {10.0 patented adding machine, 1888 • Tides {11.0	*called*
21	B	13ᵗʰ ☙. af. ℙ. • Full Sturgeon ○ • {10.2 {10.9	*him*
22	M.	ℂ on Eq. • ♂ ♄ ℂ • Tides {10.3	*Imperator.*
23	Tu.	*Genius may have its limitations, but* Gene Kelly *stupidity is not thus handicapped.* • born, 1912 •	*He*
24	W.	**St. Bartholomew** • ♀ ℂ Gr. Elong. (46° E.) • Tides {10.4 {10.2	*was*
25	Th.	Mt. Vesuvius erupted, Pompeii and New Orleans Herculaneum destroyed, A.D. 79 • founded, 1718	*pretty*
26	Fr.	Lee DeForest, Father of First baseball games Radio, born, 1873 • televised, WZX85, N.Y., 1939	*hot*
27	Sa.	ℂ at ☋ • ℂ at apo. • Mother Teresa born, 1910 • {9.1 {9.6	*stuff —*
28	B	14ᵗʰ ☙. af. ℙ. • St. Augustine of Hippo •	*and*
29	M.	Charlie "Bird" Parker *Patience is a bitter plant* born, 1920 • *but it has sweet fruit.* •	*so's*
30	Tu.	ℂ rides Telephone hot line established {8.2 high • between White House and Kremlin, 1963 {9.1	*the*
31	W.	♂ ♂ ℂ • Earthquake, Charleston, {8.1 S. C., 1886 {9.2	*temperator.*

Farmer's Calendar

Among the complex lives of the common creatures around our houses and gardens, none makes a richer narrative than that of the red eft (*Notophthalmus viridescens viridescens*). The career of this two-inch salamander is like an old-fashioned novel, full of change and shifting identities, full, above all, of journeying. Born in a pond or brook, the eft begins its active life as a quarter-inch larva, green, legless. It lives in the water during its first summer, then in the fall the mature eft leaves its native pond and goes forth on dry land to seek its fortune. It has taken on a brilliant orange color with ruby spots.

The eft lives in the moist woods and thickets. It feeds on insects, earthworms. Not a bad life, probably, but the eft's journey is far from over. It remains on land for two or three years, then makes its way back to water. There it changes color again, to an olive green, and becomes fully aquatic once more. Now, it's no longer an eft but a *newt* — same animal, different name, as though the eft had been elevated to the peerage. Back in the water it lives out its life as a newt, and in the water it reproduces, making little efts who will have the same adventures.

A curious thing about the eft is its sudden energy. I once found one hiding beneath the pea vines. It didn't run away. It seemed a slow creature. But I happened to turn it over, and it instantly flipped itself back onto its feet. I tried again with the same result. I could not put the little thing on its back; it snapped right side up more quickly than my eye could follow. I suppose I shouldn't have been surprised. The young heroes of Fielding and Smollett, too, are always nimble.

1994   SEPTEMBER, The Ninth Month

Saturn is at its brightest and closest to Earth on the 1st, when it attains opposition and is visible all night long. Mercury's greatest elongation east (26 degrees) of the entire year occurs on the 26th; it can be spotted low in the west just after sunset. Venus immensely outshines all other points in the heavens, reaching its greatest brilliancy on the 28th, in the southwest after dusk. Cygnus the Swan soars overhead in the early evening, its tail marked by the bright white star Deneb. Well to its south is Altair in Aquila the Eagle, while Vega remains high in the west. The autumnal equinox is at 1:19 A.M., EST, on the 23rd.

● New Moon	5th day	13th hour	34th min.
☽ First Quarter	12th day	6th hour	35th min.
○ Full Moon	19th day	15th hour	2nd min.
☾ Last Quarter	27th day	19th hour	24th min.

ADD 1 hour for Daylight Saving Time.

For an explanation of this page, see "How to Use This Almanac," page 30; for values of Key Letters, see Time Correction Tables, page 209.

Day of Year	Day of Month	Day of Week	☉ Rises h. m.	Key	☉ Sets h. m.	Key	Length of Days h. m.	Sun Fast m.	Full Sea Boston A.M.	P.M.	☽ Rises h. m.	Key	☽ Sets h. m.	Key	Declination of Sun ° ′	☽ Place	☽ Age
244	1	Th.	5 09	B	6 18	D	13 09	15	7¼	7½	12♈42	B	3♏30	E	8N.11	GEM	25
245	2	Fr.	5 10	B	6 17	D	13 07	16	8¼	8½	1 42	B	4 08	E	7 49	GEM	26
246	3	Sa.	5 11	B	6 15	D	13 04	16	9	9¼	2 47	C	4 44	D	7 27	CAN	27
247	4	**B**	5 12	B	6 13	D	13 01	16	9¾	10	3 54	C	5 17	D	7 05	LEO	28
248	5	M.	5 13	B	6 12	D	12 59	17	10½	10¾	5 04	D	5 50	D	6 42	SEX	0
249	6	Tu.	5 14	B	6 10	D	12 56	17	11¼	11½	6 15	D	6 22	C	6 20	LEO	1
250	7	W.	5 15	B	6 08	D	12 53	17	—	12	7 27	E	6 57	B	5 58	VIR	2
251	8	Th.	5 17	B	6 06	D	12 49	18	12¼	12¾	8 40	E	7 34	B	5 35	VIR	3
252	9	Fr.	5 18	B	6 05	C	12 47	18	1¼	1½	9 53	E	8 15	B	5 12	VIR	4
253	10	Sa.	5 19	B	6 03	C	12 44	18	2	2¼	11♈03	E	9 02	B	4 50	LIB	5
254	11	**B**	5 20	B	6 01	C	12 41	19	3	3¼	12♏09	E	9 55	B	4 27	SCO	6
255	12	M.	5 21	B	5 59	C	12 38	19	4	4¼	1 09	E	10 54	B	4 04	OPH	7
256	13	Tu.	5 22	B	5 58	C	12 36	19	5	5¼	2 01	E	11♏56	B	3 41	SAG	8
257	14	W.	5 23	B	5 56	C	12 33	20	6¼	6½	2 46	E	— —	–	3 18	SAG	9
258	15	Th.	5 24	B	5 54	C	12 30	20	7¼	7½	3 25	E	1♏01	B	2 55	SAG	10
259	16	Fr.	5 25	B	5 52	C	12 27	21	8¼	8½	4 00	D	2 06	C	2 32	AQU	11
260	17	Sa.	5 26	B	5 51	C	12 25	21	9¼	9½	4 30	D	3 10	C	2 09	AQU	12
261	18	**B**	5 27	B	5 49	C	12 22	21	10	10¼	4 59	D	4 14	D	1 46	AQU	13
262	19	M.	5 28	B	5 47	C	12 19	22	10½	11	5 27	C	5 16	D	1 22	PSC	14
263	20	Tu.	5 29	C	5 45	C	12 16	22	11¼	11½	5 55	C	6 16	D	0 59	PSC	15
264	21	W.	5 30	C	5 44	C	12 14	22	—	12	6 24	B	7 16	E	0 36	PSC	16
265	22	Th.	5 31	C	5 42	C	12 11	23	12¼	12½	6 55	B	8 15	E	0N.12	PSC	17
266	23	Fr.	5 32	C	5 40	C	12 08	23	1	1¼	7 29	B	9 13	E	0s.10	ARI	18
267	24	Sa.	5 33	C	5 38	C	12 05	23	1½	1¾	8 07	B	10 09	E	0 34	ARI	19
268	25	**B**	5 35	C	5 36	C	12 01	24	2¼	2½	8 50	B	11 03	E	0 57	TAU	20
269	26	M.	5 36	C	5 35	C	11 59	24	3	3¼	9 37	B	11♈53	E	1 20	TAU	21
270	27	Tu.	5 37	C	5 33	C	11 56	24	4	4¼	10 30	B	12♏40	E	1 44	TAU	22
271	28	W.	5 38	C	5 31	B	11 53	25	4¾	5	11♏27	C	1 23	E	2 07	GEM	23
272	29	Th.	5 39	C	5 29	B	11 50	25	5¾	6	— —	–	2 02	E	2 30	GEM	24
273	30	Fr.	5 40	C	5 28	B	11 48	25	6¾	7	12♈29	C	2♏39	D	2s.54	CAN	25

SEPTEMBER hath 30 days. 1994

Now by the brook the maple leans
With all his glory spread,
And all the sumachs on the hills
Have turned their green to red.
– *Wilfred Campbell*

D. M.	D. W.	Dates, Feasts, Fasts, Aspects, Tide Heights	*Weather* ↓
1	Th.	**St. Giles** • ♄ at ☍ • Wreckage of *Titanic* found, 1985	*Summer*
2	Fr.	Great Fire of London began, 1666 • V-J Day, 1945 • Tides {8.7 9.9	*lingers;*
3	Sa.	*If you have to kill a snake, kill it once and for all.* • Treaty of Paris ended Revolutionary War, 1783	*rain*
4	**B**	**15th S. af. P.** • George Eastman patented Kodak camera, 1888 • {9.8 10.7	*runs*
5	M.	**Labor Day** • New ● • First Labor Day Parade New York, 1882 •	*cold*
6	Tu.	**Rosh Hashanah** • ☾ on Eq. • Tides {10.9 11.2 •	*fingers*
7	W.	☌☿☾ • Boulder Dam (now Hoover Dam) began operations, 1936 •	*down*
8	Th.	**Nativity of Mary** • ☾ at perig. • ☌♀☾ • {11.2 11.6	*your*
9	Fr.	☾ at ☊ • ☌♃☾ • Elvis Presley first appeared *Ed Sullivan Show*, 1956	*spine.*
10	Sa.	Lincoln Highway opened, first coast-to-coast paved road, 1913 • Tides {10.7 11.5 •	*Now*
11	**B**	**16th S. af. P.** • Paul "Bear" Bryant born, 1913 • {10.2 11.1	*it's*
12	M.	☾ runs low • Hot, dry winds caused tree foliage to crumble, Kansas, 1882 •	*fine —*
13	Tu.	Rhinoceros first seen in New York, 1826 • Walter Reed born, 1851 • Tides {9.4 10.5 •	*in*
14	W.	**Holy Cross** • ☌♆☾ • ☌♅☾ • Tides {9.2 10.3 •	*fact,*
15	Th.	**Yom Kippur** • Jumbo the Elephant died, 1885 • Agatha Christie born, 1890	*we'd*
16	Fr.	Shawmut, Mass., renamed Boston, 1630 • B.B. King born, 1925 • {9.5 10.4 •	*call*
17	Sa.	Hank Williams born, 1923 • *Not to know is bad, but not to wish to know is worse.* • {9.8 10.4	*it*
18	**B**	**17th S. af. P.** • ☌♄☾ • Tides {10.1 10.4 •	*glorious!*
19	M.	☾ on Eq. • Full Harvest ○ • Tides {10.3 10.4 •	*Down-*
20	Tu.	**Succoth** • USS *Constitution* launched, 1797 • Guy Lafleur born, 1951	*pourious.*
21	W.	**St. Matthew** • Ember Day • Louis Joliet born, 1645 • {— 10.3 •	*Visit*
22	Th.	*Fiddler on the Roof* began 3,242-performance run in New York, 1964 • {10.0 10.3	*orchards*
23	Fr.	☾ at ☋ • Autumnal Equinox • Ember Day • {9.7 10.1 •	*humming*
24	Sa.	☾ at apo. • Ember Day • "60 Minutes" made TV debut, 1968 • {9.4 9.9	*happily,*
25	**B**	**18th S. af. P.** • -4° F Cut Bank, Montana, 1934 • {9.0 9.6 •	*come*
26	M.	☿ Gr. Elong. (26° E.) • *Abbey Road*, Beatles last album, released, 1969 •	*home*
27	Tu.	☾ rides high • *There is no cure for birth or death save to enjoy the interval.* •	*smelling*
28	W.	♀ Greatest Brilliancy • Flogging abolished, 1850 • Tides {8.3 9.1 •	*sweet*
29	Th.	**St. Michael** • ☌♂☾ • *Michaelmas rot Comes ne'er in the pot.* •	*and*
30	Fr.	**St. Jerome** • Rayon patented, 1902 • Tides {8.6 9.5	*apple-y.*

They who give have all things;
they who withhold have nothing.

Farmer's Calendar

Mourning doves, nearly always in pairs, sit in the middle of the dusty road. If you approach them in your car, they wait until the last second before annihilation to spring up and fly off. More than once I have hit the brakes when a pair of doves vanished beneath the front of my car, but they always get out in time. Daring must run in the dove family. Think of the similar antics of the mourning dove's funky urban cousin, the pigeon, who plays the same desperate game with taxis and buses all over the world.

This dove *(Zenaida macroura)* is one of the beloved birds of heraldry, with the eagle, the owl, the pelican. It is the bird of the gentle feelings: peace, devotion, constancy. Its slender, delicate form, its soft colors, its peaceful life, and its habit of flying and feeding in pairs, provoked the old writers to orgies of sentimental anthropomorphism. Audubon made sure to paint his doves as an epitome of wedded bliss, the female "listening with delight to [her mate's] assurances of devoted affection."

Its call is the dove's most famous trait — a monotone *ohh-oh-oh-ohhh.* To me that song is full of subtlety, playing on our enduring Victorian will to melancholy. Most feel the call is a sad sound, hence the bird's name. The New England ornithologist Forbush referred to it as a "pensive moan." But it's all in when you hear it. On an afternoon in September there are things to be pensive about: The year passes, time and life pass. Maybe there is a certain sadness in the season itself. But who can hear the dove's call in April without welcoming its announcement of the softer months to come? It's the same bird, the same sound. Let it remind us that, wherever else they are, the seasons are in our heart.

1994　OCTOBER, The Tenth Month

Bright Venus and Jupiter are in the same region of the southwest sky at dusk; the Moon is in conjunction with them on the 7th. At mid evening the Great Square of Pegasus hangs high in the southeast. To the upper left from the Great Square stretches Andromeda, in which shines the elongated patch of the Great Galaxy, M31. The Pleiades and Aldebaran, harbingers of fall, are low in the east. Early risers will find Mars in the southeast before dawn; binoculars show it in the midst of the Beehive star cluster on the 12th and 13th. A full Moon spoils viewing of the Orionid meteor shower this year. Daylight Saving Time ends at 2:00 A.M. on the 30th.

● New Moon	4th day	22nd hour	56th min.
☽ First Quarter	11th day	14th hour	18th min.
○ Full Moon	19th day	7th hour	19th min.
☾ Last Quarter	27th day	11th hour	45th min.

ADD 1 hour for Daylight Saving Time until 2 A.M., October 30th.

For an explanation of this page, see "How to Use This Almanac," page 30; for values of Key Letters, see Time Correction Tables, page 209.

Day of Year	Day of Month	Day of Week	☉ Rises h. m.	Key	☉ Sets h. m.	Key	Length of Days h. m.	Sun Fast m.	Full Sea Boston A.M.	Full Sea Boston P.M.	☽ Rises h. m.	Key	☽ Sets h. m.	Key	Declination of Sun ° '	Place	☽ Age
274	1	Sa.	5 41	C	5 26	B	11 45	26	7½	7¾	1ᴹ34	C	3ᴾᴹ12	D	3s.17	CAN	26
275	2	**B**	5 42	C	5 24	B	11 42	26	8¼	8¾	2 41	C	3 45	D	3 40	LEO	27
276	3	M.	5 43	C	5 23	B	11 40	26	9¼	9½	3 51	D	4 18	D	4 03	LEO	28
277	4	Tu.	5 44	C	5 21	B	11 37	27	10	10¼	5 04	D	4 52	C	4 26	VIR	0
278	5	W.	5 45	C	5 19	B	11 34	27	10¾	11¼	6 18	E	5 29	B	4 50	VIR	1
279	6	Th.	5 47	C	5 17	B	11 30	27	11½	—	7 33	E	6 10	B	5 13	VIR	2
280	7	Fr.	5 48	C	5 16	B	11 28	28	12	12¼	8 47	E	6 56	B	5 36	LIB	3
281	8	Sa.	5 49	C	5 14	B	11 25	28	12¾	1	9 57	E	7 49	B	5 59	LIB	4
282	9	**B**	5 50	C	5 12	B	11 22	28	1¾	2	11 01	E	8 47	B	6 21	OPH	5
283	10	M.	5 51	C	5 11	B	11 20	28	2¾	3	11ᴬ57	E	9 50	B	6 44	SAG	6
284	11	Tu.	5 52	C	5 09	B	11 17	29	3¾	4	12ᴾᴹ45	E	10ᴾᴹ54	B	7 07	SAG	7
285	12	W.	5 53	C	5 07	B	11 14	29	4¾	5	1 26	E	— —	—	7 29	SAG	8
286	13	Th.	5 55	C	5 06	B	11 11	29	6	6¼	2 02	D	12ᴬ00	C	7 52	CAP	9
287	14	Fr.	5 56	D	5 04	B	11 08	29	7	7¼	2 33	D	1 04	C	8 14	AQU	10
288	15	Sa.	5 57	D	5 03	B	11 06	30	8	8¼	3 02	D	2 06	D	8 36	AQU	11
289	16	**B**	5 58	D	5 01	B	11 03	30	8¾	9¼	3 30	C	3 08	D	8 58	PSC	12
290	17	M.	5 59	D	4 59	B	11 00	30	9½	10	3 57	C	4 08	D	9 20	PSC	13
291	18	Tu.	6 00	D	4 58	B	10 58	30	10¼	10½	4 26	C	5 08	D	9 42	PSC	14
292	19	W.	6 02	D	4 56	B	10 54	30	10¾	11¼	4 56	B	6 07	E	10 04	PSC	15
293	20	Th.	6 03	D	4 55	B	10 52	31	11½	11¾	5 29	B	7 05	E	10 25	ARI	16
294	21	Fr.	6 04	D	4 53	B	10 49	31	—	12	6 06	B	8 01	E	10 46	ARI	17
295	22	Sa.	6 05	D	4 52	B	10 47	31	12½	12½	6 47	B	8 56	E	11 08	TAU	18
296	23	**B**	6 06	D	4 50	B	10 44	31	1¼	1¼	7 33	B	9 47	E	11 29	TAU	19
297	24	M.	6 08	D	4 49	B	10 41	31	1¾	2	8 23	B	10 35	E	11 50	TAU	20
298	25	Tu.	6 09	D	4 47	B	10 38	31	2½	2¾	9 18	B	11 19	E	12 10	GEM	21
299	26	W.	6 10	D	4 46	B	10 36	32	3½	3½	10 16	B	11ᴬ59	E	12 31	GEM	22
300	27	Th.	6 11	D	4 44	B	10 33	32	4¼	4½	11ᴾᴹ17	C	12ᴾᴹ35	E	12 52	CAN	23
301	28	Fr.	6 12	D	4 43	B	10 31	32	5¼	5½	— —	—	1 09	D	13 12	CAN	24
302	29	Sa.	6 14	D	4 42	B	10 28	32	6	6¼	12ᴬ22	C	1 41	D	13 32	LEO	25
303	30	**B**	6 15	D	4 40	B	10 25	32	7	7¼	1 28	D	2 13	D	13 52	LEO	26
304	31	M.	6 16	D	4 39	B	10 23	32	7¾	8¼	2ᴬ38	D	2ᴾᴹ45	C	14s.11	LEO	27

OCTOBER hath 31 days. 1994

Here was October, here
Was ruddy October, the old harvester,
Wrapped like a beggared sachem in a coat
Of tattered tanager and partridge feathers . . .
– Stephen Vincent Benét

D.M.	D.W.	Dates, Feasts, Fasts, Aspects, Tide Heights	Weather ↓
1	Sa.	**St. Remigius** • ♅ stat. • Jimmy Carter born, 1924 •	*Ground*
2	**B**	**19th S. af. P.** • ♆ stat. • Tides $\frac{9.8}{10.4}$	*hardens;*
3	M.	☾ on Eq. • Johns Hopkins Univ. opened, 1876 • Chubby Checker born, 1941	*cover*
4	Tu.	**St. Francis of Assisi** • New ● • Tides $\frac{11.1}{11.1}$ •	*your*
5	W.	*In October dung your field, And your land its wealth shall yield.* • $\frac{11.7}{11.3}$ •	*gardens!*
6	Th.	☾ at perig. • ☌☿☾ • George Westinghouse born, 1846	*Evacuate*
7	Fr.	☾ at ☊ • ☌♀☾ • ☌♃☾ • Tides $\frac{11.3}{12.2}$ •	*those*
8	Sa.	George M. Cohen's *Little Johnny Jones* opened, 1904, included song, "Give My Regards to Broadway."	*ripe*
9	**B**	**20th S. af. P.** • ☿ stat. • $\frac{10.7}{11.7}$ •	*tomatoes.*
10	M.	**Columbus Day** • Thanksgiving Day (Canada) • ☾ runs low •	*Storm*
11	Tu.	☌♆☾ • ☌♅☾ • Eleanor Roosevelt born, 1884 •	*clouds*
12	W.	♀ stat. • Nikita Khrushchev pounded desk at U.N. with his shoe, 1960 • $\frac{9.5}{10.2}$ •	*usher*
13	Th.	Much rain in October, much wind in December. • White House cornerstone laid, 1792	*in a*
14	Fr.	*Winnie-the-Pooh* published, 1926 • *Many children, many cares; no children, no felicity.*	*gusher —*
15	Sa.	☌♄☾ • John Kenneth Galbraith born, 1908 • $\frac{9.7}{9.9}$ •	*mountain*
16	**B**	**21st S. af. P.** • ☾ on Eq. • $\frac{10.0}{9.9}$ •	*slusher!*
17	M.	**St. Ignatius of Antioch** • Albert Einstein arrived in U.S., 1933	*Praise*
18	Tu.	**St. Luke** • St. Luke's little summer. • Tides $\frac{10.3}{9.8}$ •	*these*
19	W.	Full Hunter's ○ • Cornwallis surrendered to Washington, 1781 Tides $\frac{10.4}{9.7}$	*days*
20	Th.	☾ at ☋ • U.S./Canada border set at 49th parallel east of Rockies, 1818 • $\frac{10.4}{9.6}$ •	*of*
21	Fr.	☿ in inf. ☌ • ☾ at apo. • "Whitey" Ford born, 1928 •	*warmth*
22	Sa.	Sam Houston became first president of Texas, 1836 • Sarah Bernhardt born, 1844 •	*and*
23	**B**	**22nd S. af. P.** • Swallows depart Capistrano. • $\frac{9.2}{10.0}$ •	*haze.*
24	M.	☾ rides high • "Black Thursday" began panic selling on N.Y. Stock Exchange, 1929 •	*Bitter*
25	Tu.	**St. Crispin** • Pablo Picasso born, 1881 • Tides $\frac{8.7}{9.5}$ •	*breeze*
26	W.	Doonesbury comic strip first appeared, 1970 • Leon Trotsky born, 1879 Tides $\frac{8.5}{9.3}$	*from*
27	Th.	*There is no opinion so absurd but that some philosopher will express it.* •	*Montreal —*
28	Fr.	**Sts. Simon and Jude** • ☌♂☾ • Tides $\frac{8.7}{9.3}$ •	*Last*
29	Sa.	☿ stat. • "Black Tuesday" marked final collapse of N.Y. Stock Exchange, 1929 •	*call*
30	**B**	**23rd S. af. P.** • ☾ on Eq. • Daylight Saving Time ends, 2 A.M. •	*for*
31	M.	**All Hallows Eve** • Harry Houdini died, 1926 • $\frac{10.3}{10.2}$ •	*fall.*

Farmer's Calendar

"For the grapes' sake, if they were all," the poet writes, "For the grapes' sake along the wall." He is imploring the warm autumn day to linger, to withhold its wind and frost and spare the year from winter one day longer. He addresses himself to the characteristic phenomena of the season: the circling crows, the falling leaves, the mists. But the wild grapes, his final image, are as eloquent as any fruit in nature's garden.

Their vines twist and writhe over the stone walls and through the woods like pythons, heavy and dark, as thick as your arm. They can climb trees, covering smaller ones entirely with their broad leaves and creating gloomy little bowers. They hang stoutly from the bigger trees, like the rigging of a tall ship. Grapes seem to thrive best along the roadsides, though, surging over the weeds there, mounting the coarse shrubs and saplings, hanging their infant clusters of fruit like green pearls, just beyond reach. Their tough leaves are deeply lobed, vigorous. By the end of summer, they're tattered and dusty. They droop beside the road.

The grapes themselves are unpredictable. Some years there will hardly be a bunch, some years their weight will make the vines bow down like willows. In a good year the grapes are fat, the size of marbles, their color a deep inky purple, rich as sin. And as forbidden, at least in the case of the grapes in my neighborhood, for as delicious as they look, they are ferociously sour. Only a partridge could be fed by them, a partridge or a poet. They make better poetry than they do jam. Best leave the October grapes alone, then, and let them, aided by art, tell the tale of this most feeling month, which cannot end, and must.

1994 NOVEMBER, THE ELEVENTH MONTH

The total eclipse of the Sun on the 3rd is visible only in southern latitudes, but all of North America gets to see a penumbral eclipse of the Moon on the night of the 17th-18th. That otherwise brilliant Moon spoils viewing of the Leonid meteor shower before dawn. Mercury is visible low in the southeast before morning's light, fairly near Spica on the 2nd and Venus on the 12th. Rapidly brightening Mars is rising in the middle of the night and is high in the south as dawn light glimmers; Saturn is the lonely planet in the south after nightfall. The Pleiades sparkle in the east after dusk, Perseus bright above them, and Cassiopeia strikes high in the north.

● New Moon	3rd day	8th hour	37th min.
☽ First Quarter	10th day	1st hour	15th min.
○ Full Moon	18th day	1st hour	58th min.
☾ Last Quarter	26th day	2nd hour	5th min.

For an explanation of this page, see "How to Use This Almanac," page 30; for values of Key Letters, see Time Correction Tables, page 209.

Day of Year	Day of Month	Day of Week	☉ Rises h. m.	Key	☉ Sets h. m.	Key	Length of Days h. m.	Sun Fast m.	Full Sea Boston A.M.	Full Sea Boston P.M.	☽ Rises h. m.	Key	☽ Sets h. m.	Key	Declination of Sun ° '	☽ Place	☽ Age
305	1	Tu.	6 17	D	4 38	B	10 21	32	8½	9	3ᴬ₍M₎50	E	3ᴾ₍M₎20	C	14s.30	VIR	28
306	2	W.	6 19	D	4 36	B	10 17	32	9½	10	5 04	E	3 59	B	14 49	VIR	29
307	3	Th.	6 20	D	4 35	B	10 15	32	10¼	10¾	6 20	E	4 43	B	15 08	VIR	0
308	4	Fr.	6 21	D	4 34	B	10 13	32	11	11¾	7 34	E	5 34	B	15 26	LIB	1
309	5	Sa.	6 22	D	4 33	B	10 11	32	—	12	8 44	E	6 32	B	15 45	SCO	2
310	6	**B**	6 24	D	4 32	B	10 08	32	12½	12¾	9 46	E	7 36	B	16 03	OPH	3
311	7	M.	6 25	D	4 30	B	10 05	32	1½	1¾	10 39	E	8 42	B	16 21	SAG	4
312	8	Tu.	6 26	D	4 29	A	10 03	32	2½	2¾	11ᴬ₍M₎24	E	9 50	B	16 38	SAG	5
313	9	W.	6 27	D	4 28	A	10 01	32	3½	3¾	12ᴾ₍M₎02	D	10ᴬ₍M₎56	C	16 56	CAP	6
314	10	Th.	6 29	D	4 27	A	9 58	32	4½	4¾	12 36	D	— —	—	17 13	AQU	7
315	11	Fr.	6 30	D	4 26	A	9 56	32	5½	5¾	1 06	D	12ᴬ₍M₎00	C	17 29	AQU	8
316	12	Sa.	6 31	D	4 25	A	9 54	32	6½	7	1 34	C	1 01	D	17 45	PSC	9
317	13	**B**	6 32	D	4 24	A	9 52	31	7½	7¾	2 01	C	2 02	D	18 01	PSC	10
318	14	M.	6 34	D	4 23	A	9 49	31	8¼	8¾	2 29	C	3 01	D	18 17	PSC	11
319	15	Tu.	6 35	D	4 22	A	9 47	31	9	9½	2 58	B	4 00	E	18 32	PSC	12
320	16	W.	6 36	D	4 22	A	9 46	31	9¾	10¼	3 30	B	4 58	E	18 47	PSC	13
321	17	Th.	6 37	D	4 21	A	9 44	31	10¼	10¾	4 06	B	5 55	E	19 02	ARI	14
322	18	Fr.	6 39	D	4 20	A	9 41	31	11	11½	4 45	B	6 50	E	19 16	ARI	15
323	19	Sa.	6 40	D	4 19	A	9 39	30	11½	—	5 29	B	7 43	E	19 30	TAU	16
324	20	**B**	6 41	D	4 18	A	9 37	30	12¼	12¼	6 18	B	8 33	E	19 44	TAU	17
325	21	M.	6 42	D	4 18	A	9 36	30	12¾	12¾	7 12	B	9 18	E	19 58	ORI	18
326	22	Tu.	6 43	D	4 17	A	9 34	30	1½	1½	8 08	B	9 59	E	20 11	GEM	19
327	23	W.	6 45	D	4 16	A	9 31	29	2¼	2¼	9 08	B	10 36	E	20 23	GEM	20
328	24	Th.	6 46	D	4 16	A	9 30	29	3	3	10 09	C	11 10	D	20 35	CAN	21
329	25	Fr.	6 47	D	4 15	A	9 28	29	3¾	4	11ᴾ₍M₎13	C	11ᴬ₍M₎41	D	20 47	LEO	22
330	26	Sa.	6 48	D	4 15	A	9 27	28	4½	4¾	— —	—	12ᴾ₍M₎12	D	20 58	SEX	23
331	27	**B**	6 49	E	4 14	A	9 25	28	5½	5¾	12ᴬ₍M₎19	D	12 42	D	21 09	LEO	24
332	28	M.	6 50	E	4 14	A	9 24	28	6¼	6¾	1 27	D	1 15	C	21 20	VIR	25
333	29	Tu.	6 51	E	4 13	A	9 22	28	7¼	7¾	2 38	E	1 50	C	21 31	VIR	26
334	30	W.	6 53	E	4 13	A	9 20	27	8	8¾	3ᴬ₍M₎51	E	2ᴾ₍M₎30	B	21s.41	VIR	27

NOVEMBER hath 30 days. 1994

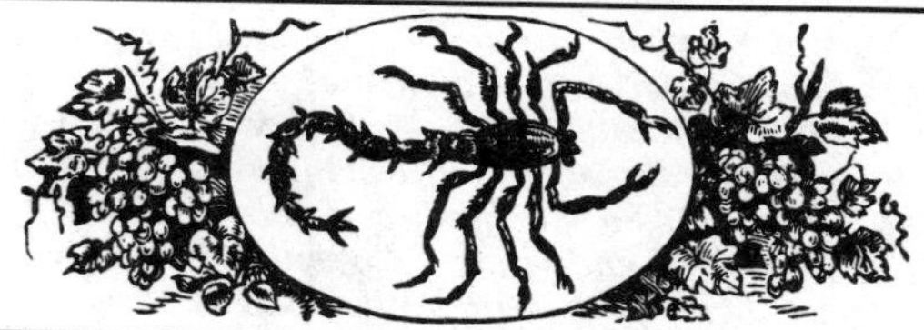

a wind has blown the rain away and blown
the sky away and all the leaves away,
and the trees stand. I think i too have known
autumn too long.

– e. e. cummings

D. M.	D. W.	Dates, Feasts, Fasts, Aspects, Tide Heights	Weather ↓
1	Tu.	**All Saints** • International Rainbow Bridge at Niagara Falls opened to public, 1941	*Snow*
2	W.	**All Souls** • ☌☿☾ • ♀ in inf. ☌ • {11.7 10.9	*comes*
3	Th.	☾ at ☊ • New ● • Eclipse of ☉ • ☾ at perig. •	*early;*
4	Fr.	*He who boasts of his descent is like the potato; the best part of him is underground.* •	*enough*
5	Sa.	☿ Gr. Elong. (19° W.) • Susan B. Anthony arrested for attempting to vote, 1875 • Tides {— 12.5	*to*
6	**B**	**24th S. af. P.** • ☾ runs low • John Philip Sousa born, 1854	*make*
7	M.	Elephant first appeared as symbol for Republican party in Thomas Nast cartoon, 1875	*a saint*
8	Tu.	☌♆☾ • ☌♅☾ • FDR elected to 4th term, 1944 • {10.3 11.2	*surly.*
9	W.	♄ stat. • Power failure caused New York City and eastern seaboard blackout, 1965 •	*Warm*
10	Th.	**St. Leo the Great** • Tommy Dorsey born, 1905 • {9.7 10.0	*reprieve,*
11	Fr.	**St. Martin** • **Veterans Day** • ☌♄☾ • Indian Summer •	*we*
12	Sa.	☾ on Eq. • ☌☿♀ • Sadie Hawkins Day • Tides {9.6 9.4 •	*do*
13	**B**	**25th S. af. P.** • Holland Tunnel under Hudson R. opened, 1927 •	*believe.*
14	M.	Claude Monet born, 1840 • *Real art is illumination; It adds stature to life.* • {9.9 9.3	*Enjoy*
15	Tu.	Arthur Dorrington became first black hockey player, 1950 • Georgia O'Keeffe born, 1887	*it*
16	W.	*The Sound of Music* premiered in New York, 1959 • W. C. Handy born, 1873 •	*while*
17	Th.	**St. Hugh of Lincoln** • ☾ at ☋ • ☌♃☉ • {10.3 9.3	*it*
18	Fr.	**St. Hilda** • ☾ at apo. • Full Beaver ○ • Eclipse of ☾ •	
19	Sa.	*If ice in November will bear a duck, There'll be nothing thereafter but sleet and muck.* •	*lasts —*
20	**B**	**26th S. af. P.** • ☾ rides high • ☌♇☉ •	*here*
21	M.	♀ stat. • Red Grange played last varsity game for U. of Ill. before turning pro, 1925 •	*come*
22	Tu.	**St. Cecelia** • President Kennedy assassinated, 1963 • Abigail Adams born, 1744	*some*
23	W.	**St. Clement** • First jukebox installed, San Francisco, 1889 • {8.9 9.7	*wintry*
24	Th.	**Thanksgiving Day** • Zachary Taylor born, 1784 • Tides {8.9 9.5	*blasts!*
25	Fr.	☌♂☾ • USS *Enterprise* aircraft carrier commissioned, 1961 • Tides {9.0 9.4	*We*
26	Sa.	*If you sleep with dogs you'll rise with fleas.* • Windstorm (105 mph gusts) in northwest, 1949 •	*just*
27	**B**	**1st S. in Advent** • ☾ on Eq. • {9.5 9.4 •	*want to*
28	M.	**Chanukah** • Ferdinand Magellan began voyage around world, 1520 • {10.1 9.6 •	*say*
29	Tu.	Louisa May Alcott born, 1832 • Busby Berkeley born, 1895 • {10.7 9.9	*thanks to*
30	W.	**St. Andrew** • ☌♀☾ • Winston Churchill born, 1874	*Squanto.*

Aim above morality. Be not simply good; be good for something. – H. D. Thoreau

Farmer's Calendar

Splitting firewood is widely appreciated as exercise for the upper body and as an aid to reflection, but the work deserves to be better known as an adventure in connoisseurship in the most rarefied realm, that of the nose. We have been given our five senses to enable us to discriminate, to mark differences and similarities between things. Smell is the finest discriminator of all; learn to use your nose while you're splitting hardwood, and it will open for you a rich volume of distinctions.

Compare the heavy smell of olives that comes from a fresh-split block of red oak with the similar but far more delicate smell of white oak or with the smoky, almost musky olive smell of butternut. Beech wood is faintly sweet; paper birch has a stronger, sweeter scent; and black birch smells like bubble gum. Maple, to me, has little character besides a kind of vague vegetative smell, and ash is odorless. No doubt a finer nose than mine could make something of the last two woods, as well.

Let no one imagine wood-sniffing is a mere frippery. The potential is there for hard financial advantage. Why couldn't a really educated woodpile nose attain the kind of refinement we read the whiskey tasters of Scotland possess? They can sniff a glass of Scotch and tell you not only which district it came from, but which glen, which brook, which distiller. Since there's a good deal of money in Scotch, a lot can hang on the findings of an expert nose. Why couldn't the same apply to wood sniffing? Firewood dealers are a tough lot, almost the last of the old-time free-booting capitalists. The buyer needs all the help he can get. A sniffer who could knock ten bucks off the price of a load for an off-scent would be a valuable man.

1994 DECEMBER, The Twelfth Month

Venus climbs higher in the east before dawn, reaching its greatest brilliancy on the 9th. Golden-orange Mars now rises in the east in the late evening, brightening to rival the glorious winter stars. The Pleiades and the arrowhead formed by Aldebaran and the Hyades in Taurus lead a throng of brilliance in the southeast. At the top is Auriga with yellow Capella, at center Orion with his three-star belt and Rigel and Betelgeuse, with the two Dog Stars, Procyon and Sirius, following. We must wait until after late moonsets to see the Geminid meteors on the 13th and 14th. There is a close conjunction of Jupiter and the Moon on the 29th. Winter begins at 9:23 P.M., EST, on the 21st.

● New Moon	2nd day	18th hour	55th min.
☽ First Quarter	9th day	16th hour	8th min.
○ Full Moon	17th day	21st hour	18th min.
☾ Last Quarter	25th day	14th hour	8th min.

For an explanation of this page, see "How to Use This Almanac," page 30; for values of Key Letters, see Time Correction Tables, page 209.

Day of Year	Day of Month	Day of Week	☉ Rises h. m.	Key	☉ Sets h. m.	Key	Length of Days h. m.	Sun Fast m.	Full Sea Boston A.M.	Full Sea Boston P.M.	☽ Rises h. m.	Key	☽ Sets h. m.	Key	Declination of Sun °	Place	☽ Age
335	1	Th.	6 54	E	4 13	A	9 19	27	9	9½	5ᴍ05	E	3ᴘ17	B	21s.50	LIB	28
336	2	Fr.	6 55	E	4 12	A	9 17	26	9¾	10½	6 18	E	4 11	B	21 59	LIB	0
337	3	Sa.	6 56	E	4 12	A	9 16	26	10¾	11½	7 26	E	5 13	B	22 07	OPH	1
338	4	B	6 57	E	4 12	A	9 15	26	11½	—	8 25	E	6 21	B	22 15	SAG	2
339	5	M.	6 58	E	4 12	A	9 14	25	12¼	12½	9 16	E	7 30	B	22 23	SAG	3
340	6	Tu.	6 59	E	4 12	A	9 13	25	1¼	1½	9 59	E	8 40	C	22 30	SAG	4
341	7	W.	7 00	E	4 12	A	9 12	24	2	2¼	10 35	D	9 47	C	22 37	AQU	5
342	8	Th.	7 01	E	4 12	A	9 11	24	3	3¼	11 07	D	10 51	D	22 44	AQU	6
343	9	Fr.	7 01	E	4 12	A	9 11	24	4	4¼	11ᴍ37	D	11ᴘ53	D	22 50	AQU	7
344	10	Sa.	7 02	E	4 12	A	9 10	23	5	5¼	12ᴍ05	C	— —	–	22 55	PSC	8
345	11	B	7 03	E	4 12	A	9 09	23	6	6¼	12 33	C	12ᴀ54	D	23 00	PSC	9
346	12	M.	7 04	E	4 12	A	9 08	22	6¾	7¼	1 01	C	1 53	E	23 05	PSC	10
347	13	Tu.	7 05	E	4 12	A	9 07	22	7¾	8¼	1 32	B	2 51	E	23 09	PSC	11
348	14	W.	7 06	E	4 12	A	9 06	21	8½	9	2 06	B	3 48	E	23 13	ARI	12
349	15	Th.	7 06	E	4 12	A	9 06	21	9¼	9¾	2 44	B	4 44	E	23 16	TAU	13
350	16	Fr.	7 07	E	4 13	A	9 06	20	9¾	10½	3 27	B	5 38	E	23 19	TAU	14
351	17	Sa.	7 08	E	4 13	A	9 05	20	10½	11	4 14	B	6 29	E	23 21	TAU	15
352	18	B	7 08	E	4 13	A	9 05	19	11¼	11¾	5 06	B	7 16	E	23 23	ORI	16
353	19	M.	7 09	E	4 14	A	9 05	19	11¾	—	6 02	B	7 59	E	23 24	GEM	17
354	20	Tu.	7 10	E	4 14	A	9 04	18	12½	12½	7 01	C	8 38	E	23 25	GEM	18
355	21	W.	7 10	E	4 14	A	9 04	18	1	1	8 02	C	9 13	E	23 25	CAN	19
356	22	Th.	7 11	E	4 15	A	9 04	17	1¾	1¾	9 05	C	9 45	D	23 25	CAN	20
357	23	Fr.	7 11	E	4 16	A	9 05	17	2½	2½	10 09	D	10 15	D	23 25	LEO	21
358	24	Sa.	7 11	E	4 16	A	9 05	16	3¼	3½	11ᴍ14	D	10 45	D	23 24	LEO	22
359	25	B	7 12	E	4 17	A	9 05	16	4	4¼	— —	–	11 16	C	23 23	VIR	23
360	26	M.	7 12	E	4 17	A	9 05	15	4¾	5¼	12ᴍ22	E	11ᴍ48	C	23 21	VIR	24
361	27	Tu.	7 13	E	4 18	A	9 05	15	5¾	6¼	1 31	E	12ᴍ24	B	23 18	VIR	25
362	28	W.	7 13	E	4 19	A	9 06	14	6¾	7¼	2 42	E	1 06	B	23 15	VIR	26
363	29	Th.	7 13	E	4 20	A	9 07	14	7¾	8¼	3 53	E	1 54	B	23 12	LIB	27
364	30	Fr.	7 13	E	4 20	A	9 07	13	8½	9¼	5 02	E	2 51	B	23 09	OPH	28
365	31	Sa.	7 13	E	4 21	A	9 08	13	9½	10¼	6ᴍ06	E	3ᴘ55	B	23s.04	OPH	29

DECEMBER hath 31 days. 1994

The Darling of the world is come,
And fit it is we find a room
To welcome Him. The nobler part
Of all the house here is the heart.
– Robert Herrick

D. M.	D. W.	Dates, Feasts, Fasts, Aspects, Tide Heights	Weather ↓
1	Th.	☾ at ☊ • First drive-in gas station opened, Pittsburgh, Penn., 1913 •	*Deck*
2	Fr.	☾ at perig. • New ● • Henry Ford unveiled Model A, 1927 • {12.3 10.7	*the*
3	Sa.	☾ runs low • Oberlin College, first coed college, opened, Oberlin, Ohio, 1833 {12.5 10.8	*malls*
4	**B**	**2nd S. in Advent** • Rain today brings rain for a week. • {12.4 —	*with*
5	M.	☌♆☾ • ☌♅☾ • *The Nutcracker* premiered, 1892 • {10.7 12.2	*plastic*
6	Tu.	**St. Nicholas** • Jefferson Davis died, 1889 • {10.6 11.7 •	*greenery,*
7	W.	*A man who does nothing never has time to do anything.* •	*stimulate*
8	Th.	**Conception of Virgin Mary** • Tides {10.1 10.4 •	*that ol'*
9	Fr.	☾ on Eq. • ☌♄☾ • ♀ Greatest Brilliancy •	*economy;*
10	Sa.	New York City's warmest winter day: 70° F, 1946 • Emily Dickinson born, 1830 •	*ice &*
11	**B**	**3rd S. in Advent** • UNICEF est., 1946 • Tides {9.5 8.9 •	*snow*
12	M.	George F. Grant patented golf tee, 1899 • First Bank of U.S. opened in Philadelphia, 1792	• *will*
13	Tu.	**St. Lucy** • ☿ in sup. ☌ • Grandma Moses died, 1961 • {9.6 8.7	*paint*
14	W.	☾ at ☋ • Temperature fell 79° F in 24 hours, Helena, Mont., 1924 • {9.8 8.7 •	*the*
15	Th.	☾ at apo. • Canadian flag adopted, 1964 • Bill of Rights passed, 1791 •	*scenery,*
16	Fr.	Boston Tea Party, 1773 • Margaret Mead born, 1901 • {10.1 8.9 •	*angels*
17	Sa.	☾ rides high • Full Cold ○ • Beware the Pogonip. • {10.2 9.0 •	*sing in*
18	**B**	**4th S. in Advent** • First photo of Moon, 1839 •	*four-*
19	M.	*All the world's a stage and most of us are desperately under rehearsed.* • Tides {10.3 — •	*part*
20	Tu.	Halcyon days. • Peter the Great reformed Russian calendar, 1699 •	*harmony.*
21	W.	**St. Thomas** • Winter Solstice • Pilgrims landed at Plymouth Rock, 1620 •	*May*
22	Th.	Colonial law required standard weight bread and pure flour, 1650 • Tides {9.2 10.0 •	*we*
23	Fr.	☌♂☾ • Colonists repealed 22-year ban on Christmas celebrations, 1681 • {9.4 9.8 •	*all*
24	Sa.	☾ on Eq. • Famous cold day, Kentucky: Ohio and Miss. rivers frozen, 1796	*sincerely*
25	**B**	**Christmas Day** • A green Christmas makes a fat churchyard. •	*strive*
26	M.	**St. Stephen** • Harry S Truman died, 1972 • Tides {10.0 9.4 •	*for*
27	Tu.	**St. John** • "Howdy Doody" show debuted, 1947 • Louis Pasteur born, 1822	*peace*
28	W.	**Holy Innocents** • ☌♀☾ • Tides {10.7 9.5 •	*on*
29	Th.	☾♃☾ • 30"+ snow on ground, Mo. and Ill., 1830 • Tides {11.2 9.7	*earth*
30	Fr.	☾ at perig. • –32° F Mountain City, Tenn., 1917 • Rudyard Kipling born, 1865	*in*
31	Sa.	☾ runs low • *Make the most of yourself for that is all there is of you.* • Tides {11.9 10.3	*'95!*

Farmer's Calendar

December 20. A big storm is coming. The forecasters are falling over one another to see who can hit the alarm bell hardest. It's early in the winter for a real snow, but indeed, outdoors it looks as though the weathermen might be right this time. The morning was palely sunny, but after lunch a gray iron sky supervened with a keen little wind out of the north. Time to get ready.

Preparing for a major storm is like preparing for war: You take thought not for what you suspect your enemy *may* do, but for what you know he *can* do. First thing, I back both cars down to the bottom of the driveway and leave them facing the road. That way the snowplow can get up the drive and I'll be able to get out after the storm without backing downhill through deep snow, a maneuver that seldom ends well. Then I bring a couple of cartloads of fuel in from the woodshed. While I'm outside, I make sure the snow shovel is gassed, oiled, and has a new plug.

Inside I fill the bathtub. Should the storm knock out the electricity, we'll have plenty of water for washing and for operating certain articles of plumbing, the importance of which is demonstrated with real force by a three-day outage. I check the flashlights to make certain all batteries are either weak or dead. They are. I ask, as I do each year, why we don't have a kerosene lamp. I try to think where the candles are. I fail.

It's nearly dark and the snow has begun. The bare patches and the steps have turned a fuzzy gray. It's supposed to snow all night. Before I quit, I always fill the birdfeeder — my last gesture of readiness, the final perfecting touch that sets the whole place safely straight and lets me enjoy the coming storm.

How to Appear to Know More Than You Really Do

Want to be admired? Considered a genius? Much sought after for dinner parties? Well, according to this expert in the art of social conversation, it's simply a matter of memorizing a few "Safe Subjects, All-Purpose Adjectives, Multifaceted Facts, and Irrefutable Opinions." by Tim Clark

– illustrated by Abby Carter

It is a familiar scene. We have just come home from a dinner party, and my wife is disconsolate. "I'm too stupid to live," she moans.

"You're not that stupid," I say. "What do you mean?" (I know exactly what she means, but for the purposes of exposition, I shall feign ignorance.)

"At dinner everyone was talking about books and movies and politics, and you all know so much about them," she says. "I just sit there like a lump. I haven't read the books or seen the movies, and politics just makes me want to scream."

Yes, she has a problem all right. But it's not the problem she thinks it is. Her shortcoming has nothing to do with her intellect, which is keen. It has everything to do with her one tragic character flaw: She is honest.

Now, in spite of this, I love her madly. But candor is a crippling deficiency in polite social intercourse. Don't misunderstand me — I'm not advocating lying. Lying is immoral. Lying is unethical. Lying can get you caught. And finally, lying is too easy. We are talking about a high art here, an art akin to bullfighting. Like the great matador, the torero of the dining-room table is marked by his ability to dodge, to weave, to dance on the edge of disaster.

I once met a man whose impudence and skill at evading the onrushing horns of his interrogators made me want to shout, "Olé!"

If, for example, someone asked him, "Have you read *Don Quixote*?" he would say, "Not recently." Of course he'd never read it at all, but why disrupt a perfectly congenial conversation?

On another occasion, when asked if he had read Dante's *Inferno,* he replied, "Not in English." I was awestruck. In three absolutely truthful words he managed to convey three distinct and misleading messages: **(1)** that he had read the book; **(2)** that he was fluent in Italian; and **(3)** that he was the sort of literary purist who would never settle for a mere translation. Glorious. I believe that, in certain countries, my friend would have been awarded the ears and tail of the person who asked the question.

But you don't have to be Manolete to sling the bull. All you have to do is memorize a few Safe Subjects, All-Purpose Adjectives, Multifaceted Facts, and Irrefutable Opinions.

SAFE SUBJECTS

☞ A safe subject is one that is interesting and provocative enough to allow you to make broad statements of dubious value (nobody wants to listen to you expound on the fine points of 19th-century German foreign policy or discuss the nuances of Kwakiutl creation myths), while at the same time obscure or complicated enough that nobody but an expert will be able to call your bluff. (It's always a good idea to circulate among the guests before dinner and engage in a little light conversation about their interests in order to know what subjects to avoid. I once held forth for 20 minutes on my interpretation of the Chinese Cultural Revolution — unencumbered by facts — all the while unaware that the man sitting next to me was the nation's leading authority on Chinese history. It was not an experience I'd care to repeat.)

Here are a few Safe Subjects you might wish to consider:

1. Quantum Physics: For ambiguity, it's hard to beat. It gave Einstein fits, and the best known part of it is something called "The Uncertainty Principle." The father of quantum physics, Niels Bohr, was famous for making cryptic remarks about the nature of reality, then giggling uncontrollably at the look on the faces of his students (see "What to Do When Confronted").

2. The Dead Sea Scrolls: Discovered in 1947, these ancient texts have been studied ever since by a small group of Biblical scholars who won't let anyone else take a look, probably because they still haven't figured out what they mean.

3. James Knox Polk: One of a series of one-term presidents preceding the Civil War, he was elected in 1844 and declined to run for a second term. Not very interesting in himself, he's a convenient guy if you get tired of somebody at the table who is yammering on about the current occupant of the White House. Then you say, "What about James Knox Polk?"

The person talking is stopped cold. "What about him?" he says belligerently.

"Well, everything you just said could also apply to James Knox Polk," you reply. "And look what happened to him. He declined to run for a second term."

Everyone nods. Who could argue with that?

ALL-PURPOSE ADJECTIVES

☞ These are descriptive terms that apply to almost anything. When asked to comment on a book, play, film, or musical composition of which you are ignorant, for example, you should say:

"I prefer his (her) earlier works. They're more pristine." (Relatively few people know what "pristine" means. It means "earlier.")

Or, alternatively:

"I prefer her (his) later works. They're more mature."

MULTIFACETED FACTS

☞ You can sound learned without being verbose. The strategic insertion of a single unusual piece of information can leave your fellow diners with a lasting impression of erudition. For example: The author D. H. Lawrence's wife, Frieda, was the sister of Baron von Richthofen, the famous German flying ace. This is a valuable piece of trivia, because it can be dropped casually into a discussion of any of the following subjects:

1. D. H. Lawrence
2. The Red Baron
3. 20th-century English literature
4. World War I
5. In-laws
6. Sex (any reference to D. H. Lawrence is appropriate in this area)
7. Snoopy

IRREFUTABLE OPINIONS

☞ At some point in any dinner conversation, someone is bound to turn to you and say, "What do you think?"

You don't want to say what you really think, because you haven't been paying attention. You have actually been thinking about the funny noise you heard in your car on the way over, or wondering why your hostess bought that hideous painting on the wall, or trying to remember the name of the actress who played Mary Ann on "Gilligan's Island." But you can't admit that. This is where you need to express an opinion that is relevant to any subject and impervious to contradiction. Here are three good ones:

"It all depends."
"You can't generalize."
"Things are different in the South."

WHAT TO DO WHEN CONFRONTED

☞ Even under the best of circumstances, there may be occasions when some rude person will try to embarrass you by pointing out that you are a fraud. Don't panic. You have three options:

1. Tell the following anecdote: The great Danish scientist, Niels Bohr, once said there are two kinds of truth: trivial and profound.

The opposite of a trivial truth is a falsehood. The opposite of a profound truth is another profound truth. Then you can excuse yourself from the table while your questioner is trying to figure out what you just said.

2. Point out the nearest window and shout, "Look at that!" hoping to distract the company's attention. The hazard in this scheme is that you may succeed too well — a friend tried it, and when everyone turned to the window, they saw two dogs sharing a moment of intimacy in the backyard.

3. Take a bite of meat and chew it thoughtfully, as if formulating your reply. Then, once it is well chewed and tucked in a corner of your mouth, simulate choking to death. Hold your breath, pointing frantically at your throat. If possible, turn blue. Rush out of the dining room and hurl yourself stomach-first against the back of a sofa or divan. You may want to do this two or three times, so that everyone will under-

stand that you are performing the Heimlich maneuver on yourself. When you judge the moment to be right, spit the concealed bit of meat into your napkin with a realistic retching sound, straighten up, turn to the horrified onlookers, and calmly say, "I'm all right." If performed persuasively, this will cause everyone present to forget the unfortunate incident that precipitated your problem and congratulate you on your presence of mind. Olé! ⬚⬚

Solving the Mysteries of *Love*

(and Sex)

For instance, a recent study shows that American women initiate two thirds of all sexual encounters. Their best pick-up line: "Hi." It works 100 percent of the time. (Men have only a 71 percent success rate with the same line.)

by Christine Schultz

As soon as she saw his photo in a catalog, she fell in love. All the other merchandise — the corsets, the garters, the studded dog collars — paled by comparison. "I am a lonely schoolteacher in the dismal hills of Idaho," she wrote to the catalog publisher. "Would you be kind enough to do your share in assisting a poor, forlorn teacher in her future happiness by sending this man advertised in your latest edition?"

Hers was a classic case of love at first sight, and though seemingly far-fetched, not one to be quickly discounted. As the philosopher Blaise Pascal once said, "The heart has its reasons which reason knows nothing of." Poets for centuries have agreed that the one certainty about love is its mystery. Today's scholars, however, armed with their studies and statistics, aren't so ready to concede. With clipboards in hand, they've taken notes on everything from the flirting sequence gesture to the copulatory gaze to the effects of diet on the libido and the "love drug" on mice. Though they have yet to crack the code, they've discovered some revealing clues about love. Our lonely Idaho schoolmistress would do well to take notes. Perhaps you would, too.

For starters, you should know that if you're a romantic, you're not alone. Scholars have mistakenly believed for too long that courtly love is a luxury invented by the 12th-century troubadours in Provence and handed down to us through Western culture. Recently they've learned (or admitted) that romantic love is, in fact, universal. Of 166 cultures surveyed by anthropologists William Jankowiak and Edward Fischer, 89 percent showed signs of romantic love. (It's true that many cultures still don't believe romantic love should be the basis of marriage, but the tide is shifting in the heart's favor.) That means you could stumble onto romance almost anywhere — in the Australian outback, in the Amazon jungle, even in the hills of Idaho.

You may wonder, nevertheless, what exactly to look for in a mate. Try measuring forearms. One study showed that men and women with the same size forearms were more likely to stay together. But if you forget your tape measure, the poets say not to worry — you'll know love when you see it. "Through the eyes love attains the heart: / For the eyes are the scouts of the heart" (Guiraut de Borneilh, ca. 1138-1200). Surprisingly, some scientists agree you should go with your instincts, since love at first sight most likely evolved to spur the mating process. "During the mating season a female squirrel needs to breed," explains anthropologist Helen Fisher. "It is not to her advantage to copulate with a porcupine. But if she sees a healthy squirrel, she should waste no time." For squirrels and humans alike, the key attraction lies in the health of the potential mate. Scholars tell us that despite all the worldwide variations, the one physical characteristic that attracts men and women in every culture is a good complexion.

But it's not just how you look, it's how you smell. Foul odors do little to induce affection. Here's why: Located in our nasal cavities are five million olfactory neurons waiting like postal workers to sort through some 10,000 recognizable odors. They mail these perfumed messages directly to the brain's emotional headquarters (what scientists call the limbic system).

Let's pretend, for instance, that the catalog model (we'll call him Marvin) meets our forlorn teacher (let's call her Myrna) in Idaho on a day when the liquid from her eccrine glands has mixed with bacteria on her skin. She hadn't really expected him to come all this way, and now that he has, it's too late to rid her body of that acrid smell. Marvin's smell sorters send nasty notes to his brain. He leaves. Poor Myrna, alone again in Idaho.

Let's give her another chance. This time when Marvin arrives at her door, she's prepared; her body smells seductively sweet. Marvin doesn't know it, but his neuron messengers have keyed into the subtle scent released from Myrna's apocrine glands located around her armpits, nipples, and groin. Had he read the 19th-century novelist Joris Karl Huysmans, he would agree that the smell of a woman's underarms "easily uncaged the animal in a man." His and Myrna's body odors hit it off after all. He understands at last what Napoleon meant when he wrote to his love, Josephine: "I will be arriving in Paris tomorrow. Don't wash." Smells can do that to a man. If you're still not convinced, try this trick used by the women in Shakespeare's day. Hold a peeled apple under your arm until the fruit becomes saturated with your scent; then present it to your lover to inhale. It'll do wonders for your relationship. Really.

Look how it works for the male black-tipped hang fly. He gets mates all the time by secreting his odor into a juicy aphid, daddy longlegs, or housefly and hanging the prize in the wind. Before long a female catches the scent and stops by for food and procreative fun.

If scented houseflies just don't do it for you, you're best to stick to chocolates. Buried amid the calories are plenty of amphetamine-related substances sure to produce the erratic behavior common to infatuation. Food for the heart.

Who can resist a little courtship feeding, the old evolutionary way for a male to show his prowess as a hunter? To keep in shape for his forays, Marvin should fill up on roughage. Lots of it. That's the advice Dr. Frederick Hollick gave back in the 1840s. "To ward off impotence," he counseled, "fill up on potatoes, celery, parsnips, onions, mushrooms, truffles if you can get them, olives, tomatoes, lima beans, and above all, asparagus. Canvasback duck also makes a potent pepper-upper." Those who need self-restraint, on the other hand, should avoid those foods and eschew coffee, particularly, the good doctor said, if they are "disposed to involuntary emissions." In all cases, he advised that lovers would do well to avoid constipation and to take care to let the stomach settle before proceeding to the bedroom. "Sexual indulgence just after eating is nearly certain to be followed by indigestion, even if it does not cause immediate vomiting."

Regrettably, not all in love is savory. If you're serious about finding love, you may wish to sample one of the many concoctions said to ignite the heart (if not the intestines). The Australian aborigines brew a love potion from kangaroo testicles; others swallow the heart of a wild duck; those in Far Eastern countries mix ginger in soft drinks, sweets, and tea; Chinese look to ginseng and rhinoceros horns. If you have trouble finding kangaroo testicles in your local supermarket, you might just try a more accessible mixture: Stir rosemary, thyme, mint, rose petals, and lemon leaves into black tea. Drink it under a waxing Moon.

During an infatuation between a man and woman, both their brains release a chemical called PEA. When scientists recently injected PEA into mice, they (the mice, that is) jumped and squealed, exhibiting "popcorn behavior."

In fact, most anything you do concerning love would be better done under the waxing or full Moon. Scientists and poets alike agree that the Moon plays a powerful role on our reproductive beings. Pliny believed that "lunar energy penetrates all things"; Aristotle noticed that the ovaries of sea urchins swell during the full Moon; Darwin wrote that "Man is subject, like other mammals, birds, and even insects, to that mysterious law, which causes certain normal processes, such as gestation, as well as the maturation and duration of various diseases to follow lunar periods."

Not only is the average menstrual cycle the same length (29.53 days) as the synodic lunar months, but the average human gestation period is ten lunar months. Furthermore, a statistically significant majority of births (seven percent) occur at full Moons, and a study by Wesleyan University's psychology department found a 30 percent increase in sexual activity at the time of ovulation, which most frequently happens during the full Moon. "Like other mammals that go into heat," writes Paul Katzeff, "women apparently grow randier at ovulation." But they're not the only ones. Researchers have also documented that men, like women, have a greater sexual appetite once a month at the time of the full Moon.

For all we know, it could just be the added light that incites us to romance. When the Moon doesn't shine, we're left groping in the dark; the darkness signals our pineal glands to produce melatonin, and that puts a damper on sperm production, ovulation, and sexual interest. During a waning Moon, we'd be better off waiting for a picnic in the Sun. Sunlight raises the excitement level by revving up the pituitary gland and turning on the ovaries and testes.

With all these cosmic forces at play on our bodies, do our brains have any say at all in the matter of love?

"If only one could tell true love from false love," said Katherine Mansfield, "as one can tell mushrooms from toadstools." But even that's not such an easy thing. If you're no mycologist, take a quick lesson in body cues. The most obvious, of course, is the human "upper smile," combined with a one-sixtieth-of-a-second eyebrow lift; it's a worldwide indicator of

interest. Don't, however, confuse the upper smile with the "nervous social smile." If Marvin, for instance, approaches with his lips pulled back to reveal his upper *and* *lower* teeth, Myrna should spot the response as one that evolved from the ancient mammalian practice of baring one's teeth when cornered. Myrna should back off.

She might try to relax Marvin with the Flirting Sequence Gesture, an age-old female courtship ploy diagrammed by ethologist Irenaus Eibl-Eibesfeldt like this: The woman smiles at her admirer, lifting her eyebrows in a swift jerky motion as she opens her eyes wide. Then she drops her eyelids, tilts her head down and to the side, and looks away. Often she will also cover her face with her hands and giggle nervously.

Marvin may now be impressed. He may wonder, though, why he hadn't been the one to initiate such advances.

Perhaps he hadn't heard of a study by Clellan Ford and Frank Beach in the 1950s that showed that in practice women around the world initiate sexual liaisons and that in another study American women initiated two-thirds of the encounters. Their best pick-up line went like this: "Hi." It worked 100 percent of the time. Men had only a 71 percent success rate with that same line. But at least it means the ball's rolling. To keep it moving, watch for the next cue. If a woman turns her toes inward, that's the meekness stance, signaling openness for approach. If the man thrusts out his chest, he's trying to impress. Males throughout the animal kingdom puff themselves up to appear attractive. If these cues click, both male and female are interested; their eyes lock for two to three seconds with the pupils dilated. Scientists call this, the most striking human courtship ploy, the Copulatory Gaze. "The gaze triggers a primitive part of the human brain," says anthropologist Helen Fisher, "calling forth one of two basic emotions — approach or retreat."

If neither backs down, then only one thing can happen next. The Kiss. Rhett Butler and Scarlett O'Hara did it best in *Gone with the Wind* — Americans rate that the most memorable kiss in movie history. (The runner-up is the beach kiss by Burt Lancaster and Deborah Kerr in *From Here to Eternity*.) Don't think for a minute that a kiss is just a kiss. On the contrary, it speaks volumes. The esteemed Dr. Bubba Nicholson wrote in the British *Journal of Dermatology* that kissing allows us to taste semiochemicals on our suitor's skin. Semiochemicals, according to Bubba, transmit biological signals of attraction and compatibility. In the

words of Carl Jung: "The meeting of two personalities is like the contact of two chemical substances; if there is any reaction, both are transformed."

So if Marvin and Myrna taste good to each other, they may well fall in love. They may find themselves dizzy with excitement, full of bumbling energy that keeps them up late into the night. They might tell you there's chemistry between them. And it would be true, literally. Michael Liebowitz of the New York State Psychiatric Institute says that during infatuation the brain releases the chemical phenylethylamine or PEA, a natural amphetamine. When scientists inject PEA into mice, they (the mice, that is) jump and squeal, exhibiting "popcorn behavior." A shot of PEA to rhesus monkeys makes them emit pleasure calls and smack their lips.

But extended romantic bliss may become too much for the brains of Marvin and Myrna. Liebowitz tells us that 18 months is about all the brain can take in this revved-up state. Then the nerve endings become habituated to the stimulants and the levels of PEA drop. A new set of brain chemicals called endorphins takes over. Endorphins calm the mind, kill pain, and reduce anxiety, leaving Myrna and Marvin comfortably settled in the attachment stage of love. Now they can talk and eat and sleep in peace. Myrna may discover for the first time that Marvin snores. Loud. She read somewhere that after sexual intercourse, male rats emit a contented high-frequency snore. Twenty-two kilohertz wouldn't be so bad. At least it wouldn't keep her awake like this jackhammer noise Marvin makes. Since she can't sleep, maybe she'll just go downstairs, do some reading, flip through a couple of catalogs to see what they have in stock. ▢▢

Why it takes legwork to flatten your stomach.

You can't reduce stomach fat by exercising abdominal muscles alone.

Research shows that exercises that work only abdominal muscles are not effective. You need a total-body workout — you need a NordicTrack. The NordicTrack total-body motion involves *all* major muscle groups. Which means you burn more fat in less time. In fact, you can burn up to 1,100 calories per hour.

Use a NordicTrack® total-body exerciser to flatten your stomach.

A NordicTrack workout gives you a smooth, vigorous motion that's easy on your joints. The patented flywheel and one-way clutch mechanism gives you a jarless, realistic cross-country skiing workout. So you feel as good as you look.

Free information.

Call or write us today. We'll send you a free brochure and video that show how NordicTrack® workouts can help you look and feel your best.

30-day in-home trial

NordicTrack
A CML Company

The World's Best Aerobic Exerciser®

©1993 NordicTrack, Inc., A CML Company • All rights reserved.

FREE Video *and* Brochure

Call **1-800-328-5888** *Ext.* **TF513**

or write: NordicTrack, Dept. TF513, 104 Peavey Road, Chaska, MN 55318

❏ *Please send me a FREE brochure*
❏ *Also a FREE VHS videotape*

Name_____Phone (   )_____

Street_____

City_____ State _____ Zip_____

by Lawrence Doorley

The Possible Secret of

OUR FOUNDING FATHERS' LONGEVITY

In 1775 a mere two percent of the populace was over 65. Yet our first ten presidents lived an average of 77.4 years. Why?

Can a person be too busy to die? Can a vital undertaking be so engrossing that there is just no time to answer the door when doomsday comes knocking? Not likely, say the geneticists, insisting that the length of one's life is mainly determined by how long his or her ancestors lived.

But Dr. Kenneth Pelletier, authority on longevity, disputes the geneticists. "Good genes give you an edge," Dr. Pelletier admits, "but that doesn't account for people who live 30 to 40 years beyond average life expectancy. A strong sense of purpose, commitment to higher values, as well as lifelong physical and mental activity play a more important role in longevity than purely biological factors such as hormonal changes." He asserts that the single most important predictor of longevity is enthusiasm for life: staying busy, being curious, feeling that you are accomplishing something worthwhile.

Proof that the "too busy to die" theory is more than wishful thinking can be found in the long and productive lives of the Founding Fathers. Life expectancy at birth in Colonial America between 1700 and 1775 was 35 years (today it is 72.2 for men and 78.9 for women). But since life expectancy is defined as the number of years an individual of a given age may expect on the average to live, once the Colonial American reached 21, odds favored his living another 20 years. And the longer one lived, the better the chance of living to a ripe old age.

Nevertheless, in 1775 a mere two percent of the populace was over 65. Yet an amazing number of Founding Fathers, all born in the perilous 18th century, achieved a longevity far beyond the average.

Our first ten presidents — Washington through Tyler — lived an average of 77.4 years, while our last ten deceased presidents — Theodore Roosevelt through Lyndon Johnson (excluding John Kennedy, whose early death would further lower the average) — lived an average of only 69.9 years.

Of the 56 signers of the Declaration of Independence, three lived to 90 or beyond (Charles Carroll of Maryland lived to 95); nine more to 80 or beyond; an additional eight to 70 or more; and another 16 reached 60 or more. Benjamin Franklin lived to 84, Paul Revere to 83, Noah Webster to 84, John Jay to 84, Samuel Adams to 81, Charles Bulfinch to 81, John Trumbull to 87, John Marshall to 80.

Some might argue that the Founders must have had long-lived ancestors (some did, but most didn't), a privileged background (less than half did), or superior medical care (it didn't exist for anyone, rich or poor).

Perhaps Benjamin Franklin had the best formula for achieving longevity. In his twenties he compiled a list of Thirteen Virtues that would govern his life. Virtue No. 6 was Industry: "Lose no time. Be always gainfully employed. Work as if you were to live a hundred years."

There it is: The Founding Fathers were industrious. They schemed, harangued, wrote, organized, fought — many of them in bloody battles — to free the Colonies. Then while some of them worked furiously to prevent the unhewn nation from falling apart, others rushed back to the workshop to pick up their tools. They were a diverse group: aristocrats, common sorts; college graduates, autodidacts; short-tempered, imperturbable; neat, sloppy; stingy, generous. Some smoked; most drank moderately, mainly wine. Some exercised diligently, others halfheartedly. But they all had one thing in common: They saw life as a heaven-sent gift, a gift to be utilized, not wasted, not squandered.

Why don't we all try this? See how it works out. □□

FIRST TEN U.S. PRESIDENTS

	BORN	DIED	AGE
George Washington	2-22-1732	12-14-1799	67
John Adams	10-30-1735	7-4-1826	90
Thomas Jefferson	4-13-1743	7-4-1826	83
James Madison	3-16-1751	6-28-1836	85
James Monroe	4-28-1758	7-4-1831	73
John Quincy Adams	7-11-1767	2-23-1848	80
Andrew Jackson	3-15-1767	6-8-1845	78
Martin Van Buren	12-5-1782	7-24-1862	79
William Henry Harrison	2-9-1773	4-4-1841	68
John Tyler	3-29-1790	1-18-1862	71

☞ *Average age at death: 77.4 years*

LAST TEN DECEASED PRESIDENTS

(Excluding John F. Kennedy)

Theodore Roosevelt	10-27-1858	1-6-1919	60
William Howard Taft	9-15-1857	3-8-1930	72
Woodrow Wilson	12-28-1856	2-3-1924	67
Warren G. Harding	11-2-1865	8-2-1923	57
Calvin Coolidge	7-4-1872	1-5-1933	60
Herbert Hoover	8-10-1874	10-20-1964	90
Franklin D. Roosevelt	1-30-1882	4-12-1945	63
Harry S Truman	5-8-1884	12-26-1972	88
Dwight D. Eisenhower	10-14-1890	3-28-1969	78
Lyndon B. Johnson	8-27-1908	1-22-1973	64

☞ *Average age at death: 69.9 years*

All sports have their famous heartbreakers, haunting defeats snatched from the jaws of certain victory. Here are a few of the most memorable (or forgettable) ones.

by Todd Balf

This is beyond devastating," said Houston Oilers cornerback Cris Dishman, hours after the most startling about-face in the 73-year history of the National Football League. "We need a new word in the English language for this." ■ On January 3, 1993, in Buffalo, New York, the Houston Oilers had a 35-3 lead over the Buffalo Bills early in the third quarter of the NFL play-off series and were en route to the sweetest moment in the franchise's hard-luck

Lost Victories

history. The victory was so secure that Houston sportswriters had already made nonrefundable plane reservations for the next round of the play-offs in Pittsburgh. ■ Then the impossible happened. Behind an unheralded second-string quarterback named Frank Reich, a man who'd thrown one pass in a play-off game, Buffalo scored the next 35 straight points and won in sudden-death overtime, 41-38. In Buffalo the comeback was hailed as a miracle. In Houston more desul-

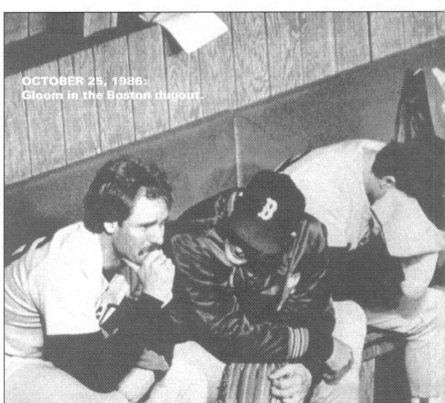

OCTOBER 25, 1986:
Gloom in the Boston dugout.

tory explanations arose. The city was cursed. Even Mayor Bob Lanier was at a loss for words. "Try as he might to think of something inspirational to say, he cannot," a spokesman reported. Meanwhile, a few Houstonians, harking back to the glory days of NASA, suggested launching all remnants of the game — pads, jerseys, a few players perhaps — on a one-way passage to Mars. ■ It may have been small consolation to the Oilers and their fans, but there were folks from Terre Haute to Tuscaloosa who knew exactly how they felt. For there is not a town or county or school in America that isn't haunted by a humdinger of a loss, a heartbreaker that has made generations rise from a perfectly good sleep years later and gently (but meaningfully) curse. Here are a few doozies . . .

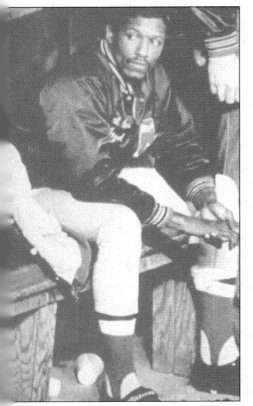

Shea Stadium, New York

The Boston Red Sox vs. the New York Mets, Game 6 of the 1986 World Series

With a 5-3 advantage in the tenth inning and two outs, Boston was one strike away from their first World Series in 68 years. Everyone thought the game was over. Red Sox pitcher Bruce Hurst had been named Series most valuable player, and 20 cases of Great Western champagne had been defoiled and delivered to the Boston clubhouse. The baseball commissioner and the NBC cameras were also in the locker room, readying for the postgame trophy presentation. The Mets' scoreboard operator prepared the message: "Congratulations, Boston Red Sox."

Of course, the game wasn't over. In circumstances that are all too familiar to New Englanders, the Mets tied the game on two singles, a broken-bat looper, and reliever Bob "Steamer" Stanley's wild pitch. Mookie Wilson's slow grounder leaked through Bill Buckner's legs into right field for the win.

Two days later, the Sox lost Game 7 and officially became the team to come closest to winning the World Series — and losing. In 1989 the late House representative Silvio Conte, apparently still reeling, read this into the Congressional Record: "Red Sox fans have felt the ecstasy of victory in their grasps so many times . . . only to be put through the agony of another lost victory. It is a ritual that has been repeated many more times than a kinder and gentler God would ever allow . . ."

MARCH 2, 1974

Chapel Hill, North Carolina

Duke vs. North Carolina, the College Basketball Season Finale

With an 86-78 lead and only 17 seconds left, perennial underdog

Duke has apparently pulled off the upset of the year against nationally ranked North Carolina. Then things go bad. The Tar Heels hit two free throws and steal two inbound passes to draw within a basket with five seconds on the clock. Duke is intentionally fouled, but misses the free throws. At the buzzer, Carolina freshman Walter Davis heaves a shot from 30 feet away, which hits high on the glass and drops in to tie the game. Carolina wins handily in the resulting overtime.

"At Duke, students today still whisper about those 17 seconds," wrote Duke graduate John Feinstein in *Forever's Team.* A few miles away, on the campus of North Carolina, they do far more than whisper. In fact, the full-court play Davis scored on is still in coach Dean Smith's playbook. It's called Duke.

JUNE 4, 1978

Marin County, California
The Dipsea Race

The eight-mile footrace across the rugged flank of Mount Tamalpais is one of the oldest running events in the country. The race locals still hum about

was the duel between Don Chassee and Russ Kierman in 1978, when the latter, tempted by what appeared to be a shortcut (but in fact was impenetrable poison oak), ended up giving away his front-running position and his best chance ever at the title. Kierman was runner-up two more times and now holds the affectionate nickname Mr. Avis (he tries harder).

DECEMBER 2, 1972

Birmingham, Alabama
Auburn University vs. Alabama, the Season Finale for the Traditional Cross-State Football Rivals

This was the year Alabama (10-0) seemed destined for the national championship. With the fourth quarter winding down, undefeated and heavily favored Alabama carried a 16-3 advantage and prepared to punt. But in the closing minutes of the annual game they call the Iron Bowl, Auburn's Bill Newton blocked two consecutive 'Bama punts, and teammate David Langer made back-to-back recoveries for 25- and 20-yard touchdown runs. Final score: Auburn 17, Alabama 16. In Auburn the team was dubbed "The Amazings." At Alabama they are condemned more than two decades later to see bumper stickers that read, "Punt, 'Bama, Punt."

MAY 31, 1967

Indianapolis Speedway, Indiana
The Indianapolis 500

In a race known for its photo finishes, Parnelli Jones had one of the

DECEMBER 2, 1972: Auburn blocks an Alabama punt.

biggest leads ever. Driving the first turbine-engine race car, the longtime Indy favorite was determined to avenge three straight years of bad-luck losses. He grabbed the pole on the second turn of the first lap and with only three laps left had an astonishing 48-second lead on the others.

Jones was actually easing his speed back when the engine suddenly (and silently) died. A $6 bearing in the transmission had failed. In seconds he went from 151 miles an hour and a spot in the winner's circle to zero. Ultimately, A. J. Foyt would win the '67 Indy 500. But what every Parnelli Jones fan remembers is their man leaving the stalled car and futilely trying to push it the final eight miles.

MARCH 21, 1953

Butler Field House, Indianapolis, Indiana

Terre Haute Gerstmeyer High vs. South Bend Central, the Indiana High School Basketball State Championship Game

Only in Indiana would a one-point defeat qualify as a collapse. But that's the way it happened. Terre Haute was led by Howard Sharpe, the dean of high-school basketball coaches. He had a flawless lineup led by identical twins Arley and Harley Andrews and their uncle Harold.

But at the start of the fourth quarter, their dream season unraveled when Arley, the team's best shooter, fouled out. The irony was that he had only four fouls, but was mistakenly assessed one belonging to his twin brother. The double irony was that in previous games, Coach Sharpe was rumored to have made the twins swap jerseys at half time if Arley was in foul trouble. "If you're one of those who believe Howard Sharpe used to pull the switch," says Ron Newlin of the Indiana Basketball Hall of Fame, "you'd have to say it came back and bit him." The final: South Bend Central 42, Terre Haute Gerstmeyer 41.

NOVEMBER 28, 1942

Fenway Park, Boston, Massachusetts

Boston College vs. Holy Cross, the Final Game of the Football Season

Boston College was en route to a national championship. They'd rolled over opponents at an alarming rate, outscoring them 249-19 in eight perfect games. Meanwhile, tiny Holy Cross, a Jesuit rival from neighboring Worcester, came into the game a mediocre 4-4-1. By the time it was over, the Holy Cross Crusaders had stunned the number one ranked Eagles 55-12, one of the most lopsided defeats in Boston College football history.

The loss was a blessing in disguise. In the wake of the humiliating defeat, BC canceled plans for a postgame celebration for team, coaches, family, and friends at the Cocoanut Grove nightclub in Boston. That night, in the second-worst fire in U.S. history, 492 people died at the Cocoanut Grove.

JUNE 19, 1966

Olympic Country Club, San Francisco, California

The U.S. Open Golf Tournament

Arnold Palmer, closing in on Ben Hogan's tournament record, had a seven-stroke lead on Billy Casper with nine holes to play. In the aftermath, Palmer would admit he got a little carried away. Always known for his daring shot-making, Palmer, with the victory seemingly in hand, gambled on the back nine in his attempt to break the mighty Hogan's record. Each gamble went awry as Arnie bogeyed the 15th, 16th, and 17th holes, losing the remaining five strokes to Casper and ending up in a tie. In the next day's playoff Palmer lost by four strokes. It was his third play-off loss at the U.S. Open in five years. □ □

Ten Little-Known Facts About the
Lewis and Clark
– E X P E D I T I O N –

Like it cost ten times the amount of money Congress had approved. (Sound familiar?) And their greatest hazard? You guessed it — bugs. BY DAYTON DUNCAN

n a rainy May afternoon in 1804, Meriwether Lewis and William Clark started up the muddy Missouri River, heading west into history. Theirs was the first American expedition to cross the continent and reach the Pacific Ocean by land, and in their wake an entire nation followed them westward, transforming the United States from the equivalent of a North American Brazil into a transcontinental power.

One hundred and ninety years later, they are still America's best-known explorers, so inextricably linked together in our memory that history students have been known to refer to the "Louis N. Clark" expedition in their term papers. And while their accomplishment stands as the country's most remarkable, successful, and far-reaching exploration, it also remains one of the most misunderstood. The following facts will help set the record straight.

Budget? What Budget?

In a secret message — to keep the plans from becoming public — President Thomas Jefferson persuaded Congress to approve the expedition on the assurance that it would cost only $2,500 and involve only a dozen men. But the crew that left the St. Louis area in 1804 numbered nearly 45 men, and the final tab to the taxpayers — not even counting services and supplies furnished by the War Department — reached $38,722.25, more than ten times the original estimate. In retrospect, this was probably still a bargain, but it also was one of the nation's earliest examples of a massive governmental cost overrun.

Jefferson's Pet Project

Even though he never personally traveled west beyond Virginia's Shenandoah Valley, Jefferson was fascinated by the West. (His library at Monticello contained the world's most extensive holding of books on western topics.) Prior to becoming president in 1800, he had tried to

organize three other expeditions for exploring the best route across the continent; none of them got off the ground. In fact, the Lewis and Clark expedition was planned and launched before the United States actually owned any of the territory Lewis and Clark explored. Lewis had already procured the expedition's supplies and was on his way to St. Louis — at the time a "foreign" city — when word arrived in the summer of 1803 that the United States had purchased the vast Louisiana Territory from France.

Lieutenant Clark

Although Lewis and Clark now share equal billing as co-commanders, in fact only Lewis held the rank of captain. Clark joined the expedition with the promise of being made a captain, but for internal, bureaucratic reasons the War Department refused the promotion. To Clark's credit, he swallowed his bitterness about this disappointment and stayed on. To Lewis's credit, he nonetheless shared the decision making with his friend and never informed the other members of the expedition, who for 2½ years referred to Lieutenant Clark as "captain."

"Empty" Spaces

The West the expedition explored was hardly an uninhabited wilderness. Several days west of St. Louis, they passed the last white settlement, but they spent nearly as much time in contact with Indians (several dozen tribes were encountered) as they did in isolation. The first winter encampment was in what is now North Dakota, in the midst of some Mandan and Hidatsa villages inhabited by about 4,000 Indians, a far larger population than St. Louis at the time, even more than Washington, D.C., in 1804! Along the Columbia River, Indians were so numerous that the men complained about the crowding. Only in what is now Montana, where the expedition saw more grizzly bears than Indians, were they essentially alone for nearly three months.

A Woman Pathfinder?

Sacagawea, the Indian woman who accompanied them west from the

Mandan-Hidatsa villages, was not brought along as a guide. With the exception of her home area, most of the terrain she traveled with Lewis and Clark was as new and unfamiliar to Sacagawea as it was to everyone else in the expedition. Her main contribution, with her French-Canadian husband Toussaint Charbonneau, was as an interpreter, especially with her native Shoshones in the Bitterroot Mountains, from whom horses were purchased for the mountain crossing. According to Clark, her presence also "reconsiles all the Indians to our friendly intentions. A woman with a party of men is a token of peace."

"Hostile Savages"

The Indian tribes the expedition encountered were almost uniformly friendly to the United States' first official envoys in the West. In fact, without the assistance of Native Americans — most notably in the food they provided at critical junctures — the expedition might well have perished. The expedition had an armed standoff with the Teton Sioux ("the vilest miscreants of the savage race," according to Clark) on the Missouri River, but no shots were exchanged. On the return journey, Lewis and a small contingent got into a fight with some Blackfoot, killing two of the Indians — the only gunplay and loss of life through hostile action during the entire expedition. (The expedition's only fatality was Sergeant Charles Floyd, who died of a ruptured appendix during the first summer.)

A Trio of Pests

Although they endured incredible hardships — a frigid winter in North Dakota, blistering heat during the summers, hailstorms that knocked the men to the ground, flash floods that nearly drowned them, grizzly bears that literally chased them across the Plains, and near starvation in the Bitterroot Mountains — what the men complained about most is familiar to all campers: bugs. Mosquitoes were "exceedingly troublesome," to use Lewis's phrase, often keeping the men awake at night and sometimes so thick they were inhaled with every breath. "Our trio of pests still invade and obstruct us on all occasions," Lewis wrote in 1805. "These are the Musquetoes, eye knats and prickley pears, equall to any three curses that ever poor Egypt laiboured under."

Man's Best Friend

For reasons not entirely clear, Lewis brought along a big, black Newfoundland dog named Seaman. Like the men, it suffered greatly from the mosquitoes and the summer heat, but Seaman earned his keep on the Upper Missouri when his barking alerted everyone to a buffalo bull that blundered into camp one night and nearly trampled some of the men. Indian dogs proved even more important to the expedition's survival. Along the Columbia River, where they were wary of eating the abundant salmon, the men purchased dogs for their meals. "For my own part I have become so perfectly reconciled to the dog that I think it an agreeable food and would prefer it vastly to lean venison or elk," Lewis wrote. Clark was the only one who never acquired a taste for roast canine.

Democracy in Action

When they reached the Pacific Ocean in November of 1805, the commanders faced an important choice: whether to encamp near the mouth of the Columbia for the winter or head back upriver immediately. They reached their decision in a most unmilitary manner: They asked every member to vote. Included in the polling were York, Clark's black slave (though black men would not be enfranchised in America for another 65 years), and Sacagawea (though Indians and women would wait another hundred years to vote in the United States). The majority voted to stay on the coast.

Success, Yet Failure

The expedition's return to St. Louis in September 1806 was greeted with wild enthusiasm. The nation, having heard no word of them for more than a year, had given them up for dead. The commanders became national heroes (Clark finally got his promotion), and the men received double pay and 320 acres of land for their efforts. But included in the report of their journey was recognition of an implicit failure. Their prime mission had been to find an easy water route across the continent — the fabled Northwest Passage that geographers insisted lay somewhere in the West. Instead, Lewis and Clark found mountains perennially covered in snow. Years later, the realization hit that no such passage exists, and the true worth of Lewis and Clark's wealth of new information would more than compensate for the initial disappointment. "It was," the historian Bernard DeVoto wrote, "the first report on the West, on the United States over the hill and beyond the sunset, on the province of the American future. . . . It satisfied desire and it created desire: the desire of the westering nation." □□

Dayton Duncan is the author of Out West: An American Journey Along the Lewis and Clark Trail *(Viking Penguin) and is working on a documentary film about the expedition with filmmaker Ken Burns.*

WINDCHILL TABLE

As wind speed increases, the air temperature against your body falls. The combination of cold temperatures and high winds creates a cooling effect so severe that exposed flesh can freeze. (Inanimate objects, such as cars, do not experience windchill.)

To gauge wind speed: at 10 mph you can feel wind on your face; at 20 small branches move, and dust or snow is raised; at 30 large branches move and wires whistle; at 40 whole trees bend.
– Courtesy of Mount Washington Observatory

Wind Velocity (MPH)	Temperature (°F)											
	50	41	32	23	14	5	–4	–13	–22	–31	–40	–49	–58
	Equivalent Temperature (°F) (Equivalent in Cooling Power on Exposed Flesh under Calm Conditions)											
5	48	39	28	19	10	1	–9	–18	–27	–36	–51	–56	–65
10	41	30	18	7	–4	–15	–26	–36	–49	–60	–71	–81	–92
20	32	19	7	–6	–18	–31	–44	–58	–71	–83	–96	–108	–121
30	28	14	1	–13	–27	–40	–54	–69	–81	–96	–108	–123	–137
40	27	12	–2	–17	–31	–45	–60	–74	–89	–103	–116	–130	–144
50	25	10	–4	–18	–33	–47	–62	–76	–90	–105	–119	–134	–148
	Little Danger			Increasing Danger			Great Danger					

Danger from Freezing of Exposed Flesh (for Properly Clothed Person)

about your *Hair* and how to make it BEAUTIFUL

by Susan Peery

We read textbooks on hair care and talked not only with hair-care professionals but also with everyday people with gorgeous hair. Here's what we learned: It's human nature to fiddle with one's crowning glory — plait it, curl it, anoint and adorn it, worry about it. After all, it's the only human body part that continually grows, degenerates, and miraculously grows again throughout life. All body hairs grow at about the same rate — roughly ½ inch a month — but vary in the length of the growth stage. Eyelash hair or forearm hair has a short life cycle (a month or less), while head hair grows for two to six years before it withers at its base and falls out (at which point the hair follicle rests for about three months and then rouses itself for another growth period).

If you are of the natural-is-best school of thought, you may believe that people should just leave their hair alone, avoid artifice, and do no more than wash and brush it when necessary. That's OK, but be aware that you are fighting powerful and ancient customs that have to do with hair as status symbol, sexual lure, and more. The ancient Assyrians, for example, wore masses of curls on their shoulders and sprinkled real gold dust in their hair. (Did everyone in ancient Assyria have naturally curly hair? No — but the nobility used curling tongs, and men set their beards with tree gum.) Egyptians of about 1200 B.C. shaved their heads and wore wigs for special occasions, stewed the leaves of the henna bush to get a red dye, or colored their hair with indigo, "dried tadpoles from the canal crushed in oil," or "tortoise shell and babgu bird boiled in oil."

Indian women, known for their lustrous hair, still use special herbal shampoos, soak their tresses in olive or coconut oil, and avoid chemicals and dryers. Beauty magazines are filled with advice

(and some misinformation) about hairstyles and hair care, although standards of beauty vary greatly. Can a person create beautiful hair? Consider the following attributes of hair:

Color

H air gets its color from the pigment melanin, the same agent that colors skin and eyes. The color is contained in the hair shaft, which is composed of long, tapering cells that have coalesced into fibrous material, in turn covered by a delicate layer of transparent, overlapping cells forming the cuticle. Hair is largely composed of the protein keratin; chemically, dark hair has more carbon and less oxygen than lighter hair. Color is inherited, along with the degree and timing of graying. Gray hair is not really gray, but is an absence of color in the hair shaft, rendering it white or opaque. Graying usually starts (or you could say that natural pigmentation usually ceases) at the hairline and progresses toward the back of the head;

Anatomy of a Hair

- Technical term for hair on head is capilli.

- Lifespan: Two to six years.

- Eighty-five percent of hairs on the head are in their growth phase at any given time.

- The average head has about 120 square inches of hair, with about 1,000 hairs per square inch.

- The outermost hair layer is the cuticle (transparent, overlapping cells); middle layer is the cortex (source of strength, elasticity, and pigment); innermost layer is the medulla.

- Hair grows 1/72" per day, or about 1/2" per month.

- Hair grows fastest between ages 15 and 30, with a sharp decline between 50 and 60. Women's hair grows faster than men's hair.

- Between 50 and 80 hairs a day are shed naturally. Shedding increases in spring and fall.

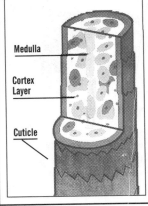

Medulla

Cortex
Layer

Cuticle

– courtesy Clairol

the "gray," unpigmented hairs tend to be coarser than the colored hairs.

Hair color can be changed and enhanced with dyes and rinses. Henna is one of the oldest hair dyes, although today's product, available in neutral, black, and brown tones as well as traditional red, is more sophisticated than that of the ancient Egyptians. Henna is not recommended for hair that is more than 15 percent gray or has already been bleached or colored. Colored hair is about ten percent weaker than untreated hair; in addition, although colorants can initially add body, they can also build up on the hair shaft and cause hair to appear dull and heavy. Color restorers, also called progressive colors, are metallic salts that build up on hair and damage it. And there's the constant problem of roots showing your true colors.

Brushing can distribute natural oils and add sheen; hairbrush bristles can be natural or synthetic as long as they have smooth ends to avoid scratching the hair cuticle (which has to remain smooth enough to reflect light).

Shape

Hair can be straight, wavy, or curly, depending on the angle and direction in which the hair shaft emerges from the follicle. The angle of the follicles, also called the hair stream, creates whorls and cowlicks and the general tendency for hair to curl out on one side of the head and curl under on the other side. In cross-section, hair can be round, oval, or flat; it was once believed that this shape was racially determined, but this belief has been discredited with research that showed significant overlap between groups. Hair shape can be changed temporarily by "permanents" and straightening, but the natural tendency will reassert itself on new growth. Curling irons and hot rollers work by using heat to make the hair shaft malleable, but must be used with care: Temperatures over 140° F can actually melt the shaft. *(continued)*

Be Your Own Boss...
IN YOUR OWN BUSINESS!

Work Part Time OR Full Time
Get Into This Booming High-Profit Business That's Easy To Learn — Easy to Do — Easy On You!

START YOUR OWN MONEY MAKING BUSINESS & BEAT INFLATION!

BE A LOCKSMITH

Never before have money-making opportunities been so great for qualified Locksmiths. Now lucrative regular lock and key business has multiplied a thousandfold as millions seek more protection against zooming crime. Yet there's only one Locksmith for every 17,000 people!

Make Up to $26.00 an Hour — even while learning! Train FAST at Home!

You're "in business" ready to earn $10 to $26.00 an hour a few days after you begin Foley-Belsaw's shortcut training. Take advantage of today's unprecedented opportunities in locksmithing for year-round EXTRA IN-COME in spare time — or full time in a high-profit business of your own. Hundreds we've trained have done it. So can YOU! All tools plus professional Key Machine given you with course. These plus practice materials and equipment, plus simple, illustrated lessons, plus expert supervision, plus business-building guidance will enable you to **KEEP THE MONEY COMING IN!** Ideal for retirement — good jobs, too.

No Extra Cost! Included With Your Locksmith Training

BURGLAR ALARM and SECURITY SYSTEMS training. Covers all phases of Burglar, Hold-Up and Fire Alarm servicing and installation. ONLY Foley-Belsaw offers such extensive training in this rapidly expanding field as a part of your Locksmith training. **PLUS... ADVANCED Locksmithing!**

How to change combinations, install and service Safe, Vault and Bank Safe-Deposit Box locks. You'll find it fascinating and highly profitable work.

Just fill in and mail coupon (or send postcard) to receive full information and details by return mail. **FOLEY-BELSAW INSTITUTE**
　　6301 EQUITABLE RD., DEPT. 12313
　　KANSAS CITY, MO. 64120

RUSH COUPON TODAY FOR THIS FACT-FILLED FREE BOOKLET!
30-DAY NO RISK TRIAL!
SEND FOR FACTS TODAY!

ALL SPECIAL TOOLS AND EQUIPMENT INCLUDED!

PRO KEY MACHINE YOURS TO KEEP!

This Pro Key Machine can alone add up to $200 a month to your income... and it won't cost you a penny extra with your training.

NO OBLIGATION... NO SALESMAN WILL CALL

FOLEY-BELSAW INSTITUTE
6301 EQUITABLE RD., DEPT. 12313
KANSAS CITY, MO. 64120

☐ YES, please send me the FREE booklet that gives full details about starting my own business in Locksmithing. I understand there is no obligation and that no salesman will call.

Name _____

Address _____

City _____

State _____ Zip _____

Thickness

Human scalps have an average of 1,000 hairs per square inch, roughly 120,000 hairs in all; age 20 marks the peak of thickness. Blond hair tends to be most numerous (140,000 hairs per head), followed by brown (110,000), black (108,000), and red (90,000). Although blonds have more hair, the individual hairs tend to be thinner than the darker tones. By age 60 half of all men are bald or balding, and 40 percent of women have experienced some hair loss. Male-pattern baldness, called alopecia, occurs when a gene triggered by age changes the hormone testosterone into a new chemical, dihydrotestosterone, which makes hair smaller and finer with each new generation of hair growth until baldness results. Traction alopecia, most commonly seen in women, is hair loss due to pulling by tight braids, heavy ponytails, and so on. The hair of pregnant women often appears especially thick and luxuriant — this is because high estrogen levels extend the growth phase and prevent hair from entering the resting phase (the down side of this is that all those hairs enter their resting phase at the same time postpartum, and hair comes out by the handful). High fevers, tranquilizers, thyroid disorders, and unusual stress (which causes high adrenaline levels) can also cause temporary hair loss.

So, How Do You Get a Beautiful Head of Hair?

We talked with hair-care professionals (Joanne Stark, head of the Keene, New Hampshire, Beauty Academy; barber Deborah Coleman of Snipper's, also in Keene), read textbooks on hair care, and interrogated friends with beautiful hair to find out their secrets. (Their expert opinions on hair care sound suspiciously like John D. Rockefeller's advice on business success: Go to work early. Stay at work late. Find oil.) The million-dollar answer on hair is: Eat well. Wash and brush hair often. Inherit the right genes.

➤ **Nutrition:** A well-balanced diet is necessary to healthy hair. Poor nutrition, especially protein deficiencies, can lead to thinning, dull, dry hair (usually reversible with a return to good eating).

PACKER'S TAR SOAP

➤ **Buy expensive shampoo** from your barber or beautician (the best modern shampoos contain plant extracts) and dilute it 50/50 with water. Shampoo daily. Avoid using very hot water. Cheap shampoos in grocery stores often contain waxes and fillers that build up on hair. Use them on your dog.

➤ **Brush hair thoroughly** twice a day, and massage your scalp to help circulation. Excessive brushing, however, can irritate the scalp and break off hairs; for some, the obligatory 100 vigorous strokes can be too much.

➤ **Get a good haircut** that makes the most of your hair's natural attrib-

utes. Remember: You can "do" the least with healthy hair. It's damaged hair that you can manipulate the most.

What to Avoid

❧ For healthiest hair, avoid styling aids, heat, and all chemical processes if possible. Permed hair is 30 percent weaker than untreated hair.

❧ Teasing or ratting hair (back-combing) roughs up and tears the cuticles and can damage hair so severely that a short haircut is the only solution.

❧ Rough treatment of the hair (hot dryers, harsh shampoos, and friction from tight barrettes and rollers) also abrades the cuticles and can cause split ends (or trichoptilosis). Contrary to advertising claims, split ends cannot be healed or glued back together; they can only be cut off.

❧ Infrequent shampooing, insufficient rinsing, improper diet, and poor scalp circulation are thought to cause dandruff, technically known as pityriasis; treatment includes scalp massage, mild shampoos, and daily use of an antiseptic scalp lotion if needed.

❧ Don't brush wet hair. Comb it out gently with a wide-tooth comb (especially for long hair), and let it dry before brushing.

Myths About Hair

❧ Race or nationality determines the basic shape (round, oval, or flat) of hair. (Truth: These categories overlap among all racial groups.)

❧ Clipping and shaving encourage hair growth. (Truth: The rate and thickness of growth is unaffected by cutting.)

❧ Ointments and oils can make hair grow faster. (Truth: These treatments only lubricate the hair shaft.)

❧ Hair grows after death. (Truth: The flesh and skin contract, causing hair to protrude slightly more. Same is true of fingernails.)

❧ Singeing the ends of the hair seals in natural oils. (Truth: The oils originate in tiny glands beside each follicle and are distributed on the outside of the hair shaft only. Singeing simply damages the hair shaft.)

❧ Baldness is inherited from the maternal side. (Truth: The timing and extent of balding can come from either side.)

❧ Hair can turn gray overnight. (Truth: This has never been documented. The pigment already in the hair is unaffected by inactive pigment cells at the root. A rare condition called alopecia areata causes pigmented hairs to fall out while gray ones stay behind, all in a short period of time.) ▢▢

Old-Fashioned Hair-Care Recipes

Egg Shampoo: Steep 1 ounce fresh rosemary in 1 pint hot water for 20 minutes. Cool. Beat in 1 egg. Massage into hair and rinse.

Herbal Rinses for Oily Hair: Steep a handful of lemon grass, nettle, peach leaves, rosemary, southernwood, or yarrow flowers in a quart of hot water. Cool and pour over wet hair after shampooing.

Herbal Rinses for Dry Hair: Steep a handful of comfrey, chamomile, clover, elder flowers, or papaya leaves in a quart of hot water. Cool and pour over wet hair after shampooing.

To Enliven Color: For blonds add lemon juice, chamomile tea, or white vinegar to the final rinse water to enhance color. For dark hair use cider vinegar, rosemary, or sage in the rinse water. Green pekoe tea used as a rinse adds reddish highlights to blond or light brown hair.

Hair Ointment: Blend 2 tablespoons castor oil, 2 tablespoons lard, and a few drops of rosemary oil. Or add several drops of rosemary oil or lemon oil to 1/4 cup almond or olive oil.

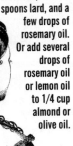

SUNDAY MORNING

NOVEMBER 12, 1933

It began in South Dakota with a clear sunrise and a crisp breeze, but by 11 A.M. the city of Sioux Falls had been plunged into darkness. Not long thereafter a plume of dust stretched from Oklahoma to the Great Lakes — and that was just the beginning . . .

by Michelle Seaton

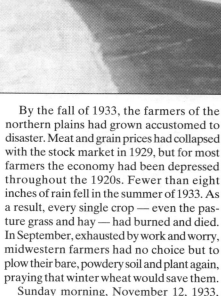

When the people of Sioux Falls, South Dakota, looked to the northern horizon on the morning of November 12, 1933, they saw a vast dark cloud, but it was not the rainstorm they would have welcomed. It was a dry plume of soil rolling toward the small town, fueled by winds of more than 50 miles per hour. They didn't know then that the dust in that cloud was thick enough to suffocate cattle or that the approaching wind was strong enough to overturn buildings. This was the storm that would usher in the Dust Bowl era, and by the time it passed, it would take several lives and set a new standard of destruction.

By the fall of 1933, the farmers of the northern plains had grown accustomed to disaster. Meat and grain prices had collapsed with the stock market in 1929, but for most farmers the economy had been depressed throughout the 1920s. Fewer than eight inches of rain fell in the summer of 1933. As a result, every single crop — even the pasture grass and hay — had burned and died. In September, exhausted by work and worry, midwestern farmers had no choice but to plow their bare, powdery soil and plant again, praying that winter wheat would save them.

Sunday morning, November 12, 1933, began with a clear sunrise and a crisp breeze. A light snowfall the week before

The Sioux Falls Storm of 1933 presaged the destruction that would create the Dust Bowl. In a later storm, a "Black Blizzard" brought darkness at noon to north Texas.

had left much of the Minnesota and eastern Dakota landscape dressed in white.

The weather bureau in Huron, South Dakota, had first noticed what it called "a disturbance moving rapidly southeastward" over Canada on Saturday morning. A bubble of low pressure, it looked to be a harmless air mass of moderate winds. Weather predictors had no way to know that it would inflict more damage than any midwestern windstorm to date.

Three types of windstorms are common along the Plains states: whirlwind storms or tornadoes; shift-wind storms or cyclones; and straight-wind storms, the rarest of the three. Straight-wind storms erupt when a point of low pressure or cyclone wanders too close to a point of high pressure or anticyclone. The clash of the two storms will raise gale-force winds as the barometric pressure fights to equalize itself.

In the early hours of November 12, that low pressure point raced south through Manitoba, past Winnipeg, all the while getting closer to a strong anticyclone east of Boise, Idaho. The point of friction between the storms occurred over South Dakota.

The wind began to rise just after the Sun

In the spring of 1934 "the farms of the Dust Bowl . . . blew clear out to the Atlantic Ocean."

Fence posts buried by blowing dust had to be dug out and raised to keep cattle in.

did, quickly reaching 35 miles per hour. It didn't take long to scatter the light covering of snow. Then, as the wind increased, it swept across the furrows, the roads and ditches, the windmills and barns like an angry broom. The first thin cloud of dust billowed up from the Dakota plain at around 8:00 A.M., then darkened quickly as the wind pushed seeds and sprouts, gravel and small rocks, tumbleweeds and sticks ahead of it. It picked up freshly plowed topsoil by the ton. That day the clouds grew to a height of 9,000 feet. The cyclone continued to move south and east, as did the windstorm. By the time it reached Sioux Falls, South Dakota, its first urban area, it had grown to a churning mass of grit and gravel 100 miles wide and was careening along at 60 miles per hour.

When seen from afar, the approaching storm looked like a dense thundercloud rolling along the ground. The Sioux Falls *Argus Leader* reported that by 11:00 A.M., the city had been "plunged into darkness."

The most striking feature of the storm was the noise. The *Argus Leader* wrote that the wind "howled throughout the day, snapping off telephone poles and trees, smashing windows, and grounding fences . . ." Dust and gravel hit the houses like fine hail, and some say that above the roaring wind and the sound of falling trees and breaking glass, they could hear birds screaming as they fluttered helplessly, trying to escape the dust. The haze became so thick that "motorists

drove with lights ablaze and Sunday merchants and housekeepers spent the day under artificial light." Outside, streetlights flickered in confusion. By noon the Sun had become a dim blue disk behind a blanket of dirt. Communities throughout the state reported zero visibility. Dust and static electricity interfered with car motors, so that drivers were forced to abandon their cars where they stopped.

The *Argus Leader* called it the most severe storm "in the memory of the white man in South Dakota." An emergency crew consisting of "every available man" worked frantically clearing trees from the streets as they fell. In mid afternoon the men had blocked off one area of the city, as the wind ripped heavy shingles off the roof of St. Joseph Cathedral and pitched them into the street.

The storm gathered momentum as it traveled south and east. In Iowa, winds were recorded at 70 miles per hour, strong enough to pry bricks from the city's chimneys. In Sioux City a woman's roof was lifted from her house and carried, intact, across the street. In Whitehall, Illinois, a man walked in front of a car while blinded by dust and was killed. In Des Moines, where the wind was clocked at 69 miles per hour, a construction worker was killed when the scaffold he was working on collapsed beneath him. As utility poles fell all around, the live wires started small grass fires. The fire department in Des Moines was called out 27 times to fight them.

The storm pressed on into Minnesota, Nebraska, Missouri, and Illinois. Throughout the region, the reports of damage were almost too bizarre to be believed. Windmills and small barns were not only toppled by the wind, but they were also said to be crumpled by it. Gusts overturned cars along the highways and rolled them into the ditches. In Tracy, Minnesota, a busful of passengers stalled four miles outside town when the motor gummed up with dust. The Associated Press reported that the wind itself pushed the bus the rest of the way into town.

As far away as Chicago, hundreds of people sought emergency eye treatment as they left the closing night of the Century of Progress exposition. By Sunday evening the plume of dust stretched from Oklahoma to the Great Lakes. The winds subsided as the cyclone continued to move east, carrying hundreds of tons of topsoil and seeds toward the seaboard. The cloud, diffused in the long trip across the country, would bring black rain to Tennessee and brown snow to New York.

In Sioux Falls the darkness lifted at around 3:00 P.M. The wind weakened and finally fell silent. The dirt hovered in the air and then slowly began to settle. In northern South Dakota the sky lightened enough for a blazing red sunset, then fell into a hazy dusk. That night the temperature dropped from 50° to 18° F.

Monday morning dawned brightly. Midwesterners woke to find their world thick with grit. Gravel, twigs, and earth had to be swept from porches and sidewalks, pushed off roofs, and scrubbed from windowpanes. Fine silt had to be shoveled from living rooms, brushed from sheets and drapes, dusted from walls, shaken from rugs, and washed from closetsful of clothes. Anywhere air could reach, the dust had gathered, either covering objects with a film or settling like a dry snow in the corners of drafty rooms. The dust was so fine that in some cases it had seeped into watch faces and gummed up the mechanisms.

Outside, the dust had settled in piles on fence posts and drifted around barns and houses. Tumbleweeds covered the barbed wire. On main streets some storefronts had caved in; even if they were intact, the displays inside — candy, groceries, flowers — were covered in a fine grit. In rural areas the damage was more permanent. Hay, corn fodder, and straw had scattered beyond salvaging. The *Argus Leader* reported that area farmers who had depended on a harvest of winter grains faced ruin: "The wind exposed the roots so that winter killing is inevitable even where the grain was not completely blown from the ground. . . . It is estimated that farmers, already hard hit by economic and climatic conditions, will not be able to receive seed back from their fields."

The *Argus Leader* could not yet report the worst news: This was just the beginning. The drought continued; farmers continued to plow the soil after each failed crop. Before long the soil had broken down completely, taking on the consistency of ash. In these conditions even slight breezes would lift dark clouds over the plains. In the spring of 1934, wrote Stuart Chase in *Rich Land, Poor Land,* "the farms of the Dust Bowl . . . blew clear out to the Atlantic Ocean, 2,000 miles away. On a single day 300 million tons of rich topsoil was lifted from the Great Plains, never to return."

In 1935 the Soil Conservation Service was established to try to halt the terrible erosion. Using techniques such as contour plowing, strip cropping, and gully control, SCS technicians worked with farmers and ranchers in a desperate attempt to keep the land from blowing away. But normal levels of rainfall didn't return until 1939. By that time, drought and blowing soil had turned 100 million acres of farmland into a wasteland of shifting sand and abandoned farmhouses. It was estimated that more than 3½ million people had lost their livelihoods. It would take several years of good rain and many millions of dollars in government aid to turn the desert back into productive land. □□

GENERAL WEATHER FORECAST
1993-1994

(For details see regional forecasts beginning on page 116.)

NOVEMBER THROUGH MARCH is expected to be warmer than normal in the Northeast and west of the Rocky Mountains and slightly warmer than normal in the eastern Great Lakes down through the Ohio River valley. The South and the lower Great Plains will be close to normal or just below. Southern California and central and southern Florida will be below normal; the upper Great Plains and western Great Lakes will be much colder than usual. Precipitation will be variable: Well above normal amounts are expected in much of New England, the Ohio River valley, and the Northwest; slightly above over the rest of the Northeast, the Great Lakes, and the far North through the northern Rockies. Much of the southern half of the country may be significantly dry, and a large part of the Great Plains may receive slightly below normal precipitation. Snowfall will be below normal in New England, the southern Sierra Nevada Mountains, and southern California, but above normal in northern California, Utah, the Cascades, most of the Rocky Mountains, and across the far north of the country through the northern Great Lakes.

APRIL THROUGH OCTOBER: Spring is anticipated to be significantly cooler than normal over most of the country; exceptions are a few sections in the South and West that will be only slightly below normal. Precipitation will be extremely variable: wet in New England, the middle Atlantic

states, the lower Great Plains, the eastern Great Plains to western Great Lakes, and across from southern California through northern Texas; dry in New York down through eastern Pennsylvania, the south Atlantic states, the western Great Plains, and northern California; and very dry in the Northwest, the lower Ohio and Mississippi River valleys, southern Texas, and Florida.

Summer will be warmer than normal from the middle Atlantic states to the Mississippi River and north through the eastern Great Lakes and the Northeast, as well as in many sections of the Northwest. The Deep South can expect hot conditions. Relatively cool weather may occur in the Great Plains, western Great Lakes, and along the California coast. Except for parts of the Northeast, much of the eastern third of the country, the Deep South, and the Northwest will be dry. Most of the rest of the country, including much of the Northeast, will receive well above normal rainfall.

Early fall will be warm east of the Mississippi River, in Texas, parts of the Rockies, and the Northwest; and cool in the northern Great Plains, northern Rockies, and California. Much of the country east of the Rockies will be fairly dry; exceptions are the northern Great Plains and sections of the Northeast, which will be wetter than normal. The Northwest will be quite wet, while other sections of the West will receive above-normal rainfall.

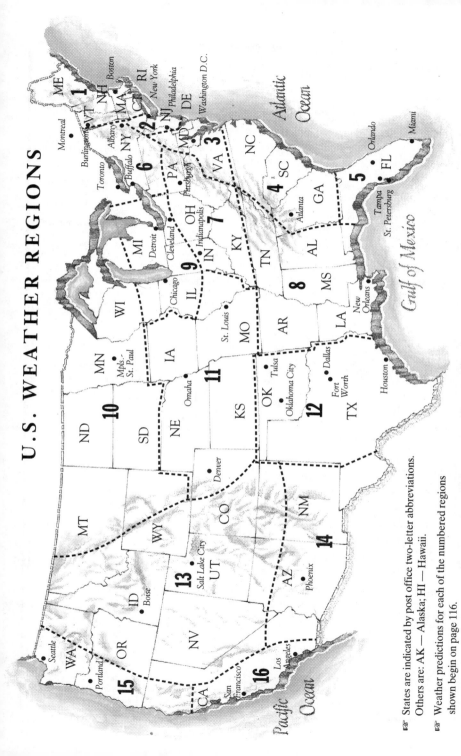

U.S. WEATHER REGIONS

☞ States are indicated by post office two-letter abbreviations. Others are: AK — Alaska; HI — Hawaii.

☞ Weather predictions for each of the numbered regions shown begin on page 116.

SUMMARY: *November through March is expected to be milder than normal, with slightly above normal precipitation in the south, but well above normal north. Snowfall may average about ten percent below normal. November through mid-December should see alternating mild and cold spells, with severe storms the end of November and mid-December. Seasonable weather will then prevail through January except for a cold wave at year's end and mild spells mid- and late January. Cold waves and snow are expected through February, with a possible Northeaster before midmonth. March may come in like a lamb, but go out like a lion.*

April through June should be slightly cooler than normal, with below-normal precipitation north but wet in the south. April may be quite wet, with above-normal snowfall at higher elevations. May should be drier than normal with near-normal temperatures the first half while cold waves and rain will alternate with sunny, warm spells the latter half. A cool mid-June will be partially offset by warm spells at the beginning and end, with heavy rains in southern sections the latter half.

July through September should see close to normal temperatures, with above-normal rainfall north, but below normal south. Few heat waves are expected, and southern sections may be fairly dry, except for heavy showers toward the end of August. In the north, heavy thundershowers in July and late August should bring ample rainfall. October may see alternating cold and warm spells before closing with a storm.

NOV. 1993: Temp. 50° (5° above avg.); Precip. 6" (1.5" above avg.). 1-5 Showers then clear & mild. 6-9 Rain, colder. 10-14 Mild; showers north. 15-18 Flurries, cold. 19-23 Sprinkles, snow mountains; then clear & cold. 24-25 Rain, snow north. 26-28 Cold. 29-30 Severe storm.

DEC. 1993: Temp. 36.5° (3° above avg.); Precip. 2.5" (1.5" below avg.; 2" above north). 1-4 Rain, snow mountains; turning cold. 5-7 Flurries. 8-10 Rain, then clearing. 11-13 Storm, gale coast. 14-16 Rain, snow mountains. 17-19 Clearing, cold. 20-23 Showers, snow inland. 24-25 Clear, milder. 26-29 Snow. 30-31 Severe cold.

JAN. 1994: Temp. 35° (6.5° above avg.); Precip. 4" (0.5" above avg.). 1-4 Clear, cold; snow. 5-6 Seasonable. 7-10 Mild, drizzle. 11-12 Snow. 13-15 Cold, flurries. 16-20 Clear & cold, then snow. 21-24 Sunny, very mild. 25-27 Rain, then turning to snow, cold. 28-31 Rain, snow inland; clearing.

FEB. 1994: Temp. 31° (1° above avg.); Precip. 4.5" (1" above avg.; 3" above north). 1-3 Snow; clearing. 4-6 Snow, rain south. 7-9 Clearing, cold. 10-12 Northeaster, snow inland. 13-15 Cold, flurries. 16-18 Mild, sprinkles. 19-21 Cold. 22-26 Sleet. 27-28 Clearing; snow north.

MAR. 1994: Temp. 38.5° (Avg.); Precip. 3.5" (Avg.). 1-2 Sunny, mild. 3-6 Flurries, cold. 7-9 Rain, snow north. 10-12 Clear, mild. 13-16 Cold; rain, snow north. 17-19 Mild; rain, snow north. 20-22 Showers. 23-25 Storm, heavy rain, snow mountains. 26-29 Freezing rain, snow north. 30-31 Clearing, cold.

APR. 1994: Temp. 49° (1° above avg.); Precip. 4" (0.5" above avg.; 2" above north). 1-2 Clear, warm. 3-7 Rain, snow north; mild. 8-10 Clear. 11-13 Warm, sprinkles. 14-16 Heavy rain. 17-21 Cloudy & rainy, mild. 22-25 Sunny, sprinkles. 26-27 Storm south, rain north. 28-30 Rain.

MAY 1994: Temp. 58.5° (0.5° above avg.; 1° below north); Precip. 4.5" (1" above avg.; 1" below north). 1-2 Sunny, warm. 3-4 Rain. 5-10 Warm, dry. 11-13 Sprinkles; clear & warm. 14-16 Rain, cold. 17-20 Clear, hot. 21-23 Cold, rain. 24-26 Warm; showers. 27-31 Rain; cool.

JUNE 1994: Temp. 65.5° (2° below avg.); Precip. 4" (1" above avg.; 1" below north). 1-3 Rain. 4-5 Clear, warm. 6-9 Cool, rainy. 10-13 Clear. 14-17 Cool, showers. 18-20 Rain, cold. 21-25 Warm, clearing; showers north. 26-28 Rain, cooler. 29-30 Sunny, warm; showers.

JULY 1994: Temp. 73.5° (Avg.; 1° below north); Precip. 1.5" (1" below avg.; 1" above north). 1-5 Rain, cool. 6-7 Sunny, warm. 8-10 Rain, cooling. 11-15 Clear, hot. 16-17 Rain, cooling. 18-19 Clear & hot. 20-23 Thunderstorms, cool. 24-26 Sprinkles; seasonable. 27-30 Clear, very warm. 31 Rain.

AUG. 1994: Temp. 70° (2° below avg.); Precip. 4" (0.5" above avg.; 2" below north). 1-2 Heavy rain, cool. 3-6 Sunny, warm; showers. 7-8 Rain, cooling. 9-11 Clear, very cool. 12-19 Some showers; sunny, warming. 20-23 Thunderstorms, then clearing; cool. 24-26 Rain, seasonable. 27-31 Sunny, then sprinkles.

SEPT. 1994: Temp. 68° (3° above avg.); Precip. 2" (1" above avg.; 1" above north). 1-4 Clear, very warm. 5-7 Cold, rain. 8-11 Sunny, then rain. 12-18 Warm & sunny, sprinkles. 19-20 Rain, seasonable. 21-24 Clear. 25-27 Cloudy, showers; warm. 28-30 Rain, cooling.

OCT. 1994: Temp. 55° (0.5° above avg.; 2° above north); Precip. 3.5" (Avg.). 1-2 Rain, cool. 3-5 Cold wave, freeze inland. 6-9 Showers, warm. 10-14 Heavy rain; clear & cold. 15-16 Rain, snow mountains; very cool. 17-20 Indian Summer-like. 21-23 Sprinkles, seasonable. 24-26 Cold wave. 27-29 Rain, milder. 30-31 Sunny, seasonable.

Be Your Own Boss and Make

$18.00 to $30.00 AN HOUR!

Find out how by sending now for your Free Lifetime Security Fact Kit!

Your FREE Lifetime Security Fact Kit tells you how to make $18.00 to $30.00 an hour in your own Foley-Belsaw Full-Service Saw and Tool Sharpening Business. Your FREE Fact Kit explains how you can:

— **be your own BOSS!**
— **work full time or part time, right at home.**
— **do work you enjoy and take pride in.**
— **operate a CASH business where 90¢ of every dollar you take in is clear cash profit.**

And it is so easy to learn. Foley-Belsaw gives you all the facts and instructions. No previous experience or special training necessary. All you need is the desire and ambition to be your own boss. Foley-Belsaw tells you everything you need to know to be successful. There's plenty of business where you live to keep you busy. It doesn't matter whether you live in a big city, small town or a small farm community.

Earn While You Learn

You'll quickly be able to develop the skills necessary to earn a steady income. You'll be able to sharpen all types of saws, garden and shop tools for home, farm and industry. Profits from your Foley-Belsaw Full-Service Sharpening Business can provide...

... **CASH for future security or supplemental income**
... **CASH for travel, vacations, fishing trips**
... **CASH for things you've always wanted!**

And you'll be able to set your own hours and not have to worry about layoffs and strikes. There are no franchise fees. Best of all — age or physical condition is no barrier — any age person can succeed.

You can be like Steve Taylor of Brookville, Ohio, who told us:
"... the first year I grossed $21,000.00."

Or James B. Jones, of Albuquerque, NM who reported:
"This past summer my sales and service amounted to almost $6,000.00 a month."

But you've got to get the FACTS before you can get started. So WRITE NOW for your FREE Lifetime Security Fact Kit. It's yours to keep with NO OBLIGATION!

FOLEY BELSAW

Foley-Belsaw Co.
6301 Equitable Rd.
Dept. 21219
Kansas City, Mo. 64120

FREE Lifetime Security FACT KIT

Foley-Belsaw Co.
6301 Equitable Rd., Dept. 21219
Kansas City, Mo. 64120

☐ **YES,** I want to know more! Please rush my FREE Lifetime Security Fact Kit. No obligation and no salesman will call.

Name _____

Address _____

City _____ State _____ Zip _____

( ) _____
Area Code   Phone

GREATER NEW YORK–NEW JERSEY

For regional boundaries, see map page 115.

SUMMARY: *November through March is expected to be warmer and considerably wetter than normal in the north, but slightly below south, with below-normal snowfall. November may begin with a heat wave, then turn cold; watch for a storm at the close of the month. December will be wet in the north, drier in the south, with cold spells at the beginning, just before Christmas, and at year's end. January will be mild and dry except for northeastern sections. In February and March, warm spells will balance cold waves, with above-normal precipitation in the north, near normal south. Snowfall is expected to be below normal.*

In April through June, frequent showers are anticipated, with northern sections receiving well above normal precipitation. Frequent warm spells will offset cold periods in April and May, but a cold wave before mid-June will bring monthly averages below normal.

July through September will average slightly warmer than normal in the north but slightly below south; rainfall may be well below normal in the north, slightly below south. Few heat waves are anticipated, but warm spells and cool periods are expected during August and September. Heavy showers are expected in eastern sections during August.

Warm periods early and late in October will easily offset cold spells during the month. Heavy rains will accompany a cold wave at mid-month. An offshore tropical storm will bring rain to coastal areas near the end of October.

NOV. 1993: Temp. 51.5° (4° above avg.); Precip. 6" (2" above avg.; avg. south). 1-2 Showers, mild. 3-7 Hot, clear. 8-10 Heavy rain. 11-14 Sunny, warm. 15-19 Cold, showers. 20-23 Rain milder then clearing. 24-25 Rain, mild. 26-28 Cold. 29-30 Heavy rain, snow mountains.

DEC. 1993: Temp. 36° (1° below avg.; 3° below south); Precip. 4.5" (1" above avg.; 1" below south). 1-3 Cold, snow north. 4-5 Cold. 6-8 Rain. 9-10 Cold. 11-15 Rain, snow north. 16-18 Clearing, cold. 19-20 Rain, snow. 21-25 Clear, cold. 26-29 Rain. 30-31 Cold, snow.

JAN. 1994: Temp. 37° (6° above avg.); Precip. 3" (Avg.; 1" below south). 1-4 Snow then freezing rain. 5-7 Sunny, cold. 8-11 Rain, mild. 12-14 Cold. 15-17 Freezing rain then clearing. 18-20 Rain, snow north. 21-26 Clear, warm. 27-28 Snow, cold. 29-31 Milder then light snow.

FEB. 1994: Temp. 33.5° (Avg.; 2° below south); Precip. 5" (2" above avg.; 0.5" above south). 1-5 Rain, snow north. 6-8 Mild then flurries. 9-10 Sunny, mild. 11-12 Rain. 13-15 Clear, cold. 16-19 Sunny, warmer. 20-26 Rain & snow, turning heavy. 27-28 Clear, cold.

MAR. 1994: Temp. 41.5° (Avg.; 2° below south); Precip. 3.5" (Avg.; 0.5 below south). 1-3 Warm, showers. 4-8 Cold, rain. 9-10 Sunny, mild. 11-12 Sprinkles, cold. 13-15 Cold. 16-19 Rain; cold south. 20-22 Cold. 23-28 Rain, snow mountains then milder. 29-31 Cold.

APR. 1994: Temp. 52.5° (1° above avg.); Precip. 5" (1" above avg.). 1-4 Rain, milder. 5-7 Clear then rain, cold. 8-13 Clear, warm. 14-19 Seasonable. 20-22 Showers, colder. 23-25 Sunny, cool. 26-27 Rain, cool. 28-30 Warm, rain.

MAY 1994: Temp. 62° (Avg.; 1° below south);

Precip. 5" (1" above avg.; 1" below south). 1-3 Rain. 4-7 Sunny & warm, showers. 8-11 Cold. 12-14 Clear & warm. 15-17 Rain, cool. 18-21 Hot, sunny. 22-25 Cold, rain. 26-28 Rain; warm then cool. 29-30 Clear, warm. 31 Rain.

JUNE 1994: Temp. 69° (2° below avg.); Precip. 3" (0.5" below avg.; 1" above south). 1-3 Cold, rain. 4-6 Clear, hot. 7-9 Rain, cool. 10-11 Clear, cool. 12-16 Rain, cool, then clearing. 17-19 Heavy rain, cool. 20-25 Clear, warm. 26-27 Rain. 28-30 Clear, warm; few showers.

JULY 1994: Temp. 76° (0.5° below avg.); Precip. 2.5" (1.5" below avg.). 1-5 Rain, cool. 6-7 Clear, warm. 8-9 Rain, cooler. 10-14 Clear. 15-17 Showers, warm. 18-19 Clear, warm. 20-23 Few thunderstorms. 24-25 Clear, warm. 26-27 Light rain. 28-30 Hot. 31 Rain.

AUG. 1994: Temp. 74.5° (1° below avg.); Precip. 5" (1" above avg.). 1 Rain, cool. 2-5 Clearing, hot. 6-10 Sunny; sprinkles south. 11-14 Rain, mild. 15-17 Thundershowers, hot. 18-19 Sunny, warm. 20-21 Thunderstorms. 22-26 Clear then rain. 27-28 Sunny, milder. 29-31 Showers, warming.

SEPT. 1994: Temp. 70° (2° above avg.; 1° above south); Precip. 2" (1.5" below avg.; 0.5" below south). 1-5 Clear, hot. 6-7 Rain, cool. 8-9 Sunny, mild. 10-11 Light rain, cooler. 12-14 Clear. 15-18 Warm. 19-20 Rain, heavy south. 21-26 Sunny, warm. 27-30 Showers, mild.

OCT. 1994: Temp. 60° (2.5° above avg.); Precip. 4" (1" above avg.; 1.5" below south). 1-5 Cool, rain. 6-9 Showers, warmer. 10-13 Storm then clearing. 14-16 Rain, cool. 17-20 Clear, warm. 21-23 Cooler. 24-26 Clear. 27-29 Rain. 30-31 Clear, warm.

MIDDLE ATLANTIC COAST

For regional boundaries, see map page 115.

SUMMARY: *November through March, despite great variability, is expected to average close to normal in temperature in central and southern sections with below-normal precipitation and warmer than normal in the north with above-normal precipitation. In November, cold waves will alternate with warm spells, ending with a snowstorm. December may be quite cold, except early in the month, with below-normal precipitation but above-normal snowfall. January will be mild with below-normal precipitation, particularly in the south. February through mid-March will be variable with cold spells being partially offset by mild ones. Above-normal precipitation is expected in the north, below normal in the south.*

April through June should be cooler than normal and drier except for a showery April. Temperatures will be particularly fickle through May and early June, with midmonth thundershowers and hail both months.

July through September is expected to see close to normal temperatures, with few heat waves. Cool periods in early and late August and September will be balanced by midmonth warm spells. Rainfall will be below normal, particularly in the north during August and September.

Early fall should be warm and dry except for a cold wave and heavy rain before mid-October and rain in coastal areas late in the month due to a possible offshore tropical storm.

NOV. 1993: Temp. 52° (2° above avg.); Precip. 3" (Avg.; 1" below south). 1-2 Warming; showers west. 3-6 Hot, clear. 7-9 Rain, cooling. 10-13 Cold snap then warming; sunny. 14-15 Rain, snow mountains. 16-18 Clear, cold. 19-21 Showers, warming. 22-23 Sunny, cool. 24-25 Rain, colder. 26-27 Cold. 28-30 Rain, snow west.

DEC. 1993: Temp. 36° (3° below avg.); Precip. 2.5" (0.5" below avg.; 1.5" below south). 1-2 Snow west; cold. 3-5 Cold. 6-7 Clearing, warm. 8-9 Rain, snow northwest; cold. 10-12 Clearing then showers, milder. 13-15 Freezing rain, snow north. 16-18 Clear, cold. 19-21 Rain & snow, seasonable. 22-25 Cold. 26-28 Mild, snow west. 29-31 Cold, flurries north.

JAN. 1994: Temp. 39.5° (4° above avg.); Precip. 1.5" (1" below avg.; 2" below south). 1-3 Cold, light snow. 4-6 Sunny, cold. 7-10 Showers then clearing; mild. 11-12 Rain turning to snow. 13-15 Milder, showers. 16-17 Clearing, cold. 18-19 Rain, mild. 20-21 Cold. 22-26 Clear, warm. 27-29 Sleet & snow. 30-31 Cold.

FEB. 1994: Temp. 36° (1.5° below avg.; avg. south); Precip. 3" (0.5" above avg.; 1" below south). 1-2 Sprinkles, mild. 3-5 Cold, snow. 6-7 Sunny, mild. 8-10 Cold. 11-12 Rain, snow west. 13-14 Cold, flurries. 15-19 Sunny, warm. 20-22 Freezing rain, snow west. 23-25 Rain & snow. 26-28 Clearing, cold.

MAR. 1994: Temp. 45.5° (1.5° below avg.); Precip. 2.5" (0.5" below avg.). 1-3 Sunny, warm; showers. 4-7 Rain. 8-12 Rain, mild. 13-15 Cold, clear. 16-18 Rain, snow west; cold. 19-21 Sunny, cold. 22-24 Rain, snow west. 25-26 Clearing, cold. 27-28 Warm. 29-31 Cold, showers.

APR. 1994: Temp. 54.5° (2° below avg.); Precip. 3" (0.5" above avg.; 0.5" below south). 1-3 Rain, heavy west; mild. 4-5 Clearing, mild. 6-7 Rain, colder. 8-10 Cold. 11-12 Clearing, milder. 13-17 Showers, mild. 18-19 Sunny,

mild. 20-22 Cold, light rain. 23-27 Few showers, cool. 28-30 Warm; showers.

MAY 1994: Temp. 65.5° (1° below avg.); Precip. 3" (0.5" below avg.; 1.5" below south). 1-2 Sprinkles, cool. 3-4 Rain, warm. 5-7 Sunny. 8-10 Cold, rain. 11-14 Sunny. 15-17 Thunderstorms, cool. 18-21 Clear, warm. 22-25 Showers, cool then warming. 26-28 Rain, cool. 29-30 Sunny, warm. 31 Rain, mild.

JUNE 1994: Temp. 72.5° (3° below avg.; 1° below south); Precip. 5" (1.5" above avg.). 1-2 Showers, cool. 3-7 Sunny, hot. 8-9 Rain, cool. 10-11 Seasonable, showers. 12-14 Thundershowers, cool. 15-16 Sunny, mild. 17-18 Rain, cool. 19-24 Sunny, cool; showers. 25-27 Showers, seasonable. 28-30 Sunny, warm; showers east.

JULY 1994: Temp. 79° (1° below avg.; 0.5° above south). Precip. 3" (1" below avg.). 1-5 Rain, warm. 6-7 Clear, warm. 8-9 Showers, cooler. 10-14 Clear, hot. 15-17 Few showers, milder. 18-19 Rain, warm. 20-24 Showers, cool. 25-27 Clear & hot. 28-29 Heavy rain, warm. 30-31 Sunny, hot.

AUG. 1994: Temp. 77.5° (1° below avg.); Precip. 4.5" (0.5" above avg.; avg. south). 1-3 Thunderstorms, milder. 4-6 Sunny & warm. 7-11 Some rain, cooler. 12-13 Clear & hot. 14-17 Showers, heavy east; warm. 18-21 Sunny, few showers. 22-26 Clear, then showers, warmer. 27-29 Clear, mild. 30-31 Thundershowers.

SEPT. 1994: Temp. 72.5° (1° above avg.); Precip. 3" (0.5" below avg.). 1-2 Thundershowers, cool. 3-5 Clear & hot. 6-7 Rain, milder. 8-9 Sunny, warm. 10-11 Showers; cooler. 12-15 Clear, mild. 16-17 Sunny & hot. 18-20 Rain, milder. 21-26 Clearing, warm. 27-30 Few showers, mild.

OCT. 1994: Temp. 63° (3° above avg.); Precip. 1.5" (1.5" below avg.). 1-2 Mild. 3-5 Cold, clear. 6-9 Sunny, warm. 10-12 Rain, cool. 13-15 Cold; showers. 16-21 Sunny, warm. 22-25 Clouds, cooler. 26-29 Rain; warmer. 30-31 Clear.

Flooding the Market with Quality and Service

The Flood Company is a family-owned firm that prides itself on the quality of its wood finishing products, including Seasonite®, a stabilizing treatment for pressure-treated wood; Dekswood®, a cleaner and brightener; and CWF-UV®, an ultraviolet-resistant clear wood finish.

Flood also prides itself in its accessibility to its customers. When customers call the toll-free number, 1-800-321-3444, they can talk to anyone in the company, including the president, Peter Flood.

First-time visitors to Flood's facilities, headquartered in Hudson, Ohio, are surprised at the barn-red buildings dotting a landscape of woods, ponds, and sprawling lawns.

The company has outgrown its original facilities, which were once a 300-acre farm complete with chicken coop, icehouse and grain-storage facility. Barns and other farm buildings were used for storage and shipping, and the century-old farmhouse served as home for Flood marketing, sales, and technical-service activities.

The company now occupies a striking, new 20,000-square-foot headquarters building whose architecture is in keeping with the Hudson area's rich Western Reserve heritage. Despite accelerated growth, Flood employees haven't lost sight of their major objectives — produce quality products and be genuinely helpful to their customers.

PIEDMONT & SOUTHEAST COAST

For regional boundaries, see map page 115.

SUMMARY: *November through March is expected to be slightly cooler and much drier than normal overall. November will see a heat wave at the beginning and severe cold at the end, with fluctuating temperatures and light showers in between. December will be mostly cold, despite warm spells near the beginning and end. Major rainfall will end the month. January will be mostly warm and dry but with several cold, wet spells. February and March will see large departures from normal temperatures, with warm, dry spells overshadowing cold, wet ones.*

April through June will be cooler and wetter than normal in the north, but near normal south. April will be colder than normal over the region, with above-normal rainfall in northern sections. May will be sunny and dry, with drought conditions developing in some sections on through early June before heavy rains arrive near midmonth.

July through September will be warmer than normal, particularly late in July and in the middle third of August, with frequent rainfall, especially in southern sections. The first half of September will be warm and dry; heavy rains will mark the second half.

Early fall is expected to be warm and dry through most of October. Watch for coastal rains late in the month due to a possible offshore tropical storm.

NOV. 1993: Temp. 52° (0.5° above avg.; 1° below south); Precip. 1.5" (1.5" below avg.). 1-5 Hot, sunny. 6-8 Heavy rain, cooler. 9-10 Clear, cold. 11-13 Sunny, warmer. 14-15 Light rain, cold. 16-18 Clear; cold nights, frost. 19-27 Showers alternating with cold snaps. 28-30 Snow then severe cold.

DEC. 1993: Temp. 38.5° (4° below avg.); Precip. 2" (1.5" below avg.). 1-4 Clear, cold. 5-6 Warming, sunny. 7-8 Heavy rain, cold. 9-12 Sunny then rain. 13-18 Cold, snow. 19-21 Sunny, cool. 22-26 Cold, flurries. 27-31 Clear & mild.

JAN. 1994: Temp. 41° (2° above avg.); Precip. 1.5" (2" below avg.). 1-3 Cold; snowstorm. 4-6 Clearing, cool. 7-8 Showers, mild. 9-11 Clear, mild; then showers. 12-14 Cold. 15-19 Showers, freezing rain. 20-21 Cold snap. 22-25 Sunny, mild; showers. 26-29 Cold, freezing rain. 30-31 Sunny, mild.

FEB. 1994: Temp. 43° (0.5° above avg.); Precip. 1.5" (2" below avg.). 1-2 Clear, mild. 3-5 Rain then snow. 6-9 Sunny, mild then cold. 10-11 Rain. 12-14 Cold, flurries. 15-19 Clear, warm. 20-21 Cold; rain, snow west. 22-23 Sunny, warm. 24-25 Rain, cool. 26-28 Clear.

MAR. 1994: Temp. 52° (1° above avg.); Precip. 3.5" (1" below avg.; 2" below south). 1-2 Sunny, warm. 3-7 Sprinkles; warm. 8-11 Rain, cool. 12-14 Clear & warm. 15-18 Cold; rain, snow west. 19-22 Clearing, cool. 23-24 Rain, cold. 25-27 Sunny, mild. 28-31 Showers, cold nights.

APR. 1994: Temp. 57.5° (2° below avg.); Precip. 4.5" (2" above avg.; 1" below east). 1-3 Heavy rain. 4-5 Clear, cold nights. 6-7 Rain, colder. 8-10 Clear, warming. 11-15 Rain then clearing, mild. 16-20 Some sun, showers. 21-23 Cold snap. 24-27 Showers, mild. 28-30 Clear, warm.

MAY 1994: Temp. 68° (0.5° above avg.); Precip. 1.5" (2" below avg.). 1-3 Showers, cool; sunny south. 4-8 Rain, hot; dry south. 9-11 Cold, showers. 12-14 Clearing, turning warm. 15-16 Showers, mild. 17-22 Sunny. 23-26 Showers then sunny. 27-29 Cool, intermittent showers. 30-31 Turning warm.

JUNE 1994: Temp. 75° (0.5° below avg.; 2° above south); Precip. 4.5" (1" above avg.). 1-2 Showers, cool. 3-7 Hot, clear. 8-11 Showers, warm. 12-14 Rain. 15-16 Sunny, warm. 17-18 Rain, heavy south. 19-20 Clear. 21-22 Heavy rain, cool. 23-25 Warming, showers. 26-30 Hot; rain south.

JULY 1994: Temp. 80° (1° above avg.); Precip. 2" (2" below avg.; 1" above south). 1-4 Rain, warm. 5-8 Showers. 9-13 Clear, warm. 14-17 Sunny, hot. 18-21 Thundershowers, mild. 22-27 Showers, sunny, hot. 28-31 Showers, hot.

AUG. 1994: Temp. 80° (2° above avg.); Precip. 3" (0.5" below avg.; 0.5" above south). 1-3 Thundershowers, cool. 4-7 Hot, intermittent showers. 8-10 Clear. 11-14 Hot; showers south. 15-17 Showers, hot & clear south. 18-21 Few showers. 22-25 Clear, hot. 26-28 Showers, warm. 29-31 Clear, warm.

SEPT. 1994: Temp. 74° (1.5° above avg.; 3° above south); Precip. 4" (0.5" above avg.). 1-2 Showers; clear & hot south. 3-7 Sunny, hot; few showers. 8-10 Rain. 11-14 Warm; cool nights. 15-17 Showers, warm. 18-21 Rain, cool. 22-25 Clearing & pleasant. 26-30 Rain, warm.

OCT. 1994: Temp. 65° (4° above avg.); Precip. 1" (2" below avg.). 1-2 Showers, warm. 3-6 Clear, cool. 7-11 Sunny, warm. 12-17 Cold, clear. 18-23 Sunny, warm. 24-27 Offshore tropical storm, heavy rain coast. 28-31 Clear, mild.

FLORIDA

For regional boundaries, see map page 115.

SUMMARY: *November through March is expected to be colder than normal, particularly in central and southern sections, and considerably drier than normal. November will be warm and dry except for chilly weather the second week and a late-month cold wave with possible hard frost. December will be particularly cold at midmonth. Rainfall will be above normal only in central sections. January through mid-February will see extremely variable temperatures with frequent cold waves and frost dominating warm spells. It will be dry overall except during early February. Mid-February to mid-March will be warm before cold returns.*

April through June will be colder than normal in central and southern sections and milder in the north. Cool spells will be partially balanced by warm periods in early and late May and through mid-June. Rainfall may be well below normal in May and June.

July through September will see slightly above normal temperatures in most areas. It will be wet in central and southern sections in July, throughout the region in early August, and over central and southern sections after mid-September.

Early fall should be warmer than normal, with several mild spells. Rainfall will be well above normal in southern sections in October due to a possible tropical storm early in the month and in northern coastal sections due to an offshore storm at the end of October.

NOV. 1993: Temp. 67° (1° below avg.; 2° below south); Precip. 0.5" (1.5" below avg.; avg. south). 1-6 Sunny, hot; scattered showers. 7-10 Cold wave, rain. 11-15 Clear, warm, sprinkles south. 16-18 Sunny, warm; cool north. 19-26 Rain, variable temperatures. 27-30 Rain, heavy south, then severe cold.

DEC. 1993: Temp. 57° (5° below avg.); Precip. 1" (1" below avg.). 1-3 Clear; cold, hard frost north. 4-6 Sunny, warm. 7-8 Rain, cool. 9-10 Clear, mild. 11-12 Rain, cooler. 13-15 Cold. 16-20 Sunny, warm; scattered showers. 21-22 Rain, cold. 23-25 Cold; frost north. 26-30 Clear, warm. 31 Scattered showers.

JAN. 1994: Temp. 59° (1° below avg.; 2° above north); Precip. 1" (1.5" below avg.). 1-4 Rain, cool. 5-10 Clearing, warm. 11-13 Cold, frost north; showers. 14-18 Sunny, warm. 19-21 Cold, showers. 22-27 Clear, warm. 28-29 Rain, cool. 30-31 Severe cold, frost north; clearing.

FEB. 1994: Temp. 60° (1.5° above avg.); Precip. 1" (2" below north; avg. south). 1-4 Clear, warm. 5-7 Rain, cold. 8-9 Cold, frost. 10-11 Mild; rain. 12-16 Cloudy, cold. 17-24 Sunny, warm; sprinkles south. 25-26 Showers, cooler. 27-28 Sunny; cold nights.

MAR. 1994: Temp. 66° (1° below avg.; 2° above north); Precip. 1" (2" below avg.). 1-3 Clear, warming. 4-8 Sunny, hot. 9-11 Sunny, warm; mild north. 12-14 Clouds, mild. 15-17 Rain. 18-21 Cold, clear. 22-25 Warming, then cold; rain north. 26-28 Sunny, mild. 29-31 Clear, mild.

APR. 1994: Temp. 69° (2° below avg.); Precip. 5" (3" above avg.; 1" below north). 1-3 Warm, then rain, cool. 4-5 Sunny, warm. 6-7 Showers. 8-9 Clear, cold nights. 10-15 Rain south, mild then cool. 16-17 Cold. 18-21 Sunny, warm. 22-24 Rain, mild. 25-30 Few showers, warm.

MAY 1994: Temp. 76° (1° below avg.; 0.5° above north); Precip. 1.5" (2" below avg.). 1-3 Light showers. 4-7 Clearing, warming. 8-9 Showers, warm. 10-12 Clear, cold nights. 13-16 Showers, mild. 17-22 Light showers, cool. 23-26 Warm, few scattered showers. 27-28 Sunny, warm; rain north. 29-31 Heavy rain.

JUNE 1994: Temp. 80° (1° below avg.; 1° above north); Precip. 4" (3" below avg.). 1-4 Sunny, hot. 5-7 Cooler, showers south. 8-11 Showers, warm. 12-13 Clear, warm. 14-16 Warm, heavy rain central. 17-18 Sunny, warm. 19-25 Thunderstorms, hot. 26-30 Sunny, hot, showers.

JULY 1994: Temp. 82° (0.5° below avg.; 1° above north); Precip. 8" (2" above avg.; 5" above central). 1-6 Sunny south, rain north. 7-8 Clear, hot. 9-14 Heavy thundershowers, light north; mild. 15-19 Clear, hot, showers south. 20-28 Thunderstorms, hot. 29-31 Sunny, hot.

AUG. 1994: Temp. 83.5° (1° above avg.); Precip. 5" (3" below avg.; 1" above central). 1-4 Showers, warm. 5-9 Thundershowers. 10-14 Sunny, hot, few showers. 15-19 Showers; sunny & hot north. 20-24 Thundershowers north, cloudy south. 25-28 Showers, hot. 29-31 Mild.

SEPT. 1994: Temp. 82° (1° above avg.; 3° above north); Precip. 8" (2" above avg.; 4" below south). 1-5 Hot then mild, showers south. 6-9 Showers; hot. 10-16 Showers south, sunny north. 17-23 Thunderstorms central & north. 24-26 Few showers, warm. 27-30 Sunny, warm.

OCT. 1994: Temp. 76° (1° above avg.; 3° above north); Precip. 4.5" (2" above avg.; 1" below south). 1-6 Rain; tropical storm south; mild. 7-12 Clear, warm. 13-15 Cold wave, showers south. 16-21 Showers, warm. 22-23 Clear, mild. 24-27 Heavy rain east from offshore hurricane; mild. 28-31 Few showers, warm.

6 UPSTATE NEW YORK

For regional boundaries, see map page 115.

SUMMARY: *November through March is expected to be warmer than normal overall with above-normal precipitation, particularly in eastern sections. Snowfall will be above normal during December but below thereafter. November should see several cold spells alternate with brief mild ones. Expect cold and snow at the end of the month. Except for a brief mild spell the second week, December will be cold with frequent snows, particularly in central and Great Lakes sections. January will be very mild, with frequent but light precipitation. February will see cold spells overshadowing mild ones, while March may see a cold latter half with increased snowfall.*

April through June will be cooler than normal, with cold spells in early and late April, and cool periods in mid-May and mid-June. Precipitation during these periods will be close to normal in eastern sections and above normal in the west, particularly in April.

July through September is expected to have close to normal temperatures due to alternating cool and warm spells throughout the period. A dry August in the west may well overshadow a fairly wet July over the region; the east will be wet in both August and September.

Early fall will be warmer than normal. Cold waves at the beginning and the middle of October may bring above-normal precipitation to eastern sections.

NOV. 1993: Temp. 44° (4° above avg.); Precip. 2.5" (0.5" below avg.; 1" above west). 1-2 Rain, mild. 3-6 Clear, warm. 7-9 Rain, cold. 10-12 Sunny, mild. 13-16 Rain & snow, colder. 17-19 Clearing, cold. 20-21 Rain, mild. 22-23 Clear, cold nights. 24-26 Snow. 27-28 Clear, cold. 29-30 Severe storm; snow mountains.

DEC. 1993: Temp. 27° (Avg.; 1° below west); Precip. 4" (1" above avg.). 1-5 Light snow, cold. 6-8 Rain, mild. 9-10 Clear, cool. 11-14 Freezing rain, then clearing, cold. 15-16 Light snow. 17-18 Sunny, mild. 19-21 Snow. 22-25 Clear, cold east. 26-28 Flurries, cold. 29-31 Cold wave.

JAN. 1994: Temp. 27° (6° above avg.); Precip. 2" (Avg.). 1-4 Snow. 5-6 Clear, cold. 7-8 Rain, snow mountains; mild. 9-10 Sunny, seasonable. 11-14 Snow, then clearing & cold. 15-16 Light snow, milder. 17-20 Clear & cold then snow. 21-22 Sunny, mild. 23-26 Rain, mild. 27-28 Cold. 29-31 Freezing rain, snow north.

FEB. 1994: Temp. 23.5° (Avg.); Precip. 3.5" (1.5" above avg.). 1-3 Light snow, cold. 4-6 Snowstorm. 7-10 Clear, cold. 11-12 Rain, snow west & north. 13-15 Cold. 16-18 Showers, milder. 19-20 Cold. 21-23 Sleet, mild. 24-26 Freezing rain, snow mountains. 27-28 Clear, cold.

MAR. 1994: Temp. 33.5° (0.5° below avg.); Precip. 3" (Avg.; 1" above west). 1-3 Rain, snow mountains; mild. 4-8 Snowstorm. 9-10 Sunny, mild. 11-13 Cold, flurries. 14-17 Clearing, mild. 18-22 Freezing rain & snow, then clearing. 23-26 Heavy snow, colder. 27-28 Freezing light rain. 29-31 Cold.

APR. 1994: Temp. 46.5° (Avg.; 1° below west); Precip. 4" (1" above avg.). 1-4 Storm, heavy rain; mild. 5-7 Freezing rain, snow mountains. 8-9 Cold; light snow. 10-14 Sunny, mild. 15-17 Rain, heavy west, seasonable. 18-23 Snow mountains; colder. 24-25 Sunny, cool. 26-30 Rain, snow mountains; very cold.

MAY 1994: Temp. 58° (0.5° above avg.); Precip. 2.5" (0.5" below avg.). 1-3 Rain, mild. 4-6 Sunny, warm. 7-10 Cold, clear. 11-13 Rain, mild east. 14-16 Heavy rain, cold. 17-20 Clearing, warm. 21-22 Sprinkles, cool. 23-24 Sunny, warm. 25-27 Rain, cooling. 28-30 Clearing, warm. 31 Rain, heavy east; mild.

JUNE 1994: Temp. 66° (1° below avg.; avg. west); Precip. 3" (0.5" below avg.). 1-3 Rain. 4-5 Clear, warm. 6-8 Sprinkles, mild. 9-12 Clear, cold nights. 13-16 Rain west, then clearing; cool. 17-19 Cold, rain. 20-25 Sunny, warm. 26-28 Rain, seasonable. 29-30 Sunny.

JULY 1994: Temp. 71° (1° below avg.); Precip. 5" (2" above avg.). 1-2 Showers, warm. 3-5 Rain, cool. 6-7 Sunny, warm. 8-9 Rain, heavy east. 10-14 Clear, warm. 15-16 Storm, cool. 17-20 Sunny, hot. 21-23 Storm, cool. 24-26 Clear then rain. 27-30 Sunny, hot. 31 Rain.

AUG. 1994: Temp. 68.5° (1° below avg.); Precip. 4.5" (1" above avg.; 3" below west). 1-2 Rain, cool. 3-5 Showers, warm. 6-8 Showers, cool. 9-12 Clear, cool; then light rain. 13-18 Sunny, warm; few showers. 19-21 Heavy rain; cool. 22-23 Clear. 24-26 Showers, cooling. 27-29 Sunny, warming. 30-31 Clear, warm.

SEPT. 1994: Temp. 63.5° (2.5° above avg.); Precip. 5" (2" above avg.; 0.5" below west). 1-3 Sunny, heat wave. 4-7 Rain, cooler. 8-9 Clearing, mild. 10-11 Rain, turning cool. 12-14 Clear. 15-16 Rain, warm. 17-19 Rainstorm. 20-25 Sunny, warm. 26-28 Cool, showers; then clearing. 29-30 Rain, turning cool.

OCT. 1994: Temp. 52° (2° above avg.; 4° above west); Precip. 4" (1" above avg.; 1" below west). 1-2 Rain, cool. 3-5 Cold, clear. 6-9 Rain, then clear and warm. 10-16 Rain, snow mountains; cold. 17-22 Sunny, warm, Indian summer-like. 23-25 Cold, clear. 26-27 Clear, warm. 28-29 Rain, cool. 30-31 Clear, cold nights.

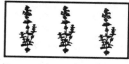

SUMMARY: *November through March is expected to be cooler than normal in the west, with near-normal precipitation, and milder than normal in the east with above-normal precipitation and snowfall. Despite some mild spells, November will turn cold and wintry, with cold and snow at midmonth and severe cold and a snowstorm at the close. December will be colder than normal, with above-normal precipitation and snowfall in the east and below normal west. January may be mild, with thaws early and midmonth. February and March will be progressively colder, particularly in the west, especially the first half of February and the latter half of March.*

April through June will be colder than normal west, but near normal east. Above-normal precipitation is expected in the east, while southern sections may be dry. April will be cool and wet east and north, cool and dry south. May through early June may see warm spells overshadowing cold waves; the cold spells will bring heavy rains in mid- and late May and the beginning of June. Mid- and late June will be wet in the east and north with frequent thunderstorms.

July through September will be cooler than normal in the west, but above normal east. Rainfall will be above normal in the north, near normal east, and below normal south. July will start out cooler and wetter than normal. August may be dry, with above-normal temperatures east. September will be warm east and south, with below-normal precipitation.

October is expected to be warmer than normal, with near-normal rainfall in northern sections but below-normal rainfall in other areas.

NOV. 1993: Temp. 46° (1° above avg.; 1° below west); Precip. 5.5" (2" above avg.; 3" above east). 1-2 Sprinkles, mild. 3-5 Sunny, warm. 6-8 Cold, rain. 9-11 Sunny. 12-14 Cold, rain turning to snow. 15-19 Clear & warm. 20-22 Rain then clearing. 23-24 Rain, mild. 25-27 Seasonable. 28-30 Severe cold, snowstorm.

DEC. 1993: Temp. 30° (4° below avg.); Precip. 2.5" (0.5" below avg.; 0.5" above east). 1-3 Snow, cold. 4-5 Sunny, warming. 6-9 Rain, snow; then clear & cold. 10-11 Snowstorm. 12-14 Flurries, very cold. 15-19 Cold, flurries. 20-22 Sunny, severe cold. 23-26 Warming, flurries. 27-28 Sunny, mild. 29-31 Cold, light snow.

JAN. 1994: Temp. 35° (6° above avg.); Precip. 4" (1.5" above avg.). 1-5 Clear, warming. 6-7 Rain, mild. 8-9 Clearing, seasonable. 10-11 Cold, snow. 12-15 Milder then sprinkles. 16-17 Sunny & mild. 18-19 Heavy rain. 20-24 Thaw. 25-26 Cold, flurries. 27-31 Snow then seasonable.

FEB. 1994: Temp. 32° (1° above avg.); Precip. 4" (1.5" above avg.). 1-2 Cold, snow. 3-5 Cold, snowstorm. 6-9 Seasonable. 10-12 Rain then snow. 13-15 Cold. 16-20 Rain then snow. 21-24 Rain, mild. 25-26 Cold. 27-28 Sunny, mild.

MAR. 1994: Temp. 42° (2° below avg.); Precip. 3.5" (0.5" below avg.; avg. east). 1-2 Clear, mild. 3-6 Cool, rain. 7-8 Rain, mild. 9-10 Sunny, warm. 11-12 Rain, cold. 13-15 Cold. 16-19 Snow, freezing rain south. 20-21 Cold. 22-23 Snowstorm. 24-26 Cold, flurries. 27-29 Mild then cold. 30-31 Seasonable.

APR. 1994: Temp. 50° (4° below avg.); Precip. 3" (0.5" below avg.; 1" above east.). 1-3 Rain, cool. 4-8 Cold; rain & snow. 9-10 Sunny, seasonable. 11-14 Rain, colder. 15-18 Freezing rain & snow. 19-21 Cold, flurries. 22-24

Milder, sprinkles. 25-26 Rain, cool. 27-28 Clear, cold. 29-30 Warm, showers.

MAY 1994: Temp. 67° (3° above avg.); Precip. 3" (1.5" below avg.; 0.5" below east). 1-3 Clear then rain. 4-6 Sunny, hot. 7-10 Rain, cold. 11-13 Clear, mild. 14-16 Cold, storm. 17-22 Clear, hot. 23-25 Cooling. 26-27 Showers, cold. 28-29 Sunny, warm. 30-31 Cold, rain.

JUNE 1994: Temp. 71° (1° below avg.; 1° above east); Precip. 2.5" (1" below avg.; 2" above east). 1-6 Clearing, hot. 7-8 Rain, cooler. 9-11 Sunny, cool. 12-15 Rain, heavy east, then clearing. 16-18 Rain, mild. 19-23 Clear, warm. 24-30 Intermittent thunderstorms.

JULY 1994: Temp. 75.5° (0.5° below avg.; 1° above east); Precip. 4" (Avg.; 2" above east). 1-4 Thundershowers, cool. 5-7 Clearing, warm. 8-9 Cold, showers. 10-13 Sunny, warm. 14-16 Heavy showers, cool. 17-21 Clear, hot. 22-25 Showers, cool. 26-28 Rain, cool. 29-31 Clear & hot.

AUG. 1994: Temp. 75.5° (0.5° above avg.); Precip. 1.5" (2" below avg.). 1-7 Sunny & hot; few showers & cooler. 8-11 Cold, clear then showers. 12-18 Clear & hot. 19-20 Showers, warm. 21-23 Sunny, warm. 24-25 Showers, mild. 26-29 Clear, cool. 30-31 Rain, mild.

SEPT. 1994: Temp. 70° (1.5° above avg.); Precip. 2.5" (0.5" below avg.). 1-5 Few showers, hot. 6-8 Cool. 9-13 Showers then clear, cool. 14-16 Showers then sunny, warm. 17-18 Rain, cooler. 19-25 Clear, warm. 26-29 Showers, cool. 30 Clear, warm.

OCT. 1994: Temp. 60° (3.5° above avg.); Precip. 2" (0.5" below avg.). 1-4 Cold, showers. 5-9 Sunny, warm. 10-12 Rain, cold. 13-15 Clear, cool. 16-22 Clear, cool nights. 23-25 Cold, sunny. 26-28 Rain, mild. 29-31 Clear, cool.

GET IN ON THE PROFITS OF SMALL ENGINE SERVICE AND REPAIR
START YOUR OWN MONEY MAKING BUSINESS & BEAT INFLATION!

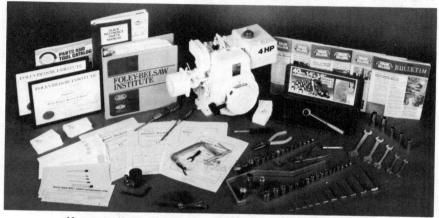

You get all this Professional equipment with your course, PLUS 4 H.P. Engine... ALL YOURS TO KEEP... All at NO EXTRA COST.

Work part time, full time right at home. In just a short time, you can be ready to join one of the fastest growing industries in America... an industry where qualified men are making from **$25.00 to $30.00 per hour.** Because the small engine industry has grown so quickly, an acute shortage of qualified Small Engine Professionals exists throughout the country. When you see how many small engines are in use today, it's easy to understand why qualified men command such high prices — as much as $49.95 for a simple tune-up that takes less than an hour.

65-million small engines are in service today!
That's right — there are over sixty-five million 2-cycle and 4-cycle small engines in service across the U.S.A.! With fully accredited and approved Foley-Belsaw training, you can soon have the skill and knowledge to make top money servicing these engines. Homeowners and businessmen will seek you out and pay you well to service and repair their lawn mowers, tillers, edgers, pow-

er rakes, garden tractors, chain saws, mini-bikes, go-carts, snowmobiles... the list is almost endless.

No experience necessary.
We guide you every step of the way, including tested and proven instructions on how to get business, what to charge, how to get free advertising, where to get supplies wholesale... all the 'tricks of the trade'... all the inside facts you need to assure success right from the start.

Send today for FREE facts!
You risk nothing by accepting this offer to find out how Foley-Belsaw training can give you the skills you need to increase your income in a high-profit, recession-proof business of your own.
Just fill in and mail coupon below (or send postcard) to receive full information and details by return mail. DO IT TODAY!

FOLEY-BELSAW INSTITUTE
6301 Equitable Rd., Dept. 52263
Kansas City, Mo. 64120

NO OBLIGATION... NO SALESMAN WILL CALL

RUSH COUPON TODAY FOR THIS FACT-FILLED
FREE BOOKLET!

Tells how you quickly train to be your own boss in a profitable Spare time or Full time business of your own PLUS complete details on our 30 DAY NO RISK Trial Offer!

DEEP SOUTH

For regional boundaries, see map page 115.

SUMMARY: *November through March is expected to be cooler and wetter than normal in the north, particularly the northeast, but warmer and drier in the south. November through early December will see warm spells alternating with cold waves bringing freezing rain and snow. The middle half of December will be cold and dry except for heavy rains in the southeast. The year will end on a warm and sunny note. January's weather will be predominantly warm and wet. Watch for flooding at the beginning and at midmonth. A cold wave in early February and a cold period after mid-March may be partially offset by warm and dry spells.*

April through June is anticipated to be cold and dry, although eastern and southern sections may receive ample rainfall. April will see frequent cool spells with heavy rains south and east, while May should be fairly warm; May will be dry to the point of drought in western and central portions. June will be cool and wet at midmonth; warm and dry at beginning and end.

July through September will be wet in the north, with near-normal temperatures, but warm and dry in the south. Watch for possible flooding in the northwest in July. August and early September will continue to be hot and dry in the south, with possible drought. The north will have close to normal rainfall, with warm temperatures the latter half of August and first half of September. Early fall will be mostly warm, with little rainfall in the south.

NOV. 1993: Temp. 55° (1° below avg.); Precip. 4" (1" below avg.; 0.5" above north). 1-5 Clear, very warm. 6-8 Cold wave; rain, snow north. 9-11 Sunny, warm. 12-14 Cold; rain, light south. 15-18 Clearing, warm. 19-26 Showers; warm to seasonable. 27-28 Very cold, heavy snow, sleet. 29-30 Clearing.

DEC. 1993: Temp. 46° (2° below avg.; 4° below north); Precip. 4" (2" below avg.). 1-5 Warming, showers east. 6-8 Cold; rain, heavy southeast. 9-11 Cold; freezing rain & snow. 12-16 Cold, clearing; showers northeast. 17-19 Showers, cold. 20-24 Cold. 25-29 Clear, warm. 30-31 Cold.

JAN. 1994: Temp. 49° (5° above avg.); Precip. 4.5" (0.5" below avg.; 2" above north). 1-3 Cold; freezing rain, snow north. 4-5 Milder. 6-8 Rain, warm. 9-10 Sunny, warm. 11-13 Cold; rain, snow north. 14-19 Rain, heavy north; warming. 20-22 Seasonable. 23-25 Warm, showers. 26-31 Cold, few showers.

FEB. 1994: Temp. 47° (1° below avg.; 3° below north); Precip. 7" (2.5" above avg.; 0.5" above north). 1-5 Warm then cold, rain turning to snow & sleet. 6-10 Sunny, warming. 11-13 Cold; rain south, snow north. 14-17 Sunny, warm. 18-20 Cold, rain. 21-22 Sunny, warming. 23-25 Warm, heavy rain, flooding. 26-28 Clear, mild.

MAR. 1994: Temp. 59° (2° above avg.; avg. north); Precip. 4" (2" below avg.). 1-4 Warm; rain north, showers south. 5-6 Clear & warm. 7-9 Milder; rain. 10-14 Sunny, warm; showers. 15-18 Cold; rain, snow north. 19-20 Clearing, milder. 21-23 Rain, cold. 24-27 Sunny, warm. 28-31 Clear, showers then heavy rain.

APR. 1994: Temp. 60.5° (4° below avg.); Precip. 7.5" (2" above avg.; 1" below north). 1-3 Rain, heavy east; cooler. 4-5 Sunny, seasonable. 6-9 Cold, rain then clearing. 10-13 Showers, warm then cooling. 14-16 Rain, cool. 17-19 Clearing,

warm. 20-22 Cool, showers south. 23-26 Warm, rain. 27-29 Clear, cool. 30 Warm, showers.

MAY 1994: Temp. 73° (1° above avg.; 1° below north); Precip. 2" (3" below avg.). 1-8 Sunny, hot, showers north. 9-11 Cold, few showers. 12-13 Sunny, seasonable. 14-16 Cold; showers. 17-25 Clear & hot. 26-27 Rain north, light south; cool. 28-31 Sunny, warming; showers north.

JUNE 1994: Temp. 80° (1° above avg.; 2° below north); Precip. 2" (1" below avg.). 1-6 Clear & hot, showers south. 7-10 Showers then clearing. 11-13 Thundershowers, warm. 14-18 Seasonable, showers. 19-21 Cooler, rain. 22-26 Showers, warm. 27-30 Hot; sunny then showers.

JULY 1994: Temp. 83° (1.5° above avg.; 1° below north); Precip. 3.5" (1" below avg.; 1" above north). 1-2 Clear & hot. 3-5 Cold, heavy rain. 6-8 Warm; heavy rain north, floods. 9-16 Sunny, hot; showers south. 17-19 Seasonable, showers. 20-25 Sunny, hot; few showers. 26-31 Clear, hot; few showers.

AUG. 1994: Temp. 84° (3° above avg.; avg. north); Precip. 3" (0.5" below avg.). 1-2 Showers, heavy south; seasonable. 3-11 Hot; few showers. 12-15 Showers, heavy north; milder. 16-19 Clear, hot. 20-22 Showers, hot. 23-24 Sunny, hot. 25-26 Thundershowers, seasonable. 27-31 Clear, turning hot.

SEPT. 1994: Temp. 79° (3° above avg.; 1° above north); Precip. 3.5" (Avg.). 1-5 Sunny, hot; showers east. 6-10 Cooling, showers. 11-13 Clear, cool nights. 14-18 Rain, turning cool. 19-24 Seasonable days, cool nights; showers west. 25-30 Few showers, seasonable.

OCT. 1994: Temp. 67° (2.5° above avg.); Precip. 1" (2" below avg.). 1-4 Cold wave, clear. 5-6 Warming; heavy rain northwest. 7-9 Clear, hot. 10-15 Cold, rain north then clearing. 16-21 Sunny, warm; few showers north. 22-26 Cold then clear & warm. 27-31 Rain.

CHICAGO & SOUTHERN GREAT LAKES

For regional boundaries, see map page 115.

SUMMARY: *November through March is expected to be slightly colder than normal with below-normal precipitation in the west but above in the east. Snowfall should be well above normal over the region. Aside from warm spells at the beginning and middle of November and one in early December, an early winter is anticipated with a cold wave and snow in mid-November, a severe snowstorm at the end of the month, frequent snows and cold in December, and a cold wave to start the New Year. Except for a brief cold snap before midmonth, January may be mostly mild. A cold and snowy period will settle in for the first half of February, followed by a mild period through mid-March before closing the season on a cold and snowy note.*

April through June may be several degrees cooler than average; precipitation and snowfall will be slightly below normal in the south and slightly above in the north. April will be cold and snowy, particularly in the north, followed by a generally warm May that may be wet in the west and cause floods in the Mississippi River valley. Aside from a warm spell in early June, most of the month will be cooler and drier than normal.

July through September is anticipated to be cooler than normal, with below-normal rainfall except for the northwest. Few heat waves are expected. Temperatures will fluctuate about the normal through July, and August will be generally cool. Watch for frequent thundershowers in July through mid-August, followed by fairly dry weather. Cold waves in September in the west will bring heavy rains. October weather will be variable, averaging out to a warm and wet month.

NOV. 1993: Temp. 40° (1.5° below avg.; 1° above east); Precip. 2" (1" below avg.; 1" above east). 1-5 Sunny, warm. 6-8 Cold, freezing rain. 9-11 Sunny, mild. 12-14 Snowstorm, cold. 15-18 Sunny, warming. 19-22 Rain; clearing. 23-27 Freezing rain, cold. 28-30 Snowstorm.

DEC. 1993: Temp. 23° (5° below avg.; 3° below east); Precip. 2.5" (Avg.). 1-4 Cold; flurries east. 5-8 Rain; clearing. 9-12 Snowstorm, cold. 13-14 Clear, cold. 15-19 Light snow, cold. 20-22 Clear, cold. 23-26 Warming, flurries. 27-28 Sunny & mild. 29-31 Cold, snow north.

JAN. 1994: Temp. 26° (4° above avg.); Precip. 1.5" (Avg.). 1-5 Cold then seasonable, clear. 6-9 Snowstorm, mild. 10-12 Cold snap; flurries. 13-15 Clear & mild. 16-19 Cold; freezing rain. 20-24 January thaw, clear. 25-30 Cold then seasonable, light snow. 31 Snowstorm east.

FEB. 1994: Temp. 22° (3° below avg.); Precip. 2.5" (1" above avg.). 1-2 Cold; snow. 3-5 Cold, snowstorm. 6-7 Clear, very cold. 8-11 Warming, snow. 12-14 Cold, flurries. 15-17 Mild; rain south, snow north. 18-19 Clear & cold. 20-24 Mild; rain, snow north. 25-28 Clearing, warming.

MAR. 1994: Temp. 35° (2° below avg.); Precip. 2.5" (Avg.). 1-3 Mild; rain north. 4-7 Snowstorm, freezing rain south. 8-10 Sunny & warm. 11-12 Cool; showers. 13-15 Cold, snow south. 16-18 Snowstorm, cold. 19-23 Clear & cold, then snowstorm. 24-26 Clear, very cold. 27-28 Milder, rain & snow. 29-31 Sunny, seasonable.

APR. 1994: Temp. 44.5° (4° below avg.); Precip. 3.5" (Avg.). 1-2 Mild, rain. 3-6 Cold, snow. 7-9 Warming, clearing. 10-12 Rain, seasonable. 13-15 Rain, colder. 16-20 Cold, snow. 21-24 Sunny, cold, rain south. 25-27 Rain, colder. 28-30 Rain, seasonable.

MAY 1994: Temp. 62° (2° above avg.; 1° above east); Precip. 5" (2.5" above avg.; 1" above east). 1-4 Rain, warm; floods. 5-6 Clear & warm. 7-10 Cold, light rain. 11-13 Sunny. 14-15 Cold, severe storm. 16-19 Sunny, hot. 20-24 Clear & warm, rain north. 25-27 Cold, rain. 28-29 Clear, warm. 30-31 Rain, cold.

JUNE 1994: Temp. 67.5° (3° below avg.); Precip. 2" (2" below avg.). 1-3 Sunny, rain east; warming. 4-7 Rain, warm. 8-11 Clear & cold. 12-15 Rain then sunny. 16-17 Showers, cold. 18-21 Clear, cold then warming. 22-24 Thundershowers, warm. 25-30 Cold then mild, rain.

JULY 1994: Temp. 73° (2° below avg.); Precip. 5.5" (2" above avg.). 1-4 Rain, cool. 5-6 Clear, warm. 7-8 Thunderstorms, cool. 9-11 Clear & warm. 12-16 Rain, cool. 17-20 Clearing & warming. 21-23 Sunny, showers. 24-26 Thundershowers. 27-29 Clear & hot. 30-31 Light showers, warm.

AUG. 1994: Temp. 70.5° (3° below avg.); Precip. 4.5" (1" above avg.; 1" below east). 1-2 Mild, rain. 3-8 Few showers; warm. 9-12 Thundershowers, cool. 13-16 Sunny, warm, few showers. 17-21 Rain, cooler. 22-25 Clear then showers. 26-28 Clear, cool. 29-31 Warming, rain.

SEPT. 1994: Temp. 66° (Avg.; 2° above east); Precip. 5" (1" above avg.; avg. east). 1-4 Sunny, warm, showers. 5-8 Cold. 9-12 Showers, some sun; cool. 13-16 Warm, showers. 17-19 Cold, rain. 20-25 Clear, warm. 26-30 Rain, cool.

OCT. 1994: Temp. 56° (2° above avg.); Precip. 3" (0.5° above avg.; 2" above east). 1-3 Cold, clear. 4-9 Warm; few showers. 10-12 Rain, cold. 13-15 Clear, cold. 16-20 Sunny, warm. 21-23 Cold, showers. 24-28 Heavy rain. 29-31 Sunny, then showers.

The Old Farmer's Almanac —
America's best-loved periodical.

NORTHERN GREAT PLAINS-GREAT LAKES

For regional boundaries, see map page 115.

SUMMARY: *November through March is expected to be colder than normal, with below-normal precipitation in the west but above in the east. Snowfall will be above normal, particularly in the north. Cold and snowy periods at mid-November and at Thanksgiving will be relieved by mild spells. December will be cold and snowy, particularly in the north and east, with a brief respite at Christmas before another snowstorm ends the year. Mild spells in early and mid-January will offset cold spells early and late in the month, while frequent snows will bring totals above normal. Watch for a possible blizzard to end the month. February will be cold the first half, milder the second half; March will be cold and blustery.*

April through June will be cold, with above-normal precipitation and snowfall in the north and east, but below southwest. April will be dry and generally cold. May will be warm, wet east but dry west. June will be quite cool and wet due to frequent rains.

July through September is expected to be cooler and wetter than normal. July will be cool except for warm spells late in the month. Warm spells early and late August and near mid-September will be offset by cool periods in between. Rainfall will be above normal except in the west, with a wet July north and east, a wet August in central sections, and a wet September in the east.

Early fall may be cooler and wetter than normal in the west, but warmer and drier in the east, with above-normal snowfall over the region.

NOV. 1993: Temp. 33.5° (0.5° above avg.); Precip. 1" (0.5" below avg.). 1-3 Cold; sunny & mild west. 4-6 Showers, warm. 7-10 Clear; cold then warming. 11-13 Cold, snow. 14-16 Cold; snowstorm east. 17-23 Mild, rain. 24-26 Snow, cold. 27-30 Cold, light snow.

DEC. 1993: Temp. 14° (4° below avg.; 1° below west); Precip. 2" (1" above avg.; 0.5" below west). 1-5 Clear, snow east. 6-10 Cold, snowstorm. 11-14 Seasonable, flurries. 15-19 Cold, light snow. 20-22 Cold, clear. 23-27 Light snow, freezing rain. 28-31 Cold, snowstorm then clearing.

JAN. 1994: Temp. 13° (1° above avg.; 2° above west); Precip. 0.5" (0.5" below avg.). 1-5 Warming, flurries central & west. 6-9 Turning cold, snow. 10-12 Mild, snow east. 13-16 Mild. 17-19 Mild, light snow. 20-23 Sunny, mild. 24-28 Cold, snow then milder. 29-31 Cold, snowstorm.

FEB. 1994: Temp. 14° (4° below avg.); Precip. 0.5" (0.5" below avg.). 1-5 Cold, flurries. 6-9 Mild, snow west. 10-13 Snow, cold. 14-16 Warm; sprinkles then cold. 17-19 Clear, mild. 20-25 Sunny, mild; flurries. 26-28 Mild, showers.

MAR. 1994: Temp. 21° (10° below avg.); Precip. 4" (2" above avg.; avg. west). 1-4 Cold, snowstorm. 5-7 Heavy snowstorm, cold. 8-9 Sunny & mild. 10-12 Cold, snow. 13-17 Milder, flurries. 18-21 Clear, cold nights; snow west. 22-24 Snow then cold. 25-28 Seasonable then cold, flurries. 29-31 Clear, mild.

APR. 1994: Temp. 39° (7° below avg.); Precip. 2" (0.5" below avg.). 1-2 Sunny, seasonable. 3-5 Cold, snow. 6-9 Clearing, seasonable. 10-19 Freezing rain, snow; variable temperatures. 20-23 Sunny, cold. 24-26 Cold, snowstorm. 27-30 Sunny, warming.

MAY 1994: Temp. 61° (2.5° above avg.); Precip. 4" (0.5" above avg.; 0.5" below west). 1-2 Seasonable, showers. 3-5 Warm, rain. 6-8 Showers, warm east. 9-11 Cold. 12-17 Sunny & warm, rain southwest. 18-24 Warm, rain. 25-27 Clear. 28-30 Rain, warm. 31 Cold.

JUNE 1994: Temp. 70.5° (3° below avg.; 6° below west); Precip. 5" (1" above avg.). 1-2 Showers, seasonable. 3-7 Cold, rain. 8-12 Sunny, warm; showers west. 13-16 Showers. 17-20 Clear & warm. 21-23 Rain, mild. 24-27 Cold, rain. 28-30 Rain, cooler.

JULY 1994: Temp. 65° (3° below avg.; 5° below west); Precip. 4.5" (1" above avg.; 0.5" below southwest). 1-9 Cool; rain. 10-12 Showers, mild. 13-16 Cold, showers. 17-19 Showers east, sunny west; seasonable. 20-25 Rain, few showers west; mild. 26-29 Few showers, warm. 30-31 Sunny, warm.

AUG. 1994: Temp. 68.5° (2° below avg.); Precip. 3.5" (Avg.; 2" above west). 1-5 Sunny, seasonable then showers. 6-8 Cool, few showers. 9-14 Cool, rain. 15-20 Cold, rain west. 21-23 Warming, showers. 24-28 Cool, showers then sunny & warm. 29-31 Showers, warm.

SEPT. 1994: Temp. 58.5° (2° below avg.); Precip. 5" (3" above avg.; 1" below west). 1-3 Light rain, warm. 4-6 Cold, sprinkles. 7-11 Seasonable then showers. 12-15 Rain east, showers west; warming. 16-19 Rain east; cool. 20-23 Sunny. 24-30 Cold; snow west, rain east.

OCT. 1994: Temp. 50° (1° above avg.; 1° below west); Precip. 1" (1" below avg.; 1" above west). 1-2 Cold, few flurries. 3-5 Sunny, warm. 6-9 Rain. 10-12 Sunny, warming. 13-16 Sunny & warm. 17-19 Showers. 20-26 Cold, freezing rain & snow. 27-28 Sunny, mild. 29-31 Cold, flurries west.

SUMMARY: *November through March is expected to be cooler than normal. Precipitation will be near normal but with above-normal snowfall in the north, while southern sections may be below normal in both precipitation and snowfall, particularly in the southeast. Except for a warm spell at the beginnning of November and mild spells after mid-November and at Christmastime, cold waves and seasonable spells will alternate through the balance of the year, with below-normal precipitation. Despite a cold wave at New Year and another a week later, January will be warm, with precipitation still below normal. The first half of February and the middle third of March should be quite wintry, resulting in above-normal precipitation, particularly in March, with heavy snows in the north.*

April through June will be cool and wet, with April rarely reaching normal temperatures. April will see frequent precipitation, snow in the north and rain south. May will be warm and wet, while June will see cold waves with heavy rainfall in the second and last weeks.

July through September will be cooler than normal with variable rainfall. Cool waves in early and late July and the second half of August will dominate, while September will see alternating warm and cool spells. Showers will be fairly uniformly distributed over the period, bringing above-normal amounts in July, well above in August, but below normal in September. Early fall is expected to have great variability in temperature and precipitation.

NOV. 1993: Temp. 40° (1° above avg.; 1° below southeast); Precip. 0.5" (1" below avg.). 1-5 Sunny, warm. 6-7 Rain, cool. 8-9 Cold. 10-11 Sunny & warm. 12-13 Showers, cold. 14-16 Cold. 17-20 Clear, warm then rain east. 21-22 Sunny, warm. 23-27 Snow, rain south. 28-30 Cold.

DEC. 1993: Temp. 20° (4° below avg.; avg. west); Precip. 0.3" (1" below avg.; 2" below southeast). 1-4 Sunny, seasonable. 5-6 Snow. 7-8 Clear, cold. 9-11 Snow, cold. 12-14 Seasonable. 15-18 Flurries. 19-24 Cold, flurries east. 25-28 Clear, mild. 29-31 Cold, flurries east.

JAN. 1994: Temp. 23° (4° above avg.; 6° above south); Precip. 0.5" (0.5" below avg.; avg. west). 1-5 Sunny, warming; flurries west. 6-7 Snow, cold. 8-10 Severe cold, flurries. 11-16 Mild, sprinkles south. 17-19 Warm, rain south. 20-23 Sunny, warm. 24-25 Cold, snow. 26-27 Mild, light snow. 28-31 Sunny, seasonable.

FEB. 1994: Temp. 20° (4° below avg.); Precip. 1" (Avg.; 0.5" below southeast). 1-4 Cold, snow. 5-9 Clear, seasonable. 10-12 Cold; snow. 13-16 Clear, warm. 17-20 Cold; snow. 21-22 Clearing, mild. 23-25 Rain south, flurries north; mild. 26-27 Sunny & mild. 28 Rain.

MAR. 1994: Temp. 31° (6° below avg.); Precip. 4" (1.5" above avg.; avg. southwest). 1-5 Rain then cool & clear. 6-7 Rain, freezing north; seasonable. 8-10 Clear, warm. 11-13 Cold, clear. 14-17 Cold; snow, heavy east. 18-20 Clear, cold. 21-24 Very cold; snow north, freezing rain south. 25-30 Mild then cold. 31 Rain.

APR. 1994: Temp. 43° (8° below avg.); Precip. 4.5" (1" above avg.; 0.5" below southwest). 1-3 Rain then snow, colder. 4-8 Clearing, warming. 9-11 Rain, seasonable. 12-14 Cold, sleet. 15-17 Snow, heavy east; cold. 18-20 Cold. 21-23 Sunny, seasonable. 24-30 Rain, snow west; cold.

MAY 1994: Temp. 63° (1° above avg.; 1° below southwest); Precip. 5.5" (2" above avg.; 5" above west). 1-5 Warm; rain. 6-9 Cooler; sunny, showers northeast. 10-12 Sunny, warming. 13-14 Rain; cold. 15-17 Clear, warm. 18-23 Rain west & north, sunny southeast. 24-26 Rain, seasonable. 27-31 Sunny, few showers.

JUNE 1994: Temp. 68° (4° below avg.); Precip. 4.5" (Avg.; 2" above west). 1-6 Rain, warm. 7-9 Cold, rain east. 10-12 Rain, cool. 13-16 Showers, seasonable. 17-20 Sunny then rain. 21-23 Rain east; seasonable. 24-30 Rain; cold.

JULY 1994: Temp. 73.5° (3° below avg.); Precip. 4.5" (0.5" above avg.; 2" above southwest). 1-4 Showers, cool. 5-7 Rain, cool. 8-13 Rain, warming. 14-17 Cold; heavy rain, flooding. 18-24 Sunny, warm, few showers. 25-27 Rain, cooler. 28-31 Showers; hot.

AUG. 1994: Temp. 72.5° (1.5° below avg.; avg. west); Precip. 5" (2" above avg.; 0.5" above northeast). 1-4 Showers, seasonable. 5-7 Sunny south, rain north. 8-11 Clearing, hot. 12-14 Rain, seasonable. 15-19 Showers then rain. 20-23 Warmer, few showers. 24-26 Rain, mild. 27-29 Showers, hot. 30-31 Rain.

SEPT. 1994: Temp. 64.5° (0.5° below avg.); Precip. 2" (1.5" below avg.; 2" above southwest). 1-4 Clear, hot. 5-7 Showers, cool. 8-9 Rain. 10-12 Showers, seasonable. 13-15 Rain then clearing, warm. 16-17 Showers. 18-20 Cold, rain south. 21-24 Clear. 25-30 Showers, cool.

OCT. 1994: Temp. 54° (0.5° above avg.); Precip. 2.5" (Avg.; 1" below west). 1-2 Sunny, cold. 3-6 Clear, warm. 7-11 Cold; rain. 12-18 Warm then showers. 19-22 Cold, light rain. 23-24 Sunny, warm. 25-26 Rain, cold. 27-29 Showers then clearing. 30-31 Rain, cool.

1994   OLD FARMER'S ALMANAC   137

TEXAS-OKLAHOMA

For regional boundaries, see map page 115.

SUMMARY: *November through March is expected to be fairly dry and to average close to normal in temperature, despite large departures due to cold waves and warm spells. November through early December may see large fluctuations in temperature, possibly ending with a severe cold wave the second week of December. Then through January mostly warmer than normal weather will prevail. These first three months may be quite dry except for portions of the east and north, with possible drought west. Cold waves, with snow north and freezing rain south, are expected early and mid-February and mid-March, with milder temperatures the rest of the period.*

April through June will be colder than normal, with below-normal precipitation in northern and southern sections, but above in central and northwestern ones. April may be particularly cold and fairly dry. May will see fewer large departures from normal. June will average close to normal due to heat waves at the beginning and end of the month being balanced by cold waves in between. It may be quite wet in central and northwestern sections in May through mid-June and in the north through much of June.

July through September will be warmer and drier than normal in central and southern sections, particularly west, but cooler and wetter than normal north. A possible off-shore hurricane near the end of August may affect the coast. Early fall will be warmer and drier than normal over much of the region, but wet in the northeast and on the south coast due to heavy rains.

NOV. 1993: Temp. 57° (Avg.); Precip. 1" (1" below avg.; 2" below north). 1-5 Sunny; cold then warm. 6-8 Cold; rain, flurries north. 9-12 Clear, warm. 13-15 Cold. 16-19 Few showers, warm. 20-23 Showers, dry west; seasonable. 24-30 Alternating warm & cold.

DEC. 1993: Temp. 48.5° (1° above avg.; avg. north); Precip. 0.3" (1.5" below avg.). 1-3 Clear, seasonable. 4-6 Sunny, warm. 7-11 Seasonable then cold, snow north. 12-16 Sunny, warm. 17-23 Clear, seasonable. 24-26 Cool, showers. 27-30 Clear, warm. 31 Cold.

JAN. 1994: Temp. 48.5° (4° above avg.; 2° above west); Precip. 1.3" (0.5" below avg.; 0.5" below north). 1-4 Cold, showers. 5-7 Rain, snow northwest. 8-10 Warm then cold; showers. 11-15 Sunny, mild. 16-18 Rain. 19-23 Sunny, warm. 24-30 Seasonable then warm; clear. 31 Cold.

FEB. 1994: Temp. 45° (4° below avg.); Precip. 3" (1" above avg.; avg. north). 1-5 Cold; freezing rain, snow west. 6-9 Clear, mild. 10-12 Cold, showers. 13-16 Clear, warm. 17-19 Cold; snow north. 20-21 Sunny, mild. 22-26 Mild, showers then clearing. 27-28 Showers north.

MAR. 1994: Temp. 58° (Avg.; 2° below north); Precip. 1.5" (1" below avg.; 0.5" above south). 1-3 Rain north; mild. 4-8 Sunny then showers. 9-11 Clear, warm. 12-15 Cold, rain. 16-20 Clearing, warmer. 21-23 Cold, showers. 24-26 Clear, warm. 27-29 Seasonable. 30-31 Rain.

APR. 1994: Temp. 62.5° (4° below avg.; 6° below north); Precip. 1.5" (2" below avg.; 1" below north). 1-2 Cold, rain ending. 3-5 Seasonable then cold. 6-8 Mild. 9-11 Cool, few showers. 12-13 Sunny, warm. 14-15 Cold, showers east. 16-22 Variable. 23-25 Cold, rain. 26-28 Clear, warm. 29-30 Showers, warm.

MAY 1994: Temp. 72° (2° below avg.); Precip. 5" (Avg.; 2" below north). 1-2 Sunny, warm; showers west. 3-5 Rain, seasonable. 6-9 Sunny, warm; showers central. 10-14 Cold, rain central & east. 15-18 Sunny, warming; showers west. 19-22 Cool; rain central & west. 23-26 Warm, showers. 27-31 Cold, showers.

JUNE 1994: Temp. 81° (0.5° below avg.; 2° below north); Precip. 5" (2" above avg.; 1" below south). 1-5 Clear & hot. 6-9 Cold, rain. 10-13 Seasonable; showers north. 14-16 Cold, rain. 17-20 Mild, showers central & north. 21-26 Hot west; showers north. 27-30 Showers, hot.

JULY 1994: Temp. 87° (1° above avg.; avg. south; 2° below north); Precip. 1" (1" below avg.; 2" above north). 1-3 Sunny, hot. 4-6 Cold; rain. 7-16 Sunny, seasonable; hot west. 17-19 Few showers, heavy north. 20-23 Clear, seasonable. 24-26 Sunny, hot. 27-31 Mild, showers.

AUG. 1994: Temp. 88° (2.5° above avg.; 1° above north, avg. south); Precip. 2" (Avg.). 1-3 Sunny, seasonable. 4-6 Clear, showers west. 7-12 Clear, hot. 13-16 Sunny, seasonable; showers north. 17-22 Sunny, hot; showers north. 23-26 Cold north, possible offshore hurricane south; heavy rain. 27-31 Hot, clear.

SEPT. 1994: Temp. 80° (2° above avg.; avg. north and south); Precip. 4" (0.5° above avg.; 2" below west). 1-9 Clear, hot. 10-13 Seasonable; rain. 14-19 Cool, rain east & south. 20-24 Clear, warm. 25-26 Cold, rain. 27-30 Warm; rain east.

OCT. 1994: Temp. 70° (2° above avg.; avg. north); Precip. 2" (1.5" below avg.; 3" above north & south). 1-2 Cold, rain east. 3-8 Sunny, warm. 9-11 Cold, showers, heavy rain north. 12-18 Sunny, warm. 19-21 Clear, cold, rain north. 22-25 Sunny, warm. 26-31 Cold, rain.

SUMMARY: *November through March is expected to be slightly warmer than normal in the north, with above-normal precipitation and snowfall, and warm and dry in southern and western sections. Warm spells in early and late November are expected to overshadow cold waves at the beginning and middle of November and in early December. The balance of December may be warm with above-normal precipitation in the north but below south. More wintry weather will evolve with the new year, particularly in early and late February and early March, with above-normal precipitation primarily as snow and particularly in the north and higher elevations.*

April through June will be cool. Precipitation will be near normal except for drier conditions in the central section. Much of April may be mild and dry. Severe cold with heavy snow at the beginning of May and further cold waves at mid-May and early June will bring below-normal temperatures and near-normal precipitation to northern and southern sections.

July through September will be cooler and wetter than normal in the east, warmer and wetter in the south, and warmer and drier north. The primary rainfall will be from monsoon rains during the latter half of July and the first week of August in south and southeastern sections. Temperatures will gradually climb to above normal during the period. October should see normal temperatures and above-normal precipitation.

NOV. 1993: Temp. 45° (4° above avg.); Precip. 2" (0.5" above avg.; avg. west; 1" below south). 1-4 Cold; rain, snow mountains; warm south. 5-10 Warming; showers then clear. 11-13 Cold; rain, snow mountains; dry south. 14-16 Clearing, cold. 17-19 Cold; freezing rain, snow. 20-25 Warming, rain, snow mountains. 26-30 Warm & dry; showers north.

DEC. 1993: Temp. 35° (5° above avg.; 8° above west); Precip. 0.5" (1" below avg.; 0.5" above north). 1-3 Partly sunny, cooling; clear, warm south. 4-9 Rain, snow mountains; cold. 10-14 Milder; rain, snow mountains; dry south. 15-17 Cold; warm south. 18-20 Scattered showers. 21-26 Flurries; clear & warm south. 27-31 Cold, light snow; sunny, mild south.

JAN. 1994: Temp. 31° (3° above avg.; avg. south); Precip. 2" (1" above avg.; 1" below south). 1-3 Warm, rain; cool south. 4-5 Cold, snow. 6-9 Snow north; mild. 10-14 Seasonable. 15-17 Warm north; snow south. 18-21 Warm; rain. 22-26 Cold then seasonable; snow. 27-31 Warming, few showers.

FEB. 1994: Temp. 34° (Avg.; 1° below west); Precip. 0.5" (0.5" below avg.). 1-4 Cold. 5-9 Warming; rain, snow mountains. 10-15 Warm; few showers. 16-20 Seasonable, few showers. 21-23 Cold, rain & snow. 24-26 Seasonable; showers north. 27-28 Cold, snow.

MAR. 1994: Temp. 37° (5° above avg.; 2° below south); Precip. 1.5" (0.5" below avg.). 1-7 Cold; snow, heavy central & south. 8-11 Clearing; cold, snow north. 12-15 Cold, flurries; warm south. 16-19 Mild; few showers. 20-21 Cold, flurries north. 22-29 Sunny, warm; sprinkles. 30-31 Mild, showers.

APR. 1994: Temp. 49.5° (0.5° below avg.; 0.5° above west); Precip. 1.5" (0.5" below avg.). 1-4 Cold, rain & snow. 5-8 Warm. 9-11 Mild; cold, rain south. 12-15 Mild then cold, snow

east. 16-22 Clear, warm. 23-25 Cold; rain south. 26-27 Clear, warm. 28-30 Cool; rain.

MAY 1994: Temp. 57° (1.5° below avg.); Precip. 2" (0.7" above avg.). 1-2 Mild; rain, heavy north. 3-5 Cold, rain, snow higher elevations. 6-9 Sunny, warm; showers north. 10-12 Warm, showers central. 13-15 Clear, warm; few showers. 16-20 Cold, rain. 21-25 Mild, showers central. 26-31 Sprinkles; hot south.

JUNE 1994: Temp. 64° (5° below avg.); Precip. 0.5" (0.5" below avg.). 1-3 Cold, few showers. 4-7 Cold, showers; clear south. 8-11 Cool; rain north. 12-16 Clear, warming; light rain. 17-23 Sunny, warm, few showers. 24-30 Mild, sprinkles; clear south.

JULY 1994: Temp. 76° (2° below avg.; 0.5° below west); Precip. 1.5" (0.5" above avg.). 1-6 Seasonable; warm south. 7-10 Warm south; cool north. 11-16 Cold, showers; seasonable south. 17-22 Clear, hot; rain south. 23-26 Cold; rain central. 27-31 Warm, rain.

AUG. 1994: Temp. 75° (0.5° below avg.; 0.5° above south); Precip. 2" (1" above avg.; 0.5" below north & west). 1-4 Rain then clearing. 5-8 Rain, cool; sprinkles north. 9-18 Sunny, warm, few showers. 19-22 Clear, hot. 23-25 Rain, cooler; clear north. 26-28 Rain north; cooler. 29-31 Seasonable; rain east.

SEPT. 1994: Temp. 65° (Avg.; 2° above west); Precip. 0" (1" below avg.; 2" above south). 1-3 Cold, rain. 4-10 Sunny, warm, showers east. 11-15 Cold wave, showers north; warm south. 16-23 Clear, warm, showers. 24-26 Cooler, few showers. 27-30 Clear, warm; showers north.

OCT. 1994: Temp. 53° (Avg.; 1° above south); Precip. 2" (0.5" above avg.; 0.5" below west). 1-3 Showers, seasonable. 4-9 Cold; rain, snow mountains. 10-14 Clear, warm. 15-19 Cold; rain north. 20-25 Warm then cold, sleet. 26-31 Cold; rain, snow mountains.

SOUTHWEST DESERT

For regional boundaries, see map page 115.

SUMMARY: *November through March is expected to be milder than normal, with well below normal precipitation in the west but only slightly below east. November and December will be warm and dry except for a cold wave with rain at mid-November and a cold spell before mid-December. The rest of the period will be variable, with cool, wet periods in early and mid-January, in early February, and from the latter part of February through early March. Interspersed will be sunny and mild periods, including several warm spells.*

April through June will be cooler and wetter than normal, except for dry conditions in the east. Cool and wet periods are expected in early and late April, early May, and after mid-May, with a sunny and warm mid-April and second week of May. Following a hot spell at the end of May and first days of June, sunny and milder weather will prevail.

July through September may be cooler and wetter than normal in northern sections, but warmer and drier south and east. Precipitation will include monsoon rains starting in mid-July, heavy rain in early August, and possibly a severe storm at the end of August and beginning of September that may cause flooding. Early fall should start on a cool note, with rain, then turn sunny and warm until a cold wave arrives at the end of October.

NOV. 1993: Temp. 65° (3° above avg.); Precip. 0" (0.6" below avg.). 1-6 Clear, warm. 7-8 Seasonable; cool east. 9-13 Clear & warm. 14-16 Cold, sunny. 17-19 Seasonable then light rain; clear east. 20-25 Clear, pleasant. 26-30 Clear, warm days.

DEC. 1993: Temp. 57° (5° above avg.); Precip. 0" (1" below avg.). 1-3 Sunny, warm. 4-8 Sunny & seasonable; cloudy east. 9-11 Cold east; clear, seasonable west. 12-15 Sunny, warm. 16-19 Slightly milder, clear. 20-29 Clear, pleasantly warm. 30-31 Cooling.

JAN. 1994: Temp. 52° (1.5° below avg.; 2° above east); Precip. 0.2" (0.5" below avg.; 0.5" above south). 1-3 Cloudy, cooler; sunny & warm east. 4-5 Rain, seasonable. 6-7 Hard frost, sunny. 8-14 Mild. 15-17 Cold, rain. 18-23 Clearing, seasonable. 24-31 Sunny, warm.

FEB. 1994: Temp. 56.5° (1° below avg.); Precip. 1.2" (0.5" above avg.). 1-4 Rain; colder. 5-6 Clear, frost. 7-11 Clear, warm. 12-15 Sunny, warm. 16-18 Showers, rain east; cooling. 19-20 Clearing; cold east. 21-26 Showers then clear, mild. 27-28 Showers, cool.

MAR. 1994: Temp. 60° (2° below avg.; 0.5° below east); Precip. 0.5" (0.4" below avg.; 0.5" above east). 1-5 Showers, cool. 6-8 Rain, snow mountains, cold. 9-11 Clear, mild. 12-14 Rain, mild. 15-17 Cold. 18-21 Clear & mild. 22-24 Cold, light frost. 25-29 Sunny, warm. 30-31 Rain, cool.

APR. 1994: Temp. 68° (2° below avg.); Precip. 1" (0.7" above avg.). 1-4 Scattered showers; frost east. 5-7 Sunny, mild. 8-11 Rain, cold; snow mountains. 12-14 Sunny & mild. 15-16 Seasonable, cold east. 17-22 Clear, warm. 23-24 Cold, rain. 25-27 Clearing, warm. 28-30 Cold, rain; sunny east.

MAY 1994: Temp. 75° (4° below avg.; 2° below east); Precip. 0.3" (0.2" above avg.). 1-2 Sunny, seasonable. 3-5 Cold, rain. 6-9 Clearing, hot. 10-15 Sunny, warm. 16-20 Cloudy; cold & rainy west, dry east. 21-24 Clear, hot. 25-27 Sunny, seasonable. 28-31 Clear, hot.

JUNE 1994: Temp. 84° (4° below avg.; avg. east); Precip. 0" (0.1" below avg.). 1-3 Sunny, hot. 4-7 Cool, clear. 8-14 Sunny, cool. 15-22 Clear, hot. 23-25 Sprinkles, hot. 26-28 Clear, milder. 29-30 Sunny, seasonable.

JULY 1994: Temp. 92° (1° below avg.; 2° above east); Precip. 1" (0.2" above avg.; 1" below south). 1-6 Clear & hot. 7-9 Seasonable, heavy rain east. 10-15 Heat wave, clear. 16-18 Few showers, seasonable. 19-23 Monsoon rains. 24-26 Hot, showers. 27-31 Heavy thundershowers, seasonably hot.

AUG. 1994: Temp. 90° (1.5° below avg.; 2° above east & south); Precip. 4" (3" above avg.; 1" below east). 1-3 Hot, showers. 4-8 Showers, cooler. 9-14 Clear & hot. 15-25 Few showers, rain south; hot. 26-29 Clear & hot, rain east. 30-31 Cold, severe storm, rain.

SEPT. 1994: Temp. 83.5° (2° below avg.; 2° above east & south); Precip. 1.4" (0.5" above avg.; 1" below east & south). 1-2 Rain ending, flooding. 3-6 Clear, warming. 7-9 Clear & hot. 10-12 Showers, seasonable. 13-16 Sunny; hot. 17-30 Sunny, hot.

OCT. 1994: Temp. 74° (0.5° below avg.; 4° above east & south); Precip. 0.6" (Avg.; 0.5" below east & south). 1-3 Rain, light east; cooler. 4-5 Sunny & warm. 6-8 Few showers, mild. 9-11 Clear, warmer; showers, cool east. 12-16 Clear, warm. 17-28 Pleasant days, cool nights; few showers east. 29-31 Cold wave; rain, heavy southeast.

Buy an extra *Almanac* for a friend.

PACIFIC NORTHWEST

For regional boundaries, see map page 115.

SUMMARY: *November through March is expected to be close to normal in temperature in central and southern sections and mild in the north, but with great variability from month to month. Precipitation may be well above normal, with heavy snowfalls at the higher elevations. Mild spells in November, December, and at the end of January will be partially offset by cold periods near mid-November, in early December, and over much of January. The whole period will be wet with heavy snows at higher elevations, particularly in November and January. Watch for a severe cold wave in early February, followed by a warm spell midmonth with heavy rains. March will be very cold, with heavy snows but near-normal precipitation.*

April through June is expected to be dry with drought developing in many sections despite a damp first half of May. Warm spells in April, and frequent brief warm periods alternating with cool spells during May and June, will result in near-normal temperatures over the period and even slightly above normal in the north.

July through September may be colder than normal in southern and central sections, above normal in the north, with frequent departures from normal. Precipitation will be well below normal, with a continuation of the spring drought. October is expected to be wet during the first week and through the latter half of the month, with an intervening warm, sunny period.

NOV. 1993: Temp. 47° (1° above avg.); Precip. 8.5" (3" above avg.; 1" above north). 1-5 Cool, heavy rain. 6-11 Showers, seasonable. 12-15 Seasonable. 16-18 Few showers, cool. 19-21 Heavy rain, snow mountains. 24-30 Warm, some rain.

DEC. 1993: Temp. 45° (5° above avg.); Precip. 6" (Avg.; 1" above north). 1-2 Rain then clearing. 3-7 Cold; rain, snow mountains. 8-15 Warm, showers. 16-17 Sunny, seasonable. 18-20 Rain, milder. 21-22 Sprinkles. 23-27 Showers, warm. 28-31 Few showers, cooler.

JAN. 1994: Temp. 42° (2.5° above avg.; avg. south); Precip. 8" (2.5" above avg.; 1.5" above north). 1-3 Rain, mild. 4-5 Warm. 6-8 Rain, snow mountains. 9-10 Sunny, mild. 11-13 Showers, seasonable. 14-27 Rain, snow mountains; seasonable. 28-31 Warm, few showers.

FEB. 1994: Temp. 41.5° (2° below avg.); Precip. 5" (1" above avg.; 2" above north & south). 1-5 Cold, clear. 6-8 Rain, seasonable. 9-10 Sprinkles. 11-15 Rain, warm. 16-18 Clearing, seasonable. 19-24 Rain, cool. 25-27 Clear, cold nights. 28 Showers, cool.

MAR. 1994: Temp. 42° (5° below avg.); Precip. 3.5" (Avg.; 1" below north & south). 1-4 Showers then clearing; cold. 5-6 Showers, snow. 7-13 Snowstorm, cold. 14-15 Warming, sprinkles. 16-20 Rain, snow mountains; seasonable. 21-24 Sunny, warm. 25-26 Scattered showers, cool. 27-31 Few showers.

APR. 1994: Temp. 53° (2° above avg.); Precip. 0.5" (2" below avg.). 1-3 Rain, snow mountains; cold. 4-10 Sunny, warm. 11-14 Clear, seasonable. 15-21 Clear, warm days. 22-23 Showers; cool. 24-30 Sunny, warm, drought.

MAY 1994: Temp. 67° (1° below avg.; 1° above north); Precip. 3" (1" above avg.; avg. north).

1-4 Cold, rain, snow mountains. 5-10 Rain, mild; sunny then showers north. 11-14 Cold then sunny & warm. 15-17 Rain, cool. 18-20 Clear, warm. 21-23 Sunny, seasonable; showers north. 24-26 Clear, hot. 27-31 Scattered showers, mild.

JUNE 1994: Temp. 62.5° (1° below avg.; avg. north); Precip. 0.5" (1" below avg.). 1-2 Few showers, cool. 3-7 Sunny & warm. 8-11 Showers, cool. 12-15 Sunny, warm days. 16-17 Light rain, seasonable. 18-20 Clear. 21-23 Sunny, seasonable. 24-26 Clear, warm. 27-30 Cool, showers north, then clear & warm.

JULY 1994: Temp. 67.5° (0.5° below avg.; 1.5° above north); Precip. 0.1" (0.5" below avg.). 1-4 Clear, hot. 5-7 Sunny, warm. 8-10 Cold, rain. 11-13 Clearing, seasonable. 14-16 Clear, hot. 17-20 Sunny, warm. 21-24 Cool, sunny. 25-27 Clear. 28-31 Cool then clear & warm.

AUG. 1994: Temp. 67° (1.5° below avg.; 0.5° below north); Precip. 0.5" (0.5" below avg.). 1-5 Clear, warm. 6-8 Sunny; seasonable, cool north. 9-12 Sunny, warm. 13-17 Cool; few showers. 18-21 Sunny, warming. 22-25 Clear, hot. 26-30 Few showers, mild. 31 Rain.

SEPT. 1994: Temp. 63° (0.5° below avg.; 1° above north); Precip. 1" (0.8" below avg.). 1-3 Rain, cool. 4-6 Clear, warm. 7-9 Sunny, warm. 10-12 Rain, cool. 13-15 Sunny. 16-20 Clear, hot. 21-23 Cooling to normal. 24-26 Clear, warm. 27-30 Cold; rain then clearing.

OCT. 1994: Temp. 55.5° (1° above avg.; 2° above north); Precip. 5" (2.5" above avg.). 1-7 Rain; cool. 8-10 Clear, showers north; mild. 11-14 Clear, warm. 15-18 Rain, seasonable. 19-21 Scattered showers, cool. 22-24 Rain, seasonable. 25-28 Rain, cool. 29-31 Clear; seasonable; warm days, cold nights.

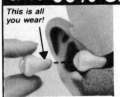
The Old Farmer's Almanac —
a year-round companion.

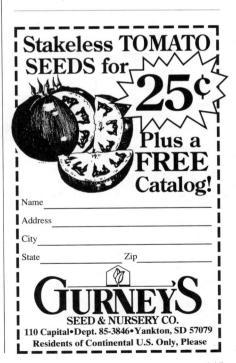

16 CALIFORNIA

For regional boundaries, see map page 115.

SUMMARY: *November through March is expected to be warmer and wetter than normal in the north, with close to normal snowfall in the Sierra Nevada mountains, but cooler than normal south and fairly dry in southern California. November will begin cool and wet, turn unusually warm and dry, then return to heavy rain and cool weather after mid-November and in the first half of December, with heavy snows in the Sierra Nevadas and flooding in the Central Valley. Following a warm spell before Christmas, cool temperatures will prevail except for warm spells during mid-February and the latter half of March. Watch for heavy rains and snows in the mountains during the latter half of January, before mid-February, and in early March.*

April through June will be cooler than normal with near-normal precipitation. April may be cool except at midmonth in the Central Valley, with little precipitation in the north and above-normal amounts in the south. The first half of May will be cold with heavy rains and snow. Little rain is expected the rest of the period. Warm spells at the end of May and in early June will be offset by cool periods during much of June except for warm weather in the upper San Joaquin Valley.

July through September will be cooler than normal along the coast and in the north, but near normal inland in the south. Warm spells are expected around the middle of each month. A few showers and heavy thundershowers in the southeast will wet the end of July and beginning of August. Early fall will start off cool along the coast and in the north, then turn warm with little rainfall until the end of the month.

NOV. 1993: Temp. 60° (5° above avg.; avg. south); Precip. 5" (2" above avg. central; 0.5" below north & south). 1-4 Rain, snow mountains, dry south. 5-10 Sunny, warm. 11-16 Cool, clear. 17-18 Rain north, snow mountains. 19-21 Showers, cool. 22-24 Rain, floods Central Valley. 25-28 Sunny, warm. 29-30 Cool.

DEC. 1993: Temp. 52.5° (3° above avg.; 0.5° below south-central); Precip. 5" (2" above avg.; 1" below south). 1-5 Cool, sprinkles. 6-9 Rain, then clearing; cool. 10-12 Rain north; warmer. 13-16 Clearing, warm. 17-19 Rain, snow mountains. 20-24 Sunny & warm. 25-27 Seasonable. 28-31 Cool, sprinkles; hot south.

JAN. 1994: Temp. 50° (1° above avg.; 2° below south); Precip. 4.5" (Avg.; 1" above north, 0.5" below south). 1-5 Clear, seasonable. 6-8 Showers, cold. 9-13 Sunny, mild. 14-16 Cold, rain, heavy snow mountains. 17-18 Sunny, warm. 19-23 Cold, rain, snow mountains. 24-26 Sunny, warmer; rain southeast. 27-31 Clear, warm.

FEB. 1994: Temp. 52° (Avg.; 2° below south & north); Precip. 3" (Avg.; 1" below inland & south). 1-3 Rain south; cool. 4-6 Sunny, warmer. 7-9 Rain, seasonable. 10-14 Sunny, warm. 15-17 Rain, snow mountains; cool. 18-20 Clear, warm. 21-24 Showers, cool. 25-28 Rain south, snow mountains; cold.

MAR. 1994: Temp. 54° (0.5° above avg.; 2° below south & north); Precip. 2" (1" below avg.). 1-5 Rain, snow mountains; cold. 6-7 Cold. 8-11 Rain, snow mountains; warming. 12-14 Showers, cold, snow mountains. 15-19 Clear, warm. 20-21 Sunny. 22-24 Clear, warm. 25-26 Cold. 27-31 Clear, warm.

APR. 1994: Temp. 53.5° (2° below avg.); Precip. 0.9" (0.5" below avg.; avg. south). 1-5 Showers, cool north. 6-10 Showers; warm south &

central. 11-15 Sunny, warm. 16-19 Cooling, warm south. 20-24 Few showers; cooler. 25-27 Sunny, cool. 28-30 Cold, rain.

MAY 1994: Temp. 57° (1° below avg.; 3° below inland); Precip. 0.7" (0.5" above avg.). 1-4 Rain, snow mountains; cold. 5-6 Showers, warm. 7-9 Cold, rain. 10-14 Clearing, warming. 15-18 Cold, rain, heavy south. 19-22 Clear, warm. 23-26 Cool. 27-30 Clear & hot. 31 Cooling.

JUNE 1994: Temp. 57.5° (4° below avg.; 1° below south); Precip. 0" (Avg.). 1-5 Seasonable; cool south. 6-8 Sunny, warm. 9-11 Cool. 12-15 Clearing, warming; cool coast. 16-18 Seasonable. 19-21 Warm inland, cool coast. 22-25 Sprinkles, cool. 26-30 Warming.

JULY 1994: Temp. 58.5° (4° below avg.; 1° below south); Precip. 0" (Avg.). 1-3 Clear, cool; warm south. 4-9 Cool north & inland. 10-13 Clear, warm. 14-20 Sunny; cool. 21-24 Warm, showers. 25-28 Cool; seasonable south. 29-31 Clear, warm.

AUG. 1994: Temp. 60.5° (3° below avg.; 1° above inland); Precip. 0" (Avg.). 1-4 Clear, warm; cool coast. 5-8 Sunny, cool. 9-11 Warmer; cool coast. 12-15 Seasonable; cool fog coast. 16-22 Clear, warm. 23-26 Showers, thunderstorms southeast; cool coast. 27-31 Sunny, warm.

SEPT. 1994: Temp. 62.5° (2° below avg.); Precip. 0" (0.3" below avg.). 1-3 Showers, cool. 4-10 Cool, rain north; warm south. 11-13 Clear, warm; cool south-central. 14-17 Sunny; cool coast. 18-20 Clear, hot. 21-25 Rain, cooler; hot south. 26-30 Clear, cool coast.

OCT. 1994: Temp. 61.5° (0.5° above avg.; 1° below north & south); Precip. 0.7" (0.5" below avg.; 0.5" above north). 1-2 Cloudy. 3-6 Rain, cool; sunny south. 7-8 Sunny. 9-12 Clear, hot. 13-15 Showers, cooler. 16-26 Warm. 27-29 Rain, cold. 30-31 Clear, seasonable.

The
WOMEN WHO
TAMED
THE WEST

*They could swing a lasso
and ride a bronco with
the best of the cowboys.
But no one knew what
to call them until Teddy
Roosevelt came along.*

BY JAMIE KAGELEIRY

"There are women in the East who think they're 'new.' They ought to see the 'newer' ones out West. Colorado has its cowboys of the feminine gender . . ."
— Boston Evening Record, *October 2, 1901*

With true cowboy grit," wrote the *Denver Times* in 1901, "Melie throws the lariat over the branching horns while the other end of the strong rawhide rope is fastened to the saddle. Then a steady pull draws the animal to a place of safety on dry ground. It's a large herd for one person to handle, but with the assistance of two well-trained dogs, she does it."

She?

History has barely glanced at the women who did (and still do) what cowboys did — roped steers, drove cattle to market, shot rustlers, ran ranches by themselves, wore pants, and cussed when they needed to. Women were "cowboying" long before there was a word for that. Many women set out to run their own cattle company or to hire on as a hand. Some, like Melie Dunn, grew up into the jobs.

The Becker sisters roped and branded cattle at their ranch in Alamosa, Colorado, 1894.

Amelia Dunn came west to Navajo country (Arizona) from Elmira, New York, with her family in 1877, when she was just a child. Mr. Dunn had consumption and thought that a herd of cattle would earn him money and keep him outdoors as well. For a while it did, but when Melie was 17, her father died. She'd been with him almost daily for seven years in his rides across the mesas, among the foothills, and through the arroyos. For several years she studied the business skills she would need to run a ranch — to know beef values, when to sell her stock, when to ship, and how to graze her herd most economically. Cattle had to be kept moving to feed well. As vaquero, Melie often traveled 200 miles from home. The years between 1889 and 1897 were hard ones even for experienced cattle ranchers in the drought-stricken Southwest. Thousands of cattle died of starvation and exhaustion. Melie had the foresight to drive her "beeves" to valleys where they fattened. By the time she was 21, cattlemen in the region considered Melie Dunn an authority.

About the same time Melie was riding the sandy wasteland with her father, ten-year-old Agnes Morley's father died, leaving the family with quite a bit of land that Mr. Morley had just purchased in Denver.

People offered to help, including, Agnes wrote later, "one persuasive and soft-spo-

Ad for Pawnee Bill's show (above); *rodeo star Mabel Strickland, ca. 1920* (below).

ken gentleman from below the Mason-Dixon line. His Southern drawl was pleasant to the ear, his bounding optimism was stimulating; his fondness for hard drinking and gambling was unsuspected." Agnes's mother married him. He convinced her to leave the city and sink most of her cash into a huge, well-stocked cattle ranch in New Mexico.

After a rugged wagon trip, the Morleys arrived in Magdalena, New Mexico, in February 1886. "Please give us a room that is not directly over the barroom," Agnes's mother stipulated to the hotel keeper. "I'm afraid those bullets will come up through the floor."

Having survived the night, the family set off the next day for their new ranch, 40 miles outside Magdalena, at the foot of the Datil mountains. It didn't take Agnes's mother long to realize the mistake of her marriage, and very shortly after, the new husband vanished. Though they didn't have a clue how to run a huge cattle ranch, the Morley family didn't have

IN THEIR OWN WORDS

learned to recognize the individuals among them as though they were people. We apportioned the herds among ourselves, each claiming as his own anywhere from a hundred head upward."

After one of the hired cowhands stuck her on a horse, "I was walking on clouds. I was a useful member of society." The horse became hers, and "we learned to ride by the simple process of riding."

Though each fall she reluctantly left the ranch to attend school, each summer Agnes grew more and more expert in roping, "riding fence," and breaking broncos. By the time she was 17, Agnes was a full-time, year-round hand, and even a local paper recognized her ability. "Miss Agnes, of the Datils, and Three-Fingered Pete are the best riders in the county," reported the *Mine and Lariat*.

More than riding skills made a good cowhand, though. Agnes became as good as any man at everything it took — except

IN THEIR OWN WORDS

much choice but to make a go of it. For Agnes and her brother Ray, she wrote later in her book, *No Life for a Lady,* the new life was the beginning of a sort of "glorified picnic."

"Cattle became the circumference of our universe," she wrote. "We

the chore of branding. "However much of an accessory to the crime I may have been in the matter of rounding up or even roping the calf," she said, "when it came to the actual applying of a hot iron to sentient flesh, I couldn't do it."

Ability with a rope was crucial. A few hundred miles north, Mrs. Victor Daniels trusted her talent with a lariat. (Apparently Mrs. Daniels was too otherwise engaged to jot down her memoirs, which may have given us her first name; the *Denver Times* called her only Mrs. Victor.)

In the 1880s the Danielses came from New Jersey and settled on a cattle ranch, 15 miles from the nearest neighbor. Mrs. Daniels's husband had gotten together a small herd of about 50 cows, and they watched over them with care. It was Mrs. Daniels's job to keep the herd together. One day, when her husband had gone 20 miles to the store, she was compelled to leave the cattle grazing while she looked after a sick baby at home. Suddenly, from behind the foothills, two men rode up and drove the cattle off, abducting the whole bunch.

She flew out of the house, mounted her bronco, and was after them. Maybe in the riot of rushing steers, the men didn't hear the hooves of Mrs. Daniels's pony as she came cantering up behind. Suddenly one of the men gave a yell and tumbled backward off his saddle with the noose of a lariat tight around his throat. Frightened, the other turned to see a furious woman facing him.

"What are you doing?" she demanded.

"Who are you?" he demanded gruffly.

"I own these cattle, and you have got to help me drive them back where you got them."

She held a cocked revolver at his head; he

IN THEIR OWN WORDS

submitted and, with her following closely, rode around the scattered herd and turned their heads homeward. The scoundrel drove the cattle the three miles back, then fled without a backward glance. His companion, reported the *Denver Times,* "choked to death and with neck broken, was found among the chaparral, but there was never any inquiry. It was enough to know that he had been engaged in cattle stealing and that summary justice had been visited upon him. . . ."

Rustlers were trouble enough, but the

landscape presented its own obstacles in the efforts to make a ranch successful. "Riding through the brush, or as we called it, 'breaking brush,' is a specialized kind of cowpuncher horsemanship, just as 'hopping

A ranch woman's life: quick meals at the cook wagon; divided skirts for riding astride.

prairie-dog holes' in Texas is another," wrote Agnes Morley. "Brush-breaking derives its name from the peculiar brittleness of the timber in the high dry altitude of the Southwest. While in pursuit of some cow critter, I have torn at top speed into a piñon tree. The rule is, if you can't dodge 'em, stick out your chest and break 'em. Usually, the momentum is enough to smack off even good-sized branches. Sometimes your chest is stuck out, and your horse is leaping a fallen log and doing it with a twisting motion to escape crashing headlong into the trunk of another tree which had not been visible. Some credit is due to fearlessness and skill, but more should go to the horse."

The worst nightmare was to have your horse fall and flatten the stirrup, trapping your foot. The chances were good that at this point the horse would decide to bolt, dragging you behind. "For this," Agnes said, "we wore six-shooters long after any other reason for doing so existed. To shoot the horse was the only answer. A six-shooter does give one a sense of security. We had a saying, 'A six-shooter makes all men equal.' I amended it to 'a six-shooter makes men and women equal.' "

But if the work of a cowhand and its risks and rewards were clear-cut, it wasn't so clear what a woman in the 1890s should wear on the job. With all this fearlessness, skill, and mastery of "man's work," one would think that what one decided to wear to work wouldn't matter. And with some it didn't. Amelia Dunn, for instance, "dressed for work," reported the *Denver Times*, "in a wide-brimmed white felt hat, long gauntlet gloves, a lariat coiled about the saddle's horn, and a revolver at her belt." More and more women who worked as ranch hands in the 1890s started wearing divided skirts and fashions more suited to their work.

"My own great concession to a new age," Agnes wrote about the 1890s, "was to abandon the sidesaddle. Why, for ten years, I continued to ride sidesaddle is a mystery to me now. I recall the steps that led to emancipation. First I discarded, or rather refused to adopt, the sunbonnet, conventional headgear of my female neighbors. When I went unashamedly about under a five-gallon Stetson, many an eyebrow was raised; then followed a double-breasted blue flannel shirt, with white pearl buttons, frankly unfeminine. In time came the blue denim knickers worn under a shortened blue denim skirt. Slow evolution toward a costume suited for immediate needs. Decadence having set in, the descent from the existing standards of female modesty to purely human comfort and convenience was swift. A man's saddle and a divided skirt (awful monstrosity that it was) were inevitable.

" 'I won't ride in the same canyon with you,' protested my brother Ray.

"He denied only a few months later ever having said it," Agnes wrote.

Agnes Morley successfully ran Morley enterprises with her brother Ray and then by herself for many years, but the West of the open range and the long trail drives was disappearing forever. By 1894 barbed wire was inexpensive, and the homesteaders who had been pouring west began to fence off their lands. The railroads extended their lines and were able to transport cattle to the distant markets. In the way that Americans tend to idealize lives that are soon to be passé, the Wild West shows were designed to show the world the soon-to-be-antiquated life on the open range.

Agnes was approached by a talent scout with the Buffalo Bill show who was impressed with her ability to keep an outlaw horse from bucking. She told him, "I can't see any sense in getting your head all but snapped from your shoulders, your spinal column whipped like a bullshacker's blacksnake, your insides turned to jelly — not if I could help it! As for making a profession of it, that was to laugh!"

Soon enough, Agnes Morley was running errands in a Model T. Years later, after the last summer of Morley ranching in 1934, one of the old hands came by to see her and mourned, "Them was the good old days. Can't ride nowheres now, 'thout runnin' into a bob-wire fence and meetin' up with some feller drivin' a Jersey cow."

"I was listening," she wrote, "with only half my mind. With the other half I was trying to span the gap between me and that young girl . . . and her life, which was not what the world calls a lady."

The country may not have had a word for women such as Melie Dunn or Agnes Morley, but it found one in the rodeo-show girls whose acts were inspired by the women who did the work of cowboys. Lucille Mulhall was roping, branding, herding, and breaking horses by the age of ten on her father's ranch. It was Teddy Roosevelt who watched her perform in a Wild West show when she was only 14 and who gave her the name that would make her famous. He called her "Cowgirl." □ □

THE DAY J. EDGAR HOOVER ARRESTED CANADA'S GREATEST CROOK

But another version has it that Hoover was hiding nearby.

BY CHRIS KELLY

By 1936 the Age of the Gangster was almost over. Bonnie and Clyde and Dillinger and Baby Face Nelson were dead. Al Capone and George "Machine Gun" Kelly were in prison. Public Enemy Number One was Alvin "Old Creepy" Karpis — born Alvin Karpowicz in Montreal in 1908.

Karpis had been leading a life of crime since he was ten years old, when he robbed a grocery store in Topeka, Kansas. He robbed stores and warehouses, bootlegged, then joined the Ma Barker Gang and moved on to bigger crimes. "My profession was robbing banks, knocking off payrolls, and kidnapping rich men," Karpis bragged. Among other achievements, he revived the art of train robbery. A celebrity criminal, Karpis had undergone facial surgery and had his fingerprints altered with acid.

In 1936 Old Creepy evaded FBI traps in three states, embarrassing the Bureau. That April, FBI Director J. Edgar Hoover was humiliated in front of a Senate subcommittee when he was asked, repeatedly, if he had ever personally made an arrest. He had not. Hoover ordered Karpis found at any cost. When agents located him, Hoover would arrest Public Enemy Number One — personally. On April 30, Karpis was spotted in New Orleans. He was placed under constant surveillance, and Hoover was called. On May 1 the FBI moved in. In Hoover's version of events, Karpis climbed behind the wheel of his 1936 Plymouth coupe for a getaway. Hoover ran up to the car and put his gun to Karpis's head, just before Old Creepy could go for a sawed-off shotgun in the backseat. "Put the cuffs on him, boys," Hoover told his agents.

There are a few problems with this story. For one, a 1936 Plymouth coupe has no backseat. For another, according to ex-agents and Karpis, it was actually an agent named Clarence Hurt who made the arrest. Hoover stayed in hiding until everything was over.

No one had remembered to bring handcuffs. They tied Karpis's hands with a necktie. Out-of-towners, they had no idea how to get to the New Orleans FBI office. Karpis had to give them directions.

Alvin Karpis served 33 years in Alcatraz and in McNeil Island Penitentiary. In 1969 he was paroled and deported back to Canada, where he died ten years later at age 71. In 1936 the director of the FBI had sat in the back of a police car and called Karpis a hoodlum. Old Creepy had corrected Hoover: "I'm a thief. I'm no lousy hoodlum." □ □

Alvin Karpis, née Karpowicz, in a 1935 mug shot.

FBI director J. Edgar Hoover, with plenty of backup firepower, hauled Public Enemy Number One into court, May 1, 1936. Karpis was convicted and sent to Alcatraz.

BUDDY, CAN YOU SPARE AN 1894-S DIME?

Of 24 dimes struck in San Francisco in 1894, only 11 have been accounted for — and the rest, somewhere around (maybe in your attic!), are worth at least $100,000 each!

BY DONN PEARLMAN

Among the most famous and valuable of all United States rare coins are the 1894 San Francisco dimes, known as the 1894-S dimes. That year the United States Mint in San Francisco produced millions of quarters, half-dollars, and silver dollars, as well as gold coins worth $5, $10, and $20. Why, after making coins with a face value of more than $25 million, did they strike only $2.40 in silver dimes? One story says that mint superintendent John Daggett made 24 dimes to balance out the fiscal-year accounts. Others have speculated that the mint struck the coins as a test in anticipation of a formal order to manufacture dimes. When no such order materialized, the dime mintage remained at 24 pieces.

Another more conspiratorial theory is that a few influential California bankers persuaded their friend, Superintendent Daggett, to make some instant rare coins for them. All the 1894-S dimes apparently were produced as "proof" specimens, specially struck with exceptionally brilliant reflective surfaces and sharpness of detail. Conflicting stories assert that the dimes were privately distributed among seven bankers, or were quietly placed into circulation, or that some were melted down.

Rare-coin historians know that three of the 1894-S dimes were given by Superintendent Daggett to his young daughter, Hallie, with instructions to keep them until she was much older because they would be valuable. According to rare-coin researcher R. W. Julian, the little girl spent one coin on the way home — to purchase a dish of ice cream!

"Hallie did keep two of the coins until 1954, when they were sold to a San Francisco rare-coin dealer," Julian explained. One of her pedigreed dimes sold at auction in Orlando, Florida, in August 1992 for $165,000. Two other specimens of the 1894-S dime are well worn, obvious victims of long circulation. Perhaps the dime deliberately spent by Hallie Daggett was eventually found in pocket change by an anonymous but astute collector who realized that the coin could buy more than just 31 flavors.

The highest price paid so far for an 1894-S dime is $275,000, a record for any United States dime that was set in January 1990 at a New York City auction conducted by Stack's Coin Company. Harvey Stack, a partner in the firm, believes there are only 11 known specimens. Over the years his firm has sold six of them. Dealer Q. David Bowers of Wolfeboro, New Hampshire, has sold four of the dimes. The first time he purchased one, in 1957, host Dave Garroway of the NBC-TV "Today Show" interviewed him, fascinated that someone would pay $4,750 for a dime. Bowers later sold it for $6,000.

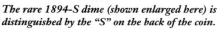

The rare 1894-S dime (shown enlarged here) is distinguished by the "S" on the back of the coin.

The 1894-S dime is deceivingly similar in appearance to the millions of common dimes struck between 1892 and 1916, the type usually described by collectors as a "Barber dime," named after its designer, former U.S. Mint chief engraver Charles E. Barber. Most Barber dimes are not scarce. They can easily be obtained from dealers, some for a dollar or two. Ronald J. Gillio, president of the Professional Numismatists Guild (an international rare-coin dealers' group) emphasized that only 1894 dimes with the distinctive San Francisco mint mark "S" on the back of the coin are the sought-after rare ones. As a public service, the Guild will provide free authentication for any newly discovered, genuine 1894-S dime.

So, take a close look at those old coins stashed in a desk drawer or hidden in the attic. Somewhere, perhaps buried in a forgotten coffee can of loose change, someone may have one of the 13 missing thin dimes, each worth a fat $100,000.

For more information about the coin search, write for a free copy of the booklet The Pleasure of Coin Collecting *to Paul L. Koppenhaver, Professional Numismatists Guild, P.O. Box 430, Van Nuys, CA 91408. For a free copy of* Coin Collecting — A Fascinating Hobby for Young and Old, *write to the American Numismatic Association, 818 N. Cascade, Colorado Springs, CO 80903. The ANA is the world's largest organization for collectors of coins, paper money, medals, and tokens.*

OTHER RARE AND "FUNNY" MONEY

1804 SILVER DOLLAR

☞ The U.S. Mint did not actually produce dollars dated 1804 in the year 1804 — but decades later some were "officially" made for special presentations, and others were produced at the mint under questionable circumstances. A total of 15 specimens are known, one of which holds the record for the highest price paid at auction for any U.S. coin: $990,000 in 1989. Another 1804 dollar, in a set with eight other coins originally given to the King of Siam in 1836, was not even known to exist until 1962. The entire set sold for $1,815,000 at a February 1993 auction in Beverly Hills, California. The whereabouts of a similar coin set given to the Sultan of Muscat (now Oman) are unknown.

(continued on next page)

1913 LIBERTY HEAD NICKEL

☞ The Philadelphia Mint started making nickels with an Indian and buffalo design in 1913, but someone produced five nickels with the previously used "Miss Liberty" motif. Three of the five are in museums. Two are in private hands, but there are persistent rumors that one of those two is unaccounted for. **Value: $500,000 to $750,000.**

1787 BRASHER DOUBLOON

☞ Produced by George Washington's neighbor, New York goldsmith Ephraim Brasher, the coin was made famous as the subject of a 1940s detective movie, *The Brasher Doubloon*. Six specimens are known; one of these was nearly tossed into a melting pot at the Philadelphia Mint in 1838. **Value: The last three offered at auctions since 1979 brought $430,000, $625,000, and $725,000.**

1893-S SILVER DOLLAR

☞ Many collectors love this coin, also called the "Morgan dollar," named after designer George T. Morgan and distributed from 1878 to 1921. Because only 100,000 Morgan dollars were struck at the San Francisco Mint in 1893, demand for them outpaces supply. Check those old silver dollars Grandma handed out at birthdays, and look for the "S" mint mark on the back below the wreath. **Value: $300 to $50,000 or more, depending on condition.** *(Note: Experts warn not to clean a rare coin. Harsh abrasives will only reduce the value.)*

1955 DOUBLED-DIE LINCOLN CENT

☞ A production error caused sharply doubled lettering around President Lincoln's portrait and the date on some 1955 cents. **Value: $200 to $3,000.**

1972 DOUBLED-DIE CENT

☞ Only coins with sharp, vivid doubling are valuable. **Value: $50 to $200.**

1870-S HALF-DIME

☞ Before there were nickels, silver half-dimes were issued from 1794 to 1873. Although there is no record of any being struck by the San Francisco Mint in 1870, one 1870-S half-dime was discovered in 1978 by a Chicago coin dealer sorting through a collection of "common" silver pieces. Are there more somewhere? **Value: The so-far unique specimen sold in 1986 for $253,000.**

1933 $10 EAGLE

☞ More than 300,000 $10 gold coins were struck in 1933, but only a few got into circulation before President Roosevelt prohibited private ownership of gold in August of that year. Each Eagle contains less than a half-ounce of gold, but the 1933 $10 coins are worth more than their weight in gold. **Value: $60,000 to $90,000.**

"FUNNY" FOLDING MONEY

☞ U.S. paper money is printed in sheets of 32 notes, and each sheet is printed

The lettering was mistakenly stamped twice on this 1972 Lincoln penny.

– photo courtesy Bowers and Merena Galleries, Inc.

three times: first the back, then the front, then the serial numbers are added. Sometimes the sheets are misfed into the high-speed presses, resulting in misplaced or upside-down serial numbers. Look at both sides of the bill, too. In 1976 a shopper in a Dallas supermarket checkout line was handed a note mistakenly printed with $20 on one side, $10 on the other. Of the 32 notes from that currency sheet, only 16 have been discovered. **Value of misprinted money: $20 to thousands of dollars, depending on the type of error and the condition of the bill.** □□

SECRETS OF THE ZODIAC

Famous Debowelled Man of the Signs

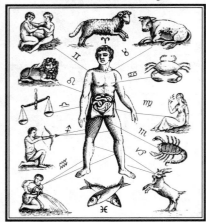

Famous Debowelled Man of the Signs

Ancient astrologers associated each of the signs with a part of the body over which they felt the sign held some influence. The first sign of the zodiac — Aries — was attributed to the head, with the rest of the signs moving down the body, ending with Pisces at the feet.

♈	Aries, head. ARI Mar. 21-Apr. 20
♉	Taurus, neck. TAU Apr. 21-May 20
♊	Gemini, arms. GEM May 21-June 20
♋	Cancer, breast. CAN June 21-July 22
♌	Leo, heart. LEO July 23-Aug. 22
♍	Virgo, belly. VIR Aug. 23-Sept. 22
♎	Libra, reins. LIB Sept. 23-Oct. 22
♏	Scorpio, secrets. SCO Oct. 23-Nov. 22
♐	Sagittarius, thighs. SAG Nov. 23-Dec. 21
♑	Capricorn, knees. CAP Dec. 22-Jan. 19
♒	Aquarius, legs. AQU Jan. 20-Feb. 19
♓	Pisces, feet. PSC Feb. 20-Mar. 20

ASTROLOGY AND ASTRONOMY

In ancient times, astrology and astronomy were the same science. "Wise men" looked into the heavens, noted the passage of planets through the vault of the sky, and summarily attached meaning to these events; their counsel was sought by kings.

During the Middle Ages and beyond, the separation of church and state and the rise of science had a negative effect on astrology. Matters of the spirit were given over to religious institutions, and the business of everyday living was subjected to the scientific model. Astronomy became solely the study of the physical properties of the universe.

Yet astrology persists. This ancient art attempts to explain human behavior and even predict the future according to the astrological placement of the two luminaries (the Sun and the Moon) and the eight known planets (Mercury, Venus, Mars, Jupiter, Saturn, Uranus, Neptune, and Pluto) in the 12 signs of the zodiac. It is important to note that *the planetary placements through the signs of the zodiac are not the same astrologically as they are astronomically.* This is because astrologers figure according to a 26,000-year cycle they have identified as the Great Ages; astronomy takes into account precession of the equinoxes and the actual placement of the planets and constellations in the heavens.

Astrologers believe we have spent the past 2,000 years in the Age of Pisces, exploring the realm of compassion and religion. We are now poised on the brink of the Age of Aquarius. Astrologers believe this age will be one of intuition and self-knowledge. As Aquarius is concerned with all of humanity, global awareness and male-female equality will increase.

ASTROLOGY AS A TOOL

Astrology is the study of cycles. Just as the Moon waxes and wanes, everything in life is in a state of flux. An astrologer can provide an individual birth chart to describe a person's initial orientation in time and space. An individual's Sun sign (the astrological sign in which the Sun was located at birth) will describe the active, conscious personality; one's work should be compatible with the qualities of this sign. The Moon, on the other hand, shows the passive personality as well as the habits. One's emotional well-being is nourished by the qualities of the sign the Moon occupied at birth.

Many readers have asked us which signs are best suited for various activities. Astrologers use Moon signs for this determination; a month-by-month chart showing appropriate times for certain activities is provided on page 162. (To find the astrological place of the Moon in the zodiac, as well as detailed gardening information, see page 164. *Do not confuse this with the astronomical position of the Moon, as listed on the Left-Hand Calendar Pages [54-80]; because of precession and other factors the astrological and astronomical zodiacs do not agree.*)

A MONTH-BY-MONTH ASTROLOGICAL TIMETABLE FOR 1994

Herewith we provide the following yearlong chart, based on the Moon signs, showing the appropriate times each month for certain activities. **BY CELESTE LONGACRE**

	JAN.	FEB.	MAR.	APR.	MAY	JUNE	JULY	AUG.	SEPT.	OCT.	NOV.	DEC.
Give up smoking	3, 27, 31	8, 27	7, 8	3, 8, 30	1, 6, 29	2, 25, 29	26	5, 23	2, 30	3, 27, 31	23, 28	20, 25
Begin diet to lose weight	3, 27, 31	8, 27	7, 8	3, 8, 30	1, 6, 29	2, 25, 29	26	5, 23	2, 30	3, 27, 31	23, 28	20, 25
Begin diet to gain weight	25, 26	12, 13, 23	21, 22	18, 19	15, 16	11, 12	8, 9	5, 6	10, 11	7, 8, 17	12, 13	9, 10
Buy clothes	4, 5, 27, 28	1, 24, 25, 28	23, 24, 27, 28	19, 20, 23, 24	17, 18, 21, 22	13, 14, 17, 18	10, 11, 15, 16	6, 7, 11, 12	3, 4, 7, 8	1, 2, 4, 5, 29	1, 2, 24, 25, 30	21, 22, 26, 27
Seek favors	13, 14	9, 10	9, 10	5, 6	2, 3	26, 27	24, 25	19, 20	16, 17	13, 14	9, 10	7, 8
Dental care	2, 3, 29, 30	19, 20, 26, 27	19, 20, 26	15, 16, 22	12, 13, 19, 20	8, 9, 15, 16	6, 7, 13	2, 3, 9, 10	5, 6, 26, 27	3, 23, 24, 31	19, 20, 26, 27	16, 17, 24, 25
End old projects	10, 11	9, 10	10, 11	9, 10	9, 10	7, 8	7, 8	5, 6	4, 5	3, 4	2, 3	1, 2
Hair care	4, 5	1, 28	1, 27, 28	23, 24	21, 22	17, 18	14, 15	11, 12	7, 8	4, 5	1, 2, 29	26, 27
Seek pleasures	6, 7	2, 3, 4	2, 3	25, 26	23, 24	19, 20	17, 18	13, 14	9, 10	6, 7	3, 4	1, 28, 29
Start a new project	12, 13	11, 12	12, 13	11, 12	11, 12	9, 10	9, 10	7, 8	6, 7	5, 6	4, 5	3, 4
Fishing	8, 9	5, 6	4, 5	1, 28, 29	25, 26	21, 22	19, 20	15, 16	11, 12	8, 9	5, 6	2, 3
Breed	6, 7	2, 3, 4	2, 3	25, 26	23, 24	19, 20	17, 18	13, 14	9, 10	6, 7	3, 4	1, 28, 29
Destroy pests/ weeds	18, 19	14, 15	13, 14	10, 11	7, 8	3, 4	1, 2, 28, 29	24, 25	21, 22	18, 19	14, 15	11, 12
Graft or pollinate	16, 17, 26	12, 13, 23	11, 12, 22	7, 8, 18	5, 14, 15	1, 2, 11, 29	8, 9, 25, 26	4, 5, 22, 23	1, 2, 18, 19	15, 16, 25, 26	12, 13, 22, 23	9, 10, 19, 20
Harvest above-ground crops	20, 21	17, 18	16, 17, 26	12, 13, 21, 22	11, 19, 20	15, 16	12, 13	9, 10	6, 18, 19	15, 16	16, 17	14, 15
Harvest root crops	2, 3, 30	26, 27	11, 30	7, 8	5, 6, 31	6, 7, 28, 29	3, 4, 30, 31	4, 27, 28	23, 24, 29	2, 3, 20, 21	26, 27	24, 25
Begin logging	11, 12	7, 8	6, 7	2, 3, 30	1, 27, 28	24, 25	21, 22	18, 19	13, 14	11, 12	7, 8	5, 6
Prune or cut hay	18, 19	15, 16	13, 14	10, 11	7, 8	3, 4	1, 2, 28, 29	24, 25	21, 22	18, 19	14, 15	11, 12
Seed grain	15, 16	12, 13, 22	21, 22	17, 18	14, 23, 24	11, 12, 20	9, 17, 18	13, 14	9, 10, 18	7, 15, 16	4, 12, 13	9, 10
Set posts or pour concrete	11, 12	7, 8	6, 7	2, 3, 30	1, 27, 28	24, 25	21, 22	18, 19	13, 14	11, 12	7, 8	5, 6
Slaughter	6, 7	2, 3, 4	2, 3	25, 26	23, 24	19, 20	17, 18	13, 14	9, 10	6, 7	3, 4	1, 28, 29
Wean	8, 9	5, 6	4, 5	1, 28, 29	25, 26	21, 22	19, 20	15, 16	11, 12	8, 9	5, 6	2, 3
Castrate animals	13, 14	9, 10	9, 10	5, 6	2, 3	26, 27	24, 25	19, 20	16, 17	13, 14	9, 10	7, 8

GARDENING BY THE MOON'S SIGN

Astrology is not the same science as astronomy. The actual sign placements of planets differ drastically between these two bodies of knowledge. For a fuller explanation of this phenomenon, see "Secrets of the Zodiac," page 160.

The *astrological* placement of the Moon, by sign, is given in the chart below. Gardeners who prefer to use this method should follow the chart.

For planting, the most fertile signs are the three water signs: Cancer, Scorpio, and Pisces. The astrological signs of Taurus, Virgo, and Capricorn would be good second choices for sowing. It should be noted that above-ground crops like to be planted between the new Moon and full Moon (waxing), whereas the root and below-ground crops prefer to be sown after the full Moon and before the new Moon (waning). The dates for the Moon's phases can be found on pages 54-80; the Outdoor Planting Table on page 206 can also be used as a guide.

Weeding and plowing are best done when the Moon occupies the signs of Aries, Gemini, Leo, Sagittarius, or Aquarius. Insect pests can also be handled at those times. Transplanting and grafting are most successful when done under a Cancer, Scorpio, or Pisces Moon. Clean out the garden shed when the Moon occupies Virgo and the work will flow along extremely smoothly. Fences or permanent beds could be nicely built or mended when Capricorn predominates. Avoid indecision when under the Libra Moon.

MOON'S PLACE IN THE ASTROLOGICAL ZODIAC

	NOV. 93	DEC. 93	JAN. 94	FEB. 94	MAR. 94	APR. 94	MAY 94	JUNE 94	JULY 94	AUG. 94	SEPT. 94	OCT. 94	NOV. 94	DEC. 94
1	GEM	CAN	LEO	LIB	LIB	SAG	CAP	PSC	ARI	GEM	CAN	LEO	LIB	SCO
2	GEM	CAN	VIR	SCO	SCO	CAP	AQU	PSC	ARI	GEM	CAN	VIR	LIB	SAG
3	GEM	LEO	VIR	SCO	SCO	CAP	AQU	ARI	TAU	GEM	LEO	VIR	SCO	SAG
4	CAN	LEO	LIB	SAG	SAG	AQU	PSC	ARI	TAU	CAN	LEO	LIB	SCO	CAP
5	CAN	VIR	LIB	SAG	SAG	AQU	PSC	TAU	GEM	CAN	VIR	LIB	SAG	CAP
6	LEO	VIR	SCO	SAG	CAP	AQU	PSC	TAU	GEM	LEO	VIR	SCO	SAG	AQU
7	LEO	VIR	SCO	CAP	CAP	PSC	ARI	TAU	GEM	LEO	LIB	SCO	CAP	AQU
8	VIR	LIB	SAG	CAP	AQU	PSC	ARI	GEM	CAN	VIR	LIB	SAG	CAP	PSC
9	VIR	LIB	SAG	AQU	AQU	ARI	TAU	GEM	CAN	VIR	SCO	SAG	AQU	PSC
10	LIB	SCO	CAP	AQU	AQU	ARI	TAU	CAN	LEO	VIR	SCO	CAP	AQU	PSC
11	LIB	SCO	CAP	PSC	PSC	ARI	TAU	CAN	LEO	LIB	SAG	CAP	PSC	ARI
12	SCO	SAG	CAP	PSC	PSC	TAU	GEM	CAN	VIR	LIB	SAG	CAP	PSC	ARI
13	SCO	SAG	AQU	PSC	ARI	TAU	GEM	LEO	VIR	SCO	CAP	AQU	PSC	TAU
14	SAG	CAP	AQU	ARI	ARI	GEM	CAN	LEO	LIB	SCO	CAP	AQU	ARI	TAU
15	SAG	CAP	PSC	ARI	ARI	GEM	CAN	VIR	LIB	SAG	AQU	PSC	ARI	TAU
16	CAP	AQU	PSC	TAU	TAU	GEM	LEO	VIR	SCO	SAG	AQU	PSC	TAU	GEM
17	CAP	AQU	ARI	TAU	TAU	CAN	LEO	LIB	SCO	CAP	AQU	ARI	TAU	GEM
18	CAP	PSC	ARI	TAU	GEM	CAN	LEO	LIB	SCO	CAP	PSC	ARI	TAU	CAN
19	AQU	PSC	ARI	GEM	GEM	LEO	VIR	SCO	SAG	AQU	PSC	ARI	GEM	CAN
20	AQU	PSC	TAU	GEM	GEM	LEO	VIR	SCO	SAG	AQU	ARI	TAU	GEM	CAN
21	PSC	ARI	TAU	CAN	CAN	VIR	LIB	SAG	CAP	PSC	ARI	TAU	CAN	LEO
22	PSC	ARI	GEM	CAN	CAN	VIR	LIB	SAG	CAP	PSC	TAU	TAU	CAN	LEO
23	PSC	TAU	GEM	LEO	LEO	LIB	SCO	CAP	AQU	PSC	TAU	GEM	CAN	VIR
24	ARI	TAU	GEM	LEO	LEO	LIB	SCO	CAP	AQU	ARI	TAU	GEM	LEO	VIR
25	ARI	TAU	CAN	LEO	VIR	SCO	SAG	AQU	PSC	ARI	GEM	CAN	LEO	LIB
26	TAU	GEM	CAN	VIR	VIR	SCO	SAG	AQU	PSC	TAU	GEM	CAN	VIR	LIB
27	TAU	GEM	LEO	VIR	LIB	SAG	CAP	AQU	ARI	TAU	GEM	LEO	VIR	LIB
28	TAU	CAN	LEO	LIB	LIB	SAG	CAP	PSC	ARI	TAU	CAN	LEO	LIB	SCO
29	GEM	CAN	VIR	—	SCO	SAG	AQU	PSC	ARI	GEM	CAN	LEO	LIB	SCO
30	GEM	CAN	VIR	—	SCO	CAP	AQU	ARI	TAU	GEM	LEO	VIR	SCO	SAG
31	—	LEO	LIB	—	SAG	—	PSC	—	TAU	CAN	—	VIR	—	SAG

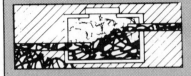
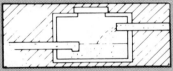

Hand-Taming Wild Birds

Like never, never swallow while a bird is on your
hand watching you. Did you know that?

I hand-fed my first wild bird, a female hedge sparrow, at the age of ten. Many years later, on a year's stay in England, I spent most of my time sketching the beautiful scenery of Epping Forest and getting friendly with the wild birds. I always carried raisins in one pocket and canary seed in another.

All you need to be successful in taming wild birds is a little know-how. You have most likely heard someone say: "She has wonderful luck with her flowers." Luck plays a very small part in success with flowers — no more than it does with birds.

Here are a few simple but very important rules you must remember if you wish to succeed with birds:

BY ALFRED G. MARTIN
– illustrated by Carolyn Croll

1   Whether you believe it or not, always try to behave as if a bird can and does reason, as if in some things it is smarter than you. If you do this, you will have little trouble in hand-taming it.

2   Never approach a wild bird without speaking to it all the time.

3   Always move very slowly around birds until they become accustomed to your presence.

4   Always try to remember that there is no such thing as a naturally tame wild bird. You are its greatest enemy until you have gained its confidence. If you should have a stray one come to your hand before you have tried to hand-tame it, you can be sure that it has been tamed by some other bird lover.

5   Never hold out your hand to a bird unless it contains food that it likes. A wild bird does not come to you because it loves you; it takes a chance because it is hungry. Holding out an empty hand to a bird is like holding out an empty hand to a child who expects to find a candy bar in it. A bird will resent it as much as a child would, and worse still, it may think you are telling it that the food is all gone and that it may leave for greener pastures.

6   Always carry some of the seed you are using as feed in your pocket; then if a bird settles on your shoulder, it will not be disappointed.

7   Never swallow while a bird is on your hand watching you. This rule is a result of consistent experience on my part. Until I realized what was wrong, I lost the opportunity to tame many birds. The sight of food makes a bird's mouth water, and it always swallows just before it starts to eat. When the bird sees you swallow while you are looking at it, it may think you are considering it for your next meal. It won't stay around to find out; the chances are very good that you will never see that bird again.

Always watch for the slightest sign of fear on a bird's face. Birds' eyes show fear in exactly the same way human eyes do. The movement of a bird's stomach also shows fear, just as the rapid movement of the vein on a man's forehead betrays his fear.

The instant you see signs of fear when a wild bird first comes to your hand, hold your breath as long as you can and keep absolutely motionless.

8 Never close your hand on a wild bird unless it is to pick up a sick or injured one. The instant you close your hand on a free bird, it is so frightened that when you open your hand again, it will fly as far away from you as fast as it can and will not return. On more than one occasion I have heard and felt the tiny heart of a poor little bird burst from fright while I held it in my hand.

9 If a bird wants to leave you while you are trying to tame it, let it go; do not follow it. The bird knows how the fox, mink, weasel, cat, and raccoon follow when they want something to eat, and when you start following it, it thinks you have the same thing in mind. Be patient and the bird will come to you when it is hungry.

10 Never overload your feeder, unless you are trying to get a large flock of new birds to come in. If you have plenty of food out all the time, you will encourage undesirable species, and you will fail in hand-taming a single bird. It is impossible to hand-tame a wild bird that can get all the food it wants on your feeder; it must be hungry before taking a chance on your hand.

11 Never allow even your best friends near your birds unless you are with them. A well-meaning friend can ruin months of work for you and may even drive off your birds for good. If you wish to let a friend feed your birds, be very sure to advise him how to do it first, and if he will not do exactly as told, get him away as fast as you can, or you may be very sorry.

You will have greater success with birds if you think of them as little people who can reason and not as brainless creatures who act only on the persuasion of some inborn instinct.

Do not feel discouraged if your first few attempts at hand-taming are failures, because this may happen to the best of naturalists. There is just as much individualism among all wild creatures as there is among people. It may be that not a single bird was tamable in the flock you worked with.

Here at my home in Great Pond, Maine, most of the pine grosbeaks will hand-tame. About 60 percent of the redpolls will take food from the hand; about 50 percent of the chickadees and 30 percent of the purple finches will hand-tame. I have never hand-tamed a red cardinal, so I cannot give you any dependable information on the bird.

Some people enjoy certain types of food more than others, and every species of bird has some kind of food it prefers above all other foods. The purple finch will kill himself on flax seed if he has the chance. The white-breasted nuthatch, the evening grosbeak, pine grosbeak, and chickadee prefer sunflower seed. The goldfinch likes thistle. The red-breasted nuthatch and the downy and hairy woodpeckers like suet. The robin and catbird are very fond of raisins and currants. If you cannot entice any one of the above birds to your hand with the food mentioned, you can be fairly certain that it is impossible to tame that individual.

Birds taken from the nest as babies and raised in a cage would come to the hand when released, but that would be like catching trout with a net. You would not be hand-taming a wild bird. It merely would be coming to feed like a barnyard chicken. □ □

A selection from the book Hand-Taming Wild Birds at the Feeder *by Alfred G. Martin, originally published in 1963. Reprinted with permission from the publisher, Alan C. Hood and Co., Inc., 28 Birge St., Brattleboro, VT 05301. Available in paperback from the publisher at $12.95 plus $2 postage and handling.*

Ways to Store Everything

SO IT STAYS FRESH

There's a good reason the Dead Sea scrolls survived in an underground cave. Dry and cool is the basic rule for storing most things. These are the conditions that postpone the deterioration of tissue by infection from foreign microbes such as bacteria or molds (their spores are everywhere!) or by self-destruction from its own metabolic processes. Deterioration is inevitable, but it can be delayed and minimized. In arranging safe storage for the necessities of life, man — and woman — has shown great imagination.

A few basic guidelines: Find a place for everything . . . and keep everything in its place as neat as a pin. And — one rotten apple does spoil the barrel. Con-

That means putting pumpkins under your bed, mushrooms in paper bags — and hockey pucks in the freezer! (And never put bread or tomatoes in the refrigerator.)

BY CYNTHIA VAN HAZINGA

trol the mold population by tossing out any moldy fruits or vegetables, and clean storage containers thoroughly from time to time.

Cool temperatures slow the biochemical activity of cells without killing them. Refrigerators are cool, but they're not dry (and not wet enough, either, for some storage); cupboards are dry, but they may not be cool. There's a lot to be said for the old-fashioned root cellar, the dug-out, underground variety common before refrigerators, where country folk kept potatoes and other root crops. In northern states the winter temperature in a root cellar can be kept just above 32° F, which is best for storing most vegetables, and the humidity can be controlled by letting in fresh air.

APPLES

To store a harvest of apples or other fall fruits and vegetables, you may want to improvise a root cellar, perhaps in an unheated space protected from freezing or by insulating the bulkhead doors over cellar stairs. Remember that fruits and vegetables need an occasional change of air — after all, they are still alive and breathing. You give them oxygen when you open the bulkhead or the cellar door from the outside, and in cold weather you may let in a bit of heat from the cellar side. Apples keep well for about six months at temperatures between freezing and 45° F. Even a simple styrofoam chest or a double cardboard box can approximate root-cellar conditions.

BATTERIES, CANDLES, FILM, SOAP, AND SIMILAR INANIMATES

Store these in a cool, dry place, out of reach of rodents and children. Professional photographers often keep their film in the refrigerator, but only when it's tightly sealed in a moisture-proof wrap.

BERRIES

Never rinse them before storage: It washes off the thin, protective epidermal layer. Store them in a cool, dry place; refrigeration favors the growth of mold as a result of condensation on their surfaces. (This is why most small fruits keep only a day or two in the refrigerator.)

(continued on next page)

BREADS

Put them in a breadbox. Staling is a temperature-dependent process that proceeds most rapidly at temperatures just above freezing and very slowly below freezing. What's going on is retrogradation of the starch molecules, molecular reordering that makes the starch and protein phases more dense and more segregated from water — not simple drying out but a change in the location and distribution of water molecules. Frozen, bread keeps well as a result of the leveling off of the decline in its water-holding capacity. In one experiment, bread stored at 46° F (a typical refrigerator temperature), staled as much in one day as bread kept at 86° F did in six. So, if you're going to freeze bread, freeze it fast; otherwise, store it wrapped at room temperature.

CUT FLOWERS

Keep them in a cool spot in water conditioned with a packaged floral preservative or one home-brewed with sugar (to replace the glucose the flowers are losing), citric acid such as lemon juice (to lower the pH), and carbonation or a bit of household bleach (to slow the growth of bacteria). Cut flowers last longest if their stems are cut with a sharp blade, either underwater or seconds before being plunged into water. The water should be warmish, never icy.

DRUGS AND REMEDIES

Ironically, the worst place to keep medicine may be in the over-the-sink bathroom medicine cabinet. Drugs and remedies should be kept cool and dry; bathrooms are often warm and steamy. Store medicines, and cosmetics, too, in a dry spot — perhaps a bedroom cabinet.

FINE CHINA

Display irreplaceable items in a glass-front cabinet or a hard-to-reach shelf, preferably one with a lip to prevent china from walking off the edge. Stack same-size plates with a piece of felt between them in piles of about four or six. Don't stack cups or bowls that can crack under the weight. Consider using cuphooks.

FRESH HERBS

Most fresh herbs (and greens) will keep best when refrigerated unwashed in tightly sealed plastic bags with enough moisture available to prevent wilting. Dill and parsley should be stored with stems immersed in a glass of water tented with a plastic bag. Instead of getting slimy, they will then keep for about two weeks. Extended storage of any living tissue in a plastic bag is not advisable; denying the plant cells oxygen makes them switch to anaerobic respiration, build up alcohol, and turn brown. Moisture- and gas-permeable paper and cellophane are better for the long run.

GRAINS AND FLOURS

Keep "dry" ingredients dry and cool in an airtight, moisture-tight container. Beans, pasta, rice, and other grains store well in tin or plastic, but beans do stale and toughen — use them up! Prevent vermin or insects from hatching in flour (or grains) by freezing for a few hours before storage.

HOCKEY PUCKS AND OTHER SPORTS STUFF

We are told that avid Canadian players deep-freeze their hockey pucks so they move faster when they hit the ice. Queried, a tennis player we know admits he keeps his tennis balls in the refrigerator for the same reason. The size of your freezer may be a consid-

eration. Our freezer is full of coffee beans and cranberries, nuts, vegetable stock, and ice cream, but keep your hockey pucks there if your children are cutting seconds off their score.

LIVE SHELLFISH

Store shellfish such as clams, mussels, and oysters in cool, well-ventilated boxes, not in airtight plastic bags or containers. Store fish on ice, briefly.

MUSHROOMS

Remove from any market wrap and keep them in the refrigerator in a paper bag. The bag absorbs some of the moisture and keeps the mushrooms from spoiling.

ONIONS

Mature, dry-skinned onions like it cool and dry — so don't store them with apples or potatoes. French-braided onions are handy and free to get some ventilation as well.

POTATOES, BEETS, CARROTS, AND OTHER ROOT CROPS

See "Apples" or store in a dark, cool place. Unlike berries, these sturdy vegetables should be brushed clean; the soil that clings to them harbors microbes. Never keep potatoes in the refrigerator; at temperatures lower than 40° F their starch will turn to sugar, making them taste strangely sweet. Don't store apples and potatoes together; the apples give off an ethylene gas that will spoil the potatoes. And, clipping the tops of parsnips, carrots, beets, and turnips will nip their tendency to use moisture in leafy growth.

PUMPKINS AND WINTER SQUASH

Squashes don't like to be quite as cool as root crops do. If you have a coolish bedroom, stashing them under the bed works well. They like a temperature of about 50° to 65° F.

SUGAR

Granulated sugar must be kept dry (and cool) or it will harden. Brown sugar contains moisture and hardens when exposed to air. Store brown sugar in an airtight container or freezer for extended storage. If it does solidify, it can be softened by exposing it to moisture. Try baking it, covered, at 200° F next to (but not with) a cup of water for about 20 minutes or storing it with a slice of apple or a citrus rind, tightly enclosed, until it's soft again.

TOMATOES AND OTHER TROPICALS

Never, ever refrigerate fresh tomatoes. It ruins their flavor and texture at once. Don't keep them on a sunny window sill, either, but at cool room temperature. Ripe tomatoes, which start life as tropical fruits, and other fruits native to warm climates do not keep well in the cold. Bananas turn black, avocados stop softening, and citrus fruit gets spotty. Think of the country of origin and store these fruits, as well as pineapples, melons, eggplants, cucumbers, peppers, and beans at about 50° F if possible.

YOUR WEDDING DRESS (OR YOUR MOTHER'S)

Any important textile calls for acid-free paper and boxes (available from dry cleaners); wood pulp disintegrates and takes the fabric with it. □□

FOR *OLD FARMER'S ALMANAC* READERS

Storage Reference Chart: Handy chart, printed on heavy stock, includes all information presented in this article — plus much more. Send $2 to Storage Chart, *Old Farmer's Almanac*, P.O. Box 520, Dublin, NH 03444.

Wife's Confession:
"I had to trick him... and he's happy I did!"

"I had really begun to wonder about him," says Sally S*, 26, who asked that her last name not be published!

"At first I thought it was another woman. Then I wondered if maybe it was something worse."

The problem was her husband, George. "We used to have such good times," Sally recalled fondly of her dating days. "We went dancing and to parties and he could stay up all night."

But, after three years together, the romance began to fade.

George was bringing home a paycheck that should have made them happy, but he was clearly leaving something behind at the job.

"I dreamed of an affair," Sally admits. "But I couldn't picture myself with anyone else."

That's when Sally heard about a pill her best friend's husband was using. "He gets it sent to the office," Laura explained, "so I won't know he buys it. Of course," Laura added with a wicked grin, "if he ever stopped using it, I'd leave him in a minute! That pill has changed my life!"

Pill for men

What was this pill? Amazingly, thousands of men, like Laura's husband, have used it ever since it was first released to men in 1981.

It is called "NSP-270" stories about it have appeared in leading publications. At one time these reports even received an evaluation by the Navy. It has been widely used by both young men and older men — in fact, there are men in their 60's and 70's who count on it.

A happy trick

Laura agreed to "borrow" a few pills for Sally — and find out where her husband was getting them.

At the market, Sally bought a bottle of ordinary vitamins, emptied them out, and put the NSP-270 inside the bottle.

The next morning at breakfast, Sally offered George a "vitamin". He took it and the rest is history.

Later that night when Sally told George what she had done, he offered to buy a six month supply. George now takes his "vitamins" regularly, Sally has her "affair," (with George, of course!), and both Sally and Laura are making extra money selling NSP-270 to their friends!

Men should know!

If a man doesn't yet know about NSP-270, it may be because, like certain personal products, you can't buy it in local stores. But you can order it by mail, if you are over 18.

Write to Frank E. Bush, Inc., Dept. NE-62, Box 5009, Monticello, NY 12701. Be sure to include your name and address. Both checks and money orders are accepted. For orders of $25 or more you may request C.O.D. if your order is to a street address (not a P.O. box).

Send $12.95 for one bottle of NSP-270 (30-day supply), $15.74 for 2 bottles, $21.36 for 3 bottles, $38.85 for 6 bottles or $58.00 for 10 bottles. The company will pay the postage & handling charges on your first order.

If you are ordering 3 bottles or more, they will also send you an interesting book about NSP-270. The product carries a 30-day money back guarantee.

Buying BY THE Gallon

Although the ultimate origin of the word *gallon* is unknown, linguists have traced it to the medieval Latin word *galleta,* a measure for wine, and related Old French and Portuguese words that meant a mug or measure for liquids. It is a measure of capacity or volume: The British imperial gallon contains 277.42 cubic inches; the standard gallon in the United States contains 231 cubic inches. A gallon can also be a dry measure equal to half a peck. A gallon can seem like a little, such as a gallon of water drawn from the sea, or a lot, such as a gallon of spilled milk. The list below is an indication of how much we'd have to pay if everything came by the gallon.

Tap water, Los Angeles	$ .001
Tap water, New York City	.00135
Crude oil, west Texas intermediate	.53
Gasoline, unleaded, 87 octane	1.30

Liquid nitrogen	2.00
Cow's milk, pasteurized, homogenized	2.50
Sheep's milk, raw	4.00
Beer, domestic	6.00
Clam chowder, reconstituted, condensed	6.00
Contact lens saline solution, generic	13.00
Rubber cement	16.00
Olive oil, pure	17.00
Blended whiskey, cheap, 70 proof	18.00
Liquid helium	30.00
Maple syrup, Grade A light amber	40.00
Tabasco sauce	65.00
Vanilla extract, pure	75.00
Champagne, Moët & Chandon "White Star," extra dry	160.00
Mercury	190.00
Amoxicillin, children's	280.00
Fountain-pen ink, permanent blue	440.00
Nail polish	780.00
Cyanoacrylate adhesive ("super glue")	4,000.00
Chanel No. 5 perfume	35,000.00
Holstein bull semen, "Mascot"	400,000.00
Interferon, alfa-N3	500,000.00

BY JON VARA

– illustrated by Margo Letourneau

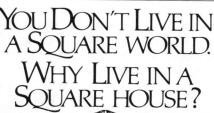

A
Handful
of
SAVORY TURNOVERS
to Try

*A long time ago,
someone got the bright
idea of tucking some
stew into a piece of
bread, folding it up,
and baking it.
Well, thank goodness,
the idea spread to the
veritable ends of the
Earth . . .*

by Ken Haedrich

– illustrated by Traci Harmon,
represented by Creative Freelancers

Back before plates, silverware, tables, or table manners, there was the savory turnover. How far back? You got me. But my guess is that it couldn't have been too long after man figured there had to be a neater way to eat his spoils du jour than by grabbing it out of the pot with his bare hands. Not only did that nasty little habit burn like heck, but all the succulent juices slipped away between his fingers.

The concept of mealtime was destined to meet at an auspicious intersection with primitive bread, those first tortilla-like rounds of dough fashioned by the village wives and daughters. Someone got the idea of tucking the stew into the bread, closing it up tight, and baking it to a turn by the fire. And just like that, gastronomy took a giant leap forward.

Not only did the idea of the savory turnover stick, but it would eventually travel to the ends of the Earth, adapting itself to local cuisines wherever it went. Consider the Italian ravioli and the Chinese wonton — both noodle-type turnovers cooked in boiling water. Or the Polish pirogi, a sometimes-boiled, sometimes-baked dumpling. Greek cookery has a number of savory turnovers — *tiropita, kreatopita,* and *spanakopita* — all wrapped with paper-thin phyllo dough. There are egg rolls, knishes, and Mexican empanadas. This category we call savory turnovers goes on and on, always encompassing the foods that are most plentiful and beloved.

So it was that the wives of Cornish miners invented the Cornish pasty (that's *pass'-tee,* not to be confused with the traditional garb of scantily dressed dancers), which arrived in this country in the mid-1800s. Big as a platter, sturdy of crust (one source claimed that a worthy crust could withstand a tumble down the mine shaft), and chock-full of meat and potatoes, the pasty was the sort of sustenance a hard-working miner could depend on to get him through a day of back-breaking labor. In *The*

Complete Book of Pastry (Simon & Schuster, 1981), Bernard Clayton writes that each miner's initials were carved into the dough, so that the men could pick their own pasty out from the many that were scattered about on the mine timbers. He says that initials are still used today, but generally only to identify the type of filling. As for dessert, the pasty even contained its own sweet corner—one last bite or two filled with fruit preserves.

Baked, boiled, steamed, or fried, filled breads and turnovers have found a happy home in this multicultural stew we call America. Take calzone for instance. *Calzoni* means, literally, pants legs. They were originally long narrow tubes of dough enclosing sausages or salami, resembling the baggy pants Neapolitan men wore in the 18th and 19th centuries. About a decade ago, before it started appearing on the menus of chic California eateries — stuffed with goat cheese, imported olives, and fresh herbs — calzone was virtually unheard of in this country. Now it is as commonplace as pizza in its adopted homeland.

Here are a handful of savory turnovers to try your hand at, including favorite versions of calzone and pasty. There's also a recipe for *vareniki,* the Russian cousin to Polish pirogi, and one for spanakopita — Greek spinach turnovers. Finally, there are fried turnovers known as *samosas.* I first ate samosas 15 years ago at an Indian restaurant in New Jersey, a place where the portions were almost as huge as the turbaned chef who worked in the closet-size kitchen. They were so hot when they arrived with their yogurt and chutney dipping sauces that you could still hear them sizzling. Serve them as a prelude to a larger Indian feast with your own favorite homemade chutney.

Try one of these turnovers, or try them all. Just be sure to keep your pasty away from mine shafts.

Vareniki

Serve a plateful of these topped with fried onions, with sour cream and hot mustard on the side to swab them in.

FOR THE DOUGH:

1 egg, lightly beaten
½ cup sour cream
½ cup cold water
1 teaspoon salt
3 cups (approximately) unbleached all-purpose flour

Whisk the egg, sour cream, water, and salt in a large mixing bowl. Add 2 cups of the flour and beat well with a wooden spoon. Add enough of the remaining flour, about ⅓ cup at a time, to make a soft, kneadable dough. Turn the dough out onto a floured surface and knead for about 7 minutes, until smooth, using flour as needed to keep the dough from sticking. Flatten the dough into a disk about ½-inch thick, flour both sides of it well, and place on a floured baking sheet. Cover with plastic and refrigerate for at least 2 hours.

FILLING AND ASSEMBLY:

2 cups sauerkraut, drained
1½ cups precooked Polish
sausage, chopped

Bring a pot of well-salted water to a boil. Cut off a quarter of the dough and return the rest to the refrigerator. Roll the dough ⅛-inch thick on a floured surface. Cut 3-inch circles of dough with a glass or biscuit cutter, keeping the cuts close together (press together the scraps and refrigerate).

Place a little pile of sauerkraut in the center of each circle and top with a bit of sausage. Moisten the edges with a wet finger or brush and fold them over, pressing the edges to seal. Set aside on a floured surface. Repeat for the remaining dough. Boil 8 to 10 at a time for 7 minutes. Remove with a slotted spoon, blot briefly on paper towels, and serve right away. If you are serving a number of people at once, cook the vareniki in 2 or 3 pots all at once. *Makes about 30 turnovers.*

Curried Chick Pea Samosas

FOR THE DOUGH:

1 cup whole wheat flour
1 cup unbleached flour
¾ teaspoon salt
¼ teaspoon baking powder
2 tablespoons oil
⅔ cup (approximately) water

Toss together the dry ingredients in a mixing bowl. Add the oil and rub it into the flour with fingertips until it is thoroughly incorporated. Stir in most of the water. If the dough fails to cohere or is dry in places, add a bit more water. When the dough coheres, knead it for 5 minutes, until smooth, using sprinkles of flour if needed to keep the dough from sticking. Wrap the dough in plastic and let it rest while you make the filling.

FILLING AND ASSEMBLY:

4 tablespoons vegetable oil
1 large onion, finely chopped
1 garlic clove, minced
3 tablespoons curry powder (or to taste)
1 teaspoon paprika
¼ teaspoon cayenne
¼ cup tomato puree
2 19-ounce cans chick peas, drained and rinsed
½ cup finely chopped cilantro or fresh parsley
juice of 1 lemon
½ cup raisins, chopped very fine
oil for frying

Heat 2 tablespoons of the oil in a large skillet and add the onion. Sauté over medium heat for 5 minutes, stirring often. Lower the heat, add the remaining oil, and stir in the garlic and spices. Cook, stirring constantly, for 1 minute, then stir in the tomato puree and chick peas. Cook another minute, then scrape into a bowl. Mash well. Stir in the cilantro or parsley, lemon juice, and raisins. Cool.

Cut off a walnut-size piece of dough, shaping it into a ball; it should be about 1½ inches in diameter. On a floured surface roll the dough into a 6-inch circle. Cut the circle in half and moisten each of the two resulting straight edges. Fold each semicircle in half and crimp with a fork or ravioli cutter where the straight edges meet.

Spoon a little of the filling into each dough packet; don't make it too full or it won't seal properly. Moisten the inside edge of one of the flaps and press the two together to seal. Crimp the edge as before. Set aside on a floured baking sheet. Repeat for the remaining samosas.

Heat about 1½ inches of oil in a deep skillet. Fry about 6 samosas at a time to a rich golden brown. Remove with a slotted spoon and blot on paper towels. Serve at once with chutney or plain yogurt. *Makes about 25 to 30 appetizers.*

Spinach & Feta Cheese Packets (Spanakopita)

1 cup small-curd cottage cheese
1 pound frozen spinach, thawed
¾ cup crumbled feta cheese
½ teaspoon dried oregano
⅛ teaspoon ground nutmeg
2 tablespoons olive oil
1 medium onion, finely chopped
pepper to taste
4 or 5 pitted Greek olives, finely chopped (optional)

8 sheets phyllo dough
6 tablespoons melted butter

Several hours ahead, place the cottage cheese in a sieve over a bowl to drain, mixing it up occasionally with a spoon. Once it has drained, pour any liquid out of the bowl. Using the back of a spoon, force the cottage cheese through the sieve and into the bowl. Squeeze the liquid out of the spinach, finely chop it, then add to the cottage cheese. Mix in the feta cheese, oregano, and nutmeg.

Heat the olive oil in a small skillet. Add the onion and sauté over medium heat, stirring, for 5 minutes. Scrape into the cheese mixture. Add pepper to taste and the olives, if using them. Lightly butter a large baking sheet.

With the sheets stacked, cut the phyllo dough in half lengthwise. Put the sheets on top of one another and cut in half again lengthwise. Stack the piles on top of one another and cover them with a piece of plastic wrap. Preheat the oven to 375° F.

Brush the top piece of phyllo with butter, then take it off the pile and lay it on the counter in front of you. Butter a second sheet and lay it on the first. (Re-cover the pile with plastic.) Put a heaping tablespoon of filling in the corner at one end of the phyllo sheets. Lift up the corner of both sheets where the filling is and fold it as you would a flag, so a triangle of phyllo covers the dough. Continue to fold,

flag-style, all the way to the top. Don't make them too snug as you fold, or the filling may burst out. Lay the packet on the baking sheet, with the seam down, and brush with butter. Repeat for the remaining packets. Work quickly so the phyllo doesn't dry out.

Bake the packets for about 30 minutes, until golden brown. Serve hot, warm, or at room temperature. *Makes about 16 small appetizers.*

Cornish Pasties

FOR THE DOUGH:

3½ cups unbleached all-purpose flour
1 teaspoon salt
½ cup chilled unsalted butter, cut in small pieces
½ cup chilled vegetable shortening
½ cup iced water (or more)

Toss the flour and salt together in a large bowl. Add the butter and shortening and cut them into the flour until the mixture resembles coarse meal. Tossing with a fork, gradually add enough of the water until the dough coheres; it will feel like pie dough. Cut the dough into four even pieces, then form them into 4 even disks about ½-inch thick. Put them on a lightly floured plate,

cover with plastic, and refrigerate for 30 minutes.

FILLING AND ASSEMBLY:

2 tablespoons butter
1 large onion, halved and thinly sliced
2 cups cabbage, thinly sliced
salt and pepper to taste
½ pound pork loin, coarsely chopped
1½ cups potatoes, peeled and cut into ½-inch cubes
optional seasonings: a little dried thyme or savory

Melt the butter in a large skillet and stir in the onion and cabbage. Cook over medium heat, stirring, about 5 minutes, until the cabbage is limp. Scrape into a bowl and season to taste with salt and pepper. Stir in the pork, potatoes, and herbs, if used. Cool to room temperature.

Roll the first disk into an 9-inch circle, trimming the edge with a knife to make it even. Repeat for the remaining disks, then refrigerate them between sheets of wax paper.

Preheat the oven to 425° F.

Remove the dough from the refrigerator one sheet at a time. Place about 1 heaping cupful of the filling on half of the dough, leaving a ¾-inch border all around. Moisten the entire perimeter with a pastry brush, then fold the empty half over the filling. Bring the bottom edge up to meet the top edge, then press them together to seal, sculpting the edge into an upstanding ridge. Transfer to a baking sheet and refrigerate. Repeat for the remaining pasties.

Prick two or three steam vents in the top crust with a fork. Bake for 15 minutes, then reduce the heat to 350° F. Bake another 45 minutes, until the pasties are nicely browned. Serve hot. *Makes 4 pasties.*

Broccoli, Cheese & Olive Calzone

FOR THE DOUGH:

1½ cups lukewarm water
1¼-ounce package active dry yeast (1 scant tablespoon)
¼ cup rye flour
½ cup whole wheat flour
1½ teaspoons salt
2 tablespoons olive oil
3¼ cups (approximately) unbleached all-purpose flour

Pour the water into a large mixing bowl and sprinkle the yeast over it. Set aside for 5 minutes to dissolve. Stir in the rye and whole wheat flours, salt, and olive oil. Add half of the unbleached flour and beat well with a wooden spoon for 1 minute. Add the remaining unbleached flour, about ⅓ cup at a time, to make a soft kneadable dough. Turn the dough out onto a floured surface and knead for 10 minutes, using a little extra flour as necessary to keep the dough from sticking. Place the dough in an oiled bowl, cover with plastic, and leave in a warm spot until doubled. Prepare the filling as the dough rises.

FILLING AND ASSEMBLY:

3 tablespoons olive oil
2 large onions, halved and thinly sliced
2 minced garlic cloves
8 cups broccoli flowers, steamed just until tender
2 cups (8 ounces) mozzarella cheese, cut into small cubes
½ cup grated Parmesan or Romano cheese
½ cup pitted olives, coarsely chopped
1 cup tomato sauce or crushed canned tomatoes in puree
4 teaspoons dried oregano

Warm the oil in a skillet. Add the onions and sauté over medium heat for 8 minutes. Stir in the garlic, sauté another minute, then remove from the heat. Preheat the oven to 450° F. Lightly oil and dust 2 baking sheets with cornmeal.

When the dough has doubled, punch it down, knead for a minute, then divide in half. Knead each half into a ball, dust with flour, and set aside on a floured work surface.

Working with one piece of dough at a time, roll it into a rectangle about 15 inches long by 10 inches wide. Draw an imaginary line down the length of the dough; keep all the filling to one side of it, leaving a 1½-inch border at the edge. Layer on half of the broccoli, the sautéed mixture, the cheeses, and olives. Dot the top with half of the tomato sauce, then sprinkle with half of the oregano. Lightly moisten the entire perimeter with a pastry brush. Without stretching the dough, fold the uncovered half of the dough over the filling and pinch to seal, curling the edge up slightly. Transfer to one of the prepared sheets and repeat for the other calzone. Bake for 30 minutes, rotating the sheets up-to-down or side-to-side about halfway through. Cool on a rack for 5 minutes, then cut each calzone in half and serve right away. *Makes 2 calzones (4 servings).*

□□

STOMACH AGONY?

UPSET STOMACH? GAS PAINS? SOUR TASTE IN MOUTH? BELCHING? SIMPLE INTESTINAL IRRITATIONS? ON A COLITIS OR ULCER DIET?*

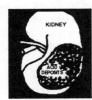

Freckles the Cow

She's going to go down in history . . .

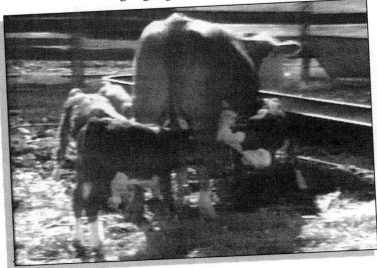

– courtesy Bruce Traber

his is no ordinary cow. As her friend Bruce Traber says, "Freckles is quite a cow. It's too bad there's not a Cow Hall of Fame, 'cause she'd be in it!" The focus of this admiration is a gentle, white-faced Hereford who lives on Robert Phillip's 40-acre farm in tiny Norris, South Carolina. On June 8, 1991, without any help from man or beast, Freckles gave birth to quadruplets. The probability of triplets in Herefords is 0.03 percent, but quadruplets are "almost unheard of in a natural setting," according to Dr. Carl Thompson, beef cattle geneticist at Clemson University.

"She just had them the way God intended," says Traber. "She didn't need a vet or any help at all."

Neighbor Joe Tankersley was bush-hogging on his adjacent land when he noticed Freckles was off by herself in the pasture and thought she might be getting ready to birth a calf. In the 15 minutes it took him to make a round, he noticed one calf had been born. He made another round and saw that a second calf had arrived. Round three brought yet another calf, but when Tankersley completed round four and discovered a fourth calf, he jumped off his tractor and ran to get his wife. Quipped one local farmer, "If Joe

hadn't quit working, there's no telling *how* many calves Freckles would have had!"

Although quadruplet births are extremely rare, it's even more unusual for the mother cow to accept more than one calf. Says Professor Thompson, "It's miraculous for her to have four live ones and for her to clean them up and for them to live. Freckles is indeed a rare cow."

For an encore, Freckles presented the quads, Eenie, Meenie, Miney, and Moe, with twin sisters on July 12, 1992. But the story of this happy family isn't over. As we go to press, Freckles is due to calve again . . .

– Deb Sanderson

The OLD FARMER'S ALMANAC 1994 ⧖ OLD AND NEW MATHEMATICAL PUZZLES

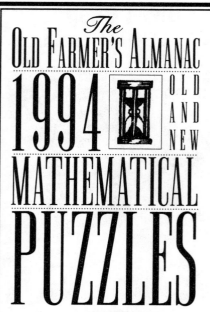

Blanton C. Wiggin, Puzzle Editor

For 1994, here are 14 classical, original, or timely puzzles from our readers. Common sense and a little agility are all you'll need; you won't need calculus, computers, alertness to tricks, or specialized knowledge, though sometimes they may be helpful.

The answers to puzzles 11 through 14 are omitted. We will award one prize of $100 for the best set of solutions to **these four** postmarked before February 15, 1994.

Each basic correct answer will earn 20 points, with up to 5 bonus points for explanations and elaboration.

Please use a separate sheet for each puzzle or puzzle anwer. Be sure to put your name and address on each sheet.

Explanations and Prize-Set answers will be sent after July 1, 1994, to anyone sending $1 and a self-addressed stamped envelope to "Puzzle Answers," *The Old Farmer's Almanac*, P.O. Box 520, Dublin, NH 03444.

We will also pay $15 for each contributed puzzle we use in *The Old Farmer's Almanac* for 1995. Closing date for submissions is February 1, 1994. Entries become the property of Yankee Publishing Incorporated and cannot be acknowledged or returned.

The 1993 winner was Robert Griffin of Montclair, New Jersey, with 98 points. An outstanding entry! Runner-up was Bob Symons, former winner, from Waterloo, Ontario. Congratulations!

Have fun with these 1994 puzzles and send your answers early. Answers to puzzles 1 through 10 appear on page 188.

1. FOUR SQUARES

Difficulty: 1

How can you move and reposition just 2 of the

a. 12 matches to make exactly 6 squares from the 5; and with the

b. 16 matches make exactly 4 squares, each equal in size to the original, from the 5.

Each pattern should have all squares contiguous and no matches or incomplete squares left over.

a.   **b.**

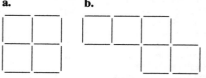

– Frank Atchison,
Charlestown, New South Wales, Australia

2. CHOICES AND ODDS

Difficulty: 1

A gambler is given 3 plain envelopes and is told one contains two $1 bills, one a $1 and a $1,000 note, and the third, two $1,000 bills. He opens one at random and, without looking, takes out a bill. It turns out to be a $1,000 note. What are the odds that the other bill is also $1,000?

– Laurie Van Tassel, Sarasota, Florida

3. MY TRUE LOVE

Difficulty: 2

On the first day of Christmas (Christmas Day), my true love gave to me a partridge in a pear tree. On the second day of Christmas my true love gave to me 2 turtle doves and another partridge in a pear tree. On the third day of Christmas my true love gave to me 3 French hens, 2 more turtle doves, and a third partridge (6 things). This was followed by 4 calling birds, 5 golden rings, 6 geese, 7 swans, 8 maids, 9 pipers, 10 drummers, 11 ladies, and 12 fiddlers, everything stopping after the twelfth day.

Unfortunately, I had no room, so I decided to return one gift each day beginning the day after Christmas (Boxing Day). When did I return the last gift?

– Sidney Kravitz, Dover, New Jersey
(Reprinted from the Journal of Recreational Mathematics with permission)

4. HOW MANY?

Difficulty: 2

If the reciprocal of "0.142,857 = W/D" is "7 Days in a Week," what do the following initials stand for? Round off answers to the nearest integer.

0.076,923 = AF/S 0.019,231 = D/C
0.041,667 = D/H   0.015,625 = CB/S
0.038,461 = A/L   0.011,364 = P/K
0.035,714 = F/D   0.011,111 = RA/D

– Jim Chandler, Scarborough, Ontario

5. LITERATE ODOMETER

Difficulty: 2

Assume an odometer with each counter wheel having 26 letters instead of the usual 10 digits. If A=1, B=2, C=3, etc., what is "OFA" worth?

– Dan Lytle, Clayton, Oklahoma

6. SHIPS IN THE LOCKS

Difficulty: 3

The Rideau Canal drops into the Ottawa River through 8 locks in a single series. Assume each lock can handle several boats, each about the same size, and that passage up or down takes about one hour. A group of boats arrives at the top to go down simultaneously with an upbound flotilla arriving at the bottom. For maximum efficiency, which pack of boats should wait for the other to pass through?

– Jolyn W. Siwa, Auburndale, Massachusetts

7. SQUARING CIRCLES

Difficulty: 3

a. Construct a perfect square using only a circle template and an unmarked straight edge, drawing a total of 8 circles and lines. Unlike the classical "squaring the circle" problem, no compass is used and tangents are permitted.

b. With how few circular 10-inch diameter pie plates can you completely cover a circular 20-inch diameter pizza? Overlapping is OK, but no cutting or folding, please.

– Bob Andersen, Athens, Tennessee

8. ABRA-CA-LADDER

Difficulty: 3

Two ladders are placed across a level alley to opposite buildings. One ladder leans against one building at a point 30 feet above the ground. The second ladder sets against the other building at a point 20 feet up. The ladders intersect at a point 12 feet high.

How wide is the alley?

– George Irish, Melbourne Beach, Florida

9. COCONUTS

Difficulty: 4

On a deserted island 5 castaways find many coconuts. Before nightfall they gather the coconuts into a pile and plan to divide it equally next morning. During the night, one man divides it into 5 equal small piles of whole coconuts, leaving 1 coconut over, which he throws to a monkey. He hides one of the small piles and combines the other 4.

Later in the night, a second, third, fourth, and fifth man each separately do the same, except the fifth man has no extra for the monkey. All piles are integer amounts. No split coconuts.

What is the smallest number of coconuts to start?

–John L. Wilson, River Vale, New Jersey

10. FISHING FOR ANSWERS
Difficulty: 4

The joys of recreation are tied up in this numerical cipher. The first number of each word is the cipher-code for the first letter. It is also a subtrahend. The second number is a minuend. The difference is the cipher-code for the second letter, and in turn this remainder is subtracted from the minuend to its right, and so on. Each word starts anew.

Develop the ciphers first and then find the message adapted from Isaac Walton. 26 = N.

21 29 27 39 30 31 29 27 36 35 32 / 21 29 24 / 12 22 / 14
22 25 40 / 19 34 / 12 22 / 14 29 / 25 42 21 14 / 8 34 29 28
42 43 29 / 19 39 28 27 / 17
36 / 18 26 34 / 26 36 34 34
11 / 12 22 / 13 18 30 50 41
/ 25 35 18 9 27 45.

– Robert Henderson,
New London,
New Hampshire

11. JIGSAWN OFA
Difficulty: 5

Here are 29 pieces, including 5 that say "OFA 94." Turning none over, can you make a flat 15x15 square that contains all 29 pieces and has the 3 black spots arranged on the midlines as shown at left?

– Don Allen,
Brossard, Quebec

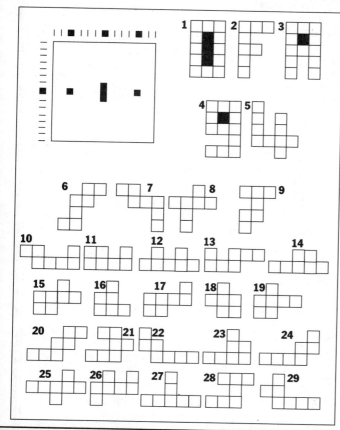

12. ALPHAMETIC ALMANAC

Difficulty: 5

Replace the letters with digits so that the following is correct. No leading zeros are allowed, but note that if A=0, it would be allowable because of the decimal point:

$$\frac{5\,(OLD + MAN + 1)}{FARM + ER} = .ALMANAC\overline{ALMANAC}$$

– Bob Lodge, Wenatchee, Washington

13. WAREHOUSE TORMENT

Difficulty: 5

A large sealed carton of goods, A, must be skidded out the door.

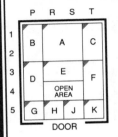

How would you slide the other 9 smaller cartons around within the room, to bring A to the door?

Please list each move, in this manner: for example, H-R4, G-R5, D-P4, in a *vertical* list, for judging. Please show *only* the floor position co-ordinates of the upper-left shaded corner of each carton *after* each move, for simple clarity.

– Al Milchen, Nashua, New Hampshire

14. COLLATZ CLASSIC

Difficulty: 5

Take *any* positive integer. If even, divide by 2; if odd, multiply by 3 and add 1. Then, to the result, do the same thing again. And again, until you repeat a result and start around a second cycle.

What is your last number before repeating?

Can you work out a set of similar operations giving a similar end? Or a family of similar series — or best — a general case of analogous operations?

From the 1984 Old Farmer's Almanac

Answers to Old and New MATHEMATICAL PUZZLES

1. a   **1. b**

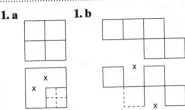

2. 1 in 2. Because one of the envelopes is eliminated, a big bill is possible only in one of the other two.

3. Christmas Eve, the following year, omitting February 29.

4. 13 Stripes/American Flag; 24 Hours/Day; 26 Letters/Alphabet; 28 Days/February; 52 Cards/Deck; 64 Squares/Checkerboard; 88 Keys/Piano; 90 Degrees/Right Angle.

5. 10,297

6. Neither. Both groups start simultaneously. Alternate locks handle up and down craft, and ships pass when adjacent locks reach the same level.

7. a.

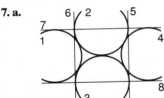

b. 7

8. Any width. Intersection always 12 feet high (less sag).

9. 2,496

10. Mathematics may be said to be so like angling that it can never be fully learnt.

11-14. Prize set. To obtain answers, see instructions on page 184.

WINNING RECIPES

in the

1993 RECIPE CONTEST

Recipes Featuring Chocolate

OLD-FASHIONED CHOCOLATE FUDGE PIE

12 tablespoons (¾ cup) unsalted butter, cut in chunks
3 ounces unsweetened chocolate, broken up
3 extra-large eggs, plus 1 extra-large egg yolk
1½ cups granulated sugar
6 tablespoons flour
¼ teaspoon salt
2 teaspoons pure vanilla extract
1 fully baked 10-inch pie shell, or 1 10-inch graham-cracker crust, baked 10 minutes

Sweet Cream Topping:

2 cups heavy whipping cream
3 tablespoons sifted confectioners' sugar
1 teaspoon pure vanilla extract

Melt the butter and chocolate in a heavy saucepan over low heat, stirring occasionally. Set aside to cool. Beat the eggs and egg yolk in a large mixing bowl until light. Add sugar, flour, and salt, and beat well. Whisk in the cooled chocolate and butter; stir in vanilla. Pour the filling into the baked pie shell and bake at 325° F for about 40 minutes, or until the filling has just set. A knife inserted 2 to 3 inches from the edge of the pie will withdraw clean. Small bubbles may appear over the surface of the baked pie, and cracks may form. Cool on a cooling rack. Whip together topping ingredients and spread over pie. Chill at least an hour. *Serves 8 to 10.*

– *Laurie Charkowsky, Cranford, New Jersey*

CHOCOLATE PEPPERMINT CREAMS

3 cups flour
1¼ teaspoons baking soda
½ teaspoon salt
¾ cup butter
1½ cups brown sugar, packed
2 tablespoons water
12 ounces semisweet chocolate chips
2 eggs

Peppermint Cream:

3 cups confectioners' sugar
⅓ cup soft butter
¼ teaspoon peppermint extract, or to taste
¼ cup milk

Sift flour, baking soda, and salt together. In a large saucepan over low heat, melt butter with brown sugar and water. Add chocolate chips and stir to melt. Remove from heat, cool slightly, and beat in eggs. Add flour mixture and mix well. Drop by heaping teaspoonfuls onto a greased cookie sheet. Bake at 350° F for 8 to 10 minutes. Cool. Prepare Peppermint Cream by blending all ingredients with a mixer until smooth. Sandwich pairs of cookies together with 1 teaspoon Peppermint Cream. *Makes about 3 dozen sandwich cookies.*

– *Roselie A. Aiello, Mount Shasta, California*

CHICKEN IN CHOCOLATE SAUCE PIQUANTE

1 chicken, cut in four pieces
1 tablespoon butter or margarine
1 teaspoon flour
½ teaspoon pepper
1 lemon wedge

Chocolate Sauce Piquante:

½ teaspoon peppercorns
1 dried chili pepper
3 whole cloves
1 clove garlic
1-inch piece fresh gingerroot, peeled
1 small onion
1 tablespoon butter or margarine
1 cup chicken stock
½ cup brewed coffee
1 tablespoon molasses
1 tablespoon tomato paste
1 tablespoon brown sugar
4 ounces semisweet baking chocolate
1 teaspoon cornstarch dissolved in
   4 teaspoons cold water

In a soup pot cover chicken with water, bring to a boil, and simmer for 20 minutes, covered. Remove, rinse with cold water, drain, cool, and pat dry. Rub with butter and sprinkle with flour and pepper. Squeeze lemon wedge over chicken pieces.

Make the sauce by grinding peppercorns, chili pepper, and cloves together in a small mill or mortar and pestle. Finely chop the garlic, gingerroot, and onion. In a small saucepan heat 1 tablespoon butter. Add chopped garlic, ginger, and onion; stir, cover, and cook on low for 3 minutes. Add the ground peppercorns, chili pepper, and cloves. Stir, cover, and cook on low for 3 minutes. Add the chicken stock and coffee. Cover and simmer for about 20 minutes.

Begin grilling chicken pieces, turning frequently until browned (10 to 15

minutes). Strain the sauce, discarding solids and reserving the liquid. Bring liquid to a simmer and add molasses, tomato paste, and brown sugar. Add the chocolate an ounce at a time, stirring constantly until dissolved. Add cornstarch mixture and continue stirring, letting mixture simmer until it thickens, about 2 minutes.

Arrange grilled chicken pieces on a plate. Spoon Chocolate Sauce Piquante over the chicken and serve hot. *Makes 4 servings.*

– Alain Lefevre, Arundel, Quebec

Announcing the 1994 Recipe Contest

Main-Dish Egg Recipes

For 1994, prizes (first prize, $50; second prize, $25; third prize, $15) will be awarded for the best original main-dish recipes featuring eggs. All entries become the property of Yankee Publishing Incorporated, which reserves all rights to the materials submitted. Winners will be announced in the 1995 edition of *The Old Farmer's Almanac.* Deadline is February 1, 1994. Address: Recipe Contest, *The Old Farmer's Almanac,* P.O. Box 520, Dublin, NH 03444.

WINNING ESSAYS

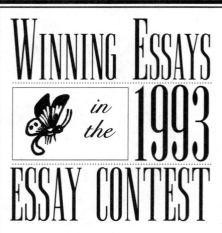

in the 1993

ESSAY CONTEST

The Best Dog I Ever Knew

FIRST PRIZE

Times were hard in the coal camps of Wharton, West Virginia, in the 1940s, and a boy owning a dog was out of the question, especially in a large family. One day I found a large, half-starved dog lying in a ditch. He couldn't move, so I carried him home, made a bed for him under the house, and then sneaked him some scraps from the table. The next morning he could stand, so I bathed him before I asked Mom if I could keep him. She said if he didn't bite. All of his bones showed, so I named him Boney. Months later a man claimed Boney and said his real name was Drum. He convinced my mom, but several weeks later he returned the dog and said he was dumb. He told Mom that he took the dog to a training school in Tennessee, but they sent him back because they couldn't teach Boney anything. On the command "sit," he would stand; "run," he would roll over. When the man left, we laughed out loud because Boney was smart: I had taught him secret commands that only we knew.

– James R. McDavid, Biloxi, Mississippi

SECOND PRIZE

One sunny afternoon my two young sons returned from play with a small, skinny, black dog. Sorry, gentlemen, we cannot keep a dog. After the boys spent two hours in the yard playing with the dog, I called them to dinner. So much for that animal. After dinner, out they went to a hungry, thirsty dog. Oh well, a little food and water couldn't hurt, then he'd be gone. Bedtime, boys asleep, dog on the porch. That's all right; by morning he'll be gone. No such luck — there he is wagging his tail as I open the door.

OK, breakfast before your journey, and then be on your way. Another day of children romping with dog in the yard. The happy sounds drifting into the house sound lovely. I do not want this or any other dog. That evening, Mother Nature stepped in and sent a rainstorm. Dog, come in and spend the night, and in the morning pack your tail and be gone. With the children asleep, rain softly falling, I snuggled on the couch to read. It was cozy and quiet and so was dog, curled at my feet fast asleep.

Since he played his part so well, we called him Sam after "Play it again, Sam." He lived with us for 13 years and became a sleek, energetic friend. This faithful friend roamed the neighborhood in search of adventure. He protected us with the fierce determination of a ten-pound warrior.

When his steps became a little slower, his hearing and sight failing, and his health failing, Sam took his final journey. He left quietly and peacefully, and I know he is entertaining some small boys somewhere. Every now and then I see a dog that reminds me of him, and I wish we could play it again, Sam.

– Nancy Nicolazzi,
North Lindenhurst, New York

There's nothing like a dog that provides for her family. Pal, née Buttercup, was such a dog. She was a compilation of more varieties of dog than Baskin-Robbins has flavors, but looked to be a 70-pound cross between a boxer and a golden retriever.

Her previous owner was a junkyard proprietor who called his dog Buttercup and kept her chained in the junkyard as a watchdog. Once adopted and renamed Pal, her true nature emerged. Pal was no watchdog. Pal was a freedom lover, a car chaser, a thief.

Those were scant years. Pal ate economy dog food for dinner; we, peanut butter and jelly, scrambled eggs, and bologna — until the day Pal brought home a Daisy ham, its cellophane wrapper intact, however soggy. My mother guiltily cooked it for dinner. It was delicious! We toasted our provider with glasses of milk. No sooner had we finished our milk than we heard Pal's familiar banging at the back door. As my mother went to let her in, we collected ham scraps to give to Pal.

Mother emerged from the back hall, incredulous, holding a Table Talk pie, still in its slightly chewed box. "She brought dessert."

Good dog, Pal.

– *Pat Breen, Ipswich, Massachusetts*

HONORABLE MENTION

(two shaggy-dog stories we couldn't resist . . .)

My aunt Barbara's father, Buck Widner, had the best bird dog I ever saw. If Mr. Widner came out of the house with a shotgun, the dog wouldn't hunt anything but quail all day. If he came out of the house with a .22 rifle, the old dog wouldn't hunt anything but rabbits all day. One day Mr. Widner walked out with a fishing pole. The old dog sat down,

scratched behind his ear, looked at Mr. Widner a while, got up, walked behind the barn, and started digging for worms.

– *George A. Nesbit, Boise, Idaho*

The best dog I ever knew was a basset hound named Sad-Eyed Sadie. He lived for eating, getting his ears rubbed, and most of all, hunting. His favorite animals to hunt were raccoons. All you had to do was put a skinning board the size of the pelt you wanted on the back porch. The next morning a dead raccoon would be lying there, exactly the size of the skinning board. Sadie would be beside it waiting to be fed and to have his ears rubbed. How he ever caught a 'coon I'll never know.

This went on 'til that fateful day when Ma decided to do her ironing on the back porch because it was so hot. Unfortunately, she forgot to put the ironing board away when she finished.

That day was the last we ever saw of that dog. I suppose he's still out there trying to find a coon to fit that ironing board.

– *John Lint, Washington Courthouse, Ohio*

Announcing the 1994 Essay Contest

One Thing I Wish I Had Never Done

For 1994, prizes (first prize, $50; second, $25; third, $15) will be awarded for the three best 200-word essays on this topic: "One Thing I Wish I Had Never Done." All entries become the property of Yankee Publishing Incorporated, which reserves all rights to the materials submitted. Winners will be announced in the 1995 edition of *The Old Farmer's Almanac*. Deadline: February 1, 1994. Address: Essay Contest, *The Old Farmer's Almanac*, P.O. Box 520, Dublin, NH 03444.

Three Muskie Tears

A Sad but True Fish Story by Mel R. Allen

They say Louie Spray's muskie weighed 69 pounds 11 ounces; Robert Malo's, 69 pounds 12 ounces; Art Lawton's, 69 pounds 15 ounces. So can you guess who holds the world's record? Oh, it's nowhere near that simple . . .

INTRODUCTION

To understand how a fish could cost one man his friends, another his reputation, and, some believe, two men their lives, you first need to understand the fish. Fishermen say that until you've fought the wily, ferocious muskellunge *(Esox masquinongy)*, a fish that has been compared to wolves, mad dogs, tigers, and sharks, you can never truly believe their passion for the fish. To muskie fishermen, theirs is the only real freshwater quarry in North America. Bass? Trout? "Rabbit hunting," they say. "Muskies are like stalking the biggest buck."

So to anyone but the muskie fisherman, this story about Louie and Chin-Whiskered Charlie, the Malo Mistake, and the Lawton Smoking Gun may seem unbelievable. But all of it is true.

Louie Spray and Chin-Whiskered Charlie

A woodsman's obsession to find the biggest fish.

Though muskies swim in lakes and rivers as far south as Alabama and west to Missouri, their fame resides in northern waters: along the St. Lawrence River, the Great Lakes, the bays of Ontario. And nobody personified the North Country's single-minded pursuit of the muskie more than Louis (Louie) Spray, a Wisconsin woodsman who ran a tavern, motel, and casino near Hayward on Rice Lake. He was a boastful, rough, and generous man, impossible to ignore. As a boy, he had hooked into a 47½-pound muskie. The stuffed mount of that boyhood fish looked down upon the bar patrons, flanked over the years by still larger specimens. In 1940 he set a new world record with a 61-pound 13-ounce muskie. He called himself "the Muskie King" and offered $2,500 to anyone who could best him.

Wisconsin woodsman Louie Spray and his trophy fish.

Living nearby was an outdoor writer named Cal Johnson. On August 24, 1949, Johnson took a 67½-pounder from Lac Court Oreilles. Johnson's friends threw a party. Spray sent this message to be read aloud: "Don't give award yet. I will catch a new world-record muskie this season. Louie Spray."

Spray had spotted a fish three years earlier in the shallows of an island in the Chippewa Flowage. He suspected the fish would still be there. He had given the fish a name, "Chin-Whiskered Charlie," and vowed to catch him. Louie was hunting more than a fish. He wanted to regain what one fishing writer called "the greatest jackpot in Wisconsin fishing history."

He set off from Herman's Landing each morning during the month of October 1949. He found Charlie on a cold, rainy afternoon, October 20. After a 40-minute fight, the fish came close enough to the boat for George Quentmeyer, a local guide, to shoot it, in those days the accepted and legal method for dispatching the thrashing, sharp-toothed predator.

Charlie weighed 69 pounds 11 ounces and took the place of honor on the tavern wall. Louie Spray was king once again.

The controversy began almost immediately. Rumors started: He had bought the fish from a well-known gangster, one writer claimed. Spray added to the controversy by insisting he had caught the fish within sight of Herman's Landing, at a spot known as Fleming's Bar. Reporters spoke to people who had been fishing at Fleming's Bar that day and never sighted Louie Spray. Spray's defenders insisted he was merely protecting his secret hole, a timeless tradition.

The innuendo surrounding what should have been Spray's finest moment left him bitterly disappointed. Five years later, on a summer morning in 1954, an Ontario man named Robert Malo bested Chin-Whiskered Charlie by a few ounces on a Wisconsin lake. When Spray saw pictures of the new "biggest muskie," he fired off letters to newspapers and outdoor magazines, saying it was impossible that this short, fat fish could be a record beater. The Malo Muskie was indeed disallowed

as a world record. But in 1957, a 69-pound 15-ounce specimen was caught in the St. Lawrence River. Spray hollered foul again, but this time a new official muskie record was claimed by Art Lawton.

After that, life went downhill for Louie Spray. The same year that Art Lawton became muskie king, fire destroyed Spray's tavern, and his treasured muskie trophies burned to ashes. To whoever would listen, he professed doubts that anyone had ever caught a bigger muskie than he had, but to most outdoor writers, Louie Spray had become, as one said, "old news."

Hobbled by arthritis, he retired to the Arizona desert, a lifetime away from the northern waters he loved. In 1984 the one-time "Muskie King" killed himself.

But that would not end the story of Louie Spray and the fish he called Charlie. Because three years later, in 1987, Larry Ramsell, the muskie historian, resurrected the ghost of the Malo muskie.

Robert Malo's Mistake

A short, fat fish, caught by a duffer, weighed on an uncertified scale.

W
hen Robert Malo left his factory job in Thunder Bay, Ontario, for a quick weekend trip to Sportsman's Lodge on Middle Eau Claire Lake in Bayfield County, Wisconsin, he could not have cared less about catching fish.

"I just wanted to take it easy," he says today.

At 4 A.M. on Sunday, June 6, 1954, Robert Malo was in a rowboat nursing a hangover, wondering how he had let a friend, George Cruise, coax him out.

After about an hour of rowing and trolling, he felt his rod tug. The next day's news accounts quoted Malo:

"We moved toward a short sand beach, and when I got the fish in shallow water, it slapped the boat once. Then I jumped out of the boat and kept nosing the fish into the beach. George got out. He had the pistol in his jacket and let fly with two shots. The fish quit fighting and started to quiver. We just stood there and sweated awhile." They quickly motored back to Sportsman's Lodge and woke owner Hank Boroo.

"Never had I seen such a fish, and we've had some big ones," Boroo said. By 7:30 A.M. Boroo had hustled Malo and Cruise to a Duluth, Minnesota, taxidermist named George Flaim.

Flaim placed the fish on a flat bathroom-type scale. The needle stopped just short of 70 pounds. The four men agreed on 69 pounds 12 ounces. The fish measured 55½ inches long and had a tremendous 33-inch girth that stretched almost to the tail. It was a sumo wrestler's body on a fish.

Malo gave the fish to Boroo in return for a lifetime of free lodging. A few days later, realizing that the taxidermist's scale was not officially "certified," Boroo, Cruise, and a group of reporters had it checked by Minnesota's chief weights and measurements inspector.

Over and over the inspector checked the scale — each time it registered the same: a half pound slow. The Malo fish was actually *at least* 70 pounds, heavier than anyone had thought.

Word spread rapidly through the muskie community. Cal Johnson, the former world record holder, accused the taxidermist of doctoring the fish's appearance to make it look larger.

"There was so much commotion because of that fish, I figured it killed him. His widow, Hilda, wouldn't let anyone see it..."

The formal procedure to get a fish recognized as a world record was to send photos of the fish and affidavits from witnesses to the catch and weighing to *Field and Stream* magazine, then the arbiter of record fish. Malo did that. The magazine rejected the fish. Because the scale was not certified, wrote the editor, "we have no recourse but to refuse acceptance of your entry." The taxidermist always believed that the magazine was intimidated by a threatened lawsuit by Louie Spray.

Over 30 years later Larry Ramsell investigated the Malo muskie. He came up with 28 "Possible Negative Influencing Factors." Chief among them was the disbelief among muskie diehards that a record fish could be caught by an unknown fisherman, who knew next to nothing about muskies, in a lake not known to harbor muskies.

Today Robert Malo says, "I wish I'd just stayed in bed that day. I lost lots of friends. Other people lost friends, what with all the blame thrown around. Everything just got screwy."

Hank Boroo displayed the muskie at his lodge. A few years later the lodge burned down. Many suspected arson. Boroo suffered a heart attack. Says Bob Kutz, longtime spokesman for the National Freshwater Fishing Hall of Fame in Hayward, today's keeper of muskellunge records, "There was so much commotion because of that fish, I figured it killed him. His widow, Hilda, wouldn't let anyone see it. It wound up in her basement." When Hilda died, her estate sold it to a sporting lodge some 25 miles east of Hayward for a reported $5,000. Today a sign hangs outside: "World's Largest Muskellunge."

Ramsell concluded his Malo muskie

study by recommending to the Fishing Hall of Fame that "the official recognized weight of Robert Malo's muskie should be 70 pounds even."

The Hall ruled against the Malo muskie. In defense of its ruling it cited that after 33 years a biologist had posed a basic, yet overlooked question: "How could a 55-inch-long fish of a flat girth wider than the bathroom-type scale be weighed . . . The fact that a board may have been used to support the fish during weighing, but never was mentioned in any report of the procedure, is the prime reason to disqualify the fish as a record contender."

Ramsell replied: "I knew the fish had been weighed on a board. They put the board on the scale and re-zeroed the scale. In essence the board became part of the scale. It was probably a 70-pound fish. But people have to be willing to accept it, and they're not."

The Hall did agree to list Malo's fish as an "unofficial" 70-pound muskie. Until 1992 it continued to recognize the world-record 69-pound 15-ounce muskie caught by Art Lawton in the St. Lawrence River on September 22, 1957, a fish that had been weighed on a certified locker-plant scale.

Art Lawton's Smoking Gun

A fish magnified by muskie fever.

Art Lawton of New York had muskie fever as badly as Louie Spray. In September of 1957 it was as though he possessed an almost supernatural ability to catch muskies. On a weeklong fishing trip up the St. Lawrence, Art and his wife, Ruth, boated 30 muskies weighing 18 to 49 pounds.

His luck held, and a week later, on September 22, he caught the 69-pound

15-ounce muskie. The next day he took it to a slaughterhouse for weighing on a certified scale. He had five witnesses. He then cut up the fish into fillets. He sent affidavits and photos to *Field and Stream.* Amazingly, an Easterner was the new muskie king.

Midwestern fishermen looked at the published photo and said the fish didn't seem hefty enough, especially in the tail. Spray wrote to *Field and Stream* professing his doubts. The magazine hired Pinkerton detectives who said they thought Lawton had bought the fish from Indians who had nets on the river. But lacking proof, the magazine let the record stand, and it stood, unchallenged, until 1992.

After Larry Ramsell's intensive study of the Malo muskie, John Dettloff, a Wisconsin fishing guide, history buff, and writer for *Musky Hunter Magazine,* took on the legacy of the late Art Lawton.

Only two photos of the record fish were known to exist, but aided by a Lawton relative, Dettloff stumbled upon a scrapbook filled with previously unknown photos, among them what Dettloff would call the "smoking gun" photo.

The photo Lawton used to convince *Field and Stream* seemed to show a fish identical to the 49-pounder Lawton had caught and photographed a week earlier. Dettloff sent copies of the photos to various

Art Lawton and his muskie, in the photo he sent to Field and Stream.

experts around the country who scrutinized the two fish. They concluded that the fish were identical, down to the most minute blood and slime spots! The record was a fraud. And the witnesses? Dettloff found they were a nephew, two brothers-in-law, the husband of a niece, and a close friend. Larry Ramsell, a longtime friend of Lawton's, sadly concluded that Lawton "had probably stored the 49-pound fish in a cooler. Took it out a week later, added weight to it, and proudly displayed it to his unsuspecting relatives."

Says Ramsell, "I think back to something he said to me in 1977, shortly before he died. He said he had proved that he could take a fish and photograph it in a certain way to make it look bigger. I think he was probably trying to confess something."

In 1992, armed with Dettloff's findings, the Fishing Hall of Fame stripped Art Lawton's name from its record books. The Hall has again officially recognized Louie Spray's Chin-Whiskered Charlie as the undisputed world-record muskellunge.

And so we are back where we began — on the water with the undisputed muskie king, Louie Spray.

Oh, did I say undisputed? In the world of muskies there's no such thing. The other arbiter of such matters, the International Game Fish Association, does not accept Spray's fish because it was shot before landing. They say that even though it was legal at the time it was "not sporting."

Their choice? Cal Johnson's 1949 fish, the one that started Louie Spray on his October quest. □ □

BEST FISHING DAYS, 1994

(and other fishing lore from the files of The Old Farmer's Almanac*)*

Probably the best fishing time is when the ocean tides are restless before their turn and in the first hour of ebbing. All fish in all waters — salt or fresh — feed most heavily at that time.

Best temperatures for fish species vary widely, of course, and are chiefly important if you are going to have your own fish pond. Best temperatures for brook trout are 45° to 65° F. Brown trout and rainbows are more tolerant of higher temperatures. Smallmouth black bass do best in cool water. Horned pout take what they find.

Most of us go fishing when we can get off, not because it is the best time. But there are best times:

☞ One hour before and one hour after high tide, and one hour before and one hour after low tide. (The times of high tides are given on pages 54-80 and corrected for your locality on pages 204-205. Inland, the times for high tides would correspond with the times the Moon is due south. Low tides are halfway between high tides.)

☞ "The morning rise" — after sunup for a spell — and "the evening rise" — just before sundown and the hour or so after.

☞ Still water or a ripple is better than a wind at both times.

☞ When there is a hatch of flies — caddis or mayflies, commonly. (The fisherman will have to match the hatching flies with *his* fly — or go fishless.)

☞ When the breeze is from a westerly quarter rather than north or east.

☞ When the barometer is steady or on the rise. (But, of course, even in a three-day driving northeaster the fish isn't going to give up feeding. His hunger clock keeps right on working, and the smart fisherman will find something he wants.)

☞ When the Moon is between new and full.

MOON BETWEEN NEW & FULL			
January	11-27	July	8-22
February	10-25	August	7-21
March	12-27	September	5-19
April	10-25	October	4-19
May	10-24	November	3-18
June	9-23	December	2-17

200   OLD FARMER'S ALMANAC   1994

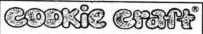

THE TWILIGHT ZONE

How to Determine the Length of Twilight and the Times of Dawn and Dark

Twilight begins (or ends) when the Sun is about 18 degrees below the horizon, and the latitude of a place, together with the time of year, determines the length of the twilight. To find the latitude of your city, or the city nearest you, consult the **Time Correction Tables,** page 209. Check the figures against the chart at right for the appropriate date, and you will have the length of twilight in your area.

It is also possible to determine the times dawn will break and darkness descend by applying the length of twilight taken from the chart at right, to the times of sunrise and sunset at any specific place. (Follow the instructions given in "How to Use This Almanac," page 30, to determine sunrise/sunset times for a given locality.) **Subtract** the length of twilight from the time of sunrise for dawn. **Add** the length of twilight to the time of sunset for dark.

Latitude	25° N to 30° N	31° N to 36° N	37° N to 42° N	43° N to 47° N	48° N to 49° N
	H M	H M	H M	H M	H M
Jan. 1 to Apr. 10	1 20	1 26	1 33	1 42	1 50
Apr. 11 to May 2	1 23	1 28	1 39	1 51	2 04
May 3 to May 14	1 26	1 34	1 47	2 02	2 22
May 15 to May 25	1 29	1 38	1 52	2 13	2 42
May 26 to July 22	1 32	1 43	1 59	2 27	—
July 23 to Aug. 3	1 29	1 38	1 52	2 13	2 42
Aug. 4 to Aug. 14	1 26	1 34	1 47	2 02	2 22
Aug. 15 to Sept. 5	1 23	1 28	1 39	1 51	2 04
Sept. 6 to Dec. 31	1 20	1 26	1 33	1 42	1 50

	Boston, MA (latitude 42° 22')	Fresno, CA (latitude 36° 44')
Sunrise, August 1	4:36 A.M.	5:08 A.M.
Length of twilight	−1:52	−1:38
Dawn breaks	2:44 A.M., EST	3:30 A.M., PST
Sunset, August 1	7:04 P.M.	7:10 P.M.
Length of twilight	+1:52	+1:38
Dark descends	8:56 P.M., EST	8:48 P.M., PST

TIDAL GLOSSARY

Apogean Tide: A monthly tide of decreased range that occurs when the Moon is farthest from the Earth (at apogee).

Diurnal: Applies to a location that normally experiences one high water and one low water during a tidal day of approximately 24 hours.

Mean Lower Low Water: The arithmetic mean of the lesser of a daily pair of low waters, observed over a specific 19-year cycle called the National Tidal Datum Epoch.

Neap Tide: A tide of decreased range occurring twice a month when the Moon is in quadrature (during the first and last quarter Moons, when the Sun and Moon are at right angles to each other relative to the Earth).

Perigean Tide: A monthly tide of increased range that occurs when the Moon is closest to the Earth (at perigee).

Semidiurnal: Having a period of half a tidal day. East Coast tides, for example, are semi-

diurnal, with two highs and two lows in approximately 24 hours.

Spring Tide: Named not for the season of spring, but from the German *springen* (to leap up). This tide of increased range occurs at times of syzygy (q.v.) each month. A spring tide also brings a lower low water.

Syzygy: Occurs twice a month when the Sun and Moon are in conjunction (lined up on the same side of the Earth at the new Moon) and when they are in opposition (on opposite sides of the Earth at the full Moon, though usually not so directly in line as to produce an eclipse). In either case, the gravitational effects of the Sun and Moon reinforce each other and tidal range is increased.

Vanishing Tide: A mixed tide of considerable inequality in the two highs or two lows, so that the "high low" may become indistinguishable from the "low high" or vice versa. The result is a vanishing tide, where no significant difference is apparent.

Times, Tides, Frosts, and When to Plant

TIDE CORRECTIONS

Many factors affect the time and height of the tides: the coastal configuration, the time of the Moon's southing (crossing the meridian) at the place, and the phase of the Moon. This table of tidal corrections is a sufficiently accurate guide to the times and heights of the high water at the places shown. (Low tides occur approximately 6.25 hours before and after high tides.) No figures are shown for the West Coast or the Gulf of Mexico, since the method used in compiling this table does not apply there. For such places and elsewhere where precise accuracy is required, consult the Tide Tables published annually by the National Ocean Service, 1305 E. West Highway, Silver Spring, MD 20910; telephone 301-713-2815.

The figures for Full Sea on the Left-Hand Calendar Pages 54-80 are the times of high tide at Commonwealth Pier in Boston Harbor. (Where a dash is shown under Full Sea, it indicates that time of high water has occurred after midnight and so is recorded on the next date.) The heights of these tides are given on the Right-Hand Calendar Pages 55-81. The heights are reckoned from Mean Lower Low Water, and each day listed has a set of figures — upper for the morning, lower for the evening. To obtain the time and height of high water at any of the following places, apply the time difference to the daily times of high water at Boston (pages 54-80) and the height difference to the heights at Boston (pages 55-81).

	Time Difference: Hr. Min.	Height Feet
MAINE		
Bar Harbor	−0 34	+0.9
Belfast	−0 20	+0.4
Boothbay Harbor	−0 18	−0.8
Chebeague Island	−0 16	−0.6
Eastport	−0 28	+8.4
Kennebunkport	+0 04	−1.0
Machias	−0 28	+2.8
Monhegan Island	−0 25	−0.8
Old Orchard	0 00	−0.8
Portland	−0 12	−0.6
Rockland	−0 28	+0.1
Stonington	−0 30	+0.1
York	−0 09	−1.0
NEW HAMPSHIRE		
Hampton	+0 02	−1.3
Portsmouth	+0 11	−1.5
Rye Beach	−0 09	−0.9

	Time Difference: Hr. Min.	Height Feet
MASSACHUSETTS		
Annisquam	−0 02	−1.1
Beverly Farms	0 00	−0.5
Boston	0 00	0.0
Cape Cod Canal:		
East Entrance	−0 01	−0.8
West Entrance	−2 16	−5.9
Chatham Outer Coast	+0 30	−2.8
Inside	+1 54	*0.4
Cohasset	+0 02	−0.07
Cotuit Highlands	+1 15	*0.3
Dennis Port	+1 01	*0.4
Duxbury (Gurnet Pt.)	+0 02	−0.3
Fall River	−3 03	−5.0
Gloucester	−0 03	−0.8
Hingham	+0 07	0.0
Hull	+0 03	−0.2
Hyannis Port	+1 01	*0.3
Magnolia (Manchester)	−0 02	−0.7
Marblehead	−0 02	−0.4
Marion	−3 22	−5.4
Monument Beach	−3 08	−5.4
Nahant	−0 01	−0.5
Nantasket	+0 04	−0.1
Nantucket	−0 56	*0.3
Nauset Beach	+0 30	*0.6
New Bedford	−3 24	−5.7
Newburyport	+0 19	−1.8
Oak Bluffs	+0 30	*0.2
Onset (R.R. Bridge)	−2 16	−5.9
Plymouth	+0 05	0.0
Provincetown	+0 14	−0.4
Revere Beach	−0 01	−0.3
Rockport	−0 08	−1.0
Salem	0 00	−0.5
Scituate	−0 05	−0.7
Wareham	−3 09	−5.3
Wellfleet	+0 12	+0.5
West Falmouth	−3 10	−5.4
Westport Harbor	−3 22	−6.4
Woods Hole Little Harbor	−2 50	*0.2
Oceanographic Institute	−3 07	*0.2
RHODE ISLAND		
Bristol	−3 24	−5.3
Sakonnet	−3 44	−5.6
Narrangansett Pier	−3 42	−6.2
Newport	−3 34	−5.9
Pt. Judith	−3 41	−6.3
Providence	−3 20	−4.8
Watch Hill	−2 50	−6.8
CONNECTICUT		
Bridgeport	+0 01	−2.6

	Time Difference: Hr. Min.	Height Feet
Madison	−0 22	−2.3
New Haven	−0 11	−3.2
New London	−1 54	−6.7
Norwalk	+0 01	−2.2
Old Lyme (Highway Bridge)	−0 30	−6.2
Stamford	+0 01	−2.2
Stonington	−2 27	−6.6
NEW YORK		
Coney Island	−3 33	−4.9
Fire Island Lt.	−2 43	*0.1
Long Beach	−3 11	−5.7
Montauk Harbor	−2 19	−7.4
New York City (Battery)	−2 43	−5.0
Oyster Bay	+0 04	−1.8
Port Chester	−0 09	−2.2
Port Washington	−0 01	−2.1
Sag Harbor	−0 55	−6.8
Southampton (Shinnecock Inlet)	−4 20	*0.2
Willets Point	0 00	−2.3
NEW JERSEY		
Asbury Park	−4 04	−5.3
Atlantic City	−3 56	−5.5
Bay Head (Sea Girt)	−4 04	−5.3
Beach Haven	−1 43	*0.24
Cape May	−3 28	−5.3
Ocean City	−3 06	−5.9
Sandy Hook	−3 30	−5.0
Seaside Park	−4 03	−5.4
PENNSYLVANIA		
Philadelphia	+2 40	−3.5
DELAWARE		
Cape Henlopen	−2 48	−5.3
Rehoboth Beach	−3 37	−5.7
Wilmington	+1 56	−3.8
MARYLAND		
Annapolis	+6 23	−8.5
Baltimore	+7 59	−8.3
Cambridge	+5 05	−7.8
Havre de Grace	+11 21	−7.7
Point No Point	+2 28	−8.1
Prince Frederick (Plum Point)	+4 25	−8.5
VIRGINIA		
Cape Charles	−2 20	−7.0
Hampton Roads	−2 02	−6.9
Norfolk	−2 06	−6.6
Virginia Beach	−4 00	−6.0
Yorktown	−2 13	−7.0
NORTH CAROLINA		
Cape Fear	−3 55	−5.0
Cape Lookout	−4 28	−5.7
Currituck	−4 10	−5.8

	Time Difference: Hr. Min.	Height Feet
Hatteras:		
Ocean	−4 26	−6.0
Inlet	−4 03	−7.4
Kitty Hawk	−4 14	−6.2
SOUTH CAROLINA		
Charleston	−3 22	−4.3
Georgetown	−1 48	*0.36
Hilton Head	−3 22	−2.9
Myrtle Beach	−3 49	−4.4
St. Helena Harbor Entrance	−3 15	−3.4
GEORGIA		
Jekyll Island	−3 46	−2.9
Saint Simon's Island	−2 50	−2.9
Savannah Beach:		
River Entrance	−3 14	−5.5
Tybee Light	−3 22	−2.7
FLORIDA		
Cape Canaveral	−3 59	−6.0
Daytona Beach	−3 28	−5.3
Fort Lauderdale	−2 50	−7.2
Fort Pierce Inlet	−3 32	−6.9
Jacksonville Railroad Bridge	−6 55	*0.10
Miami Harbor Entrance	−3 18	−7.0
St. Augustine	−2 55	−4.9
CANADA		
Alberton, P.E.I.	−5 45**	−7.5
Charlottetown, P.E.I.	−0 45**	−3.5
Halifax, N.S.	−3 23	−4.5
North Sydney, N.S.	−3 15	−6.5
Saint John, N.B.	+0 30	−8.0
St. John's, Nfld.	−4 00	−6.5
Yarmouth, N.S.	−0 40	+3.0

* Where the difference in the "Height/Feet" column is so marked, height at Boston should be multiplied by this ratio.

** Varies widely; accurate only within 1½ hours. Consult local tide tables for precise times and heights.

Example: The conversion of the times and heights of the tides at Boston to those of Fall River, Massachusetts, is given below:

Sample tide calculation July 1, 1994:

High tide Boston (p. 70)	5:00 A.M., EST
Correction for Fall River	−3:03 hrs.
High tide Fall River	1:57 A.M., EST
Tide height Boston (p. 71)	8.9 ft.
Correction for Fall River	−5.0 ft.
Tide height Fall River	3.9 ft.

OUTDOOR PLANTING TABLE

1 9 9 4

The best time to plant flowers and vegetables that bear crops above the ground is during the *light* of the Moon; that is, between the day the Moon is new to the day it is full. Flowering bulbs and vegetables that bear crops below ground should be planted during the *dark* of the Moon; that is, from the day after it is full to the day before it is new again. The dates given here are based on the safe periods for planting in areas that receive frost and the Moon's phases for 1994. Consult page 208 for dates of frosts and length of growing season. See calendar pages 54-80 for the exact days of the new and full Moons.

☞ Above-Ground Crops Marked (*) ☞ E means Early ☞ L means Late

	Planting Dates	Moon Favorable	Planting Dates	Moon Favorable	Planting Dates	Moon Favorable
*Barley	5/15-6/21	5/15-24, 6/9-21	3/15-4/7	3/15-27	2/15-3/7	2/15-25
*Beans (E)	5/7-6/21	5/10-24, 6/9-21	4/15-30	4/15-25	3/15-4/7	3/15-27
(L)	6/15-7/15	6/15-23, 7/8-15	7/1-21	7/8-21	8/7-31	8/7-21
Beets (E)	5/1-15	5/1-9	3/15-4/3	3/28-4/3	2/7-28	2/7-9, 2/26-28
(L)	7/15-8/15	7/23-8/6	8/15-31	8/22-31	9/1-30	9/1-4, 9/20-30
*Broccoli (E)	5/15-31	5/15-24	3/7-31	3/12-27	2/15-3/15	2/15-25, 3/12-15
Plants (L)	6/15-7/7	6/15-23	8/1-20	8/7-20	9/7-30	9/7-19
*Brussels Sprouts	5/15-31	5/15-24	3/7-4/15	3/12-27, 4/10-15	2/11-3/20	2/11-25, 3/12-20
*Cabbage Plants	5/15-31	5/15-24	3/7-4/15	3/12-27, 4/10-15	2/11-3/20	2/11-25, 3/12-20
Carrots (E)	5/15-31	5/25-31	3/7-31	3/7-11, 3/28-31	2/15-3/7	2/26-3/7
(L)	6/15-7/21	6/24-7/7	7/7-31	7/7, 7/23-31	8/1-9/7	8/1-6, 8/22-9/4
*Cauliflower (E)	5/15-31	5/15-24	3/15-4/7	3/15-27	2/15-3/7	2/15-25
Plants (L)	6/15-7/21	6/15-23, 7/8-21	7/1-8/7	7/8-22, 8/7	8/7-31	8/7-21
*Celery Plants (E)	5/15-6/30	5/15-24, 6/9-23	3/7-31	3/12-27	2/15-28	2/15-25
(L)	7/15-8/15	7/15-22, 8/7-15	8/15-9/7	8/15-21, 9/5-7	9/15-30	9/15-19
*Collards (E)	5/15-31	5/15-24	3/7-4/7	3/12-27	2/11-3/20	2/11-25, 3/12-20
(L)	7/1-8/7	7/8-22, 8/7	8/15-31	8/15-21	9/7-30	9/7-19
*Corn, Sweet (E)	5/10-6/15	5/10-24, 6/9-15	4/1-15	4/10-15	3/15-31	3/15-27
(L)	6/15-30	6/15-23	7/7-21	7/8-21	8/7-31	8/7-21
*Cucumber	5/7-6/20	5/10-24, 6/9-20	4/7-5/15	4/10-25, 5/10-15	3/7-4/15	3/12-27, 4/10-15
*Eggplant Plants	6/1-30	6/9-23	4/7-5/15	4/10-25, 5/10-15	3/7-4/15	3/12-27, 4/10-15
*Endive (E)	5/15-31	5/15-24	4/7-5/15	4/10-25, 5/10-15	2/15-3/20	2/15-25, 3/12-20
(L)	6/7-30	6/9-23	7/15-8/15	7/15-22, 8/7-15	8/15-9/7	8/15-21, 9/5-7
*Flowers (All)	5/7-6/21	5/10-24, 6/9-21	4/15-30	4/15-25	3/15-4/7	3/15-27
*Kale (E)	5/15-31	5/15-24	3/7-4/7	3/12-27	2/11-3/20	2/11-25, 3/12-20

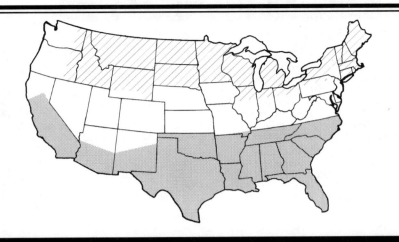

	Planting Dates	Moon Favorable	Planting Dates	Moon Favorable	Planting Dates	Moon Favorable
*Kale (L)	7/1-8/7	7/8-22, 8/7	8/15-31	8/15-21	9/7-30	9/7-19
Leek Plants	5/15-31	5/25-31	3/7-4/7	3/7-11, 3/28-4/7	2/15-4/15	2/26-3/11, 3/28-4/9
*Lettuce	5/15-6/30	5/15-24, 6/9-23	3/1-31	3/12-27	2/15-3/7	2/15-25
*Muskmelon	5/15-6/30	5/15-24, 6/9-23	4/15-5/7	4/15-25	3/15-4/7	3/15-27
Onion Sets	5/15-6/7	5/25-6/7	3/1-31	3/1-11, 3/28-31	2/1-28	2/1-9, 2/26-28
*Parsley	5/15-31	5/15-24	3/1-31	3/12-27	2/20-3/15	2/20-25, 3/12-15
Parsnips	4/1-30	4/1-4/9, 4/26-30	3/7-31	3/7-11, 3/28-31	1/15-2/4	1/28-2/4
*Peas (E)	4/15-5/7	4/15-4/25	3/7-31	3/12-27	1/15-2/7	1/15-27
(L)	7/15-31	7/15-22	8/7-31	8/7-21	9/15-30	9/15-19
*Pepper Plants	5/15-6/30	5/15-24, 6/9-23	4/1-30	4/10-25	3/1-20	3/12-20
Potato	5/1-31	5/1-9, 5/25-31	4/1-30	4/1-9, 4/26-30	2/10-28	2/26-28
*Pumpkin	5/15-31	5/15-24	4/23-5/15	4/23-25, 5/10-15	3/7-20	3/12-20
Radish (E)	4/15-30	4/26-30	3/7-31	3/7-11, 3/28-31	1/21-3/1	1/28-2/9, 2/26-3/1
(L)	8/15-31	8/22-31	9/7-30	9/20-30	10/1-21	10/1-3, 10/20-21
*Spinach (E)	5/15-31	5/15-24	3/15-4/20	3/15-27, 4/10-20	2/7-3/15	2/10-25, 3/12-15
(L)	7/15-9/7	7/15-22, 8/7-21, 9/5-7	8/1-9/15	8/7-21, 9/5-15	10/1-21	10/4-19
*Squash	5/15-6/15	5/15-24, 6/9-15	4/15-30	4/15-25	3/15-4/15	3/15-27, 4/10-15
Sweet Potatoes	5/15-6/15	5/25-6/8	4/21-30	4/26-30	3/23-4/6	3/28-4/6
*Swiss Chard	5/1-31	5/10-24	3/15-4/15	3/15-27, 4/10-15	2/7-3/15	2/10-25, 3/12-15
*Tomato Plants	5/15-31	5/15-24	4/7-30	4/10-25	3/7-20	3/12-20
Turnips (E)	4/7-30	4/7-9, 4/26-30	3/15-31	3/28-31	1/20-2/15	1/28-2/9
(L)	7/1-8/15	7/1-7, 7/23-8/6	8/1-20	8/1-6	9/1-10/15	9/1-4, 9/20-10/3
*Watermelon	5/15-6/30	5/15-24, 6/9-23	4/15-5/7	4/15-25	3/15-4/7	3/15-27
*Wheat, Winter	8/11-9/15	8/11-21, 9/5-15	9/15-10/20	9/15-19, 10/4-19	10/15-12/7	10/15-19, 11/3-18, 12/2-7
Spring	4/7-30	4/10-25	3/1-20	3/12-20	2/15-28	2/15-25

FROSTS AND GROWING SEASONS

Courtesy of National Climatic Center

Dates given are normal averages for a light freeze (32° F); local weather and topography may cause considerable variations. The possibility of frost occurring after the spring dates and before the fall dates is 50 percent. The classification of freeze temperatures is usually based on their effect on plants, with the following commonly accepted categories: **Light freeze:** 29° F to 32° F — tender plants killed, with little destructive effect on other vegetation. **Moderate freeze:** 25° F to 28° F — widely destructive effect on most vegetation, with heavy damage to fruit blossoms, tender, and semihardy plants. **Severe freeze:** 24° F and colder — heavy damage to most plants.

CITY	Growing Season (Days)	Last Frost Spring	First Frost Fall	CITY	Growing Season (Days)	Last Frost Spring	First Frost Fall
Mobile, AL	272	Feb. 27	Nov. 26	North Platte, NE	136	May 11	Sept. 24
Juneau, AK	133	May 16	Sept. 26	Las Vegas, NV	259	Mar. 7	Nov. 21
Phoenix, AZ	308	Feb. 5	Dec. 15	Concord, NH	121	May 23	Sept. 22
Tucson, AZ	273	Feb. 28	Nov. 29	Newark, NJ	219	Apr. 4	Nov. 10
Pine Bluff, AR	234	Mar. 19	Nov. 8	Carlsbad, NM	223	Mar. 29	Nov. 7
Eureka, CA	324	Jan. 30	Dec. 15	Los Alamos, NM	157	May 8	Oct. 13
Sacramento, CA	289	Feb. 14	Dec. 1	Albany, NY	144	May 7	Sept. 29
San Francisco, CA	*	*	*	Syracuse, NY	170	Apr. 28	Oct. 16
Denver, CO	157	May 3	Oct. 8	Fayetteville, NC	212	Apr. 2	Oct. 31
Hartford, CT	167	Apr. 25	Oct. 10	Bismarck, ND	129	May 14	Sept. 20
Wilmington, DE	198	Apr. 13	Oct. 29	Akron, OH	168	May 3	Oct. 18
Miami, FL	*	*	*	Cincinnati, OH	195	Apr. 14	Oct. 27
Tampa, FL	338	Jan. 28	Jan. 3	Lawton, OK	217	Apr. 1	Nov. 5
Athens, GA	224	Mar. 28	Nov. 8	Tulsa, OK	218	Mar. 30	Nov. 4
Savannah, GA	250	Mar. 10	Nov. 15	Pendleton, OR	188	Apr. 15	Oct. 21
Boise, ID	153	May 8	Oct. 9	Portland, OR	217	Apr. 3	Nov. 7
Chicago, IL	187	Apr. 22	Oct. 26	Carlisle, PA	182	Apr. 20	Oct. 20
Springfield, IL	185	Apr. 17	Oct. 19	Williamsport, PA	168	Apr. 29	Oct. 15
Indianapolis, IN	180	Apr. 22	Oct. 20	Kingston, RI	144	May 8	Sept. 30
South Bend, IN	169	May 1	Oct. 18	Charleston, SC	253	Mar. 11	Nov. 20
Atlantic, IA	141	May 9	Sept. 28	Columbia, SC	211	Apr. 4	Nov. 2
Cedar Rapids, IA	161	Apr. 29	Oct. 7	Rapid City, SD	145	May 7	Sept. 29
Topeka, KS	175	Apr. 21	Oct. 14	Memphis, TN	228	Mar. 23	Nov. 7
Lexington, KY	190	Apr. 17	Oct. 25	Nashville, TN	207	Apr. 5	Oct. 29
Monroe, LA	242	Mar. 9	Nov. 7	Amarillo, TX	197	Apr. 14	Oct. 29
New Orleans, LA	288	Feb. 20	Dec. 5	Denton, TX	231	Mar. 25	Nov. 12
Portland, ME	143	May 10	Sept. 30	San Antonio, TX	265	Mar. 3	Nov. 24
Baltimore, MD	231	Mar. 26	Nov. 13	Cedar City, UT	134	May 20	Oct. 2
Worcester, MA	172	Apr. 27	Oct. 17	Spanish Fork, UT	156	May 8	Oct. 12
Lansing, MI	140	May 13	Sept. 30	Burlington, VT	142	May 11	Oct. 1
Marquette, MI	159	May 12	Oct. 19	Norfolk, VA	239	Mar. 23	Nov. 17
Duluth, MN	122	May 21	Sept. 21	Richmond, VA	198	Apr. 10	Oct. 26
Willmar, MN	152	May 4	Oct. 4	Seattle, WA	232	Mar. 24	Nov. 11
Columbus, MS	215	Mar. 27	Oct. 29	Spokane, WA	153	May 4	Oct. 5
Vicksburg, MS	250	Mar. 13	Nov. 18	Parkersburg, WV	175	Apr. 25	Oct. 18
Jefferson City, MO	173	Apr. 26	Oct. 16	Green Bay, WI	143	May 12	Oct. 2
Fort Peck, MT	146	May 5	Sept. 28	Janesville, WI	164	Apr. 28	Oct. 10
Helena, MT	122	May 18	Sept. 18	Casper, WY	123	May 22	Sept. 22
Blair, NE	165	Apr. 27	Oct. 10	*Frosts do not occur every year			

TIME CORRECTION TABLES

The times of sunrise/sunset, moonrise/moonset, and the rising and setting times of the planets and bright stars, are given for **Boston only** on pages 54-80 and 40-43. Use the **Key Letter** shown to the right of each time on those pages with these tables to find the number of minutes that should be added to or subtracted from Boston time to give the correct time for your city. The answer will not be as precise as that for Boston, but will be within approximately five minutes. If your city is not listed, find the city closest to you in both latitude and longitude and use those figures. **Boston's latitude is 42° 22' and longitude is 71° 03'.** Canadian cities appear at the end of the list. For a more complete explanation of the usage of Key Letters and these tables, see "How to Use This Almanac," page 30.

Time Zone Code: Atlantic Std. is -1; Eastern Std. is 0; Central Std. is 1; Mountain Std. is 2; Pacific Std. is 3; Alaska Std. is 4; Hawaii-Aleutian Std. is 5.

City	North Latitude ° '	West Longitude ° '	Time Zone Code	Key Letters A min.	B min.	C min.	D min.	E min.
Aberdeen, SD	45 28	98 29	1	+37	+44	+49	+54	+59
Akron, OH	41 5	81 31	0	+46	+43	+41	+39	+37
Albany, NY	42 39	73 45	0	+ 9	+10	+10	+11	+11
Albert Lea, MN	43 39	93 22	1	+24	+26	+28	+31	+33
Albuquerque, NM	35 5	106 39	2	+45	+32	+22	+11	+ 2
Alexandria, LA	31 18	92 27	1	+58	+40	+26	+ 9	− 3
Allentown-Bethlehem, PA...	40 3	75 28	0	+25	+20	+17	+13	+10
Amarillo, TX	35 12	101 50	1	+85	+73	+63	+52	+43
Anchorage, AK	61 10	149 59	4	−46	+27	+71	+122	+171
Asheville, NC	35 36	82 33	0	+67	+55	+46	+35	+27
Atlanta, GA	33 45	84 24	0	+79	+65	+53	+40	+30
Atlantic City, NJ	39 22	74 26	0	+23	+17	+13	+ 8	+ 4
Augusta, GA	33 28	81 58	0	+70	+55	+44	+30	+19
Augusta, ME	44 19	69 46	0	−12	− 8	− 5	− 1	0
Austin, TX	30 16	97 45	1	+82	+62	+47	+29	+15
Bakersfield, CA	35 23	119 1	3	+33	+21	+12	+ 1	− 7
Baltimore, MD	39 17	76 37	0	+32	+26	+22	+17	+13
Bangor, ME	44 48	68 46	0	−18	−13	− 9	− 5	− 1
Barstow, CA	34 54	117 1	3	+27	+14	+ 4	− 7	−16
Baton Rouge, LA	30 27	91 11	1	+55	+36	+21	+ 3	−10
Beaumont, TX	30 5	94 6	1	+67	+48	+32	+14	0
Bellingham, WA	48 45	122 29	3	0	+13	+24	+37	+47
Bemidji, MN	47 28	94 53	1	+14	+26	+34	+44	+52
Berlin, NH	44 28	71 11	0	− 7	− 3	0	+ 3	+ 7
Billings, MT	45 47	108 30	2	+16	+23	+29	+35	+40
Biloxi, MS	30 24	88 53	1	+46	+27	+11	− 5	−19
Binghamton, NY	42 6	75 55	0	+20	+19	+19	+18	+18
Birmingham, AL	33 31	86 49	1	+30	+15	+ 3	−10	−20
Bismarck, ND	46 48	100 47	1	+41	+50	+58	+66	+73
Boise, ID	43 37	116 12	2	+55	+58	+60	+62	+64
Brattleboro, VT	42 51	72 34	0	+ 4	+ 5	+ 5	+ 6	+ 7
Bridgeport, CT	41 11	73 11	0	+12	+10	+ 8	+ 6	+ 4
Brockton, MA	42 5	71 1	0	0	0	0	0	− 1
Brownsville, TX	25 54	97 30	1	+91	+66	+46	+23	+ 5
Buffalo, NY	42 53	78 52	0	+29	+30	+30	+31	+32
Burlington, VT	44 29	73 13	0	0	+ 4	+ 8	+12	+15
Butte, MT	46 1	112 32	2	+31	+39	+45	+52	+57
Cairo, IL	37 0	89 11	1	+29	+20	+12	+ 4	− 2
Camden, NJ	39 57	75 7	0	+24	+19	+16	+12	+ 9
Canton, OH	40 48	81 23	0	+46	+43	+41	+38	+36
Cape May, NJ	38 56	74 56	0	+26	+20	+15	+ 9	+ 5
Carson City–Reno, NV	39 10	119 46	3	+25	+19	+14	+ 9	+ 5

City	North Latitude ° ′		West Longitude ° ′		Time Zone Code	Key Letters				
						A min.	B min.	C min.	D min.	E min.
Casper, WY......................	42	51	106	19	2	+19	+19	+20	+21	+22
Chadron, NE.....................	42	50	103	0	2	+ 5	+ 6	+ 7	+ 8	+ 9
Charleston, SC.................	32	47	79	56	0	+64	+48	+36	+21	+10
Charleston, WV................	38	21	81	38	0	+55	+48	+42	+35	+30
Charlotte, NC..................	35	14	80	51	0	+61	+49	+39	+28	+19
Charlottesville, VA..........	38	2	78	30	0	+43	+35	+29	+22	+17
Chattanooga, TN..............	35	3	85	19	0	+79	+67	+57	+45	+36
Cheboygan, MI.................	45	39	84	29	0	+40	+47	+53	+59	+64
Cheyenne, WY	41	8	104	49	2	+19	+16	+14	+12	+11
Chicago-Oak Park, IL	41	52	87	38	1	+ 7	+ 6	+ 6	+ 5	+ 4
Cincinnati-Hamilton, OH..	39	6	84	31	0	+64	+58	+53	+48	+44
Cleveland-Lakewood, OH..	41	30	81	42	0	+45	+43	+42	+40	+39
Columbia, SC...................	34	0	81	2	0	+65	+51	+40	+27	+17
Columbus, OH	39	57	83	1	0	+55	+51	+47	+43	+40
Cordova, AK	60	33	145	45	4	−55	+13	+55	+103	+149
Corpus Christi, TX...........	27	48	97	24	1	+86	+64	+46	+25	+ 9
Craig, CO	40	31	107	33	2	+32	+28	+25	+22	+20
Dallas-Fort Worth, TX.....	32	47	96	48	1	+71	+55	+43	+28	+17
Danville, IL......................	40	8	87	37	1	+13	+ 9	+ 6	+ 2	0
Danville, VA.....................	36	36	79	23	0	+51	+41	+33	+24	+17
Davenport, IA	41	32	90	35	1	+20	+19	+17	+16	+15
Dayton, OH	39	45	84	10	0	+61	+56	+52	+48	+44
Decatur, AL......................	34	36	86	59	1	+27	+14	+ 4	− 7	−17
Decatur, IL.......................	39	51	88	57	1	+19	+15	+11	+ 7	+ 4
Denver-Boulder, CO	39	44	104	59	2	+24	+19	+15	+11	+ 7
Des Moines, IA	41	35	93	37	1	+32	+31	+30	+28	+27
Detroit-Dearborn, MI	42	20	83	3	0	+47	+47	+47	+47	+47
Dubuque, IA.....................	42	30	90	41	1	+17	+18	+18	+18	+18
Duluth, MN	46	47	92	6	1	+ 6	+16	+23	+31	+38
Durham, NC	36	0	78	55	0	+51	+40	+31	+21	+13
Eastport, ME	44	54	67	0	0	−26	−20	−16	−11	− 8
Eau Claire, WI	44	49	91	30	1	+12	+17	+21	+25	+29
El Paso, TX	31	45	106	29	2	+53	+35	+22	+ 6	− 6
Elko, NV	40	50	115	46	3	+ 3	0	− 1	− 3	− 5
Ellsworth, ME	44	33	68	25	0	−18	−14	−10	− 6	− 3
Erie, PA............................	42	7	80	5	0	+36	+36	+35	+35	+35
Eugene, OR	44	3	123	6	3	+21	+24	+27	+30	+33
Fairbanks, AK	64	48	147	51	4	−127	+ 2	+61	+131	+205
Fall River– New Bedford, MA.........	41	42	71	9	0	+ 2	+ 1	0	0	− 1
Fargo, ND	46	53	96	47	1	+24	+34	+42	+50	+57
Flagstaff, AZ....................	35	12	111	39	2	+64	+52	+42	+31	+22
Flint, MI...........................	43	1	83	41	0	+47	+49	+50	+51	+52
Fort Randall, AK	55	10	162	47	4	+62	+99	+124	+153	+179
Fort Scott, KS	37	50	94	42	1	+49	+41	+34	+27	+21
Fort Smith, AR.................	35	23	94	25	1	+55	+43	+33	+22	+14
Fort Wayne, IN.................	41	4	85	9	0	+60	+58	+56	+54	+52
Fort Yukon, AK................	66	34	145	16	4	+30	−18	+50	+131	+227
Fresno, CA	36	44	119	47	3	+32	+22	+15	+ 6	0
Gallup, NM	35	32	108	45	2	+52	+40	+31	+20	+11
Galveston, TX	29	18	94	48	1	+72	+52	+35	+16	+ 1
Gary, IN............................	41	36	87	20	1	+ 7	+ 6	+ 4	+ 3	+ 2
Glasgow, MT	48	12	106	38	2	− 1	+11	+21	+32	+42
Grand Forks, ND	47	55	97	3	1	+21	+33	+43	+53	+62
Grand Island, NE.............	40	55	98	21	1	+53	+51	+49	+46	+44
Grand Junction, CO	39	4	108	33	2	+40	+34	+29	+24	+20
Great Falls, MT	47	30	111	17	2	+20	+31	+39	+49	+58

City	North Latitude ° '	West Longitude ° '	Time Zone Code	Key Letters A min.	B min.	C min.	D min.	E min.
Green Bay, WI	44 31	88 0	1	0	+ 3	+ 7	+11	+14
Greensboro, NC	36 4	79 47	0	+54	+43	+35	+25	+17
Hagerstown, MD	39 39	77 43	0	+35	+30	+26	+22	+18
Harrisburg, PA	40 16	76 53	0	+30	+26	+23	+19	+16
Hartford-New Britain, CT..	41 46	72 41	0	+ 8	+ 7	+ 6	+ 5	+ 4
Helena, MT	46 36	112 2	2	+27	+36	+43	+51	+57
Hilo, HI	19 44	155 5	5	+94	+62	+37	+ 7	−15
Honolulu, HI	21 18	157 52	5	+102	+72	+48	+19	− 1
Houston, TX	29 45	95 22	1	+73	+53	+37	+19	+ 5
Indianapolis, IN	39 46	86 10	0	+69	+64	+60	+56	+52
Ironwood, MI	46 27	90 9	1	0	+ 9	+15	+23	+29
Jackson, MI	42 15	84 24	0	+53	+53	+53	+52	+52
Jackson, MS	32 18	90 11	1	+46	+30	+17	+ 1	−10
Jacksonville, FL	30 20	81 40	0	+77	+58	+43	+25	+11
Jefferson City, MO	38 34	92 10	1	+36	+29	+24	+18	+13
Joplin, MO	37 6	94 30	1	+50	+41	+33	+25	+18
Juneau, AK	58 18	134 25	4	−76	−23	+10	+49	+86
Kalamazoo, MI	42 17	85 35	0	+58	+57	+57	+57	+57
Kanab, UT	37 3	112 32	2	+62	+53	+46	+37	+30
Kansas City, MO	39 1	94 20	1	+44	+37	+33	+27	+23
Keene, NH	42 56	72 17	0	+ 2	+ 3	+ 4	+ 5	+ 6
Ketchikan, AK	55 21	131 39	4	−62	−25	0	+29	+56
Knoxville, TN	35 58	83 55	0	+71	+60	+51	+41	+33
Kodiak, AK	57 47	152 24	4	0	+49	+82	+120	+154
LaCrosse, WI	43 48	91 15	1	+15	+18	+20	+22	+25
Lake Charles, LA	30 14	93 13	1	+64	+44	+29	+11	− 2
Lanai City, HI	20 50	156 55	5	+99	+69	+44	+15	− 6
Lancaster, PA	40 2	76 18	0	+28	+24	+20	+17	+13
Lansing, MI	42 44	84 33	0	+52	+53	+53	+54	+54
Las Cruces, NM	32 19	106 47	2	+53	+36	+23	+ 8	− 3
Las Vegas, NV	36 10	115 9	3	+16	+ 4	− 3	−13	−20
Lawrence-Lowell, MA	42 42	71 10	0	0	0	0	0	+ 1
Lewiston, ID	46 25	117 1	3	−12	− 3	+ 2	+10	+17
Lexington-Frankfort, KY.	38 3	84 30	0	+67	+59	+53	+46	+41
Liberal, KS	37 3	100 55	1	+76	+66	+59	+51	+44
Lihue, HI	21 59	159 23	5	+107	+77	+54	+26	+ 5
Lincoln, NE	40 49	96 41	1	+47	+44	+42	+39	+37
Little Rock, AR	34 45	92 17	1	+48	+35	+25	+13	+ 4
Los Angeles incl. Pasadena and Santa Monica, CA..	34 3	118 14	3	+34	+20	+ 9	− 3	−13
Louisville, KY	38 15	85 46	0	+72	+64	+58	+52	+46
Macon, GA	32 50	83 38	0	+79	+63	+50	+36	+24
Madison, WI	43 4	89 23	1	+10	+11	+12	+14	+15
Manchester-Concord, NH..	42 59	71 28	0	0	0	+ 1	+ 2	+ 3
McAllen, TX	26 12	98 14	1	+93	+69	+49	+26	+9
McGrath, AK	62 58	155 36	4	−52	+42	+93	+152	+213
Memphis, TN	35 9	90 3	1	+38	+26	+16	+ 5	− 3
Meridian, MS	32 22	88 42	1	+40	+24	+11	− 4	−15
Miami, FL	25 47	80 12	0	+88	+57	+37	+14	− 3
Miles City, MT	46 25	105 51	2	+ 3	+11	+18	+26	+32
Milwaukee, WI	43 2	87 54	1	+ 4	+ 6	+ 7	+ 8	+ 9
Minneapolis-St. Paul, MN	44 59	93 16	1	+18	+24	+28	+33	+37
Minot, ND	48 14	101 18	1	+36	+50	+59	+71	+81
Moab, UT	38 35	109 33	2	+46	+39	+33	+27	+22
Mobile, AL	30 42	88 3	1	+42	+23	+ 8	− 8	−22
Monroe, LA	32 30	92 7	1	+53	+37	+24	+ 9	− 1
Montgomery, AL	32 23	86 19	1	+31	+14	+ 1	−13	−25

City	North Latitude ° '	West Longitude ° '	Time Zone Code	Key Letters A min.	B min.	C min.	D min.	E min.
Muncie, IN	40 12	85 23	0	+64	+60	+57	+53	+50
Nashville, TN	36 10	86 47	1	+22	+11	+ 3	− 6	−14
New Haven, CT	41 18	72 56	0	+11	+ 8	+ 7	+ 5	+ 4
New London, CT	41 22	72 6	0	+ 7	+ 5	+ 4	+ 2	+ 1
New Orleans, LA	29 57	90 4	1	+52	+32	+16	− 1	−15
New York, NY	40 45	74 0	0	+17	+14	+11	+ 9	+ 6
Newark-Irvington- East Orange, NJ	40 44	74 10	0	+17	+14	+12	+ 9	+ 7
Nome, AK	64 30	165 25	4	−48	+74	+132	+199	+271
Norfolk, VA	36 51	76 17	0	+38	+28	+21	+12	+ 5
North Platte, NE	41 8	100 46	1	+62	+60	+58	+56	+54
Norwalk-Stamford, CT	41 7	73 22	0	+13	+10	+ 9	+ 7	+ 5
Oakley, KS	39 8	100 51	1	+69	+63	+59	+53	+49
Ogden, UT	41 13	111 58	2	+47	+45	+43	+41	+40
Ogdensburg, NY	44 42	75 30	0	+ 8	+13	+17	+21	+25
Oklahoma City, OK	35 28	97 31	1	+67	+55	+46	+35	+26
Omaha, NE	41 16	95 56	1	+43	+40	+39	+37	+36
Orlando, FL	28 32	81 22	0	+80	+59	+42	+22	+ 6
Ortonville, MN	45 19	96 27	1	+30	+36	+40	+46	+51
Oshkosh, WI	44 1	88 33	1	+ 3	+ 6	+ 9	+12	+15
Parkersburg, WV	39 16	81 34	0	+52	+46	+42	+36	+32
Paterson, NJ	40 55	74 10	0	+17	+14	+12	+ 9	+ 7
Pendleton, OR	45 40	118 47	3	− 1	+ 4	+10	+16	+21
Pensacola, FL	30 25	87 13	1	+39	+20	+ 5	−12	−26
Peoria, IL	40 42	89 36	1	+19	+16	+14	+11	+ 9
Philadelphia-Chester, PA	39 57	75 9	0	+24	+19	+16	+12	+ 9
Phoenix, AZ	33 27	112 4	2	+71	+56	+44	+30	+20
Pierre, SD	44 22	100 21	1	+49	+53	+56	+60	+63
Pittsburgh-McKeesport, PA.	40 26	80 0	0	+42	+38	+35	+32	+29
Pittsfield, MA	42 27	73 15	0	+ 8	+ 8	+ 8	+ 8	+ 8
Pocatello, ID	42 52	112 27	2	+43	+44	+45	+46	+46
Poplar Bluff, MO	36 46	90 24	1	+35	+25	+17	+ 8	+ 1
Portland, ME	43 40	70 15	0	− 8	− 5	− 3	− 1	0
Portland, OR	45 31	122 41	3	+14	+20	+25	+31	+36
Portsmouth, NH	43 5	70 45	0	− 4	− 2	− 1	0	0
Presque Isle, ME	46 41	68 1	0	−29	−19	−12	− 4	+ 2
Providence, RI	41 50	71 25	0	+ 3	+ 2	+ 1	0	0
Pueblo, CO	38 16	104 37	2	+27	+20	+14	+ 7	+ 2
Raleigh, NC	35 47	78 38	0	+51	+39	+30	+20	+12
Rapid City, SD	44 5	103 14	2	+ 2	+ 5	+ 8	+11	+13
Reading, PA	40 20	75 56	0	+26	+22	+19	+16	+13
Redding, CA	40 35	122 24	3	+31	+27	+25	+22	+19
Richmond, VA	37 32	77 26	0	+41	+32	+25	+17	+11
Roanoke, VA	37 16	79 57	0	+51	+42	+35	+27	+21
Roswell, NM	33 24	104 32	2	+41	+26	+14	0	−10
Rutland, VT	43 37	72 58	0	+ 2	+ 5	+ 7	+ 9	+11
Sacramento, CA	38 35	121 30	3	+34	+27	+21	+15	+10
Salem, OR	44 57	123 1	3	+17	+23	+27	+31	+35
Salina, KS	38 50	97 37	1	+57	+51	+46	+40	+35
Salisbury, MD	38 22	75 36	0	+31	+23	+18	+11	+ 6
Salt Lake City, UT	40 45	111 53	2	+48	+45	+43	+40	+38
San Antonio, TX	29 25	98 30	1	+87	+66	+50	+31	+16
San Diego, CA	32 43	117 9	3	+33	+17	+ 4	− 9	−21
San Francisco incl. Oakland and San Jose, CA	37 47	122 25	3	+40	+31	+25	+18	+12
Santa Fe, NM	35 41	105 56	2	+40	+28	+19	+ 9	0
Savannah, GA	32 5	81 6	0	+70	+54	+40	+25	+13

City	North Latitude °	'	West Longitude °	'	Time Zone Code	A min.	B min.	C min.	D min.	E min.
Scranton–Wilkes Barre, PA.	41	25	75	40	0	+21	+19	+18	+16	+15
Seattle-Tacoma-Olympia, WA	47	37	122	20	3	+ 3	+15	+24	+34	+42
Sheridan, WY	44	48	106	58	2	+14	+19	+23	+27	+31
Shreveport, LA	32	31	93	45	1	+60	+44	+31	+16	+ 4
Sioux Falls, SD	43	33	96	44	1	+38	+40	+42	+44	+46
South Bend, IN	41	41	86	15	0	+62	+61	+60	+59	+58
Spartanburg, SC	34	56	81	57	0	+66	+53	+43	+32	+23
Spokane, WA	47	40	117	24	3	−16	− 4	+ 4	+14	+23
Springfield, IL	39	48	89	39	1	+22	+18	+14	+10	+ 6
Springfield-Holyoke, MA	42	6	72	36	0	+ 6	+ 6	+ 6	+ 5	+ 5
Springfield, MO	37	13	93	18	1	+45	+36	+29	+20	+14
St. Johnsbury, VT	44	25	72	1	0	− 4	0	+ 3	+ 7	+10
St. Joseph, MO	39	46	94	50	1	+43	+38	+35	+30	+27
St. Louis, MO	38	37	90	12	1	+28	+21	+16	+10	+ 5
St. Petersburg, FL	27	46	82	39	0	+87	+65	+47	+26	+10
Syracuse, NY	43	3	76	9	0	+17	+19	+20	+21	+22
Tallahassee, FL	30	27	84	17	0	+87	+68	+53	+35	+22
Tampa, FL	27	57	82	27	0	+86	+64	+46	+25	+ 9
Terre Haute, IN	39	28	87	24	0	+74	+69	+65	+60	+56
Texarkana, AR	33	26	94	3	1	+59	+44	+32	+18	+ 8
Toledo, OH	41	39	83	33	0	+52	+50	+49	+48	+47
Topeka, KS	39	3	95	40	1	+49	+43	+38	+32	+28
Traverse City, MI	44	46	85	38	0	+49	+54	+57	+62	+65
Trenton, NJ	40	13	74	46	0	+21	+17	+14	+11	+ 8
Trinidad, CO	37	10	104	31	2	+30	+21	+13	+ 5	0
Tucson, AZ	32	13	110	58	2	+70	+53	+40	+24	+12
Tulsa, OK	36	9	95	60	1	+59	+48	+40	+30	+22
Tupelo, MS	34	16	88	34	1	+35	+21	+10	− 2	−11
Vernal, UT	40	27	109	32	2	+40	+36	+33	+30	+28
Walla Walla, WA	46	4	118	20	3	− 5	+ 2	+ 8	+15	+21
Washington, DC	38	54	77	1	0	+35	+28	+23	+18	+13
Waterbury-Meriden, CT	41	33	73	3	0	+10	+ 9	+ 7	+ 6	+ 5
Waterloo, IA	42	30	92	20	1	+24	+24	+24	+25	+25
Wausau, WI	44	58	89	38	1	+ 4	+ 9	+13	+18	+22
West Palm Beach, FL	26	43	80	3	0	+79	+55	+36	+14	− 2
Wichita, KS	37	42	97	20	1	+60	+51	+45	+37	+31
Williston, ND	48	9	103	37	1	+46	+59	+69	+80	+90
Wilmington, DE	39	45	75	33	0	+26	+21	+18	+13	+10
Wilmington, NC	34	14	77	55	0	+52	+38	+27	+15	+ 5
Winchester, VA	39	11	78	10	0	+38	+33	+28	+23	+19
Worcester, MA	42	16	71	48	0	+ 3	+ 2	+ 2	+ 2	+ 2
York, PA	39	58	76	43	0	+30	+26	+22	+18	+15
Youngstown, OH	41	6	80	39	0	+42	40	+38	+36	+34
Yuma, AZ	32	43	114	37	2	+83	+67	+54	+40	+28
CANADA										
Calgary, AB	51	5	114	5	2	+13	+35	+50	+68	+84
Edmonton, AB	53	34	113	25	2	− 3	+26	+47	+72	+93
Halifax, NS	44	38	63	35	−1	+21	+26	+29	+33	+37
Montreal, PQ	45	28	73	39	0	− 1	+ 4	+ 9	+15	+20
Ottawa, ON	45	25	75	43	0	+ 6	+13	+18	+23	+28
Saint John, NB	45	16	66	3	−1	+28	+34	+39	+44	+49
Saskatoon, SK	52	10	106	40	1	+37	+63	+80	+101	+119
Sydney, NS	46	10	60	10	−1	+ 1	+ 9	+15	+23	+28
Thunder Bay, ON	48	27	89	12	0	+47	+61	+71	+83	+93
Toronto, ON	43	39	79	23	0	+28	+30	+32	+35	+37
Vancouver, BC	49	13	123	6	3	0	+15	+26	+40	+52
Winnipeg, MB	49	53	97	10	1	+12	+30	+43	+58	+71

VEGETABLES

Can Win a

BLUE RIBBON

at the Fair

BY POLLY BANNISTER

We asked a half dozen expert judges to reveal the criteria for prizewinners — and a few secrets for growing and presenting picture-perfect vegetables.

Agricultural judging is a mainstay at county and state fairs across the country. Competitions include everything from best sheaf of barley in the straw to best quart of soybeans, best display of cut comb honey, best plate of five red slicing tomatoes. In most cases, the coveted first prize is simply a blue ribbon. Might not sound like much, but winning is a real honor, an achievement some folks work toward for months.

According to fair managers, the fastest-growing category is garden vegetables. Judging is based on condition (free from disease and insect damage), quality (ripeness, including skin color and texture), uniformity (when more than one specimen is being shown), size, and true-to-typeness (specimen's color, size, and form are in keeping with its variety). We asked long-time judges at some of the biggest and best fairs in the country to give us specific advice on growing and presenting a winner.

ROBERT IRELAND

New York State Fair judge, ten years

BEST HEAD OF CABBAGE

Any gardener is a potential prizewinner — the secret is knowing how to select the right specimen and prepare it for exhibit. We look for a nice, round, symmetrical head with no sun fading or bleaching on the outer leaves. We like to see leaves trimmed away except for a couple of layers of shiny green wrapper leaves. We like deep color, a firm, solid body, crispness, and no sign of insect damage or disease.

"For competition, plant a minimum of half a dozen plants. Cabbage is easy to grow and easy to show. A good green-

leaf variety is Stonehead, because it remains symmetrical. For red cabbage, Ruby Ball is a good choice. If you can, leave an extra foot between plants to assure the wrapper leaves enough space to develop symmetrically. Plants shouldn't be placed where cabbages or their relatives were planted in the previous year because of soil-borne disease. Insect damage from cabbageworm caterpillars is easily controlled with early dusting of *Bacillus thuringiensis*. As soon as you see a white butterfly, dust or spray. To prevent the cabbage heads from splitting, keep the soil uniformly moist.

"When you're ready for the fair, carefully cut the stalk well beneath the head, leaving on most of the outer leaves. Closer to show time, trim the stem to about half an inch. Make sure about four wrapper leaves remain on. At the fairgrounds, gently buff them to a sheen."

The New York State Fair is held each year in Syracuse for the 12 days preceding Labor Day. It draws over 800,000 people; 315-487-7711.

Robert Ireland is national judging chairman for the Gardeners of America. Their *Judges Manual* includes criteria for judging flowers, fruits, and vegetables and tips for preparing horticultural specimens. Available for $7.50 plus shipping from Gardeners of America, Inc., 5560 Merle Hay Rd., P.O. Box 241, Johnston, IA 50131; 515-278-0295.

WILLIAM FOUNTAIN, PH.D.
Kentucky State Fair judge, ten years

BEST DOZEN GREEN SNAP BEANS

W hen you enter a vegetable, give us the ultimate — something that looks so luscious and perfect, you're likely to find teeth marks on it. You've got to be first among equals. With snap beans, we want a bright green, tender bean, not so young that it is flabby or wilted, and not so mature that we see swollen seeds through the pod. The degree of maturation for all 12 should be the same. Uniformity is important here — it should look like one bean with 11 mirrors around it. The beans should be similar in length and nestled to-

gether with the curve in the same direction to the same degree. Try not to have more than a millimeter or two variation in length. A little trick is to place beans from largest to smallest on the plate — this helps to diminish the size variation.

"To get a perfect plateful, count on harvesting about half a bushel, so plant at least 25 feet of bush beans. Note your dates and aim to pick before peak maturation. Here in Kentucky, Blue Lake and White Half-Runner are good choices. Check with your county extension agent for a variety appropriate to your region. Early pest control is key, so watch for aphids and Japanese beetles.

"When harvesting, use needlenose clippers, and gently snip off the stem. Don't pull — you might hurt the pod or tear the plant. Wipe the bean clean with a soft cloth, but minimize handling to avoid washing off the waxy bloom. This is desirable and worth points in the judges' eyes. Wrap your exhibit in paper toweling and be sure to have a couple of spare beans."

The Kentucky State Fair in Louisville runs for ten days at the end of August. Attendance is over 675,000; 502-367-5000.

William Fountain is a horticultural specialist at the University of Kentucky in Lexington and program chairman of the National Junior Horticultural Association. He has written a 4-H booklet, "Exhibiting and Judging Vegetables"; single copies are available from the Department of Horticulture, N-318 Ag. Science Building-North, University of Kentucky, Lexington, KY 40546-0091. Include a large, self-addressed envelope with 52¢ postage for shipping. 606-257-3320.

CLARA BARTLEY
Illinois State Fair judge, 20 years

BEST FIVE GREEN BELL PEPPERS

W ith peppers, five are placed in a circle on a plate. It is hard to get five looking exactly alike, but we've seen them come close. First off, we look for condition — no water streaks, bacterial speckles, scratches, or dirt. We like a brilliant green color with no sun scald or yellow or red on the shoulders. We hold the pepper to feel its weight, looking for a nice, heavy pepper with thick walls. A good size is three to four inches long and close to three inches wide. We look for an equal number of lobes on the bottom of each pepper in the exhibit. Often uniformity is the determining factor in a winner.

"For a good harvest, plant a minimum of a dozen plants in well-drained soil. Gardeners with a short growing season should choose early varieties, because even these need over two months to mature. Overfertilizing is a common mistake. For a better yield with bigger fruit, pinch back when the plant is about six inches. When harvesting, always cut with pruning shears so as not to injure the plant or fruit. For showing, cut the stem flush with shoulders and wipe the fruit with a soft chamois cloth or paper towel. Peppers don't store well: To avoid shriveling, transport them in a cooler to keep them crisp. Wrap each one carefully in tissue paper, then newspaper."

The Illinois State Fair in Springfield is held for nine days in August. The annual attendance is over 700,000; 217-782-6661.

Clara Bartley is a farm wife and mother who always judges in a team with her husband, John, a soybean breeder. Having been married for 50 years, she says they've learned to agree on a lot, including vegetables!

ELDON EVERHART, PH.D.

Iowa State Fair judge, eight years

BEST FIVE RED SLICING TOMATOES

Every year there seems to be a greater number of vegetable entries — last year I think we had 60 to 70 plates of tomatoes. For standard slicing tomatoes, we want uniformity among the five, all fully ripe but still firm. We look for a shiny red color with no green shoulders, no blotchy ripening or yellow pigment (which develops in too much heat). There can be no cracking at the stem or blossom ends, and no blemishes. They have to be picture-perfect, so the hardest thing for us is to keep from tasting them!

"Here in Iowa, the variety Jet Star does consistently well as a winner. Supersonic and Mountain Pride are good for resistance to cracking. Your county extension agent should know what grows best in your area. Look for varieties that are resistant to common tomato problems — verticillium, fusarium, nematodes, and tobacco mosaic virus. Seed packets will list the initials V.F.N.T. in varieties bred for resistance.

"For a good yield, cultivate at least five or six plants; space them two to three feet apart. And stake or cage them for optimum sunlight and air circulation. Plants sprawled on the ground are more susceptible to disease, and you'll get a higher number of culls. You'll want uniform moisture, so use a good clean mulch of some organic matter like straw or wood chips. (Avoid mulching with yard clippings if you've used the lawn herbicide 2,4-D or Dicamba, because tomatoes are sensitive to them.) Mulching is important in preventing blossom-end rot, a calcium deficiency.

"Harvest tomatoes slightly before ripe by gently lifting until the stem snaps. Wipe clean and wrap individually in paper towels and newspaper for protection. Keep cool until the exhibit."

The Iowa State Fair, held in Des Moines, runs for ten days in mid-August. Attendance is nearly 900,000. The fair is one of the oldest in the country — 136 years old; 515-262-3111.

Eldon Everhart works as a commercial horticultural field specialist for 37 counties and teaches vegetable judging with the Master Gardeners training program at the county extension service.

VICTOR MILLER, PH.D.

Arizona State Fair judge, ten years

BEST FIVE CARROTS, TOPPED

Carrots are divided into classes according to length: three to four inches, five to seven inches, and eight to nine inches. An exhibit calls for five roots, and these should be straight with a nice taper. Some varieties are stumpy, shaped with a blunt end; the judge will know what to expect. Roots shouldn't be knobby or gnarled, and they should be as uniform as possible. Tops should be trimmed to within an inch. We want to see a deep orange-colored root, with no green or purple on the shoulders.

"For growing winners, you have to have well-limed, loose, deep, sandy, stoneless soil with no obstructions. If you know you've got shallow, rocky soil, it is a good idea to select varieties with shorter roots. Plant at least a ten-foot row for about a seven-pound yield. Thin early to at least two inches, as overcrowding causes small and misshapened roots. When thinning, don't stand directly on the soil — this will compact the dirt and cause roots to become gnarled. Before planting, thoroughly spade in a 5-10-10 fertilizer. Harvest carefully with a spading fork. Brush clean, but don't disturb the skin."

The Arizona State Fair is held in Phoenix, starting on the second Thursday of October and running 18 days. It is rated among the top ten fairs in the country, is over 100 years old, and attracts one million people annually; 602-252-6771.

Victor Miller is a retired professor of horticulture who hosts an Arizona State University cable TV program, "Gardening for Fun." For 20 years he wrote a gardening column for the *Arizona Republic*.

RICHARD KASSABIAN

The Big Fresno (Calif.) Fair judge, 18 years

BEST HEAD OF LETTUCE

Fresno County grows about 18,000 acres of lettuce. We have a harvest in both the spring and fall. At the fair in October, we'll see Butterheads, Iceberg, and Bibb, among others. Most heads should be at least six to eight inches in diameter, except Bibb, which is smaller and can start at four inches. We look for a well-shaped, round head that is firm, but has a slight give, indicating crispness. If it feels real tight, the lettuce is overmature, not tender. Iceberg is firmer and will have a tighter head than Butterhead. Their colors differ according to variety, but we look for bright green outer leaves, free from insect damage or disease. Stems should be trimmed to about half an inch and still have a fresh, white color.

"True head lettuce, Iceberg, is not common to many home gardeners because it requires a special temperature range — cool nights with an average daytime temperature of 70° F. Most gardeners will have more luck with looser-leaf varieties like Buttercrunch and Summer Bibb. Plant at least a 15-foot row for a harvest of about 15 heads. Lettuce is a cool-season crop and does well before the full heat of summer. It needs partial shade during the hottest season, so provide some sort of screening, like cheesecloth. Check for slugs, which like lettuce, and remove immediately.

"If possible, harvest early in the morning of judging day and cover your plants with a moist towel. Don't transport the entries in a plastic bag unless there are plenty of air holes for breathing or the lettuce will sweat and break down."

The Big Fresno Fair, Fresno, California, is held the first three weeks in October and attracts 700,000 visitors; 209-453-3247.

Richard Kassabian has worked for the Fresno County Department of Agriculture for 29 years. Fresno County is the leading agricultural county in the country, with 250 crop varieties grown for international distribution. The Big Fresno Fair has 25,000 agricultural entries each year! □ □

RAINY DAY AMUSEMENTS

On pages 242-243.

A QUIZ YOU SHOULD REALLY HUM THROUGH

1. Basin Street
2. Ventura Highway
3. The Road to Mandalay
4. Flatbush Avenue
5. Primrose Lane
6. Boulevard of Broken Dreams
7. Slaughter on 10th Avenue
8. Santa Claus Lane
9. The Yellow Brick Road
10. The Long and Winding Road
11. 77 Sunset Strip
12. Lonely Street
13. State Street
14. Route 66
15. Twelfth Street and Vine
16. On Broadway
17. King of the Road
18. On the Avenue — Fifth Avenue
19. Penny Lane
20. Under the Boardwalk
21. South Street
22. Thunder Road
23. *The Saint of Bleecker Street*
24. 59th Street Bridge
25. Dancin' in the Street

FUNNY PEOPLE

1) F; 2) I; 3) G; 4) B; 5) H; 6) A; 7) D;
8) J; 9) E; 10) C.

FOUR IN NINE

1. anARCHism
2. arBOREtum
3. gaBARDine
4. inCENTive
5. reCORDing
6. inDENTure
7. inDUCTion
8. peDOMEter
9. inFIRMity
10. inFORMant
11. reGISTrar
12. arMISTice
13. caPILLary
14. coPARTner
15. coROLLary
16. peRIMEter
17. diSPARity
18. opTOMEtry
19. poTENTial
20. inVENTory

AN ADJECTIVAL BESTIARY: QUIZ & PRIMER

1) P, snake — *anguis* is a Latin word for snake.

2) B, bee — *apis* is Latin for bee.

3) H, eagle — *aquila*, Latin for eagle, also lends its name to a small star group northeast of Sagittarius.

4) G, donkey — this is relatively easy since the Latin *asinus* eventually became *ass*, another word for donkey.

5) D, cow — *bovis* is Latin for cow. *Bovine* is also used when referring to oxen.

6) K, goat — one of the two goat words — Capricorn, the zodiac sign, derives from the Latin *caper* for goat and *cornu*, for horn.

7) F, deer — from the Latin *cervus*.

8) P, snake — *colubra* is another Latin word for snake.

9) E, crow — *corvus*, Latin for raven or crow, is also the name of a rectangular constellation just south of Virgo.

10) L, horse — from the Latin *equus*.

11) K, goat — a great word for when you're hurling invectives, since it refers especially to the smell attached to the goat. *Hircus* is Latin for he-goat.

12) M, lion — *leo* is Latin for lion.

13) Q, wolf — the Latin *lupus* also became the Spanish word for wolf, *lobo*.

14) O, sheep — *ovis* is Latin for sheep.

15) I, fish — another giveaway from the zodiac, *pisces* is the plural of *piscis*, Latin for fish.

16) N, pig — *porcus* is Latin for pig.

17) C, bull — *taurus*, Latin for bull, also became the Spanish *toro*.

18) A, bear — *ursus*, Latin for bear.

19) J, fox — from the Latin *vulpes*, for fox.

SCORING

14 or more — You're probably a veterinarian, biologist, Latin scholar, or really dull person who reads too much.

9-13 — You're someone who really likes language, who reads a lot about animals, or who can guess really well.

5-8 — About average.

0-4 — Give yourself credit for *canine* and *feline* and see if that doesn't move you up a notch.

TAKING YOUR

CHANCES

An Examination of Risk Assessment and the Psychology of Worry

Your chances of getting hit by lightning: 1 in 2 million. Being killed in a car crash: 1 in 4,000. But is anyone afraid of cars? BY JON VARA

Forty years ago, on the afternoon of November 30, 1954, a 32-year-old woman named Ann Elizabeth Hodges was napping on the living-room couch in her home in Sylacauga, Alabama. Suddenly there was a thunderous boom, and Mrs. Hodges felt a numbing pain in her right hip. The room filled with splinters of wood and plaster dust. Mrs. Hodges and her mother, who had been sewing in the next room, rushed outside, thinking the gas heater had exploded. A few minutes later they cautiously ventured back inside and discovered a blackened rock about the size of a bowling ball lying on the floor.

The stone, of course, was a meteorite. Mrs. Hodges, who died in 1972 (of other causes) is the only confirmed human actually to be struck by a falling extraterrestrial body. (A dog, however, was killed by a three-pound meteorite that fell on Egypt in 1911.)

Mrs. Hodges beat some impressive odds. According to one risk-assessment authority, your annual risk of being cut down by a celestial brickbat is on the order of one chance in 17 billion. (Near misses, how-

ever, are more common than you might think. In an average year, half a dozen small meteorites strike the Earth close enough to human observers to be recovered.)

Scientists have come to realize that our own planet, like our satellite the Moon, is marked by giant impact craters, probably more than once thought. Geologists have already identified about 140 so-called hypervelocity impact craters. By calculating the dates of these craters, scientists estimate that a massive (two-kilometer-wide) meteor hits the Earth once every half million years, causing unimaginable destruction. Of course, they don't follow any sort of schedule — the next big hit could happen this year or a million years from now.

Paradoxically, your risk of being struck by a small meteorite — an event known to have happened at least once in this century — is utterly dwarfed by the risk of a globally catastrophic asteroid strike — an event that has not occurred in all of recorded history. If the scientists are right, there's one chance in 500,000 that we'll see a major impact during any given year. Over the course of a 70-year human lifetime, that adds up to

One hour of riding a motorcycle is as

runs a risk equal to 35 mrem of radiation exposure.

one chance in 7,000. It's about the same as your chance of dying of bronchitis and three times as great as your chance of dying in a commercial airline crash.

But cheer up. Bronchitis, asteroid impacts, and air crashes combined increase your risk of death by — at most — one in several thousand. Your chances of dying of something else are nothing short of excellent.

For instance, which worries you more: the prospect of dying in a car accident or developing a fatal cancer from a radiation leak at the nuclear power plant? The possibility of dying in a fall at home or being eaten by a shark while swimming at the beach? Dying of heart disease or being killed by a tornado?

If we think for a moment, most of us can correctly identify the first item in each pair as the statistically greater risk. But most of us would also agree that the second-named items, while less dangerous (in fact, tens of thousands of times less dangerous), are somehow more threatening and fearsome.

This kind of thinking frustrates professional risk analysts no end. As they see it, our difficulty in making rational judgments about risk often leads us to make foolish choices that may actually increase our exposure to risk. We misjudge risk for several reasons, including:

Ignorance: We're not good at estimating the relative frequencies of causes of death, especially uncommon ones. In one survey of well-educated adults, tornadoes were seen as more frequent killers than asthma (asthma actually causes 20 times as many deaths); accidental deaths were thought to be as frequent as deaths from disease (disease actually causes 15 times as many deaths); and death from botulism was thought to be more common than death by lightning (lightning is actually 52 times as dangerous).

Obstinacy: If we learn to fear something, we fear it. If not, we don't. If you grow up believing that automobile travel is safe, you'll go on thinking that, even after you find out that it causes 45,000 deaths a year in the United States alone. When we are confronted with evidence that challenges our beliefs, we find a way to dismiss it as misleading or unreliable.

> *The average coffee habit, over the lifetime of a healthy 30-year-old, implies a six-day reduction in life expectancy.*

Disaster Potential: To a statistician, risk is simply a matter of numbers. A risk that causes 7,300 deaths in a single disastrous event once every 20 years is no different from one that kills one person every day for 20 years. The average person, on the other hand, tends to be much more fearful of mass disaster than of scattered individual deaths. We are apt to see the mere possibility of disaster, however remote, as more threatening than definite but more diffuse risks, however severe. The certainty that air pollution kills 20,000 people a year in the eastern United States worries us less than the theoretical possibility of a Bhopal-style disaster at a single pesticide factory.

risky as one hour of being 75 years old.

Avoidability: We're remarkably complacent about risks we expose ourselves to voluntarily, but we have a low tolerance for risks imposed on us. One study showed that we are willing to accept voluntary risks (downhill skiing, for example) that are roughly a thousand times greater than risks from involuntary hazards (such as the presence of preservatives in our food), given equal benefits.

In the face of such widespread irrationality, you have to admire risk analysts for even trying to get through to us. They are always on the lookout for new and imaginative ways of presenting the numbers. For a risk analyst, disaster is a way of life, but hope springs eternal.

Alcohol use is responsible for about 50 percent of all motor-vehicle deaths, 20 percent of all other accidents, suicides, and homicides, and ten percent of cancers of the esophagus and oral cavity. On the average each of these deaths shortens life by about 20 years for the individual.

RISK FACTS

Life Expectancy Lost (in Minutes) as a Consequence of Individual Action

Action	Minutes
Smoking a cigarette	10
Eating calorie-rich dessert	50
Drinking nondiet soft drink	15
Drinking diet soft drink	0.15
Crossing a street	0.4
Extra driving	0.4 per mile
Not fastening seat belt	0.1 per mile
1 mrem of radiation	1.5
Coast-to-coast drive	1,000
Coast-to-coast flight	100
Skipping annual Pap test	6,000
Move to unfavorable state	800,000
Buying a small car	7,000

Average Annual Risk of Death to an Individual from Various Natural and Human-Caused Accidents

Motor vehicle	1 in 4,000
Falls	1 in 10,000
Fires and hot substances	1 in 25,000
Drowning	1 in 30,000
Firearms	1 in 100,000
Air travel	1 in 100,000
Falling objects	1 in 160,000
Electrocution	1 in 160,000
Lightning	1 in 2,000,000
Tornadoes	1 in 2,500,000
Hurricanes	1 in 2,500,000
All accidents combined	1 in 1,600

Seven percent of all males versus four

Risks Estimated to Increase the Probability of Death in Any Year by One Chance in a Million

(The activities described in this list are all equally risky but for differing reasons: i.e., smoking 1.4 cigarettes increases your risk of cancer and heart disease by one in a million in any year; traveling ten miles by bicycle or 300 miles by car or 1,000 miles by plane are equally risky in terms of possible fatal accidents.)

Activity	Risk
Smoking 1.4 cigarettes	Cancer, heart disease
Drinking .5 liter of wine	Cirrhosis of the liver
Spending 1 hour in a coal mine	Black lung disease
Spending 3 hours in a coal mine	Accident
Living 2 days in New York or Boston	Air pollution
Traveling 6 minutes by canoe	Accident
Traveling 10 miles by bicycle	Accident
Traveling 300 miles by car	Accident
Flying 1,000 miles by jet	Accident
Flying 6,000 miles by jet	Cancer caused by cosmic radiation
Living 2 months in Denver	Cancer caused by cosmic radiation
Living 2 months in average stone or brick building	Cancer caused by natural radioactivity
One chest X-ray taken in good hospital	Cancer caused by radiation
Living two months with cigarette smoker	Cancer, heart disease
Eating 40 tablespoons of peanut butter	Liver cancer caused by aflatoxin B
Drinking Miami water for 1 year	Cancer caused by chloroform
Drinking 30 12-ounce cans diet soda	Cancer caused by saccharin

Life Expectancy Lost (in Days) Due to Various Causes

Cause	Days	Cause	Days	Cause	Days
Being unmarried — male	3,500	Dangerous job — accidents	300	Falls	39
Cigarette smoking — male	2,250	Pipe smoking	220	Accidents to pedestrians	37
Heart disease	2,100	Motor-vehicle accidents	207	Safest job — accidents	30
Being unmarried — female	1,600	Alcohol use	130	Fire — burns	27
Being 30 percent overweight	1,300	Accidents in home	95	Illicit drug use (U.S. average)	18
Being a coal miner	1,100	Suicide	95	Firearms accidents	11
Cancer	980	Diabetes	95	Natural radiation	8
Being 20 percent overweight	900	Being murdered (homicide)	90	Medical X-rays	6
Eighth-grade education	850	Legal drug misuse	90	Coffee	6
Cigarette smoking — female	800	Average job — accidents	74	Oral contraceptives	5
Living in unfavorable state	500	Drowning	41	Pedal-cycle accidents	5
Cigar smoking	330	Job with radiation exposure	40	Diet drinks	2

N.B.: The above tables are taken from three different scientific studies published over the last two decades by the Nuclear Regulatory Commission, *Technology Review*, and the University of Pittsburgh.

Getting to Know the Toad That Lives in Your Garden

wo years ago, while cutting the grass in my backyard with a power mower, I happened to run over a toad. I do not regard myself as a sentimental person, but I was troubled as I bent down to examine it. It wasn't just that I had unwittingly killed an ally against the hordes of mosquitoes, gnats, and flies that plague our summers. It was mostly the rush of blood that affected me, making it dramatically clear that what at first glance looked to be a clod of earth was actually a living being, quite unlike the cold, formaldehyde-filled frogs we had dissected in high school biology class.

TOAD *Evolution* and the Difference Between Toads and Frogs

If the scientists are right, we owe the toad a great debt: His forebears, as the first vertebrates to leave the water some 300 million or more years ago, led us all up onto dry land. Since the Devonian period, however, the toad has not always been treated with the honor due a pioneer. With many enemies and minimal defenses, he has survived by adapting to fill almost any available biological niche. This is no doubt why there are still over 2,500 surviving variations on the basic toad-frog animal. Some of them live entirely in or near water, some live in trees; some live on land, while others spend most of their time underground. They populate forests, mountains, and even deserts from the tropics right up to the permafrost line at the Arctic Circle.

The formal taxonomy of the class Amphibia is extremely complex and subject to continuing debate and disagreement. The order of tailless amphibians, Anura, includes frogs and toads. The toad, *Bufo* (of the family Bufonidae), except for its tadpole stage and breeding period, is primarily terrestrial. Its skin is drier and rougher than that of a frog, and its hind legs are shorter and weaker, so that it can only hop rather than leap. No country kid would hesitate to call a toad a toad.

Compared with his nearest rival, the frog, the toad reacts more promptly and learns more readily. Toads can figure out a maze far more quickly than frogs can. When set on a high table, toads will peer cautiously over the edge, appearing to estimate the drop, and then refuse to jump. Frogs will fling themselves off anything.

Toads once led us living
creatures onto dry land. Witches
and princes have been known to
turn into them.
If a baseball pitcher spots one
in the outfield, he'll surely win that day.
Now read on for more . . .
by Robert M. DeGraaff

– Illustrated by Robert Crawford

TOAD *Music*

When the toad's amphibian ancestors first crawled out of the water, they must have entered a very quiet world. There probably was little more than the sound of the wind in the reeds and ferns until the voice of the toad — Earth's primeval music — was heard in the land. The calls of some species of toads are as melodious as those of any bird. Secondly, unlike birds, toads make their music with genuine vocal cords; they are in a class with the best.

A linked chain of bubbling notes,
When birds have ceased their calling,
That lulls the ear with soothing sound
Like voice of water falling.
It is the knell of winter dead;
Good-by, his icy fetter.
Blessings on thy warty head:
No bird could do it better.

— John Burroughs, "The Song of the Toad"

> **So strong is the mating drive that some males have been discovered grasping lumps of mud along the shorelines.**

Having migrated to the mating pools in early spring, the males put all this vocal equipment to work in the breeding chorus, whose sound may carry as much as a half mile or more, guiding the egg-heavy females to the right pools, the right species (each species has a distinctive call), and possibly even to the right males. Some evidence suggests not only that the deeper voices of the larger males are more attractive to females, but also that larger males may seek out and defend sites on land or in water whose cooler temperatures will help them get the most out of their bass range.

Sometimes the female gets drowned in the melee, and a male may embrace the dead body for several days. So strong is the mating drive that some males have even been discovered grasping attractive lumps of mud along the shorelines.

TOAD *The Hunter*

Despite its slow and clumsy gait, the speed and accuracy of the toad's tongue make it a formidable hunter. Many observers of feeding toads report seeing nothing except the sudden and mysterious disappearance of insects in the toad's immediate vicinity. They bear witness to the amazing speed of the tongue-flip, which has been shown to take, from opening mouth to impact on prey, about 16 one-thousandths of a second.

While vision is undoubtedly the key sense in a feeding toad, it has been found that toads will eat in extremely dim light, even in absolute darkness. Blind toads are alerted by the sound of prey movements, but apparently do not stalk prey and eat only those insects that actually bump into them.

A particular toad's home range has been shown to be as much as a square mile, and a displaced toad may return to that range from more than a mile away.

TOAD *The Hunted*

The smaller they are, the more vulnerable, but toads of all sizes are preyed upon by reptiles, birds, and mammals. Why, since most toads are toxic, do they have so many enemies? The answer seems to be that for every species of toad that developed toxic potency, nature evolved several species of enemies who are either immune to the poison or have found a way of avoiding it. The glands that secrete the poison are localized in the skin behind the ear drums. The warts on a toad's back also produce poison, but most toads seem to excrete the venom only in response to physical pressure on the skin.

Thus, sea gulls have learned to flip the toad over and eat everything but the dorsal skin. Raccoons have adopted a similar strategy with the Colorado River toad, whose poison has been known to kill large dogs who have only mouthed it for a moment. The skunk tumbles the toad over and rubs its back vigorously in the grass until the poison is both excreted and rubbed away, leaving a palatable dinner.

The most voracious toad eaters are those varieties of snakes that are impervious to the poison; and certain it is that they strike terror into toad hearts. Observers have reported toads apparently impersonating possums, rolling over and playing dead when threatened by snakes — only it turned out they weren't playing, but had suffered some sort of temporary heart failure and had literally passed out.

The Pharmaceutical

"Experience has proven the toad to be endowed with valuable qualities. If you run a stick through three toads, and, after having dried them in the sun, apply them to any pestilent tumor, they draw out all the poison, and the malady will disappear."
– Martin Luther, *Table-Talk*

The most obvious chemical use of *Bufo* — to poison somebody — was recognized early in the Greco-Roman-Arabian tradition. The ultimate effect of ingesting toad poison is death — a fact that is well known by the various Indian tribes of South America who have traditionally tipped their blow darts with toad venom extracts.

The Chinese seem to have been aware of the medical possibilities of toad venom, ch'an su, for hundreds of years and to have used its digitalis-like prop-

erties in treating heart ailments, among other things. Pellets of dried toad venom may still be bought today from Chinese druggists, who prescribe it for external treatment of canker sores, sinusitis, and many local inflammatory conditions, in the relief of toothache, and in the arrest of hemorrhages from the gums.

In the early medicine of many cultures the toad was commonly used to treat edema and tumors. British medicine of the 16th and 17th centuries also gave much credit to powdered toad or toad ashes, as in William Salmon's London Dispensatory of 1702, which stated that "the poudre of a dry'd toad taken 5ss [scruples] at a time or more, cures almost incurable dropsies [edema], carrying away the water by urine."

The Evil Medieval

Most classical Western writers on the animal worlds, such as Aristotle and Aelian, do little more than list the toad as a poisonous land-dwelling counterpart to the frog. Only the elder Pliny (*Natural History*, Book 32) goes into some detail, defining the toad as a frog who lives only in brambles, a "bramble-toad," and as large, horned, and full of poison. He also includes a few of the marvelous stories about toads that were to proliferate throughout the Middle Ages: that the presence of a toad will cause a meeting of people to fall silent; or if worn as an amulet, a toad will act as an aphrodisiac.

The real barometric virtues of toads, however, were first recorded by Samuel Hartlib in the 17th century, when he wrote to Robert Boyle "concerning a weather prophet whose remarkably successful predictions were made by observing the changing colors of the skin of a toad which he kept in captivity."

During the Middle Ages and the Renaissance, and in folklore persisting into our own day, witches and toads have been closely connected. For one thing, as Topsell points out, "the women-witches of ancient time which killed by poysoning, did much use Toads in their confections."

So did some of the men-witches, and they occasionally came to a bad end. Hugues Geraud, bishop of Cahors, admitted in 1317 to having made several attempts on the life of Pope John XXII "by poison and by sorcery with wax images, ashes of spiders and toads, the gall of a pig, and the like substances."

The first notable English trial for witchcraft occurred in 1566 at Chelmsford, Essex, and much of it concerned the antics of Elizabeth Francis's white spotted cat — Sathan by name — who occasionally took the form of a toad. In 1599 Oliffe Bartham was executed for practicing devilish and wicked witchcraft upon one Joan Jordan, having sent three toads "to trouble her in her bed." John Palmer confessed at St. Albans in 1649 that he had gone so far as to turn himself into a toad in order to torment one of his victims.

TOAD
The Enduring

Bufophiles may rejoice: Not only have centuries of abuse failed to wipe out the toad, but there are even signs in modern times of a trend to clear his good name. The inimitable Henri de Toulouse-Lautrec used a toad to serve as a model for the illustration "Le Crapaud" that he contributed to his friend Jules Renard's *Histoire Naturelle*; we know that he fed it and gave it free run of his Paris studio and that he felt some regret when it disappeared.

Improved human-toad relations are reflected not only in the literature of the past hundred years (including sympathetic toad poems by Kipling, Robert Browning, Emily Dickinson, and others), but also in the realm of folk wisdom: "Kill a toad and your cows will give bloody milk." Other dire results of toad murder

might be that you will stub your toe or that your house will catch fire. Once regarded as poisoners of the drinking water, toads are now coveted as well residents who guarantee the water's purity. The toad even has a romantic role: "A toad crossing the road in front of you indicates that you will see your sweetheart that day." And if a pitcher finds a toad in the outfield before a game, he is sure to win.

TOADS
Real
in Real Gardens

One practical reason for the turn in public opinion is the fact that toads eat bugs. In his pamphlet "Usefulness of the American Toad," A. H. Kirkland reports observing toads' feeding habits closely for two years; one summer he actually sliced open 149 toad stomachs and analyzed their contents. Of the toads' total food, 62 percent was made up of harmful insects, though "should ants be included as injurious, as many housekeepers would think proper, this figure would be increased to 81 percent."

Kirkland found that toads would fill their stomachs to capacity up to four times in a single night, accounting for as many as 55 army worms, 37 tent caterpillars, 65 gypsy moth caterpillars, or 77 thousand-legged worms. Kirkland conjectures that in a three-month summer period, a single mature toad might wipe out almost 10,000 noxious insects. It seems clear that these self-activating natural vacuum cleaners can in fact replace often-dangerous chemical pesticides.

Childhood is a toad in the garden,
  a happy toad.

– William Carlos Williams, "Romance Moderne"

□□

Excerpts taken from *The Book of the Toad* by Robert M. DeGraaff (professor of Victorian literature at St. Lawrence University in Canton, N.Y.). Published by Park Street Press, Rochester, VT 05767; available in paperback ($22.50, including shipping; call 800-488-2665).

CLASSIFIED ADVERTISING

ASTROLOGY/OCCULT

BIORHYTHMS. Your physical, emotional, intellectual cycles charted in color. Interpretation guide. Six months $10. Twelve months $15. Send name, birth date. CYCLES, Dept. FAB, 2251 Berkley Ave., Schenectady NY 12309

LEARN WITCHCRAFT for protection, success, and serenity. Gavin and Yvonne Frost, world's foremost witches, now accepting students. Box 1502-0, Newbern NC 28563

WORLD'S LARGEST OCCULT, mystic arts, new age, witchcraft, voodoo. Largest supply of good luck talismans and amulets for every purpose. Thousands of rare, unusual curios and gifts. Set of 3 fascinating 1994 catalogs, $2. By airmail, $3. Worldwide Curio House, Box 17095-A, Minneapolis MN 55417

FREE BOOKLETS: Life, Death, soul, resurrection, pollution crisis, hell, judgment day, restitution. Bible Standard (OF), PO Box 67, Chester Springs PA 19425

WITCHCRAFT POWERS bring success. World's foremost occult school offers six home-study courses and personal training. Free information. Box 1366, Nashua NH 03061; 603-880-7237

COMPUTERIZED TAROT Readings eliminate guesswork. The wisdom of ages, harnessed by technology. Master the present. Command the future. Send questions, age, description, $10 to: TAROT 2000, PO Box 202059, Kettering OH 45429-9998

ONE MAGIC SPELL! No charge! Tell me what you need! B. Zenor, 18533 Roscoe, Northridge CA 91324-4632

VOODOO, oldest organization. Catalog $15. Ritual work by request. T.O.T.S., Suite 310, North San Fernando Blvd., Burbank CA 91504

FREE LUCKY NUMBERS. Send birth date, self-addressed stamped envelope. Mystic, Box 2009-R, Jamestown NC 27282

MAGICAL & SPIRITUAL NEEDS

Catalog. Herbs, oils, incense, books, etc. $2. Joan Teresa Power Products, Box 442, Mars Hill NC 28754

AMAZING OCCULT Discoveries develop supernatural powers safely, easily! Free experiments. Publisher, Box 3483-FAM, New York NY 10008

ASTROLOGY. Personalized, comprehensive natal chart $10. Progressed chart for current year $10. Both $15. Send name, birth date, birth time, birthplace. CYCLES, Dept. FAA, 2251 Berkley Ave., Schenectady NY 12309

FREE PERSONAL Horoscope from Anna Riva. Send name, birth date, time, place, and $1 for p/h to: Stardust Dist., 2222 Foothill Blvd., Suite E305-0, La Canada CA 91011

FREE COMPUTER Horoscope. Send birth date, time, city, and country to: Horoscope, Box 4467, Columbia SC 29240

AUTOMOTIVE

VAPOR CARBURETOR Triples MPG! Save big $ on gasoline. Free information. H&A, R20FA, Bowling Green MO 63334

AUTOMOBILE LITERATURE. Wanted: 1900-1975. I buy automobile sales brochures, manuals, etc. Walter Miller, 6710 Brooklawn, Syracuse NY 13211; 315-432-8282

BEER & WINE MAKING

FREE HOME BEER-MAKING Catalog. Middlesex Brewing, 25-13 Old Kings Highway North, Darien CT 06820

WINEMAKERS-BEERMAKERS. Free illustrated catalog. Fast service. Large selection. Kraus, Box 7850-YB, Independence MO 64054; 816-254-0242

POWERFUL WINE without fruit. Amazing easy recipe. $5. International Concepts, 60 Martin Creek Ct., Stockbridge GA 30281

BOAT KITS & PLANS

BOAT KITS & PLANS. Boatbuilding supplies. 250 designs. Catalog only $3. Clarkcraft, 16-29 Aqualane, Tonawanda NY 14150

BOOKS/MAGAZINES/CATALOGS

LEARN TAXIDERMY. Easy book, kit, or video method. Send for free information. VanDyke's, Dept. 88, Box 278, Woonsocket SD 57385

"HOW-TO" Books and Videos on self-reliance, practical survival, and dozens of other subjects! 56-page catalog describes over 500 titles. Send $1 to: Paladin Press, PO Box 1307-4AZ, Boulder CO 80306

PUBLISH YOUR BOOK! Join our successful authors. All subjects invited. Publicity, advertising, beautiful books. Send for fact-filled booklet and free manuscript report. Carlton Press, Dept. OA, 11 West 32 St., New York NY 10001

GOLFERS: Short game killin' you? New secret systems cut strokes. Guaranteed. Free details. LARGS Publishing, Box 3128, Urbana IL 61801-8128

HOW-TO REPORTS! Clear, concise reports show how others have saved time, money. Free catalog. How to attract, avoid, buy, build, improve, learn, profit, start, succeed, use. Free Spirit Company, PO Box 685-FA4, Winsted CT 06098-0685

DIRECTORY, 64 PAGES listing over 1,001 free items. For directory and valuable gift, send $5 P/H to: Simmons Publishing Co., PO Box 12691, New Bern NC 28562

FREE! NOVELTY CATALOG, world's most unusual. 2000 things you never knew existed. Johnson-Smith, Box 25500, BS008, Bradenton FL 34206

BUILD, RESTORE, REPAIR, refinish! Carvings, moldings, brass, hardwood, veneers, upholstery, caning, lamps. $1 for unique wholesale catalog. VanDyke's, Dept. 89, Box 278, Woonsocket SD 57385

BUSINESS OPPORTUNITY

$80,000 FROM ONE ACRE! Grow ginseng. Sell $60/pound. Free information: 5712-FA Cooper Rd., Indianapolis IN 46208

LET THE GOVERNMENT finance your small business. Grants/loans to $500,000 yearly. Free recorded message: 707-448-0270. (KEI)

ALUMINUM SCRAP. Recycle yourself. Make $25/pound! Free information: Ameriscrap-FA94, Alexandria Bay NY 13607-0127

ALL TYPES GREETING CARDS, Christmas card catalog - imprint. Fund-raising, gift items. Charm Cards, Dept. A, Box 187, Austell GA 30001-0187; 404-941-4312

HOMEWORKERS WANTED. Earn money-making musical teddy bears. All materials supplied with refundable deposit. No selling. For free brochure send SASE to: Jo-El Enterprises Inc., PO Box 590296, Orlando FL 32859-0296 or call 407-857-9518

LEARN VCR REPAIR. Great profits. Home study. P.C.D.I., Atlanta, Georgia. Free literature. 800-362-7070, Dept. VK554.

$1000'S MONTHLY POSSIBLE processing mail! Free supplies/postage. SASE. STL, Box 120, W Nyack NY 10994

MAKE BUNK BEDS at home in spare time. $239 bunk takes 2 hours, costs $48 to make. Earn $200 per day easily. Free details. Bunks, Dept. XE, PO Box 24705, Minneapolis MN 55424

BUSINESS IDEA PUBLICATIONS. Catalog. Send a large SASE to: PO Box 416, Denver CO 80201

STUFF ENVELOPES for average $140/100. Send SASE to: Taylor's, Green Acres Rd. #18, Jacksonville AR 72076

REAL ESTATE APPRAISER Careers. Home study. P.C.D.I., Atlanta Georgia. Free career literature. 800-362-7070, Dept. RK554.

RECORD VIDEOTAPES at home. $5,000 monthly possible. No pornography. Free details. Write: CMS Video Company, Dept. 51, 210 Lorna Sq. #163, Birmingham AL 35216

JOIN HOME-WORKER'S Association. Get free lists! Legitimate companies offering home employment! Write: Association-FA94, Alexandria Bay NY 13607-0250

HOMEWORKERS WANTED.

Earn money assembling "Bunny Rabbits." All materials supplied with refundable deposit. For free brochure send SASE to: Kerray Products Inc., PO Box 590325, Orlando FL 32859-0325 or phone 904-855-8355

$600/WEEK AT HOME. Legitimate. We need you. Free report: Skyline, Box 336A, Geneseo NY 14454

WE BUY newspaper clippings. $781.23 weekly. Send stamped envelope. Edwards, Box 467159FA, Atlanta GA 30346

BECOME A HOME INSPECTOR. Approved home study. Free literature. P.C.D.I., Atlanta Georgia. 800-362-7070, Dept. PK554.

EARN WEEKLY PAYCHECKS! Mail advertisements from home! Midwest Direct (#FA-94), 3400 111th, Chicago IL 60655

UNBELIEVABLE RECRUITING system and program. Sweeping the country. Fantastic Upline Help. Send: Name, address, phone #, and best time to call. JP Enterprises, 35 Bennington Rd., Hancock NH 03449

HOME ASSEMBLY WORK available! Guaranteed easy money! Free details! SASE. Homework-FA, Box 520, Danville NH 03819

LEARN GUNSMITHING. Rifles, shotguns, pistols. Professional level home study. Free career literature. 800-362-7070, Dept. GK554.

MAKE BIG PROFITS! Sell over 3,000 fast-selling items at flea markets, stores, parties, etc. $5 brings giant catalog, refundable with first order. Gift World, 598 Valley Rd., Dept. FA1, Walpole NH 03608

STUFF ENVELOPES for $140/100. Send stamp to: Advanced Mailing, 6732 State #144F, Fort Wayne IN 46815

BE A PLUMBER. Make huge profits. Free literature. American Plumbing Association, 33227 Bainbridge, Cleveland OH 44139

CARNIVOROUS PLANTS

CARNIVOROUS (Insect-Eating) plants, seeds, supplies, and books. Peter Paul's Nurseries, Canandaigua NY 14424

CRAFTS

INDIAN CRAFTS. Free brochure showing materials used. Recommended to Indian guides, scout troops, etc. Cleveland Leather, 2629 Lorain Ave., Cleveland OH 44113

BETTER LACE TRIMS, 144 yards $13.50. Twelve delightful patterns. Oppenheim's, Department 578, North Manchester IN 46962-0052

FUN AND EASY to make, high-quality composite fishing lures for pennies each. For detailed and illustrated instruction booklet send $5 to: Taclbk, 411 South Boundary Ave., Proctor MN 55810

EDUCATION/INSTRUCTION

COLLEGE DEGREES without classrooms. Complete information on hundreds of accredited schools. Free recorded message: 707-447-3053. (6KE1)

GREAT NEWS! Non-federal sources of scholarships: for college or trade school. For application: LAMFA, Box 149, Millersburg OH 44654-0149

BECOME A VETERINARY Assistant/Animal-care specialist. Home study. Free career literature. 800-362-7070, Dept. CK554.

IF YOU NEED INFORMATION about financial assistance and scholarships write to: Manlio Lopez, Box 5212, Roanoke VA 24012

COLLEGE DEGREE BY MAIL, Associate to Ph.D. Catalog $1. Christian Bible College, Station Sq., Suite 227, Rocky Mount NC 27804. 919-442-1211. (Accredited)

HIGH SCHOOL AT HOME. No classes. Low monthly payments. Information free. Our 97th year. Call 1-800-228-5600 or write American School, Dept #348, 850 E. 58th St., Chicago IL 60637

UNIVERSITY DEGREES without classes! Accredited Bachelor's, Master's, Doctorates. Free revealing facts! Thorson-FR4, Box 470886, Tulsa OK 74147

BECOME A PARALEGAL. Work with attorneys. Lawyer-instructed home study. Free catalog. 800-362-7070, Dept. LK554.

GRIP-TDC 2000 BALL PEN. Revolutionary design with unique contoured finger grip for easy and comfortable writing only $1.89, 2 for $3.50, or best buy, 3 for $4.50. Add $1 s/h. Mail to: Leonard, PO Box 43138, Detroit MI 48243

FARM AND GARDEN

KRICKETT KRAP. Organic fertilizer; roses/tomatoes love it. Free catalog. 824 Sandbar FA., Augusta GA 30901

RARE SEEDS CATALOG/peter, female, or squash pepper seed sample. Send $1. E.T. Seeds, Rte. 3 Box 1894, Retreat TX 75110

FREE CATALOG, Lowest Prices. Pots, flats, lights. Wholesale-retail. Two stamps postage. Plant Collectibles, 103FAM Kenview, Buffalo NY 14217

LEARN LANDSCAPING at home. Free brochure. Call 800-326-9221 or write: Lifetime Career Schools, Dept. OBO114, 101 Harrison St., Archibald PA 18403

EVERGREEN TREE SEEDLINGS. Direct from grower. Free catalog. Carino Nurseries, Box 538, Dept. AL, Indiana PA 15701

FRUIT, NUT TREES, FIGS, berry, grape plants. Free catalog. Wells Nursery, Box 606, Lindale TX 75771

GREENHOUSE PLASTIC. Superstrong, ripstop woven polyethylene. Resists windstorms, yellowing. Sample: Bob's Greenhouses, Box 42FA, Neche ND 58265; 204-327-5540

FLAGS

FLAGPOLE, Commercial Grade Aluminum, 20' – 3 pc. shipment via UPS with 3' x 5' U.S. embroidered nylon flag. $212 plus tax. Visa/MC. Bartol Company, Inc., PO Box 670F, Kenton OH 43326; 1-800-537-4143

FOOD AND RECIPES

FINGER FOODS, FRUIT DIP, Tex-Mex Meatballs. SASE and $3. Kendrick, 11354 Jeff Ave., Lakeview Terr. CA 91342-6822

TEN SAUSAGE RECIPES. Italian, kielbasa, breakfast, bratwurst, etc. Send $2 and SASE to: Roland J. Scarinci, 793 Cherry Hill Ln., Pottstown PA 19464

WORLD'S FINEST COFFEE. Sample $1. Bumper stickers: HIV negative $2. Buttons $2. Manno, 4026 Carpenter Ave., Bronx NY 10466

DELICIOUS EAST-INDIAN Recipes. Send $3 plus SASE. SEVA, 4080 Paradise #15-251, Las Vegas NV 89109

FOR THE HOME

ROACHES KILLED with home remedy. Cheap to make, will eliminate roaches. Complete recipe $5, plus SASE. Roaches, 1013 Pickens Dr., Hueytown AL 35023

"CHOSEN VALLEY Treasures," nostalgic farm scenes are the unique gift. Free information. Call 1-800-848-0130, ext. 120.

CUCKOO CLOCKS: hand-carved with birds, squirrels, deer. Catalog $1. Terre Celeste, Box 4125F, Kenmore NY 14217

GINSENG AND HERBS

RELAX! FLORSED VALERIAN, a registered, over-the-counter plant medicine, relieves anxiety and nervous stress. It works as a sedative, muscle relaxant, and sleep aid without addiction or withdrawal symptoms! Flora Laboratories Inc., 151 Little Mountain Rd., Trout Lake WA 98650; 509-395-2765

GINSENG! GOLDENSEAL! Profitable, good demand. Quality planting stock. Comfrey. Information $1. William Collins, Viola IA 52350

COLD AND FLU RELIEF from Florammune Echinacea, a full-strength medicine for defense against cold and flu viruses, not just symptoms! This safe, over-the-counter alternative to petrochemical drugs uses only the finest Echinacea plants without side effects! Flora Laboratories Inc., 151 Little Mountain Rd., Trout Lake WA 98650; 509-395-2765

GOVERNMENT SURPLUS

GOVERNMENT SEIZED Vehicles! Buy dirt cheap! Your area! Free details. Surplus, Box 3321, Ft. Smith AR 72913

GREETING CARDS

GREETING CARDS. 1994 All-Occasion scripture, 25 per box $5.95. Cards, PO Box 13506(F), Roanoke VA 24033

HEALTH/BEAUTY

AMAZING SECRETS for restoring health, beauty, and longevity! Free details. Publisher, Box 3483-FA, New York NY 10008

STOP ARTHRITIS pain and inflammation. Dr.-recommended natural molar VII dissolves spurs, sharp crystals, deposits, with rehabilitation and more. Month's supply $25; 3 months $45. ARP, 855 Mohawk, Ukiah CA 95482. Over 50 successful years.

FREE HERBS & More Remedies brochure. Stamped envelope. Pharmacist Champion, Box 26363-FA, Memphis TN 38126

FREE CATALOG! Name-brand vitamins: Kal, Schiff, Twinlab, and more! 20% to 60% off! 1-800-858-2143

ASTHMA/HAYFEVER Sufferers. Free information. Nephron Pharmaceutical Corporation, Dept. NPCFA, PO Box 616344, Orlando FL 32861-6344

NEW HEMORRHOID MEDICAL device uses low temperatures, shrinking hemorrhoids, ending pain. American Products, Dept. FA, 2j Fairways Cir., St. Charles MO 63303

HELP WANTED

EXCELLENT INCOME! Assemble easy craft products at home. Easy work! Legitimate! Program guaranteed. 800-377-6000, x-590.

READ BOOKS FOR PAY. $95 each. Free reports! Send LSASE: B.E.S., Box 8187-MF, Pittsburgh CA 94565-8187

WATKINS. Famous vanilla, liniments, health aids, spices. Independent representatives needed, top profits! Free catalog, details. Watkins, Box 440392-F, Kennesaw GA 30144. 404-974-4400

INVENTIONS/PATENTS

INVENTIONS, IDEAS, New Products! Presentation to industry, national exposition. 1-800-288-IDEA

LEARN HOW TO offer your invention for sale or license. Free booklet outlines procedures, royalty rates, requirements. Kessler Sales Corporation, C-429-4, Fremont OH 43420

LOANS BY MAIL/FINANCIAL

FREE $25,000 CASH grants! Never repay. Virtually guaranteed approval. Application: $1. Universal, 4011-FA4 Valleyview, Crystal Lake IL 60012-2105

FINANCIAL AID for college resources. 904-892-2811, leave message. HBC Services, PO Box 1138, Defuniak FL 32433

MUSIC/RECORDS/TAPES

ACCORDIONS, CONCERTINAS, button boxes. New, used, buy, sell, trade, repair. Hohners, Martin guitars, lap harps, hammered dulcimers. Catalog $5. Castiglione, Box 40, Warren MI 48090; 313-755-6050

FIDDLE INSTRUCTION VIDEO. By studio pro. No music. Makes learning easy. Guaranteed! Fiddler's catalog free! $33.45 postpaid. Ridgerunner FA-94, 84 York Creek, Driftwood TX 78619

FIDDLING, FOLK music instruction, recordings, free catalog: Captain Fiddle, 4 Elm Ct., Newmarket NH 03857; 603-659-2658

GUITAR STRINGS – Discount. Martin, Fender, more. Harmonicas, guitars, songbooks, accessories. Free catalog. Maxwell Music Company, Box 1173, Waco TX 76703

OF INTEREST TO ALL

STUDENTS! Get free scholarships and grants galore. Write Scholarships Now, Box 4735-A, Wichita KS 67204

JEWELRY. 14KT GOLD bracelets, earrings, necklaces and rings. Big savings. For brochure, call toll free 1-800-729-2521. 24-hour service.

HYDROELECTRIC SYSTEMS AC/DC components, 100 watts to 5 megawatts. Since 1973. Free brochure. Send $15 for Engineering Guide/Catalog. Water Power Machinery Company, c/o Box 9723, Midland 08, Texas; 915-697-6955

FOUNDATION GRANTS for individuals to $180,000 for widely varied uses. Free recorded message: 707-448-2668. (2KE1)

GEORGIA PECANS fresh from our orchards! 5 lbs. mammoth halves, $28.95. 5 lbs. fancy pieces, $27.95. Postpaid. Quantity discounts available. Visa, MC, checks, MO. Merritt Pecan, Hwy. 520, Weston GA 31832; 1-800-762-9152

HOME CANNERS: Order everything you need: canners, jars, rubber rings, spices, more. Send $1 for catalog. Home Canning Supply, PO Box 1158-OF, Ramona CA 92065

BELLS IN YOUR EARS? Amazing natural remedy. 100 capsules $13.50. International Concepts, 6 Martin Creek Ct., Stockbridge GA 30281

MAGIC TRICKS, sets, novelties catalog $2. Includes free trick, $5 discount coupon. KMS, Box 2785K, Fairlawn NJ 07410

HORSE RACING FORMULA, Free. Hit exacta, quinellas, daily doubles consistently. $2.25 postage/handling to: Bledsoe Products, 720 Meadowlark, Sallisaw OK 74955

FLOURSACK DISH TOWELS, large, white cotton, washed, hemmed, pressed. 14 For $20., includes shipping, USA. Olson Towels, 10299 Nightingale, Coon Rapids MN 55433

FREE SHOPPING CATALOG. Limited supply. Minimum order $75. Products Unique, 210 Fifth Ave., New York NY 10010

PERFUME OILS. 100+, designers included! List, plus free sample. Send SASE: Amore Oils Fabulous Fragrances, PO Box 1232, Brooklyn NY 11202

COPPER BRACELETS: Solid copper chain link. Beautifully hand polished. Specify 8-, 9-, or 10-inch length. $12.50 each. Touch of Excellence, 75 Forest Ridge Dr., Worthington OH 43235

BE A HERO! Kids love making these paperfold poppers. Just $4.95 gets reusable popper, pattern, smiles! Funfold, 75 Ledger St., Hartford CT 06106

GRACE LIVINGSTON HILL Collectors! Write for our free list. Arnold Publication-A, 2440 Bethel Rd., Nicholasville KY 40356. 800-858-8571

50 FABULOUS HORSE/RIDER tips. $5. EZRIDER, Dept. 185, 4902 Carlisle Pike, Mechanicsburg PA 17055

SING BEAUTIFULLY, EASILY! Exciting, inexpensive manual shows how. Convincing free proof. Publisher, Box 3483-FA, New York NY 10008

TWELVE-MONTH BIORHYTHM charts. $5. Send birth date and year. John Morgan, 1208 Harris, Bartlesville OK 74006

CHESS FOR 2/3/4 PLAYERS: 64 solid chess men on 21" board with 160 squares. $29, check, M.O. SASE for free color brochure. Intense Games, 4 Park Ave. 9U, New York NY 10016

CELEBRITY ADDRESSES 25¢ each. Name plus a SASE. KF, Dept. A, PO Box 248, Sandy OR 97055

"JUST MARRIED" bumper stickers quickly decorate newlyweds' getaway cars. Weatherproof. Easy to remove. Four/$4.95 postpaid. U.S. funds only. 1776 Enterprises, Box 374FB, Sudbury MA 01776

PERSONALS

LATIN AND ORIENTAL LADIES seek friendship, marriage. Free photo brochure. "Latins," Box 1716-FR, Chula Vista CA 91912

NEED HELP DESPERATELY? Mrs. Stevens, Astrologer. Lonely? Unlucky? Unhappy? Helps all. Marriage, love, business, health, stress. I will give you options you never considered, never dreamed of. Immediate results. Call or write now. 803-682-9889. Mrs. Stevens, PO Box 207, Laurens SC 29360

SISTER HOPE SOLVES all problems. Specializing in love affairs. Are you sick? Having bad luck? Bothered by evil spells? Whatever your problem may be, call today 800-548-0023 or 706-353-9259

SISTER ADAMS, spiritual healer, will solve problems in love, marriage, business, health, evil influences. If you have talked with others and are disappointed, contact me. 8287 Spanish Fort Blvd., Spanish Fort AL 36527. Immediate results. 205-626-7997

MOTHER DOROTHY, reader and adviser. Advice on all problems — love, marriage, health, business, and nature. Gifted healer, she will remove your sickness, sorrow, pain, bad luck. ESP. Results in 3 days. Write or call about your problems. 404-755-1301. 1214 Gordon St., Atlanta GA 30310

NEW AGE contacts, occultists, circles, wicca, companionship, love, etc. America/worldwide. Dollar bill: Dion, Golden Wheel, Liverpool L15 3HT, England

BRITISH-AMERICAN Christian. Pen Pal Club, PO Box 581, Cypress CA 90630. Self-addressed stamped envelope.

NICE SINGLES with Christian values wish to meet others. Free magazine. Send age, interest. Singles, Box 310-OFA, Allardt TN 38504

ASIAN WOMEN desire romance! Overseas, sincere, attractive. Free details, photos! Sunshine International Correspondence, Box 5500-YH, Kailua-Kona HI 96745; 808-325-7707

JAPANESE, ASIANS, Europeans seek friendship, correspondence! All ages! Free information: Inter-Pacific, Box 304-K, Birmingham MI 48012

BEAUTIFUL ORIENTAL LADIES desire correspondence, romance! Free color brochure! P.I.C., Box 461873(FA), Los Angeles CA 90046; 213-650-1994

MOTHER ANDERSON wants to help you with all your problems — large or small, 65 years experience. 404-382-2143. PO Box 1465, Cartersville GA 30120

FREE LIST of discreet, adventurous ladies, local/nationwide. Mailed discreetly. Lori, PO Box 20001-F4, Columbus OH 43220

FREE PHOTO MAGAZINE for singles. Send name, address, age. Send no money. Exchange, Box 2425, Loveland CO 80539

FREE PHOTOS! Meet pretty Latin ladies. World, Box 7358-FR, Moreno Valley CA 92552

SPECIALIZES IN LOVE. Mrs. Bell reunites lovers immediately. Reveal and control your lover's future! Removes evil that's causing corruption. Changes the course of your life. Restores peace of mind! Helps all problems. 803-429-3693. PO Box 1260, Union SC 29379

ATTENTION: SISTER LIGHT, Spartanburg, S.C. One free reading when you call. I will help in all problems; 803-576-9397

SISTER RUBY gives advice about love, business, and all problems. Removes suffering and bad luck. 912-776-3069.2602 US Hwy. 82W, Sylvester GA 31791

MRS. KING will set you free from evil. Need positive help? Need counseling? 1-205-263-1199.3900 Birmingham Hwy., Montgomery AL 36108

POSTCARDS

OLD PICTURE POSTCARDS. Free information on buying, selling, collecting, plus large directory of more than 300 dealers. Send large SASE with two stamps to: Postcard Federation, Box 1765, Manassas VA 22110

POULTRY

GOSLINGS, DUCKLINGS, CHICKS, turkeys, guineas, bantams, pheasants, quail, swans. Equipment, books. Hoffman Hatchery, Gratz PA 17030

GOSLINGS, DUCKLINGS, CHICKS, turkeys, guineas, books. Illustrated catalog $1, deductible. Visa/MC. Pilgrim Goose Hatchery, OF-94, Williamsfield OH 44093

REAL ESTATE

GOVERNMENT LAND now available for claim. Up to 160 acres/person. Free recorded message: 707-448-1887. (4KE1)

CHAMPAGNE VILLAGE, North San Diego county. Active 5-Star senior resort, gated. Dine, dance, swim, tennis, golf, more. Beautiful area, shopping, airport/freeway convenience. Free map, prices, land ownership. Welk Village Realty, 8875 Lawrence Welk Dr., Escondido CA 92026. 619-749-1000/6404, John Oliver.

ARKANSAS LAND — Free List! Farms, ranches, homes, recreational acreages. Gatlin Farm Agency, Box 790, Waldron AR 72958; 800-562-9078 Ext. OFA

OZARK MOUNTAIN OR LAKE acreages. From $30/month, nothing down, environmental protection codes, huge selection. Free catalog. Woods & Waters, Box 1-FA, Willow Springs MO 65793. 417-469-3187

UPSTATE N.Y. Catskills, Adirondacks vacation land, houses. For list & packet, send $2 + #10 SASE to: G.M.C., Box 335, Highmount NY 12441. Buyers Broker.

ARKANSAS — Free Catalog. Natural beauty. Low taxes. The good life for families and retirement. Fitzgerald-Olsen Realtors, PO Box 237-A, Booneville AR 72927. Call toll-free 800-432-4595, Ext. 641A.

RELIGION

FREE. Booklet of Bible verses. Vernon, 11613 N. 31st Dr., Phoenix AZ 85029-3201

FREE BIBLE-STUDY COURSE. Adults or children. Project Philip, Box 35A, Muskegon MI 49443

TRADITIONAL CATHOLIC Calendar, 1994, only $8.95. Box 428, Black Eagle MT 59414. Relive the good old days!

WHO IS A CHRISTIAN? Called for what purpose? Is God trying to convert the world now? Free booklet. Clearwater Bible Students, PO Box 8216, Clearwater FL 34618

FREE BIBLE COURSE. Zion Faith College, PO Box 804, Caldwell ID 83606-0804

SEEDS

RARE HILARIOUS peter, female, and squash pepper seeds. $3 per pkg. Any two $5. All three $7.50. And over 100 more rare peppers, etc. Seeds, Rte. 2 Box 246, Atmore AL 36502

FREE CATALOG: Unusual seed varieties. Giant Belgium, evergreen, pineapple tomatoes and more. We make gardening fun. Gleckler Seedman, Metamora OH 43540

TOBACCO, Home-Growing Kit, 50-seed pkg. Instructions included. Smoking, chewing. $10. Homegrown Seeds, PO Box 4205, Pasco WA 99302-4205

WANTED

OLD FIRECRACKER PACKS, labels, boxes, catalogs, related memorabilia wanted! Brian, PO Box 3193, New Britain CT 06050. 203-223-8872

SLOT MACHINES, old juke boxes, music boxes, nickelodeons. Cash. Frank Zygmunt, PO Box 542, Westmount IL 60559; 708-985-2742

WANTED: OLD MARBLES, sulphides, swirls. Top prices paid. Bertram Cohen, 169 Marlborough St., Boston MA 02116

WANTED: AUTOGRAPHS, signed photos, letters, documents of famous people. Herb Gray, Box 5084, Cochituate MA 01778 or 617-426-4912

WORK CLOTHES

WORK CLOTHES. Save 80%. Shirts, pants, coveralls. Free folder. Write: Galco, 4004 East 71st St., Dept. OF-1, Cleveland OH 44105

MISCELLANEOUS

CASH FOR OLD RECORDS! Illustrated 72-page catalog, including thousands of specific prices we pay for 78s on common labels (Columbia, Decca, Victor, etc.), information about scarce labels, shipping instruction, etc. Send $2 (refundable). Discollector, Box 691-35 (FA), San Antonio TX 78269

LET THE GOVERNMENT finance your career in writing or the arts. Free recorded message: 707-448-0200. (5KE1)

BURIED TREASURE. Sensitive equipment allows locating from distance. Brochure free. Simmons, Box 10057-PA, Wilmington NC 28405

FREE BOOK CATALOG! Health, nutrition, alternative medicine, fitness, herbology, homeopathy, women's health, more! SONNCO, Dept. OFA94, Box 656, El Cerrito CA 94530

ANECDOTES *and* PLEASANTRIES

A motley collection of amazing (if sometimes useless) facts, strange stories, and questionable advice kindly sent to us during 1993 by readers of this 202-year-old publication.

Three Questions to Ask at Dinner Tonight

Especially if people at the table love pets. And think they know all about them . . .

Courtesy of Mark Sunlin, Saratoga, California

1. Why do kitties scratch the furniture?

No, not to sharpen their claws.

One of the most deeply in-grained beliefs pertaining to animal behavior is that it is the desire to sharpen their claws that motivates cats to rake them along tree bark or whatever else happens to be handy. The theory, however attractive it may be, is in error. As zoologist E. G. Appelman wrote in a footnote to Joy Adamson's book, *Born Free,* when a cat runs its claws along a tree trunk or your favorite sofa, it is actually exercising the tendons that cause its claws to retract. This seems to stimulate the tendons and thereby enhances the cat's ability to unsheathe and retract the claws, although the primary motivation is probably a matter of, "If it feels good, do it." Sort of like running the back of your fingernails along a corrugated box or rubbing your face when tired.

2. Do birds sing because they're happy?

Basically, there are two schools of thought on this one.

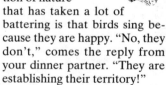

Since Robert Ardrey's book *The Territorial Imperative* brought the word "territory" into small talk, one common observation of nature that has taken a lot of battering is that birds sing because they are happy. "No, they don't," comes the reply from your dinner partner. "They are establishing their territory!"

For some reason this seems rather like telling a small child on Christmas Eve that there is no Santa Claus. But as it happens, it may be more than a little off the mark. Attributing the motivation behind a bird's song directly to a territorial proclamation is making a wide leap between cause and effect. It is perhaps more likely that birds do in fact give vent to song when they are feeling secure and content, and they are much more likely to feel secure and content when on their own familiar territory — a fact that other birds recognize and respect: "There is a self-assured individual living here." Thus, while the songs of birds may not be actually motivated by territoriality, it does have this cumulative effect, but the birds themselves, blissfully unaware of this, continue to sing primarily because they are happy.

I don't think King Solomon could have handled that one any better.

3. Why do dogs have whiskers?
Can you believe they're like your finger?

All mammals have whiskers. But *why* all mammals have whiskers is not quite as simple to state. It is the smaller mammals who generally have the most prominent set of facial hairs, or vibrissae, and this might seem to bear out the theory that such whiskers serve as a sort of tactile radar when the animal is scurrying through the grass or bushes. However, the mouse, who spends much of his life brushing through tunnels, would hardly seem to need a set of facial antennae to tell him that he is about to rub shoulders with grass stems or tunnel walls — he does so all the time, regardless. If the whiskers transmitted signals every time this happened, he might become a rather neurotic rodent. In fact, mice and other mammals tend to pull their whiskers back along their cheeks when making their way through such claustrophobic terrain in order to avoid making contact.

Then what use are whiskers?

It seems that the real reason for whiskers is not as radar, but rather to detect wind direction. Most mammals have senses of smell so profound that they are unfathomable to humans. When using such sophisticated olfactory equipment as this, it is very useful to know from which direction the wind, and along with it the scents it carries, is coming. In this sense whiskers serve as a weather vane, a moistened index finger held aloft to detect the breeze. Since wind is considerably weaker close to the ground, smaller animals need correspondingly larger sets of whiskers in order to detect it.

Well . . . so now you know.

How to Start a Ford

Just for the record, this is how it was 70 years ago . . . (i.e., confusing).

Submitted by Janet J. Baer,
Washington, Ohio

I recently found the following among my late husband's papers. He wrote it in 1924 at age ten. His title was simply "How to Start an Automobile . . ."

"The way to start a Ford is this. First, you get into the driver's seat, put the key into the keyhole, and turn to the right. Put your foot on the starter. If it won't start, pull out the choke. If it still won't start, then turn the key to the left. Then when it starts, turn the key back to the right. Now put your foot halfway in on the left pedal. Then push the hand brake forward. When that is done, push clear in on the pedal you have your foot on.

"You will go forward. Push the throttle down a little bit, which is on the right and side of the steering gear. When you are going well, let out on the pedal you have your foot on. If you want to stop, first put your foot halfway in on the left pedal and put your other foot on the right pedal. If you want to back up, put your foot halfway on the left-hand pedal and your other foot on the middle pedal.

"The left-hand pedal is low, the middle reverse, and the right is the foot brake."

The Best Way to Cook a Carp

We included a carp recipe (carp are more or less huge goldfish) in last year's Almanac and nobody seemed to like it. So we tested this one by the late Euell Gibbons (remember him — the fellow who liked to eat bark?) and found it to be truly delicious.

Courtesy of Alan C. Hood Co., Inc., Brattleboro, Vermont, publisher of Euell Gibbons's book, Stalking the Wild Asparagus

It was my brother who finally devised a method of cooking carp that made it not only fit for human consumption, but also actually delicious. First, instead of merely scaling the fish, he skinned them. Then, taking a large pinch, where the meat was thickest, he worked his fingers and thumb into the flesh until he struck the median bones, then he worked his thumb and fingers together and tore off a handful of meat. Using this tearing method, he could get two or three good-sized chunks of flesh from each side of the fish. He then heated a pot of bland vegetable shorten-

ing, rubbed the pieces of fish with salt, and dropped them into the hot fat. He used no flour, meal, crumbs, or seasoning other than salt. They cooked to a golden brown in a few minutes, and everyone pronounced them "mighty fine eating." The muddy flavor seemed to have been eliminated by removing the skin and the large bones. The forked bones were still there, but they had not been multiplied by cutting across them, and one only had to remove several bones still intact with the fork from each piece of fish.

A Weird Way to Save Money on Your Cow

Most people don't own cows anymore. But when those who do can save money in feed costs, then we all benefit from lower milk and beef prices. (Don't we?) So pass along the following trick to anyone you know who does own a cow.

Based on a New York Times clipping submitted by A. R. Brewster, Spring Valley, New York

Like humans, cows need roughage such as hay in their diet for good health. Hay, however, is very low in calories. For a cow to gain weight, it needs to eat high-calorie stuff like corn, which doesn't provide much roughage. So the more corn it eats, the less hay it eats. But without the roughage hay provides, the cow will lose its appetite and eat less overall, thus negating the increase in high-calorie corn. It seems a cow's first (of four) stomach, called

the rumen, needs the stimulation of roughage to induce a good appetite. So what to do? Well, according to an article published by Dr. Steven Loerch of Ohio State University last year in *The Journal of Animal Science,* you should make your cow eat a plastic pot scrubber. The kind you use when you wash the dishes. Actually, few cows or steers will volunteer. So you need to wrap the pot scrubber in digestible tape and then place it on the back of the

A Cure for Jet Lag

All it takes is sunshine . . . plus a pretty good memory.

Courtesy of R. C. Gagnon, Philadelphia, Pennsylvania

Irecently read a newspaper item about a Dr. Alfred J. Lewy of the Oregon Health Science Center in Portland in which he suggests a cure for jet lag that utilizes sunshine — or simple outdoor daylight. Here's what you do . . .

Crossing Six or Fewer Time Zones

East to West (like from New York to California): Expose yourself to sunlight in the late afternoon of the day of your arrival. This will help reset your body clock to the later bedtime and subsequent wake-up time the next morning.

West to East (like from New York to London): Expose yourself to sunlight immediately upon arrival early in the morning, if possible. Your body rhythm will then adjust to the new bedtime that night.

Crossing More Than Six Time Zones

West to East (like from Oregon to London): Morning light upon arrival will delay the body's clock 16 hours instead of advancing it eight hours, and you'll have jet lag for up to two weeks. So, avoid morning sunshine or daylight upon arrival at your destination, and instead, expose yourself to sunshine at noon.

East to West (like from New York to Tokyo): Get out in the midday sunshine as soon as possible after arrival but, above all, avoid sunshine or daylight in the late afternoon of that day.

If You Can't Remember the Above

East to West or West to East (any number of time zones): Mix ⅓ glass of brandy, ⅓ vermouth (sweet), and ⅓ port. Sip very slowly for approximately 30 minutes on day of arrival. (This is not part of Dr. Lewy's jet-lag cure, but rather one offered to travelers at the Bailey Restaurant at 2 Duke Street in Dublin, Ireland.)

Important Vacuum Cleaning Statistics

People who vacuum once a day	9 percent
four to six times a week	14 percent
once a week	37 percent
never	0.06 percent

. . . and Facts About Holidays

Holidays are more hassle than fun, a study found. Americans spend 17 minutes planning Christmas purchases — and six hours shopping; in the last week before the big day, the average person spends ten minutes a day bickering (with someone) over what parties to attend, what to wear, and whether to leave early.

tongue. (The cow's tongue, silly.) Once swallowed, the tape is digested and the pot scrubber remains in the rumen — for life. And apparently the coarseness of the scrubber as well as the bacteria that build up on the surface of it all combine to act as roughage in the digestive process. Your cow can eat more corn, gain weight, and you don't have to provide — and pay for — roughage feed like hay. The savings, according to Dr. Loerch, can be up to $50 (less the cost of the scrubber) per cow without in any way jeopardizing the animal's health.

Ten Tantalizing Tongue Twisters of Tenuous Taste

1. The seething sea ceaseth and thus the seething sea sufficeth us.

Used by legendary radio newscaster Lowell Thomas as a warm-up for his shows.

2. Betty Botter bought a bit of butter. "But," she said, "this butter's bitter. If I put it in my batter, it will make my batter bitter. But a bit of better butter will make my batter better." So Betty Botter bought a bit of better butter, and it made her batter better.

Lord Laurence Olivier's favorite "warm-up" tongue twister.

3. Three gray geese in the green grass grazing: Gray were the geese and green was the grazing.

Favorite of the late Metropolitan opera star Ezio Pinza.

4. Moses supposes his toeses are roses, but Moses supposes erroneously. For Moses he knowses his toeses aren't roses, as Moses supposes his toeses to be.

Sophia Loren's English teacher made her practice this one.

5. The sixth sick sheik's sixth sheep's sick.

The most difficult one-line tongue twister, according to the Guinness Book of World Records.

6. Iqaqa laziqikaqika kwaze kwaqhawaka uqhoqhoqha.

The most difficult one-line foreign language tongue twister, according to the Guinness Book of World Records. *Translated from the South African dialect Xhosa, it means: "The skunk rolled down and ruptured its larynx."*

7. She sells seashells by the seashore, etc., etc.

Because actor Boris Karloff had a bit of a lisp, this was the one he'd practice saying on a regular basis.

8. Amidst the mists and coldest frosts, with barest wrists and stoutest boasts, he thrust his fist against the posts, and still insists he sees the ghosts.

A favorite of many dentists who make patients with new dentures practice by saying tongue twisters.

9. Theophilus Thistle, the thistle-sifter, sifted a sieve of unsifted thistles. If Theophilus Thistle, the thistle-sifter, sifted a sieve of unsifted thistles, where is the sieve of unsifted thistles Theophilus Thistle, the thistle sifter, sifted?

Many tongue-twister buffs agree this is the toughest one of them all.

10. Truly rural. (*Or* Preshrunk shirt. *Or* Peggy Babcock. *Or* Sixty-six sick chicks.)

These are the shortest.

Courtesy of Frederick John, Honolulu, Hawaii

Forecasting the Weather by Observing a Leech in a Jar

If you don't believe it can be done, well . . . gee . . . what's the matter with you?

Courtesy of Bridget Boland and her book,
Gardener's Magic and Other Old Wives' Lore

You've heard, surely, that when a frog is pale yellow, the weather will be fine. The same frog will, of course, turn brown or green before a storm. Everyone knows those things. Hear a crow before dawn and expect rain. Well, along the same line, here's how to predict the weather with leeches (or, as some call them, bloodsuckers), available in most freshwater ponds.

First of all, put the leech in a large glass jar about two-thirds filled with water. Change the water once a week during the summer and once a fortnight during the winter. Now, according to the early Victorian encyclopedia *Enquire Within,* "If the weather is to be fine, the leech lies motionless in the bottom of the glass; if rain may be expected, it will creep up to the top of its lodgings and remain there till the weather is settled; if we are to have wind, it will move through its habitation with amazing swiftness and seldom goes to rest till it begins to blow hard."

If heavy storms are to be expected, "it will lodge for some days before, almost continually out of the water, and discover great uneasiness in violent throes and convulsive motions; in frost as in clear summer weather, it lies constantly at the bottom; and in snow as in rainy weather, it pitches its dwelling at the very mouth of the phial. The top [of the jar] should be covered with a piece of muslin."

Help for the Russians

(Or maybe "Déjà Vu All Over Again")

The American steamer Indiana lately sailed from Philadelphia with about 4,000 tons of grain and flour, the generous gift of the citizens of that noble town to the suffering people in Russia. The railroads transported the cargo free, and all who dealt with it, from truckmen and stevedores down to insurance companies, rendered free service. This ship was soon followed by the steamer Missouri from New York, carrying about 3,000 tons more of meal and flour to the famine-stricken Russians, the generous contributions of Western millers and farmers. The use of the steamer was also given free of charge by the Atlantic Transport Line. The total contributions to the Russians, so far, reach the sum of about half a million dollars.

Reprinted from the March 19, 1892, issue of Scientific American *and sent to us by Donald Armistead of Madison, Connecticut*

ANECDOTES and PLEASANTRIES *(continued)*

In Support of Old Wives' Tales

After years of pooh-poohing, scientists are finally acknowledging that maybe kids do grow in "spurts." Some recent studies showed that some children can grow as much as five-eighths of an inch overnight. So there. Just what Grandma said all along.

A Question for Us All to Ponder

Solve this one problem and we've solved thousands of horrendous problems throughout the world. But how do we solve this one problem?

Courtesy of Guy Murchie, author of
The Seven Mysteries of Life *and many other books*

A million years ago there were probably less than a hundred thousand men and women on Earth. They were furry, apelike creatures living in the most fertile parts of Africa, Asia, and probably Europe. They did not think of themselves as much different from the animals around them, for no one had ever heard of human beings. They could grunt, murmur, and communicate better than the dumb beasts and slowly evolved what we call real languages that enabled them to articulate ideas and outwit their enemies. By 8000 B.C., their numbers had grown to an estimated three million, most of them hunters but many also skilled herdsmen, and quite a few beginning to learn to sow and reap, which enabled them to live in villages.

In succeeding millennia man's population kept on increasing and accelerating, no doubt stimulated by such developments as his marvelous discovery that he could persuade cattle, horses, and buffalo to plow, the wind to sail a ship, and flowing water to grind grain. By 2300 B.C., his number was approaching 100 million and in Roman times about 300 million, reaching 500 million only in the 17th century. Then his invention of the steam engine, with its massive cheap power that launched the industrial revolution, surged man's population again, pushing it to a billion by the mid-19th century. From there it accumulated to two billion in the 1920s, three billion about 1960, four billion in 1976, and five billion in 1988.

Summing up, the explosion of man's population in the 20th century amounts to a thousandfold increase in its growth rate: from less than .002 percent increase a year before the advent of farming to two percent today.

How can this dire explosion be brought under control? That's the question for us all to ponder.

RAINY DAY AMUSEMENTS

Answers appear on page 219

A QUIZ YOU SHOULD REALLY HUM THROUGH

Can you come up with the musical address (song title or lyric) to match these clues? Example: Kris Kringle's address is Santa Claus Lane.

– Jamie Kageleiry

1. The best address for blues with Miss Bessie

2. A road America has traveled

3. "Where the flyin' fishes play . . ."

4. "Just give me the Moon over Brooklyn . . ."

5. "Life's a holiday" here

6. A place where Tony Bennett lamented

7. From the Rodgers and Hart musical *On Your Toes*

8. Kris Kringle's address

9. Follow this, "because, because, because, because, because . . ."

10. You can be sure: This "road that leads to your door will never disappear"

11. Here, you might just hear

Connie Stevens singing, "Kookie, Kookie, lend me your comb"

12. Heartbreak Hotel sits right at the end

13. "That great street"

14. Possibly the best place to "get your kicks"

15. Where you stand with your "Kansas City Baby (and a bottle o' Kansas City wine)"

16. "They say the lights are always bright . . ."

17. "Man of means, by no means . . ."

18. Where "the photographers will snap us"

19. A place with a lot of colorful characters. For instance, "There is a fireman with an hourglass, and in his pocket is a portrait of the queen"

20. You might just drift here to get "out of the Sun"

21. "Where all the hep cats meet"

22. Directions to the "promised land," according to the E Street Band

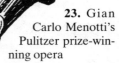

23. Gian Carlo Menotti's Pulitzer prize-winning opera

24. Here's the address if you're "lookin' for fun and feelin' groovy . . ."

25. Martha and the Vandellas did this all over the country

FUNNY PEOPLE

Match the oldie cartoon characters at left with the names of their comic strips at right.   *– Milt Hammer*

1. Hans and Fritz   **A.** Napoleon
2. Dragon Lady   **B.** Joe Palooka
3. Major Hoople   **C.** The Gumps
4. Anne Howe   **D.** Mutt and Jeff
5. Captain Easy   **E.** Li'l Abner
6. Uncle Elby   **F.** The Captain and the Kids
7. Cicero   **G.** Our Boarding House
8. King Guz   **H.** Wash Tubbs
9. Daisy Mae   **I.** Terry and the Pirates
10. Uncle Bim   **J.** Alley Oop

FOUR IN NINE

In each case below, build another noun around the given one to match the hint shown there. We think 17 correct is a good average.

Example: <u>a</u> <u>c</u> C O R D <u>i</u> <u>o</u> <u>n</u> (instrument).
        – George O. Pommer

1. _ _ A R C H _ _ _ (revolution)
2. _ _ B O R E _ _ _ (botanical preserve)
3. _ _ B A R D _ _ _ (fabric)
4. _ _ C E N T _ _ _ (motive)
5. _ _ C O R D _ _ _ (tape)
6. _ _ D E N T _ _ _ (contract)
7. _ _ D U C T _ _ _ (initiation)
8. _ _ D O M E _ _ _ (counter)
9. _ _ F I R M _ _ _ (debility)
10. _ _ F O R M _ _ _ (source)
11. _ _ G I S T _ _ _ (record keeper)
12. _ _ M I S T _ _ _ (treaty)
13. _ _ P I L L _ _ _ (vessel)
14. _ _ P A R T _ _ _ (partaker)
15. _ _ R O L L _ _ _ (inference)
16. _ _ R I M E _ _ _ (boundary)
17. _ _ S P A R _ _ _ (difference)
18. _ _ T O M E _ _ _ (for eyes)
19. _ _ T E N T _ _ _ (possibility)
20. _ _ V E N T _ _ _ (list)

AN ADJECTIVAL BESTIARY: QUIZ & PRIMER

In a language as rich in borrowed words as English, the terminology in a given field is not always straightforward. The adjective associated with *dog*, for instance, is *canine*, from the Latin *canis*. Life would be a lot simpler if *doglike* were the word everybody used, but it wouldn't be nearly as interesting. Likewise, the cat's adjective is *feline*, from the Latin, *felis*.

A lot of common animals have similar, Latin-based adjectives. Here's your chance to see how many you can pick out of a crowd. See if you can match the adjective at left with the animal named on the right.   *– Rob Simbeck*

1. Anguine   **A.** Bear
2. Apian   **B.** Bee
3. Aquiline   **C.** Bull
4. Asinine   **D.** Cow
5. Bovine   **E.** Crow
6. Caprine   **F.** Deer
7. Cervine   **G.** Donkey
8. Colubrine   **H.** Eagle
9. Corvine   **I.** Fish
10. Equine   **J.** Fox
11. Hircine   **K.** Goat (2)
12. Leonine   **L.** Horse
13. Lupine   **M.** Lion
14. Ovine   **N.** Pig
15. Piscine   **O.** Sheep
16. Porcine   **P.** Snake (2)
17. Taurine   **Q.** Wolf
18. Ursine
19. Vulpine

by Lawrence Doorley

A Eulogy for

The WISH BOOK

Born: August 15, 1893 • Died: January 25, 1993

O n January 25, 1993, the Chicago headquarters of Sears, Roebuck and Co. announced it was abandoning publication of its 100-year-old catalog. The 1993 spring edition would be the last. After the shock had subsided — and it took time — many Americans were forced to admit that the stalwart friend and mentor had been ailing for many years. Still, it hurt. "What next?" grieved a little Nebraska newspaper. "Pave the prairie?"

Newspapers all over America devoted columns to the catalog's obituary, the mood being particularly sad in the hundreds of small-town papers where the Wish Book — also called the Dream Book, the Big Book, and the Farmer's Bible — had been held in such love and reverence. Not only had the magical catalog nourished and invigorated the body, but the spellbinding plot changed twice a year. Most obituary writers agreed that the death of the catalog meant the end of an era, the severing of the last link to the Good Old Days, the incredible period from the late 1890s to the Roaring Twenties when America exploded as the world's greatest industrial nation.

In truth, the Good Old Days had been pretty rough for most Americans of the time.

As late as 1890 more than two-thirds of the country's population lived on farms. With no control over the prices they received for their crops or over prices charged for the goods they bought, constantly at the mercy of the boom-and-bust cycle, most farm families scraped by. Anger — at the railroads, Wall Street bankers, the middle man — had seethed for years. In the late 1880s, urged on by fiery agitators who thundered against "ten cent [a bushel] corn and ten percent mortgages," farmers began to organize, but hard times continued.

It was in this turbulent period that Richard Warren Sears began what was to become one of the all-time American success stories. Sears was born in 1863 on a Minnesota farm; his father had prospered, overexpanded in a boom, and lost everything when the inevitable bust came. Young Sears went to work as a telegrapher at age 16.

By 1886 he was the railroad station agent in North Redwood, Minnesota, and his family lived with him above the station. An energetic, ambitious go-getter — the locals called him a "humdinger" — Sears jumped at the chance to take over a large shipment of engraved pocket watches that a local merchant had refused to accept. Telegraphing other agents up and down the line, he sold the entire shipment in three weeks at a profit of $375. He was on his way. He ordered more watches, advertised in rural papers, and in six months had a nest egg of $4,500.

Resigning his job and taking his family along, he moved to Minneapolis. He was 23 years old (actually, rather long in the tooth for the typical Horatio Alger Pluck and

Richard Warren Sears

Luck hero), a handsome, dark-haired chap. He decided to go into the watch business in a big way. Naturally, a few of the watches malfunctioned. To fix them, he hired another ex-farm boy, a 24-year-old watchmaker named Alvah Curtis Roebuck, a practical, cautious fellow, quite the opposite of audacious, venturous Sears.

Business was great. Sears made Roebuck a partner, and in 1888 they put out the R.W. Sears Watch Company mail order catalog. They did so well that they moved to Chicago in 1893 and incorporated as Sears, Roebuck and Co. on August 15. The company issued its first catalog late that year, featuring watches and other goods. But it was the 1894 catalog that changed the mail order business forever. Sears knew that there was an enormous untapped market along the railroad lines of rural America, a market desperate to be freed from the clutches of the general storekeeper and his 100-percent markup.

Proclaiming itself the "Cheapest Supply House on Earth," the 1894 Sears catalog contained more than 300 pages of well-illustrated, detailed descriptions of hundreds of items: pianos, organs, guns, revolvers, silverware, farm implements, bicycles, clothing, sewing machines, buggies. Every single item was of high quality, sold at a low price, and came with a money-back guarantee.

Sears wrote every ad himself. Actually he dictated them to young lady "type writers," as stenographers were called back then. He spewed out words at a furious pace while rushing around the plant, exhorting employees — many of them young women in their first job — to greater effort.

Sears's prose tended to the flamboyant, bordering on hyperbole. He was so dazzled by what he was doing that his frenzied optimism frequently outran common sense.

timid girl out in the high plains of South Dakota wondered if Mr. Sears knew of anything that would give her a bigger bust. Next year came not one but two Princess Bust Developers.

Through ads in small-town papers and farm journals, farmers learned of the Sears catalog. Leaving nothing to chance, Sears raced around the Middle West hiring eager kids to pass out flyers announcing the catalog. Persistent stories from that time allege that local merchants, horrified by the low prices, let it be known that they would pay a nickel for every catalog the kids brought to them, undelivered.

Sears couldn't have picked a worse time to start a mail order business targeting farmers. The Panic of 1893 had intensified and farm prices were at rock bottom. But the catalog's low factory prices and promise to eliminate the middleman often proved irresistible. Coffee cans containing nickels, dimes, a few quarters, came out of hiding, and after nights of agonized scanning of the catalog, a choice would be made. Pa would hitch up and drive to town, where the pursed-lipped postmaster (who was often also the storekeeper) would make out the money order for Item No. 10R10 — "Our Handsomest, Cheapest, Most Durable Iowa Plow Horse Harness" at $9.95. As postmaster, the general storekeeper would make a small fee for filling out the money order, but he lost the profit he would have made had Pa been forced to buy from him.

The Panic hung on, but nothing daunted Sears. He added more pages to the 1895 catalog, and in 1896 went up to a breath-taking 732 pages crammed with thousands of items, all illustrated and exhaustively described. It paid off. Orders flowed into Chicago, forcing Sears to lease ever-larger quarters, hire more employees, line up suppliers. Poor Roebuck, the doer, the shipper, responsible for everything but the catalog and the ordering, collapsed under the mad pace. The final blow was an avalanche of orders for Item No. 45R216 — "Men's Three-Piece Wool Navy Blue Serge Suit; Equal to the Finest of New York City Haberdashery"— at $5.75. Sears had featured it in the 1895 catalog, but had neglected to order the suits from the supplier.

Roebuck resigned, selling out for $25,000. Sears got the money from two Chicago businessmen, Aaron Nusbaum and Julius Rosenwald, who formed a new company on August 23, 1895, injecting fresh capital and experienced management into Sears, Roebuck and Co.

The year 1897 brought a boom of epic proportions. Corn went from eight cents a bushel to an incredible 57 cents. Wheat exploded from an abysmal 12 cents to 98 cents. Those prices would stay until the end of World War I; the post-war plummet caught the farmers again and presaged the Great Depression. But while it lasted, the farmer basked in the prosperity of the Good Old Days. Sears put out two catalogs a year, reaching millions.

The Wish Book became not only a marvelous cornucopia from which thousands of goods cascaded, but also an encyclopedia, a friend. Schoolteachers used it for spelling, reading, and arithmetic (calculating railroad prices per pound). On long winter nights the Book was a wonderful source of entertainment. The company's archives contain hundreds of letters to "Dear Mr. Sears." A timid girl out in the high plains of South Dakota wondered if Mr. Sears knew of anything that would give her a bigger bust. Next year out came not one but two Princess Bust Developers: One was a nickel and aluminum hand-operated device that looked like a drain plunger; the second, a "delicately perfumed" massage cream for creating "a plump, full, rounded bosom, perfect neck and arms" by nourishing the "bust glands." "If Nature Hasn't Favored You," said Sears in at least 750 words, these superb items would do the trick.

"Isn't there a more powerful windmill?" wrote an Iowa farmer. There was — and Sears found it. A distressed young lady in Pennsylvania wailed that her complexion was making her a wallflower at school dances. The next catalog extolled the virtues of No. 8R99, "Dr. Rose's French Arsenic Wafers," 100 treatments for 67 cents. A wafer a day was guaranteed to give even the most unprepossessing girl "a transparency and pellucid clearness of complexion . . . free from any spot or blemish whatever."

There were testimonials, too. A Sunday school teacher from Wyoming wrote to say that when she asked her class, "Where did the Ten Commandments come from?" a dear little child answered, "From the Sears, Roebuck catalog." Thousands of lonely people wrote, and Sears and his "type writers" answered all letters.

Congress established Parcel Post in 1913, intending it to encourage city dwellers to order fresh produce from farmers, who would then mail it back by Parcel Post. Although this romance never quite caught on, a perfect marriage resulted between Sears, Roebuck and Parcel Post. Sears's customers got their packages quickly and reliably, and Parcel Post's revenues soared. In the first year of operation, Sears, Roebuck received five times as many orders as it had in the previous year!

Meanwhile, Richard Warren Sears had suddenly resigned in November 1908. He was simply exhausted. He died in Waukesha, Wisconsin, at the age of 50 on September 28, 1914, leaving behind a book that had changed America. In its heyday, the Wish Book sold everything from the cradle to the grave. You could buy a Royal Blue Vermont Marble Tombstone weighing 206 pounds for $7.65 in 1916. It almost paid to die.

Alvah Curtis Roebuck

The automobile and good roads started the Book's downhill slide. Sears helped to kill its own catalog by building retail stores. But the catalog hung on, selling everything from hairpins to whole houses (100,000 were sold, most still standing).

Now it's gone, but this icon of America will not be forgotten. Someday perhaps there'll be a Wish Book musical on Broadway. A young untried singer from Broken Bow, Nebraska, will bring down the house as the true-life Sears clerk to whom Lady Luck directed a plaintive order from a lonely Montana rancher seeking a spouse "like the girl at the top of page 97." The clerk jumped up, grabbed her hat, took the first train to Montana, and married the rancher. And, no doubt, raised a family, furnishing the ranch house with up-to-date goods from the wonderful Wish Book. □□

1 9 9 3

JANUARY
S	M	T	W	T	F	S
—	—	—	—	—	1	2
3	4	5	6	7	8	9
10	11	12	13	14	15	16
17	18	19	20	21	22	23
24	25	26	27	28	29	30
31						

FEBRUARY
S	M	T	W	T	F	S
—	1	2	3	4	5	6
7	8	9	10	11	12	13
14	15	16	17	18	19	20
21	22	23	24	25	26	27
28						

MARCH
S	M	T	W	T	F	S
—	1	2	3	4	5	6
7	8	9	10	11	12	13
14	15	16	17	18	19	20
21	22	23	24	25	26	27
28	29	30	31			

APRIL
S	M	T	W	T	F	S
—	—	—	—	1	2	3
4	5	6	7	8	9	10
11	12	13	14	15	16	17
18	19	20	21	22	23	24
25	26	27	28	29	30	—

MAY
S	M	T	W	T	F	S
—	—	—	—	—	—	1
2	3	4	5	6	7	8
9	10	11	12	13	14	15
16	17	18	19	20	21	22
23	24	25	26	27	28	29
30	31					

JUNE
S	M	T	W	T	F	S
—	—	1	2	3	4	5
6	7	8	9	10	11	12
13	14	15	16	17	18	19
20	21	22	23	24	25	26
27	28	29	30	—	—	—

JULY
S	M	T	W	T	F	S
—	—	—	—	1	2	3
4	5	6	7	8	9	10
11	12	13	14	15	16	17
18	19	20	21	22	23	24
25	26	27	28	29	30	31

AUGUST
S	M	T	W	T	F	S
1	2	3	4	5	6	7
8	9	10	11	12	13	14
15	16	17	18	19	20	21
22	23	24	25	26	27	28
29	30	31	—	—	—	—

SEPTEMBER
S	M	T	W	T	F	S
—	—	—	1	2	3	4
5	6	7	8	9	10	11
12	13	14	15	16	17	18
19	20	21	22	23	24	25
26	27	28	29	30	—	—

OCTOBER
S	M	T	W	T	F	S
—	—	—	—	—	1	2
3	4	5	6	7	8	9
10	11	12	13	14	15	16
17	18	19	20	21	22	23
24	25	26	27	28	29	30
31						

NOVEMBER
S	M	T	W	T	F	S
—	1	2	3	4	5	6
7	8	9	10	11	12	13
14	15	16	17	18	19	20
21	22	23	24	25	26	27
28	29	30	—	—	—	—

DECEMBER
S	M	T	W	T	F	S
—	—	—	1	2	3	4
5	6	7	8	9	10	11
12	13	14	15	16	17	18
19	20	21	22	23	24	25
26	27	28	29	30	31	—

1 9 9 4

JANUARY
S	M	T	W	T	F	S
—	—	—	—	—	—	1
2	3	4	5	6	7	8
9	10	11	12	13	14	15
16	17	18	19	20	21	22
23	24	25	26	27	28	29
30	31					

FEBRUARY
S	M	T	W	T	F	S
—	—	1	2	3	4	5
6	7	8	9	10	11	12
13	14	15	16	17	18	19
20	21	22	23	24	25	26
27	28	—	—	—	—	—

MARCH
S	M	T	W	T	F	S
—	—	1	2	3	4	5
6	7	8	9	10	11	12
13	14	15	16	17	18	19
20	21	22	23	24	25	26
27	28	29	30	31	—	

APRIL
S	M	T	W	T	F	S
—	—	—	—	—	1	2
3	4	5	6	7	8	9
10	11	12	13	14	15	16
17	18	19	20	21	22	23
24	25	26	27	28	29	30

MAY
S	M	T	W	T	F	S
1	2	3	4	5	6	7
8	9	10	11	12	13	14
15	16	17	18	19	20	21
22	23	24	25	26	27	28
29	30	31	—	—	—	—

JUNE
S	M	T	W	T	F	S
—	—	—	1	2	3	4
5	6	7	8	9	10	11
12	13	14	15	16	17	18
19	20	21	22	23	24	25
26	27	28	29	30	—	—

JULY
S	M	T	W	T	F	S
—	—	—	—	—	1	2
3	4	5	6	7	8	9
10	11	12	13	14	15	16
17	18	19	20	21	22	23
24	25	26	27	28	29	30
31						

AUGUST
S	M	T	W	T	F	S
—	1	2	3	4	5	6
7	8	9	10	11	12	13
14	15	16	17	18	19	20
21	22	23	24	25	26	27
28	29	30	31	—	—	—

SEPTEMBER
S	M	T	W	T	F	S
—	—	—	—	1	2	3
4	5	6	7	8	9	10
11	12	13	14	15	16	17
18	19	20	21	22	23	24
25	26	27	28	29	30	—

OCTOBER
S	M	T	W	T	F	S
—	—	—	—	—	—	1
2	3	4	5	6	7	8
9	10	11	12	13	14	15
16	17	18	19	20	21	22
23	24	25	26	27	28	29
30	31					

NOVEMBER
S	M	T	W	T	F	S
—	—	1	2	3	4	5
6	7	8	9	10	11	12
13	14	15	16	17	18	19
20	21	22	23	24	25	26
27	28	29	30	—	—	—

DECEMBER
S	M	T	W	T	F	S
—	—	—	—	1	2	3
4	5	6	7	8	9	10
11	12	13	14	15	16	17
18	19	20	21	22	23	24
25	26	27	28	29	30	31

1 9 9 5

JANUARY
S	M	T	W	T	F	S
1	2	3	4	5	6	7
8	9	10	11	12	13	14
15	16	17	18	19	20	21
22	23	24	25	26	27	28
29	30	31				

FEBRUARY
S	M	T	W	T	F	S
—	—	—	1	2	3	4
5	6	7	8	9	10	11
12	13	14	15	16	17	18
19	20	21	22	23	24	25
26	27	28	—	—	—	—

MARCH
S	M	T	W	T	F	S
—	—	—	1	2	3	4
5	6	7	8	9	10	11
12	13	14	15	16	17	18
19	20	21	22	23	24	25
26	27	28	29	30	31	—

APRIL
S	M	T	W	T	F	S
—	—	—	—	—	—	1
2	3	4	5	6	7	8
9	10	11	12	13	14	15
16	17	18	19	20	21	22
23	24	25	26	27	28	29
30						

MAY
S	M	T	W	T	F	S
—	1	2	3	4	5	6
7	8	9	10	11	12	13
14	15	16	17	18	19	20
21	22	23	24	25	26	27
28	29	30	31	—	—	—

JUNE
S	M	T	W	T	F	S
—	—	—	—	1	2	3
4	5	6	7	8	9	10
11	12	13	14	15	16	17
18	19	20	21	22	23	24
25	26	27	28	29	30	—

JULY
S	M	T	W	T	F	S
—	—	—	—	—	—	1
2	3	4	5	6	7	8
9	10	11	12	13	14	15
16	17	18	19	20	21	22
23	24	25	26	27	28	29
30	31					

AUGUST
S	M	T	W	T	F	S
—	—	1	2	3	4	5
6	7	8	9	10	11	12
13	14	15	16	17	18	19
20	21	22	23	24	25	26
27	28	29	30	31	—	—

SEPTEMBER
S	M	T	W	T	F	S
—	—	—	—	—	1	2
3	4	5	6	7	8	9
10	11	12	13	14	15	16
17	18	19	20	21	22	23
24	25	26	27	28	29	30

OCTOBER
S	M	T	W	T	F	S
1	2	3	4	5	6	7
8	9	10	11	12	13	14
15	16	17	18	19	20	21
22	23	24	25	26	27	28
29	30	31	—	—	—	—

NOVEMBER
S	M	T	W	T	F	S
—	—	—	1	2	3	4
5	6	7	8	9	10	11
12	13	14	15	16	17	18
19	20	21	22	23	24	25
26	27	28	29	30	—	—

DECEMBER
S	M	T	W	T	F	S
—	—	—	—	—	1	2
3	4	5	6	7	8	9
10	11	12	13	14	15	16
17	18	19	20	21	22	23
24	25	26	27	28	29	30
31						

I. The Old Farmer's Almanac Great Americans Hall of Fame 250

T he profiles in this series portray people whose lives changed all our lives since this Almanac was first published 202 years ago. These people are chosen for the ways their particular genius shaped and reshaped the everyday lives of Americans. For 1994, Hall of Famers include clipper ship builder Donald McKay; pioneer geneticist Barbara McClintock; public servant Albert Gallatin; Standard Time-keeper William F. Allen; social architect Jane Addams; conservationist and forester Gifford Pinchot; and lyric songwriter Stephen Foster, America's "beautiful dreamer."

From time to time the editors of this Almanac will nominate other American men and women to *The Old Farmer's Almanac* Great Americans Hall of Fame.

II. A Reference Compendium 266

Great Americans Hall of Fame

by Lawrence Doorley

DONALD McKAY
Clipper Ship Leonardo
(1810-1880)

She was a breathtaking beauty: Incredibly tall, sleek, thin-waisted, draped in billowy garments of purest white. Writers waxed lyrical over her. Her magnificent prow, arching toward the heavens, was frequently adorned with a full-figured angel, but she was no angel. She was racy and reckless, bold and brazen, an unabashed Lorelei — in it for the quick buck and to hell with the risks.

She was the glorious, gorgeous, wonderful, dazzling, grand, majestic American clipper ship. She enthralled everyone who ever saw her sleek hull, her deeply arched bow, her acres of canvas swelling above her decks. She was born in America at a time when England's merchant fleet dominated world trade, and while this uniquely American beauty reigned for only a short while, she wrested control of the seas from Great Britain, ignited a roaring prosperity, and gave surging America another reason to throw out its chest and brag, "We're Number One."

Henry Wadsworth Longfellow was so enchanted with the clipper that he spent months composing a poem, "The Making of a Ship." He was one of the notables on hand in Boston on April 15, 1851, when Donald McKay, 19th-century America's greatest shipbuilder, launched the largest clipper ever built up until then, the *Flying Cloud.*

Donald McKay's vision of harnessing the wind was realized in the sleek, racy clippers he designed.

In the poem, Longfellow called McKay the "Master Builder." Others called him the "Leonardo of the Clip-

McKay's Flying Cloud, *canvas billowing "New York style," raced from New York to San Francisco's gold fields in 89 days in 1851, beating the time of McKay's first clipper, the* Stag Horn, *by 20 days.*

per," but such praise made the unpretentious McKay squirm. He always insisted he was a "mere mechanic."

Born in Nova Scotia, McKay was a poor farm boy whose family sent him to New York in 1826, at the age of 16, with the hope that he would be the means of providing a better future for them. He became a laborer at the East River shipyard of Webb and Allen and made such a good impression that the company offered to make him an apprentice in shipbuilding. Thus he became indentured for five years, bound to work a 12-hour day, six days a week, for $2.50 a week and a new set of clothes each year.

After his apprenticeship, McKay found work at a nearby yard as a full-fledged shipwright, earning a decent salary as a member of a respected profession. He also met and married a genuine jewel, an amazing young lady named Albenia Martha Boole, the daughter of a prominent shipbuilder. Miss Albenia

Martha knew the shipbuilding business from stem to stern and spent many evenings teaching her husband the mathematics and engineering his limited education had denied him.

Donald McKay quickly made a name for himself, and by the age of 34, he had his own shipyard in East Boston. With the expansion of world trade and the huge requirements of the California gold rush, American shipowners were demanding ever-faster vessels. Thanks to innovative, audacious designers such as McKay, the result was the fabled clipper. Though her narrow hull reduced cargo and passenger space, and the enormous amount of sail required a large crew, the clipper was far superior to the plodding steam-driven cargo ship.

The clipper's fuel was the wind. It was free, but it was fickle. Old-time captains shortened sail in a hurry when winds became gale force, but not the clipper captains. The stronger the gale, the more the sail. They would push their ships down faraway coasts, with sails shrieking and hulls squealing — their reckless drive becoming known as "carrying sail New York style."

McKay's first clipper, the *Stag Horn,* cost her Boston owners $70,000. She sailed from New York in December 1850 and reached San Francisco 109 days later, showing a profit of $85,000. Ten months to the day, having circumnavigated the globe, she was back in New York, her decks loaded with tea. When the cargo was sold, the jubilant owners calculated that the marvelous ship had not only paid the cost of her construction, but had made a net profit of $90,000.

McKay's clippers became the talk of the shipping industry. When the *Flying Cloud* sailed from New York in June 1851, history was in the making. While conventional ships were averaging 159 days for the trip to San Francisco, the clipper flew into the Golden Gate in 89 days, 8 hours. (That record would be broken only once by a sailing ship — when the *Flying Cloud* herself cut 13 hours from the time.) She then sailed for China, loaded up with tea, and came racing home to New York, smashing 20 days off the record. The city went wild as the great clipper sailed into the harbor.

McKay, his reputation established, expanded his yard, hired more workers, and built even bigger and faster ships. There was *Lightning,* which crossed a storm-tossed North Atlantic from Boston to Liverpool in 14 days, during which she logged an incredible 436 miles in 24 hours, still a record for a sailing ship. There was the *Great Republic,* which carried 16,000 yards of white cotton duck, which today would cover a two-lane highway for over a mile. Americans who saw that mammoth white ship roaring up from the south with a screaming gale behind her never

forgot the sight. There was the *Flying Fish,* which flew around the Horn in an unheard-of seven days. There were over a hundred others. Some historians claim McKay built 120 clippers.

But black clouds were forming. Competing yards meant smaller profits, a financial "panic" dried up orders, and iron steamships, profiting from McKay's radical designs and engineering technology, had made tremendous advances. By 1859 the wooden clipper's short but glorious reign was over, and McKay, holding out to the last, was finally forced to close his yard in 1869.

His lovely ships changed America from a net importing to a net exporting country, but more than that, as historian Samuel Eliot Morison wrote, "Never in these United States has the brain of man conceived, or the hand of man fashioned, so perfect a thing as the clipper ship."

BARBARA McCLINTOCK
Pioneer Geneticist
(1902-1992)

It takes an enormous amount of courage for someone who is preeminent in a particular field, respected and admired by his or her peers, to come forth with a revolutionary new theory, one that contradicts a belief held sacred for many years. History has shown that rough times await those who announce that a fundamental axiom is false.

Martin Luther had the right idea. He nailed his 95 theses on the door of the castle church in Wittenberg, then headed for the hills. Others, like Galileo, barely escaped the Inquisition. No human being likes to have his basic beliefs challenged, and scientists, in particular, do

By studying patterns of corn kernel coloration, Dr. Barbara McClintock set genetics research on its ear.

not like to be told they have been worshipping at the wrong shrine.

It is July 1951 at a place called Cold Spring Harbor on Long Island, and eminent biologists from around the world have gathered at the Long Island Biological Laboratories for the annual Cold Harbor symposium on the latest developments in the field of genetics. Forty-nine-year-old Barbara McClintock is about to address the gathering. Engaged in genetic research since the 1930s, inducted into the National Academy of Sciences in 1944, elected president of the Genetics Society in 1945, she has published dozens of papers on the function of chromosomes as the basis for heredity and has begun to be compared to both Gregor Mendel and Thomas Hunt Morgan as the most influential person in the history of genetics.

Dr. McClintock is about to drop a

bombshell. Years of diligent research have given her the confidence necessary to stand before her colleagues and tell them that the basic dogma of genetics, that genes "are as permanently ordered on the chromosome as are pearls on a necklace," is all wrong. Segments of DNA — the molecular basis for heredity — purposefully, not randomly as the theory of evolution holds, move around (Dr. McClintock's term is "jumping genes"), deliberately inserting themselves into genetic material and altering it.

A private person, a loner, Dr. McClintock is somewhat apprehensive as she finishes her monumental talk; she anticipates wild applause and hopes for a muted response. "Muted" is hardly the word. Dead silence reigns. Not one of the brilliant scientists has understood. What in the world does this woman mean by "jumping genes — transposable elements?" Later, there are snickers. The old girl has finally gone over the edge.

"The old girl," Barbara McClintock, was born on June 16, 1902, in Hartford, Connecticut, the third of four children born to a young physician, whose parents were English immigrants, and his wife, who came from old Yankee stock. Her mother had a hard time coping with four children and limited finances, so Barbara was sent to live with a paternal uncle and aunt in Massachusetts, years she always remembered as "wonderfully enjoyable." When she finally rejoined her family after they moved to New York, relations with her mother remained distant, and although she excelled scholastically, she made few friends. All her life she was to remain a solitary person.

Against her mother's wishes, but with the tacit approval of her father, Barbara enrolled in Cornell University in 1919, hoping to study plant breeding. But the university was not yet ready to allow women to enter such a specialized field. Instead she took botany and was so outstanding that by her junior year, she was allowed to take genetics courses and work with Cornell's noted researchers.

After receiving her Ph.D. in 1927, Barbara remained at Cornell as a research associate in plant breeding. Corn was the organism she used for the study of plant genetics, and she discovered that chromosomes not only break, but also recombine to create genetic changes. With these and other discoveries, she became well known in her field, and after serving as assistant professor at the University of Missouri, she was wooed by the Carnegie Institute in 1941 to the research facility at Cold Spring Harbor. There she would remain for over 50 years.

Dr. McClintock continued her work with corn, studying the patterns of coloration in the kernels over generations of carefully controlled crosses. Slowly, over the years, it became apparent to her that, contrary to all she had learned, sometimes a piece of genetic material would break free, deliberately inserting itself into the pigment gene. Working alone, without even a telephone, she gathered an enormous amount of data, forcing her to the revolutionary conclusion that genetic material is not fixed, but moves at will. She initially postponed announcing her discovery, but by the 1951 symposium she had decided that by withholding her knowledge, she was permitting the whole field of genetics to continue on the wrong course.

The cruel rejection of her theory made Barbara McClintock even more reclusive, but after further tests continued to vindicate her findings, she made one more attempt to reach her colleagues by publishing an article in as simple a language as the complicated science permitted, explaining that "jumping genes," or "transposons," are DNA segments that can change location, affecting the genetic code. She concluded by stating that heredity is much more complicated than previously believed. Although the journal went to several thousand subscribers in her field, she received exactly three requests for reprints. That did it. She retreated further into her shell, growing more eccentric — but she continued to work, alone. "I knew I was right," she said later.

Then a new science, molecular biology, evolved. And in the transition from classical to molecular genetics, the biologists found mounting evidence that Barbara McClintock was right; genes move, cause deletions, translocations, inversions. Exactly what she had said in the 1951 symposium.

Honors and prizes descended on her. Israel's Wolf Prize in Medicine, the Albert Lasker Basic Medical Research Award, the MacArthur Laureate Award — all in 1981; then in 1983, the Nobel Prize in Physiology and Medicine. She became the first woman to win an unshared prize in this category and only the third woman to win an unshared Nobel prize.

When Barbara McClintock died in September 1992, at the age of 90, eulogies came from all over the world. Today's ever-expanding genetics industry, with breakthroughs in all phases of life, owes her a tremendous debt. Perhaps credit must also go to a "jumping gene" that broke away from the DNA in 1902, changing what might have become a dutiful, reclusive daughter to a brilliant, dedicated, courageous scientist.

ALBERT GALLATIN
A Most Astonishing Man
(1761-1849)

Sometime in 1783, 47-year-old Patrick Henry, just elected to his second term as governor of Virginia, met 22-year-old Albert Gallatin, an impecunious land speculator who was attempting to buy 120,000 acres in western Virginia. Henry had encountered dozens of similar chaps and was not easily fooled. When, after this meet-

During his years of public service, Gallatin was able to put his democratic ideals into practice.

— courtesy Independence National Historical Park

ing, Henry announced, "I have just met a most astonishing man," one can only conclude that even then, young Gallatin was an unusual person.

He was born in Geneva, Switzerland, in 1761, to an aristocratic family. Even as a boy Gallatin was an independent thinker, and by the time he graduated with honors from Geneva University, he had become imbued with the philosophy of Jean Jacques Rousseau, which stated that all conflict was due to the unnatural distribution of power and wealth, that modern society (this was the mid-18th century) had corrupted the "noble savage," and that mankind must return to the rural life and live harmoniously with nature.

Afire with these tenets, Gallatin refused command of mercenary troops being raised to fight the rebellious American colonists, fleeing instead to America in 1780. He headed for rural Maine, but nature in the raw soon sent him scurrying back to Boston. Only slightly disillusioned — he would remain a practical, commonsense Rousseauian all of his life — Gallatin managed to secure a position at Harvard, and there he was remembered as a brilliant, refined, sensitive individual who delighted in spirited discussions of complex subjects.

After Harvard, Gallatin was hired as interpreter and minority partner by a French land speculator and eventually ended up with a large tract of land in what is now Fayette County, Pennsylvania, just north of the West Virginia line. There he built a large house, Friendship Hill, and later a store, glass factory, sawmill, gristmill, even an ammunition plant, while continuing to engage in land speculation. His home became a meeting place for the backwoods settlers, and his extraordinary talents made him the logical person to represent the area at the September 1788 conference held in Harrisburg, Pennsylvania, for the purpose of revising the United States Constitution.

Gallatin proved to be the most outspoken delegate against the granting of strong powers to the federal government. He proposed amendments for the strict limitation of Congress's powers, for giving rural areas equal representation with urban areas, and for the election of Con-

gressmen by the voters, but his unortho-
dox suggestions were voted down.

That did not change Gallatin, still
seething with concern for the common
man. After the death of his young wife,
while still in mourning, he represented the
backwoods voters at the 1789-1790 convention called to discuss changes in the
Pennsylvania Constitution. Again he dominated the proceedings, presenting brilliant arguments in favor of universal suf-
frage, universal education, reduction of
the state debt, and an improved judiciary.
In October 1790, he was elected to the
state legislature and was reelected the next
two years. Of his numerous accomplishments, the main one was his unrelenting
insistence that Pennsylvania live within
its means, pushing through legislation that
put the state on a sound financial basis.

In 1793 a new United States senator
was chosen by the state legislature. Although the legislature was dominated by
the Federalist party, Gallatin, a Democ-
ratic-Republican, was overwhelmingly
elected. But the Federalists, supporters of
a strong central government, saw a formidable threat in the young "states
rights" advocate from Pennsylvania and
voted to deny Gallatin his seat on the
grounds that he was not yet an American
citizen. Ever the gentleman, Gallatin
took his defeat gracefully, and he and his
second wife returned to Friendship Hill.

Meanwhile, turmoil had broken out.
Congress, in the winter of 1791, passed a
bill taxing all distilled spirits. Whiskey was
big business in the western counties of all
the states south of New York, and almost
every farmer had a distillery. Violence
erupted, tax collectors were attacked —
the new nation was on the verge of collapse. President George Washington
called out the militia.

History has recorded that Albert Gallatin prevented the outbreak of civil war

in western Pennsylvania, holding meetings with the leaders of the rebellion, ar-
guing against violence, and urging mod-
eration. His common sense prevailed, and
by the time the federal troops reached
the hinterlands the rebellion was over.

A hero now, Gallatin was elected to
the House of Representatives in 1795.
He served three terms, during which he
created and chaired the still-powerful
Ways and Means Committee. He also
became Minority Leader and was so successful in thwarting the persistent assaults
of the Federalists on the federal budget
that when Jefferson was elected president, he made Gallatin his Secretary of
the Treasury in 1801.

His first priority was the national debt,
regarding any refusal to pay it as "a fla-
grant and pernicious break of public faith
and national morality." He halved the
army and navy budgets and demanded all
government departments operate as if
"they were spending their own money."
Jefferson, and later Madison, came to depend on Gallatin's judgment in all matters.

Gallatin was Treasury secretary for 12
years, longer than anyone else. During
that time he halved the debt and financed
the Louisiana Purchase, the war with the
Barbary pirates, the Cumberland Road,
and many other internal projects.

After his retirement from Treasury, he
drew up the treaty ending the War of 1812,
and became Minister to France and later
to England. His accomplishments in the
world of diplomacy were as remarkable
as his domestic achievements. At the age
of 68, Gallatin retired from public service,
and he and his wife moved to New York.
There he became president of the National Bank of New York. He also was in-
strumental in founding the University of
New York and was elected president of
the New York Historical Society.

This astonishing man was active until

his death in 1849 at the age of 88. Besides authoring many articles, he produced a mammoth book on American Indian tribes, which attracted so much attention he became known as "the Father of American ethnology." Gallatin ranks with Washington, Jefferson, and Madison as savior, guardian, and leader of the struggling little country. Without such brilliant men, America might not have survived the monumental problems that confronted it during its uncertain beginning.

WILLIAM F. ALLEN
Father of Standard Time
(1846-1915)

P rior to Sunday, November 18, 1883, "the day of two noons," an anxious out-of-towner arriving in Pittsburgh for an important 1:45 P.M. appointment had better be

William Allen made order from chaos with his system of Standard Time and time zones.

certain he knew what that particular 1:45 P.M. Pittsburgh time meant. Back then, the city, its six railroads, and the Allegheny Observatory each observed its own time, with a variance of as much as 22 minutes. But this was simplicity compared with other places. In 1882 the *Chicago Tribune* listed 27 local times in Michigan, 38 in Wisconsin, and 27 in Illinois. Prior to 1883 the railroads alone used 101 different times.

Time was fought over as if it were a precious commodity, every town and railroad insisting that theirs was the correct reckoning. People missed train connections, million-dollar deals collapsed, grooms were late for their weddings. Even the law ran into trouble: one apocryphal anecdote recounted the sad tale of an execution performed at Sing Sing because the governor of New York, operating on Albany's time, was too late with the reprieve.

That kind of confusion didn't mean too much in the early days of the Republic, but with the advent of the Industrial Revolution, life speeded up and chaos soon prevailed. Something had to be done. Some brave fellow had to come forward and straighten out the mess. Someone did. His name was William Frederick Allen.

Allen was born in New Jersey in 1846, the son of a railroad official. After receiving an excellent education, he began his engineering experience with the railroads, becoming resident engineer of the West Jersey Railroad at age 22, a tenure that brought him widespread recognition in the industry.

The railroads — there were at least 250 — had begun to realize that some sort of order was overdue. Shippers and passengers were becoming incensed at the complicated timetables and the confusion and inconvenience that resulted.

Railroads cooperated in bringing forth the *Official Railway Guide,* and William Allen was chosen to shape and edit the complicated book. Soon to become known as the "Railroad Man's Bible," the publication would eventually contain over 1,600 pages, and even today is the standard reference book in the industry.

All the while, there had been agitation from many sources for a complete overhaul of the confusing time system, and in 1875 Allen was made secretary of the General Time Convention, charged with the responsibility of creating a standard time for the entire nation. Even before Allen began his work on the vexing problem, there had been unsuccessful efforts by a number of others — mainly by Samuel Langley (the future Secretary of the Smithsonian Institution) and Charles F. Dowd. Allen was well aware of the monumental task confronting him. Things had become so complicated that a bewildered traveler journeying from Boston to San Francisco was forced to change his watch 21 times! And life in the cities was just as vexing, the time difference between Chicago's Loop and western suburbs being 67 seconds.

But many vested interests opposed standardization. In addition to sundial, clock, and watch manufacturers, each town of consequence had its "Time Ball" system — a sacred institution. Each day at official noon for that location, a rubber ball was dropped from a high mast. As it fell, all townsfolk adjusted their timepieces to noon. Many protested the assault on such hallowed practices. Boston was outraged, word having leaked out that it would have to share the same time as backwoods West Virginia.

The farmers, particularly in the West, were furious, condemning the plan as but one more infamous trick of the railroads to keep them in debt. Opposition from the clergy was almost unanimous, pulpits thundering with fiery sermons denouncing "this blasphemous tampering with God's time, the Sun."

Poor Allen! He had expected some mild opposition, but not this firestorm. However, never one to shirk responsibility, he embarked on an arduous campaign to explain the need for standard time. It lasted eight long years.

He enlisted universities in the cause, prevailing on academics to write articles in defense of standard time; he lectured before all sorts of groups; he addressed city and town councils. He held symposiums. He took great pains to make himself available to the press. He made headway. But just when it would seem that he had persuaded a city to the cause, a dissenting voice would be heard, someone would have second thoughts.

Back and forth went Allen — every railroad had him as a passenger — explaining, persuading, calm, always polite, lining up new recruits, rushing back and forth over the miles to put out smoldering embers that he had long thought extinguished.

Finally, opposition crumbled (not all — some diehards never did change). Elated, Allen presented two maps to the General and Southern Railway Time Conventions in 1883. One depicted 50 different local railroad times, the other, in four colors, represented zones corresponding to Greenwich meridians — today's Eastern, Central, Mountain, and Pacific time zones. The second map was unanimously adopted.

Ironically, the Allegheny Observatory in smoky Pittsburgh was the institution chosen to provide the new time because its director, Samuel Langley, had been transmitting telegraphic time from there to the Pennsylvania Railroad for years. The day chosen was November 18,

1883, which became known as "the day of two noons." In the eastern part of each time zone came the noon based on Sun time. Then, clocks and watches were set back from one to 30 minutes when the new Standard Time reached twelve o'clock. Predictions that all sorts of dire happenings would occur proved groundless. It went without a hitch. In fact, Standard Time proved to be so successful in the United States that it soon expanded to create time zones throughout the world.

William Allen remained active in railroad and scientific circles until his death in 1915. The "Father of Standard Time" was praised as "a man of great ability, possessed of a forceful but amiable character which endeared him to all who knew him."

JANE ADDAMS
Humanitarian
(1860-1935)

I n 1874 a dire prediction regarding young women who aspired to higher education was issued by no less an authority than Dr. Edward H. Clarke, a professor at Harvard Medical School. In his book, *Sex in Education,* Dr. Clarke pontificated that college would have a deleterious effect on women's delicate anatomy; it might even disable their reproductive faculties.

It is doubtful that the young ladies at the Rockford Female Seminary in Illinois would have known of

Dr. Clarke and his pronouncement, but if they had, they probably would have giggled, although perhaps with an inward uncertainty. Still, whatever the hazards, many women were eager to further their education and compete with men in the workaday world. Jane Addams was one of those pioneers.

Jane was born September 6, 1860, to a wealthy family in Cedarville, Illinois. By the time she entered Rockford Female Seminary in 1877, she had received the usual formal education in the local school, supplemented in the cultural aspects of life by her socially conscious stepmother. She had also devoured the entire circulating library of Cedarville — not a tough task since it operated out of the Addams home.

The four-year seminary taught the Bible, Greek, Latin, domestic science, and a smattering of mathematics and science. Daily chapel was mandatory. The young ladies were exhorted to remain pure, pious, and morally superior — noble sentiments but poor preparation for the real world. Jane graduated in 1881 at the top of her class. In her valedictory address, she stressed that "woman's mind must grow strong and intelligible by the thorough study of science . . . and must pass from . . . the arts of pleasing to the development of her capabilities for direct labor."

The graduates ap-

– Sophia Smith Collection, Smith College

Jane Addams's vision led first to Hull House and broadened to a crusade for social reform.

plauded enthusiastically. They didn't plan to be pampered butterflies, fluttering aimlessly through life. Marriage? Later. First they were going to have careers, using their brains and education, "become somebody," as Jane Addams later wrote.

Alas, reality came quickly. Jane Addams and her colleagues found their liberal education had prepared them for opportunities that didn't exist. Grade-school teaching was about all that was available.

Unhappy, disillusioned, Jane spent several miserable years drifting aimlessly. Not wishing to teach, she thought a career in medicine might be the answer, but one year at a medical college in Pennsylvania proved otherwise. After undergoing an operation to correct a spinal curvature, she was bedridden for six months and spent two years in a monstrous steel contraption, suffering from chronic exhaustion and nervous prostration. She wrote Ellen Starr, a college classmate, that "I am a failure in every sense. I have constantly lost confidence in myself, have gained nothing, improved in nothing."

Her condition became so serious her alarmed stepmother took her off to Europe for a dose of "culture." This helped for awhile, but once back home, Jane relapsed into futility and despair.

Then, in 1887, she and Ellen Starr decided that another trip abroad might somehow show the way. It did. They found the answer in London's squalid East End where a group of Oxford men, appalled at the suffering brought on by exploding industrialization, had established Toynbee Hall, the world's first settlement house. The women were inspired. They raced home, avidly discussing plans for a similar institution. They felt Chicago was the logical choice for a site since its slums were equal, if not superior, to those of London!

With Jane providing the money, they rented a huge abandoned mansion once owned by a wealthy real estate speculator named Charles J. Hull. It took awhile to clean up the place, but on September 18, 1889, the doors of Hull House opened. At long last Jane Addams had found her niche.

At first Jane and Ellen, with the help of volunteers, provided food, shelter, and literary readings. Gradually the focus changed. Kindergartens were established, English classes and classes in cooking, carpentry, mechanical drawing, and nursing were begun. As immigrant women found sweatshop jobs, a day nursery was established; a gymnasium was built. More buildings were rented. Hull House became an enormous operation.

A visitor described it as a "salon of democracy, filled with a procession of fruit vendors, university professors, club women, washerwomen . . . all sorts and conditions of men and women." It could easily have foundered under the well-meaning but inexperienced management of Jane Addams and her staff of naive do-gooders.

But it didn't founder. Slowly, gaining confidence from each new crisis, Jane became a superb administrator, an expert fund-raiser, and a calm, smiling inspiration to all involved in Hull House.

The fame of the settlement house brought a new breed of female "do-gooder" to Chicago. Outspoken and confident, these women soon convinced Jane that her efforts were little more than stopgaps and that the real problems — child labor, women's rights, housing, educational reform, universal medical care, the eight-hour day, workmen's compensation — must be addressed. Jane became a crusader and reformer, fighting for these and other issues — factory safety, minimum wage, the vote for women.

By early this century Jane Addams

was a national heroine. A leading suffragist as well as a mighty force against injustice, she also campaigned against war and prior to World War I was elected president of the International Women's Peace Party. Even when the United States entered the war, she refused to support the war effort and came under vicious attack.

Undeterred, she continued to decry war and in 1931 was awarded the Nobel Peace Prize (sharing it with Nicholas Murray Butler). Her antiwar efforts were gradually forgotten, overshadowed by her monumental accomplishments on behalf of the downtrodden.

Jane Addams, who had wailed that she was "a failure in every sense," died at the age of 74 in 1935. She was mourned by millions, and in over 400 settlement houses across the country, memorials were held in her honor. In 1993 the National Women's Hall of Fame elected her one of the ten most influential women of the 20th century, second only to Eleanor Roosevelt.

One wishes Dr. Edward H. Clarke could have been listening.

GIFFORD PINCHOT
Pragmatic Conservationist
(1865-1946)

L ong before the spotted owl made its appearance on the six o'clock news as the unintentional cause célèbre between the environmentalists and the Northwest lumber industry, the fight to save America's forests had been raging for years. Back then, though, the owl would have been in real trouble, for even such a dedicated conservationist as Gifford Pinchot, the U. S. Forest Service's first chief, would have sided with the lumber industry.

Pinchot's insistence on scientific forest management and conservation led to the creation of the U.S. Forest Service.

Pinchot, who time and again insisted that America's forests should be used for the "greatest good of the greatest number in the long run," who fought the lumber companies' cut-and-run practices, was firmly against having the forests "taken out of circulation and locked up." Nevertheless, all living species — spotted owls, gray wolves, human beings — owe a tremendous debt to Gifford Pinchot. He saved our magnificent forests.

For generations Americans had regarded our natural resources, especially our forests, as inexhaustible. People felt there could never be a shortage of anything, particularly land and trees. But by the end of the 19th century, New England and the northeastern states were denuded and Wisconsin and Minnesota were losing forests at the rate of a township a week. With the consequent degradation of the land and rivers and the destruction of habitats, voices were finally raised in alarm.

The loudest voice was that of Gifford Pinchot, scion of the rich. Once steeped in laissez-faire Republicanism, the 25-year-old had returned to America in 1890 after a year studying silviculture in Europe. Pinchot wrote: "The American Colossus is fiercely intent on exploiting . . . the richest of all continents . . . reaping where he had not sown, wasting what he thought would last forever."

Gifford Pinchot was born into great wealth on August 11, 1865, in Simsbury, Connecticut. He was raised in luxury, and it was at one of the family's vacation homes in the Adirondacks where the boy experienced his first taste of the beauty and majesty of the forest. Following the family tradition, he attended Phillips Exeter Academy and Yale, and it was at the latter that he decided, at his father's suggestion, to study forestry. (Perhaps a guilty conscience gnawed at the elder Pinchot, since *his* father had made a fortune cutting down half the oak, elm, and chestnut trees of eastern Pennsylvania.) However, since there was no forestry school at Yale (nor at any other American university), Gifford studied meteorology, geology, and astronomy "because science underlies the forester's knowledge of the woods."

With his father's encouragement, he went to Europe after graduation, studying under famous foresters in France, Germany, and Switzerland. He witnessed European conservation, which found a use for pencil-sized scraps of wood, and returned to America imbued with a messianic drive to save its forests.

This was 1890, when magnificent stands of oak or chestnut could be bought for $2.50 an acre; when millions of acres of western timberland had been given to the railroads. One, Northern Pacific, had received from the government timberlands exceeding the combined areas of Pennsylvania, New York, New Jersey, and Rhode Island. These beautiful tracts were being decimated at a hideous rate, resulting, east of the Mississippi, in massive soil erosion.

Pinchot became a forestry consultant, devoting himself to writing and lecturing. His first job came through his friendship with Frederick Law Olmsted, the famous landscape architect, who was creating a massive estate, Biltmore, for George W. Vanderbilt near Asheville, North Carolina. Pinchot's work at Biltmore brought other contracts. He prepared forestry management plans for privately owned tracts, and in 1898 he was appointed head of the U. S. Forest Reserve. His first effort at the Reserve was to lobby to have the division transferred from Interior to the Department of Agriculture, but it was not until Theodore Roosevelt became president in 1901 that he was able to effect the transfer.

Roosevelt, who had done more than his share in depleting the world's big game herds, had become an ardent arboreal conservationist, upset at the timber industry for devastating the big-game habitats. He and Pinchot were old friends, and he agreed wholeheartedly with him that the federal government had been woefully negligent in protecting public lands. Against bitter opposition, Roosevelt pushed a bill through Congress, transferring all the lands to the Agriculture Department under a new office — the U. S. Forest Service. Gifford Pinchot became the nation's first Chief Forester.

He inherited a mess. With few employees and a meager budget, the department's chief function was to rubber-stamp the demands of the private timber companies. Pinchot changed things in a hurry, hiring competent people with authority to get things done and inaugurating programs for cooperative forest management; with Roosevelt's cooperation, he had millions of acres brought back under federal control. He publicized the need for forest conservation, established fire-fighting facilities, and constantly preached "tree farming" to the timber companies. His watchword, "Conservation," to him meant "wise use" of the forests.

Pinchot was Chief Forester only five years. He disagreed with the new president, Taft, and outraged Republicans, who felt he was a traitor to his party. When Pinchot accused the Interior Secretary of fraudulent deals with private business interests over Alaskan public lands, he was fired.

Gifford Pinchot later served (1923-1927, 1933-1935) as governor of Pennsylvania, a tenure marked by his commitment to protecting the state's forests and for construction of the famous "Pinchot roads," paved roads in rural areas that brought the farmer out of the mud.

Pinchot's utilitarian conservationism (and impatience with starry-eyed preservationists, including John Muir) would be anathema to many of today's environmentalists. If he were alive today, the more belligerent might be tempted to hang him from the nearest Douglas fir — forgetting that if it were not for Gifford Pinchot, there might not be a Douglas fir.

Stephen Collins Foster

America's Troubadour

(1826-1864)

It is late July 1850 on the Oregon Trail, somewhere on the high plains between Independence Rock and South Pass. Far off, beyond the Wind River Mountains, the twilight sky is ablaze with color, but very few of the emigrants in the wagon train can admire the display. It has been another arduous day and the train is behind schedule. Finally night comes, and supper over and campfires glowing, someone brings out a banjo. Soon the tired voices are raised in song and the immense emptiness rings with the strains of: "Oh! Susanna, do not cry for me/ I come from Alabama wid my banjo on my knee."

At the same time, far on the other side of the world, in a waterfront bar in Canton, China, a rowdy crew from a Boston tea clipper is belting out "Oh! Susanna," and soon they are joined by other disreputable denizens.

A New York newspaperman reported in 1850 that he had heard the song sung by a Hindu in Delhi, an Arab in North Africa, and whistled by a chestnut vendor in Paris. One Indiana mother walking the Oregon Trail wrote in her diary: "'Oh! Susanna' kept us going, no matter what." However, there is no evidence to support the oft-told story that the coyotes along the trail joined in the nightly campfire sing-alongs. (There were a lot of wild tales along the Oregon Trail.)

The composer of "Oh! Susanna," Stephen Collins Foster, was born on July 4, 1826, in Lawrenceville, now part of Pittsburgh, Pennsylvania, the ninth of 12 children. Stephen's boyhood was idyllic, but he did not appear to show much aptitude for business, preferring to stay

Great Americans Hall of Fame

black-face minstrel shows, which he sold for $50 apiece. Then "Oh! Susanna," which had become popular in Pittsburgh, was picked up by the famous Christy Minstrels and became the rage of the music halls. Foster sold the rights to the song for $100 and rushed back to Pittsburgh to write more: "Camptown Races," "Dolly Day," "Ring de Banjo," and others. In 1852, now with a wife and daughter, Foster joined friends for a month's voyage to New Orleans. This would be the only time he would visit the South, of which he wrote so feelingly.

With "Oh! Susanna" sweeping the country (although Foster had only earned $100 for it), he was contacted by a prominent New York publishing company, Firth and Pond. A contract was signed and the company would eventually publish over 80 of Foster's songs, including "My Old Kentucky Home," "Swanee River," "Old Folks at Home," "Laura Lee," and "Gentle Annie." All were noteworthy not only for their musical content but also for the gradual elimination of the black dialect, so prominent in all the minstrelsy dominating the times. In fact, the "Nelly" of "Nelly Was a Lady" is a slave who dies of a broken heart when her husband is sold to a faraway plantation. The theme was revolutionary and belies the prevalent belief that Foster favored slavery and that his songs made fun of poor, ignorant black people. While he did initially imitate the comical songs of the Christy Minstrels, as early as 1848 his "Uncle Ned" was a poignant requiem for an old, faithful slave who dies in the cotton field with no possessions, but finds peace in heaven among the angels.

Foster's knowledge of black people came from the fact that Pittsburgh was a stop on the Underground Railroad and that, in good times, his family had "bound

Foster's musical gift was his ability to combine haunting melody with simple, heartfelt lyrics.

home and scribble down songs. In 1845 he joined with other young men in the neighborhood to form "The Knights of the Square Table," meeting each week to write verse, sing songs, and put on plays. Soon they were joined by the neighborhood girls, and Stephen was in his element, dashing off songs for the Knights to serenade the belles. ("Oh! Susanna" was dedicated to one of the young ladies, but later in life she sternly denied any romantic connection.) In time his songs were sung all over Pittsburgh.

The family fortunes having taken a nosedive, Stephen had to join his brothers in Cincinnati and start work as a bookkeeper. However, he continued to publish songs, mostly "plantation type," similar to those sung in the popular

264   OLD FARMER'S ALMANAC   1994

servants." He also learned much from the many southern travelers who visited the city. He was a decent man, torn between his family's philosophy of states' rights and anti-abolitionism, and his humanitarian feelings for the downtrodden blacks. His songs of the South were more of a yearning for the "Good Old Days" that never existed, instead of comical songs designed purely to make money.

"Jeanie with the Light Brown Hair," one of Foster's loveliest ballads, was written in honor of his wife, Jane, but he was far from a perfect husband, and the couple separated. He moved to New York to be close to his publisher, who promoted him aggressively and paid him well, but eventually Foster asked to be released from his contract, feeling he could do better on his own.

It proved to be a bad move. Not only had Foster begun to drink heavily, but the country was plunged into a severe depression, and sheet music sales collapsed. His "serious" songs, born of his aspirations to reach classical music heights, were unsuccessful. He found temporary solace in the companionship of a friend, George Cooper, who not only encouraged him to go back to the old ways of songwriting, but also helped with the words. Together they wrote 21 songs.

On a cold January day in 1864, Foster fell in his hotel room, the result of undernourishment and alcohol abuse. Cooper rushed him to Bellevue Hospital where he died, never regaining consciousness. His pockets contained a few cents and some scraps of wrapping paper on which he'd scribbled words and music. When the scribblings were deciphered and published, there emerged his last song, "Beautiful Dreamer." Like most of his 280 songs, it has endured through the years, its haunting beauty still tugging at the heart.

Foster is unique in that his words blended so perfectly with his music. His songs are still sung all over the world. Thousands come to the University of Pittsburgh's Stephen Foster Memorial, the only museum devoted to an American composer. They come, anxious to pay their respects to our country's first songwriter, "America's Troubadour."

□□

This year's nominees to The Old Farmer's Almanac
Great Americans Hall of Fame join this illustrious company:

Johnny Appleseed	Rachel Carson	Emily Post
Francis Asbury	Emily Dickinson	Henry Martyn Robert
Benjamin Banneker	Duke Ellington	Knute Rockne
Irving Berlin	Fanny Farmer	Margaret Sanger
Mary McLeod Bethune	Joseph Glidden	Samuel Slater
Clarence Birdseye	Mother Jones	Noah Webster
Nathaniel Bowditch	Chief Joseph	Paul Dudley White
Mathew Brady	Mary Lyon	John Greenleaf Whittier
Luther Burbank	George Mowbray	

Useful Year-Round

Time Zones and Area Codes

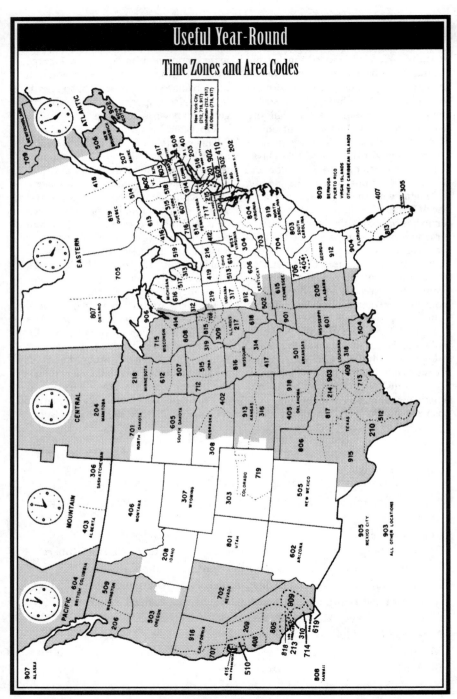

Abbreviations approved by the U.S. Postal Service to be used in addressing mail.

Alley	Aly.
Arcade	Arc.
Avenue	Ave.
Boulevard	Blvd.
Branch	Br.
Bypass	Byp.
Causeway	Cswy.
Center	Ctr.
Circle	Cir.
Court	Ct.
Courts	Cts.
Crescent	Cres.
Drive	Dr.
Estates	Est.
Expressway	Expy.
Extension	Ext.
Freeway	Fwy.
Gardens	Gdns.
Grove	Grv.
Heights	Hts.
Highway	Hwy.
Lane	Ln.
Manor	Mnr.
Place	Pl.
Plaza	Plz.
Point	Pt.
Road	Rd.
Rural	R.
Square	Sq.
Street	St.
Terrace	Ter.
Trail	Trl.
Turnpike	Tpke.
Viaduct	Via.
Vista	Vis.

U.S. Postage Rates

Single-Piece Letter Rates

First ounce $0.29
Each additional
  ounce 0.23

For pieces not exceeding (oz.) — The rate is

For pieces not exceeding (oz.)	The rate is
1	$0.29
2	0.52
3	0.75
4	0.98
5	1.21
6	1.44
7	1.67
8	1.90
9	2.13
10	2.36
11	2.59

For pieces over 11 ounces consult postmaster.

Card Rates

Single postcards $0.19

Note: To qualify for card rates, a card may not be larger than 4¼ by 6 inches, nor smaller than 3½ by 5 inches. The thickness must be uniform and not less than 0.007 of an inch.

Size Standards for Domestic Mail

Minimum Size

Pieces that do not meet the following requirements are prohibited from the mails:

a. All pieces must be at least 0.007 inch thick.

b. All pieces (except keys and identification devices) that are ¼ inch or less in thickness must be:

1) Rectangular in shape,
2) At least 3½ inches high, and
3) At least 5 inches long

Note: Pieces greater than ¼ inch thick can be mailed even if they measure less than 3½ by 5 inches.

Nonstandard Mail

First-Class Mail, except Presort First-Class and carrier route First-Class, weighing one ounce or less, and all single-piece rate Third-Class Mail weighing one ounce or less, is nonstandard (and subject to a $0.10 surcharge in addition to the applicable postage and fees) if:

1) Any of the following dimensions are exceeded:

   Length — 11½ inches,
   Height — 6⅛ inches,
   Thickness — ¼ inch, or

2) The length divided by the height is not between 1.3 and 2.5, inclusive.

Useful Year-Round

International Postage Rates

Letters and Letter Packages

Weight not over	Canada	Mexico	All other countries	
	Airmail Rates			Surface Rates
0.5 ozs.	$0.40	$0.35	$0.50	$0.50
1	.40	.45	.95	.70
1.5	.63	.55	1.34	.95
2	.63	.65	1.73	.95
2.5	.86	.90	2.12	1.20
3	.86	.90	2.51	1.20
3.5	1.09	1.15	2.90	1.45
4	1.09	1.15	3.29	1.45
4.5	1.32	1.40	3.68	1.70
5	1.32	1.40	4.07	1.70
5.5	1.55	1.65	4.46	1.95
6	1.55	1.65	4.85	1.95

International Card Rates

Canada	$0.30
Mexico	$0.30
All other (surface)	$0.35
All other (airmail)	$0.40

Aerogrammes

$0.45 each

Table of Measures

Apothecaries'

1 scruple = 20 grains
1 dram = 3 scruples
1 ounce = 8 drams
1 pound = 12 ounces

Avoirdupois

1 ounce = 16 drams
1 pound = 16 ounces
1 hundredweight = 100 pounds
1 ton = 2,000 pounds
1 long ton = 2,240 pounds

Cubic Measure

1 cubic foot = 1,728 cubic inches
1 cubic yard = 27 cubic feet
1 cord = 128 cubic feet
1 U.S. liquid gallon = 4 quarts = 231 cubic inches
1 Imperial gallon = 1.20 U.S. gallons = 277.420 cubic inches
1 board foot = 144 cubic inches

Dry Measure

2 pints = 1 quart
4 quarts = 1 gallon
2 gallons = 1 peck
4 pecks = 1 bushel

Liquid Measure

4 gills = 1 pint
2 pints = 1 quart
4 quarts = 1 gallon
63 gallons = 1 hogshead
2 hogsheads = 1 pipe or butt
2 pipes = 1 tun

Linear Measure

1 foot = 12 inches
1 yard = 3 feet
1 rod = 5½ yards
1 mile = 320 rods = 1,760 yards = 5,280 feet
1 nautical mile = 6,076.1155 feet
1 knot = 1 nautical mile per hour
1 furlong = ⅛ mile = 660 feet = 220 yards

1 league = 3 miles = 24 furlongs
1 fathom = 2 yards = 6 feet
1 chain = 100 links = 22 yards
1 link = 7.92 inches
1 hand = 4 inches
1 span = 9 inches

Square Measure

1 square foot = 144 square inches
1 square yard = 9 square feet
1 square rod = 30¼ square yards = 272¼ square feet
1 acre = 160 square rods = 43,560 square feet
1 square mile = 640 acres = 102,400 square rods
1 square rod = 625 square links
1 square chain = 16 square rods
1 acre = 10 square chains

Household Measures

120 drops of water = 1 teaspoon

Useful Year-Round

What Should You Weigh?

Women (Medium Frame)		Men (Medium Frame)	
Height	Weight	Height	Weight
5' 0"	113 - 126 lbs.	5' 2"	131 - 141 lbs.
5' 2"	118 - 132 lbs.	5' 4"	135 - 145 lbs.
5' 4"	124 - 138 lbs.	5' 6"	139 - 151 lbs.
5' 6"	130 - 144 lbs.	5' 8"	145 - 157 lbs.
5' 8"	136 - 150 lbs.	5' 10"	151 - 163 lbs.
5' 10"	142 - 156 lbs.	6' 0"	157 - 170 lbs.
6' 0"	148 - 162 lbs.	6' 2"	164 - 178 lbs.

---

60 drops thick fluid = 1 teaspoon
2 teaspoons = 1 dessertspoon
3 teaspoons = 1 tablespoon
16 tablespoons = 1 cup
2 cups = 1 pint
2 pints = 1 quart
4 quarts = 1 gallon
3 tablespoons flour = 1 ounce
2 tablespoons butter = 1 ounce
2 cups granulated sugar = 1 pound
3¾ cups confectioners' sugar = 1 pound
2¾ cups brown sugar = 1 pound
3½ cups wheat flour = 1 pound
5⅓ cups dry coffee = 1 pound
4 cups cocoa = 1 pound
6½ cups dry tea = 1 pound
2 cups shortening = 1 pound
1 stick butter = ½ cup
3 cups cornmeal = 1 pound
2 tablespoons sugar = 1 ounce
2⅜ cups raisins = 1 pound
3½ cups walnuts (chopped) = 1 pound

9 eggs = 1 pound
8 egg whites = 1 cup
16 egg yolks = 1 cup
1 ounce yeast = 1 scant tablespoon
3 cups fresh, sliced peaches = 1 pound
60 pounds potatoes = 1 bushel
52 pounds onions = 1 bushel
24 pounds string beans = 1 bushel
56 pounds tomatoes = 1 bushel
55 pounds turnips = 1 bushel
54 pounds sweet potatoes = 1 bushel
45 pounds parsnips = 1 bushel
50 pounds carrots = 1 bushel
60 pounds beets = 1 bushel
60 pounds beans = 1 bushel
48 pounds apples = 1 bushel
196 pounds flour = 1 barrel

Metric

1 inch = 2.54 centimeters
1 centimeter = 0.39 inch
1 meter = 39.37 inches
1 yard = 0.914 meters
1 mile = 1,609.344 meters = 1.61 kilometers
1 kilometer = .62 mile
1 square inch = 6.45 square centimeters
1 square yard = 0.84 square meter
1 square mile = 2.59 square kilometers
1 square kilometer = 0.386 square mile
1 acre = 0.40 hectare
1 hectare = 2.47 acres
1 cubic yard = 0.76 cubic meter
1 cubic meter = 1.31 cubic yards
1 liter = 1.057 U.S. liquid quarts
1 U.S. liquid quart = 0.946 liter
1 U.S. liquid gallon = 3.78 liters
1 gram = 0.035 ounce
1 ounce = 28.349 grams
1 kilogram = 2.2 pounds
1 pound avoirdupois = 0.45 kilogram

States of the U.S.

State		State Nickname	Capital	Entered Union
Alabama	(AL)	Heart of Dixie State; Camellia State	Montgomery	Dec. 14, 1819
Alaska	(AK)	The Last Frontier State	Juneau	Jan. 3, 1959
Arizona	(AZ)	Grand Canyon State	Phoenix	Feb. 14, 1912
Arkansas	(AR)	Land of Opportunity State	Little Rock	June 15, 1836
California	(CA)	Golden State	Sacramento	Sept. 9, 1850
Colorado	(CO)	Centennial State	Denver	Aug. 1, 1876
Connecticut	(CT)	Nutmeg State; Constitution State	Hartford	Jan. 9, 1788
Delaware	(DE)	First State; Diamond State	Dover	Dec. 7, 1787
Florida	(FL)	Sunshine State	Tallahassee	Mar. 3, 1845
Georgia	(GA)	Peach State; Empire State of the South	Atlanta	Jan. 2, 1788
Hawaii	(HI)	Aloha State	Honolulu	Aug. 21, 1959
Idaho	(ID)	Gem State; Spud State	Boise	July 3, 1890
Illinois	(IL)	Prairie State	Springfield	Dec. 3, 1818
Indiana	(IN)	Hoosier State	Indianapolis	Dec. 11, 1816
Iowa	(IA)	Hawkeye State	Des Moines	Dec. 28, 1846
Kansas	(KS)	Sunflower State; Jayhawk State	Topeka	Jan. 29, 1861
Kentucky	(KY)	Bluegrass State	Frankfort	June 1, 1792
Louisiana	(LA)	Pelican State; Creole State	Baton Rouge	Apr. 30, 1812
Maine	(ME)	Pine Tree State	Augusta	Mar. 15, 1820
Maryland	(MD)	Old Line State; Free State	Annapolis	Apr. 28, 1788
Massachusetts	(MA)	Bay State; Old Colony	Boston	Feb. 6, 1788
Michigan	(MI)	Great Lake State; Wolverine State	Lansing	Jan. 26, 1837
Minnesota	(MN)	North Star State; Gopher State	St. Paul	May 11, 1858
Mississippi	(MS)	Magnolia State	Jackson	Dec. 10, 1817
Missouri	(MO)	Show-Me State	Jefferson City	Aug. 10, 1821
Montana	(MT)	Treasure State	Helena	Nov. 8, 1889
Nebraska	(NE)	Cornhusker State; Beef State	Lincoln	Mar. 1, 1867
Nevada	(NV)	Sagebrush State; Battle-Born State	Carson City	Oct. 31, 1864
New Hampshire	(NH)	Granite State	Concord	June 21, 1788
New Jersey	(NJ)	Garden State	Trenton	Dec. 18, 1787
New Mexico	(NM)	Land of Enchantment; Sunshine State	Santa Fe	Jan. 6, 1912
New York	(NY)	Empire State	Albany	July 26, 1788
North Carolina	(NC)	Tar Heel State; Old North State	Raleigh	Nov. 21, 1789
North Dakota	(ND)	Peace Garden State	Bismarck	Nov. 2, 1889
Ohio	(OH)	Buckeye State	Columbus	Mar. 1, 1803
Oklahoma	(OK)	Sooner State	Oklahoma City	Nov. 16, 1907
Oregon	(OR)	Beaver State	Salem	Feb. 14, 1859
Pennsylvania	(PA)	Keystone State	Harrisburg	Dec. 12, 1787
Rhode Island	(RI)	Ocean State; Little Rhody	Providence	May 29, 1790
South Carolina	(SC)	Palmetto State	Columbia	May 23, 1788

Useful Once in a While

State		State Nickname	Capital	Entered Union
South Dakota	(SD)	Coyote State; Rushmore State	Pierre	Nov. 2, 1889
Tennessee	(TN)	Volunteer State	Nashville	June 1, 1796
Texas	(TX)	Lone Star State	Austin	Dec. 29, 1845
Utah	(UT)	Beehive State	Salt Lake City	Jan. 4, 1896
Vermont	(VT)	Green Mountain State	Montpelier	Mar. 4, 1791
Virginia	(VA)	Old Dominion	Richmond	June 25, 1788
Washington	(WA)	Evergreen State	Olympia	Nov. 11, 1889
West Virginia	(WV)	Mountain State	Charleston	June 20, 1863
Wisconsin	(WI)	Badger State	Madison	May 29, 1848
Wyoming	(WY)	Equality State	Cheyenne	July 10, 1890

General Rules for Pruning

What	When	How
Apple	Early spring	Prune moderately. Keep tree open with main branches well spaced. Avoid sharp V-shaped crotches.
Cherry	Early spring	Prune the most vigorous shoots moderately.
Clematis	Spring	Cut weak growth. Save as much old wood as possible.
Flowering Dogwood	After flowering	Remove dead wood only.
Forsythia	After flowering	Remove old branches at ground. Trim new growth.
Lilac	After flowering	Remove diseased, scaly growth, flower heads, and suckers.
Peach	Early spring	Remove half of last year's growth. Keep tree headed low.
Plum	Early spring	Cut dead, diseased branches; trim rank growth moderately.
Rhododendron	After flowering	Prune judiciously. Snip branches from weak, leggy plants to induce growth from roots.
Roses (except climbers)	Spring, after frosts	Cut dead and weak growth; cut branches or canes to four or five eyes.
Roses, climbers	After flowering	Cut half of old growth; retain new shoots for next year.
Rose of Sharon	When buds begin	Cut all winter-killed wood to swell growth back to live wood.
Trumpet Vine	Early spring	Prune side branches severely to main stem.
Virginia Creeper	Spring	Clip young plants freely. Thin old plants and remove dead growth.
Wisteria	Spring, summer	Cut new growth to spurs at axils of leaves.

Gestation and Mating Table

	Proper age for first mating	Period of fertility, in years	No. of females for one male	Period of gestation in days Range	Average
Ewe	90 lbs. or 1 yr.	6		142-154	147 / 151[8]
Ram	12-14 mos., well matured	7	50-75[2] / 35-40[3]		
Mare	3 yrs.	10-12		310-370	336
Stallion	3 yrs.	12-15	40-45[4] / Record 252[5]		
Cow	15-18 mos.[1]	10-14		279-290[6] 262-300[7]	283
Bull	1 yr., well matured	10-12	50[4] / Thousands[5]		
Sow	5-6 mos. or 250 lbs.	6		110-120	115
Boar	250-300 lbs.	6	50[2] / 35-40[3]		
Doe goat	10 mos. or 85-90 lbs.	6		145-155	150
Buck goat	Well matured	5	30		
Bitch	16-18 mos.	8		58-67	63
Male dog	12-16 mos.	8			
She cat	12 mos.	6		60-68	63
Doe rabbit	6 mos.	5-6		30-32	31
Buck rabbit	6 mos.	5-6	30		

[1]Holstein & Beef: 750 lbs.; Jersey: 500 lbs. [2]Handmated. [3]Pasture. [4]Natural. [5]Artificial. [6]Beef; 8-10 days shorter for Angus. [7]Dairy. [8]For fine wool breeds.

Bird and Poultry Incubation Periods, in Days

Chicken	21	Goose	30-34	Guinea	26-28
Turkey	28	Swan	42	Canary	14-15
Duck	26-32	Pheasant	22-24	Parakeet	18-20

Gestation Periods, Wild Animals, in Days

Black bear	210	Seal	330
Hippo	225-250	Squirrel, gray	44
Moose	240-250	Whale, sperm	480
Otter	270-300	Wolf	60-63
Reindeer	210-240		

Maximum Life Spans of Animals in Capitivity, in Years

Box Turtle (Eastern)	138	Elephant	84	Oyster
		Giant Tortoise	190	(Freshwater)	80
Bullfrog	16	Giraffe	28	Pig	10
Camel	25	Goat	17	Polar Bear	41
Cat (Domestic)	23	Gorilla	33	Rabbit	13
Cheetah	16	Grizzly Bear	31	Rattlesnake	20
Chicken	14	Horse		Reindeer	15
Chimpanzee	37	(Domestic)	50	Sea Lion	28
Cow	20	Kangaroo	16	Sheep	20
Dog (Domestic)	22	Lion	30	Tiger	25
Dolphin	30	Moose	20	Timber Wolf	15
Eagle	55	Owl	68	Toad	36
				Zebra	25

Reproductive Cycle in Farm Animals

	Recurs if not bred	Estrual cycle incl. heat period (days)		In heat for		Usual time of ovulation
	Days	Ave.	Range	Ave.	Range	
Mare	21	21	10-37	5-6 days	2-11 days	24-48 hours before end of estrus
Sow	21	21	18-24	2-3 days	1-5 days	30-36 hours after start of estrus
Ewe	16½	16½	14-19	30 hours	24-32 hours	12-24 hours before end of estrus
Goat	21	21	18-24	2-3 days	1-4 days	Near end of estrus
Cow	21	21	18-24	18 hours	10-24 hours	10-12 hours after end of estrus
Bitch	pseudo-pregnancy	24		7 days	5-9 days	1-3 days after first acceptance
Cat	pseudo-pregnancy		15-21	3-4 if mated	9-10 days in absence of male	24-56 hours after coitus

Manure Guide

Type of Manure	Water Content	Primary Nutrients (pounds per ton)		
		Nitrogen	Phosphate	Potash
Cow, horse	60%-80%	12-14	5-9	9-12
Sheep, pig, goat	65%-75%	10-21	7	13-19
Chicken: Wet, sticky, and caked	75%	30	20	10
Moist, crumbly to sticky	50%	40	40	20
Crumbly	30%	60	55	30
Dry	15%	90	70	40
Ashed	none	135	100	

Type of Garden	Best Type of Manure	Best Time to Apply
Flower	cow, horse	early spring
Vegetable	chicken, cow, horse	fall, spring
Potato or root crop	cow, horse	fall
Acid-loving plants (blueberries, azaleas, mountain laurel, rhododendrons)	cow, horse	early fall or not at all

Which Burns More Calories, Scrubbing Floors or Bowling?

Activity	Calories burned per hour
Bicycling (5 miles per hour)	150-250
Bowling	200-250
Cooking	125-200
Dancing	250-450
Gardening	250-325
Jogging (5 miles per hour)	450-500
Making beds	200-250
Reading	75-125
Scrubbing floors	200-250
Skiing (downhill)	350-500
Swimming	230-325
Tennis (doubles)	250-350
Typing	75-125
Walking (3 miles per hour)	200-250
Washing dishes (by hand)	125-200
Watching television	75-125

Safe Ice Thickness *

Ice Thickness	Permissible load
2 inches	one person on foot
3 inches	group in single file
7½ inches	passenger car (2-ton gross)
8 inches	light truck (2½-ton gross)
10 inches	medium truck (3½-ton gross)
12 inches	heavy truck (8-ton gross)
15 inches	10 tons
20 inches	25 tons
30 inches	70 tons
36 inches	110 tons

* Solid clear blue/black pond and lake ice

☞ Slush ice has only one-half the strength of blue ice.

☞ Strength value of river ice is 15 percent less.

Source: *American Pulpwood Association*

Where the Sun Rises and Sets

By using the table below and a compass, you can determine accurately where on the horizon the Sun will rise or set on a given day. The top half of the table is for those days of the year, between the vernal and autumnal equinoxes, when the Sun rises north of east and sets north of west. March 21 through June 21 are listed in the left column, June 21 through September 22 appear in the right column. Similarly arranged, the bottom half of the table shows the other half of the year when the Sun rises south of east and sets south of west. Here's how it works. Say you live in Gary, Indiana, and need to know where the Sun will rise or set on October 10. Use the Time Correction Tables (see "Contents") to determine the latitude of your city or the listed city nearest to you. Gary is at 41° latitude. Find the 40° latitude column and you see that on October 10 the Sun rises 8° south of east and sets 8° south of west. Of course, you can determine figures for other latitudes and days not actually shown in the table by using extrapolation.

Latitude / Date	0°	10°	20°	30°	40°	50°	60°	Latitude / Date
Mar. 21	0°	0°	0°	0°	0°	0°	0°	Sept. 22
Mar. 31	4° N	4° N	4° N	4° N	5° N	6° N	8° N	Sept. 14
Apr. 10	8° N	8° N	8° N	9° N	10° N	12° N	15° N	Sept. 4
Apr. 20	11° N	12° N	12° N	13° N	15° N	18° N	23° N	Aug. 24
May 1	15° N	16° N	16° N	17° N	20° N	23° N	31° N	Aug. 14
May 10	17° N	18° N	19° N	20° N	23° N	28° N	37° N	Aug. 4
May 20	20° N	21° N	21° N	23° N	26° N	32° N	43° N	July 25
June 1	22° N	22° N	23° N	26° N	29° N	36° N	48° N	July 13
June 10	23° N	24° N	24° N	27° N	31° N	37° N	51° N	July 4
June 21	23½° N	25° N	25° N	27° N	31° N	38° N	53° N	June 21
Sept. 22	0°	0°	0°	0°	0°	0°	0°	Mar. 21
Oct. 1	3° S	3° S	3° S	3° S	4° S	5° S	6° S	Mar. 14
Oct. 10	6° S	7° S	7° S	7° S	8° S	10° S	13° S	Mar. 5
Oct. 20	10° S	11° S	11° S	12° S	13° S	16° S	20° S	Feb. 23
Nov. 1	15° S	15° S	15° S	16° S	18° S	22° S	29° S	Feb. 12
Nov. 10	17° S	18° S	18° S	20° S	22° S	27° S	36° S	Feb. 2
Nov. 20	20° S	21° S	21° S	23° S	26° S	31° S	42° S	Jan. 23
Dec. 1	22° S	23° S	23° S	25° S	29° S	35° S	48° S	Jan. 13
Dec. 10	23° S	24° S	24° S	27° S	30° S	37° S	51° S	Jan. 4
Dec. 21	23½° S	25° S	25° S	27° S	31° S	38° S	53° S	Dec. 21

1994 Atlantic Hurricane Names

Alberto	Helene	Oscar
Beryl	Isaac	Patty
Chris	Joyce	Rafael
Debby	Keith	Sandy
Ernesto	Leslie	Tony
Florence	Michael	Valerie
Gordon	Nadine	William

Beaufort's Scale of Wind Speeds

"Used Mostly at Sea but of Help to all who are interested in the Weather"

A scale of wind velocity was devised by Admiral Sir Francis Beaufort of the British Navy in 1806. The numbers 0 to 12 were arranged by Beaufort to indicate the strength of the wind from a calm, force 0, to a hurricane, force 12. This adaptation of Beaufort's scale is used by the U.S. National Weather Service.

Force	Description	Statute Miles Per Hour
0	Calm	less than 1
1	Light air	1 to 3
2	Light breeze	4 to 7
3	Gentle breeze	8 to 12
4	Moderate breeze	13 to 18
5	Fresh breeze	19 to 24
6	Strong breeze	25 to 31
7	Moderate gale	32 to 38
8	Fresh gale	39 to 46
9	Strong gale	47 to 54
10	Whole gale	55 to 63
11	Storm	64 to 73
12	Hurricane	more than 73

Wind/Barometer Table

Barometer (Reduced to Sea Level)	Wind Direction	Character of Weather Indicated
30.00 to 30.20, and steady	westerly	Fair, with slight changes in temperature, for one to two days.
30.00 to 30.20, and rising rapidly	westerly	Fair, followed within two days by warmer and rain.
30.00 to 30.20, and falling rapidly	south to east	Warmer, and rain within 24 hours.
30.20 or above, and falling rapidly	south to east	Warmer, and rain within 36 hours.
30.20 or above, and falling rapidly	west to north	Cold and clear, quickly followed by warmer and rain.
30.20 or above, and steady	variable	No early change.
30.00 or below, and falling slowly	south to east	Rain within 18 hours that will continue a day or two.
30.00 or below, and falling rapidly	southeast to northeast	Rain, with high wind, followed within two days by clearing, colder.
30.00 or below, and rising	south to west	Clearing and colder within 12 hours.
29.80 or below, and falling rapidly	southeast to northeast	Severe storm of wind and rain imminent. In winter, snow or cold wave within 24 hours.
29.80 or below, and falling rapidly	east to north	Severe northeast gales and heavy rain or snow, followed in winter by cold wave.
29.80 or below, and rising rapidly	going to west	Clearing and colder.

Note: *A barometer should be adjusted to show equivalent sea-level pressure for the altitude at which it is to be used. A change of 100 feet in elevation will cause a decrease of $\frac{1}{10}$ inch in the reading.*

Guide to Lumber and Nails

Lumber Widths and Thickness in Inches

NOMINAL SIZE	ACTUAL SIZE Dry or Seasoned
1 x 3	¾ x 2½
1 x 4	¾ x 3½
1 x 6	¾ x 5½
1 x 8	¾ x 7¼
1 x 10	¾ x 9¼
1 x 12	¾ x 11¼
2 x 3	1½ x 2½
2 x 4	1½ x 3½
2 x 6	1½ x 5½
2 x 8	1½ x 7¼
2 x 10	1½ x 9¼
2 x 12	1½ x 11¼

Nail Sizes

The nail on the left is a 5d (penny) finish nail; on the right, 20d common. The numerals below the nail sizes indicate the approximate number of common nails per pound.

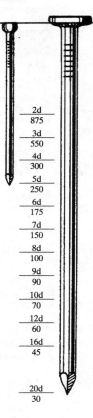

2d	875
3d	550
4d	300
5d	250
6d	175
7d	150
8d	100
9d	90
10d	70
12d	60
16d	45
20d	30

Lumber Measure in Board Feet

Size in Inches	LENGTH 12 ft.	14 ft.	16 ft.	18 ft.	20 ft.
1 x 4	4	4⅔	5⅓	6	6⅔
1 x 6	6	7	8	9	10
1 x 8	8	9⅓	10⅔	12	13⅓
1 x 10	10	11⅔	13⅓	15	16⅔
1 x 12	12	14	16	18	20
2 x 3	6	7	8	9	10
2 x 4	8	9⅓	10⅔	12	13⅓
2 x 6	12	14	16	18	20
2 x 8	16	18⅔	21⅓	24	26⅔
2 x 10	20	23⅓	26⅔	30	33⅓
2 x 12	24	28	32	36	40
4 x 4	16	18⅔	21⅓	24	26⅔
6 x 6	36	42	48	54	60
8 x 8	64	74⅔	85⅓	96	106⅔
10 x 10	100	116⅔	133⅓	150	166⅔
12 x 12	144	168	192	216	240

Not Particularly Useful but Interesting Nonetheless

Formula for Determining the Date of Easter for Any Year in the Gregorian Calendar

Step	N=Numerator	Denominator	Equation	Quotient	Remainder
1.	N=The Year	19	N/19	Discard	a
Example:	N=1994		1994/19		a=18
2.	N=The Year	100	N/100	b	c
	N=1994		1994/100	b=19	c=94
3.	N=b	4	N/4	d	e
	N=19		19/4	d=4	e=3
4.	N=(b+8)	25	N/25	Discard	f
	N=27		27/25		f=2
5.	N=(b-f+1)	3	N/3	g	Discard
	N=18		18/3	6	
6.	N=(19a+b-d-g+15)	30	N/30	Discard	h
	N=366		366/30		h=6
7.	N=c	4	N/4	i	j
	N=94		94/4	i=23	j=2
8.	N=(32+2e+2i-h-j)	7	N/7	Discard	k
	N=76		76/7		k=6
9.	N=(a+11h+22k)	451	N/451	L	Discard
	N=216		216/451	L=0	
10.	N=(h+k-7L+114)	31	N/31	m	n
	N=126		126/31	m=4	n=2

m = Month in which Easter occurs: m = 4 = April   n + 1 = Day of month on which Easter occurs: n + 1 = 3
Hence, Easter 1994 occurs on April 3.

March 22 is the earliest possible date for Easter. It has not been celebrated that early since March 22, 1818, and will not be again until 2285. The latest date on which Easter can fall is April 25, on which it was celebrated in 1943 and will be next in 2038.

Is It Raining, Drizzling, or Misting?

	Drops (per sq. ft. per second)	Diameter of Drops (mm)	Intensity (in. per hr.)
Cloudburst	113	2.85	4.00
Excessive Rain	76	2.40	1.60
Heavy Rain	46	2.05	.60
Moderate Rain	46	1.60	.15
Light Rain	26	1.24	.04
Drizzle	14	.96	.01
Mist	2,510	.10	.002
Fog	6,264,000	.01	.005

How to Find the Day of the Week for Any Given Date

**To compute the day of the week for any given date
as far back as the mid-18th century, proceed as follows:**

Add the last two digits of the year to one-quarter of the last two digits (discard any remainder if it doesn't come out even), the given date, and the month key from the key-box below. Divide the sum by seven; the number left over is the day of the week (one is Sunday, two is Monday, and so on). If it comes out even, the day is Saturday. If you go back before 1900, add two to the sum before dividing; before 1800, add four; and so on. Don't go back before 1753.

Example: **The Dayton Flood was on Tuesday, March 25, 1913.**

KEY

Last two digits of year:	13
One-quarter of these two digits:	3
Given day of month:	25
Key number for March:	4
Sum:	45

45/7 = 6, with a remainder of 3. The flood took place on Tuesday, the third day of the week.

	KEY
Jan.	1
leap yr.	0
Feb.	4
leap yr.	3
Mar.	4
Apr.	0
May	2
June	5
July	0
Aug.	3
Sept.	6
Oct.	1
Nov.	4
Dec.	6

How to Order Two Bun Halves Filled with Cheese, Meat, Onions, Peppers, and Other Stuff

Place	Name
Norfolk, VA	Submarine
Akron, OH	"
Jacksonville, FL	"
Los Angeles, CA	"
Philadelphia, PA	Hoagie
Ann Arbor, MI	"
Knoxville, TN	"
Newark, NJ	"
Providence, RI	"
Des Moines, IA	Grinder
Hartford, CT	"
Chester, PA	"
Cleveland, OH	"

Not Particularly Useful but Interesting Nonetheless

A Table Foretelling the Weather Through All the Lunations of Each Year (Forever)

This table is the result of many years' actual observation and shows what sort of weather will probably follow the Moon's entrance into any of its quarters. For example, the weather for the week following October 19, 1994, would be windy and rainy because the Moon becomes full that day at 7:19 A.M., EST.

Editor's note: *While the data in this table are taken into consideration in the yearlong process of compiling the annual long-range weather forecasts for* The Old Farmer's Almanac, *we rely far more on our projections of solar activity.*

Time of Change	Summer	Winter
Midnight to 2 A.M.	Fair	Hard frost, unless wind is south or west
2 A.M. to 4 A.M.	Cold, with frequent showers	Snow and stormy
4 A.M. to 6 A.M.	Rain	Rain
6 A.M. to 8 A.M.	Wind and rain	Stormy
8 A.M. to 10 A.M.	Changeable	Cold rain if wind is west; snow if east
10 A.M. to noon	Frequent showers	Cold with high winds
Noon to 2 P.M.	Very rainy	Snow or rain
2 P.M. to 4 P.M.	Changeable	Fair and mild
4 P.M. to 6 P.M.	Fair	Fair
6 P.M. to 10 P.M.	Fair if wind is northwest; rain if south or southwest	Fair and frosty if wind is north or northeast; rain or snow if wind is south or southwest
10 P.M. to midnight	Fair	Fair and frosty

This table was created more than 160 years ago by Dr. Herschell for the Boston Courier; *it first appeared in* The Old Farmer's Almanac *in 1834.*

Place	Name
Madison, WI	Garibaldi
Norristown, PA	Zeppelin
Mobile, AL	Poor Boy
Sacramento, CA	"
Houston, TX	"
Montgomery, AL	"
New Orleans, LA	Poor Boy or Musalatta
Gary, IN	Submarine or Torpedo
Allentown, PA	Hoagie or Italian Sandwich
Cheyenne, WY	Hoagie or Submarine or Rocket
Cincinnati, OH	"
Buffalo, NY	" or Bomber
Dublin, NH	Two Bun Halves Filled with Cheese, Meat, Onions, Peppers, and Other Stuff

Not Particularly Useful but Interesting Nonetheless

Full Moon Names

The native Indians of what are now the northern and eastern United States kept track of the seasons by distinctive names given to each recurring full Moon, these names being applied to the entire month in which it occurred. With some variations, the same Moon names were used throughout the Algonquin tribes from New England to Lake Superior.

Name	Month	Other Names Used
Full Wolf Moon	January	Full Old Moon
Full Snow Moon	February	Full Hunger Moon
Full Worm Moon	March	Full Crow Moon, Full Crust Moon, Full Sugar Moon, Full Sap Moon
Full Pink Moon	April	Full Sprouting Grass Moon, Full Egg Moon, Full Fish Moon
Full Flower Moon	May	Full Corn Planting Moon, Full Milk Moon
Full Strawberry Moon	June	Full Rose Moon, Full Hot Moon
Full Buck Moon	July	Full Thunder Moon, Full Hay Moon
Full Sturgeon Moon	August	Full Red Moon, Full Green Corn Moon
Full Harvest Moon*	September	Full Corn Moon
Full Hunter's Moon	October	Full Travel Moon, Full Dying Grass Moon
Full Beaver Moon	November	Full Frost Moon
Full Cold Moon	December	Full Long Nights Moon

* The Harvest Moon is always the full Moon closest to the autumnal equinox. If it occurs in October, the September full Moon is usually called the Corn Moon.

Acceptable Two-Letter Words in Scrabble™

aa	aw	do	fa	it	my	op	sh	we
ad	ax	ef	go	jo	na	or	si	wo
ae	ay	eh	ha	ka	no	os	so	xi
ah	ba	el	he	la	nu	ow	ta	xu
ai	be	em	hi	li	od	ox	ti	ya
am	bi	en	ho	lo	oe	oy	to	ye
an	bo	er	id	ma	of	pa	un	
ar	by	es	if	me	oh	pe	up	
as	da	et	in	mi	om	pi	us	
at	de	ex	is	mu	on	re	ut	